THE SHOW BIZ LIFE

An Anecdotal History of Stage, Screen, and Television

—

ROBERT HENDRICKSON

CONTEMPORARY BOOKS

Library of Congress Cataloging-in-Publication Data

Hendrickson, Robert, 1933–
　　The show biz life : an anecdotal history of stage, screen, and television / Robert Hendrickson.
　　　　p.　　cm.
　　Includes index.
　　ISBN 0-8092-3083-6
　　1. Performing arts—Miscellanea.　　2. Performing arts—Anecdotes.
I. Title.
PN1584.H46　　1999
791—dc21　　　　　　　　　　　　　　　　　　　　　　　　98-49866
　　　　　　　　　　　　　　　　　　　　　　　　　　　　　　　CIP

Interior design by Precision Graphics

Published by Contemporary Books
A division of NTC/Contemporary Publishing Group, Inc.
4255 West Touhy Avenue, Lincolnwood (Chicago), Illinois 60712-1975 U.S.A.
Copyright © 1999 by Robert Hendrickson
All rights reserved. No part of this book may be reproduced, stored in a retrieval system, or transmitted in any form or by any means, electronic, mechanical, photocopying, recording, or otherwise, without the prior written permission of NTC/Contemporary Publishing Group, Inc.
Printed in the United States of America
International Standard Book Number: 0-8092-3083-6
99　00　01　02　03　04　HP　19　18　17　16　15　14　13　12　11　10　9　8　7　6　5　4　3　2　1

To my son-in-law, Tony S. Kafeiti

Contents

	Preface	vii
	Acknowledgments	ix
I	An Actor's Life for Me	1
II	The Supporting Cast: From Stage Mothers to Computers	59
III	Playwrights and Their Muses and Mates	85
IV	Moguls, Mavens, and Momzers (Including Producers, Directors, and Screenwriters, et al)	133
V	Animal Actors, Cartoon Characters, and Movie Monsters	175
VI	Of Barns and Palaces: Famous Theaters and Movie Houses	207
VII	Fanatics, Fires, and Murders Most Foul	227
VIII	Oscars, Tonys, Pulitzers, and Other Prestigious Prizes	253
IX	Scurrilous Critics and Insidious Censors	333
X	Entertaining Words and Memorable Lines	357
XI	Final Cuts and Curtain Falls: The Strange Deaths and Last Words of Famous Thespians	389
	Bibliography	413
	Index	419

Preface

The Show Biz Life is intended as an entertaining social history of stage and screen from earliest times to the present, told in the form of brief biographies, amusing and edifying anecdotes, quotations, quips, quizzes, lists, and interesting and revealing statistics. Though it might be called a broad anecdotal history of the theater, its hundreds of stories, at least touching on the most important aspects of theatrical life, are primarily meant to entertain, just as its subjects entertained or are still entertaining today. I've tried to be fair-minded and evenhanded in making my selections from the trove of tales I could have told. Now that it's time to raise the curtain and let the story unfold upon this off-Broadway stage, I hope that my book brings pleasure not only to theater, movie, and television fans but to all those thespians, from bright-eyed extras to stars of the first magnitude, who have brought so much pleasure to me.

Acknowledgments

I would like to thank all of the many people who have helped me over a period of several years in researching and writing this book. Especially appreciated are the valuable suggestions of my editor, Susan Schwartz, and those of copyeditor Kathleen Fridella. There are so many friends and research librarians across the country who provided material that it is impossible to list them in this short space, but I owe special thanks to Lauren Walsh, Karen Kafeiti, Joseph Hallstein, and my son, Brian Hendrickson. As for my wife, Marilyn, I can only say that, once again, this book is as much hers as it is mine.

I

AN ACTOR'S LIFE FOR ME

Actors on Acting

"We must stir ourselves! Move on! Work! Work! . . . Must move on! Must work!" —*dying words of Eleonora Duse*

"The true artist will let his wife starve, his children go barefoot, his mother drudge for his living at seventy, sooner than work on anything but his art." —*George Bernard Shaw*

"We had a hunger for something more important than fame. Food." —*George Burns*

Thespis: Every Actor's Ancestor

"Thespis, the first professor of our art
At country wakes sang ballads from a cart"
—*John Dryden*

A *thespian* is, of course, an actor, and as an adjective the word means "pertaining to tragedy or dramatic art." Both meanings pay tribute to the world's first professional actor. According to legend, Thespis was a Greek poet of the latter sixth century B.C. who recited his poems at festivals of the gods around the country; he is even said to have invented tragedy and to have created the first dialogue spoken on the stage in the form of exchanges between himself as an actor reading poems and responses by a chorus. Thespis is probably a semilegendary figure, his name possibly an assumed one. The popular story that he went around Attica in a cart in which his plays were acted is of doubtful authenticity but may be based on truth.

In recent times *thesping* has become a synonym for acting. No one really knows exactly when the first tragic and comic thespians performed on the stage in Greece. The word *comedy* may derive from the Greek word *kome* for "village," because the first comic thespians were scorned in the cities and had to wander about rural villages to give performances. This was Aristotle's belief, but others say *comedy* comes from the Greek *komas*, meaning "revel," because it first was performed by revelers at festivals.

Tragedy comes from the Greek *tragodia*, which means "goat singer," but we don't know exactly why. As historian Richard C. Trench wrote in an essay a century ago,

> There is no question that tragedy is the song of the goat, whether because a goat was the prize for the best performance of the song in which the germs of the future tragedy lay, or because the first actors were dressed, like satyrs, in goatskins, is a question which has stirred abundant discussion and will remain unsettled to the end.

A Cry of Players: Collective Names for Thespians

Collectively actors and actresses have been called *companies*, *casts*, *troupes*, and even *entrances*. In the Middle Ages a troupe was called a *cry*, and in more recent times, during the heyday of the Hollywood studios, there were *stables* of actors and writers. A number of *angels* financially backing a play might be called a *host of angels* and a collection of critics a *frown*.

Rome's Greatest Actors

Roman actor Quintus Gallus Roscius (c. 126–62 B.C.) was born a slave but became the greatest performer of his time. Excelling in comedy roles, he was so esteemed that the golden-tongued orator Cicero took lessons from him and became his friend, the two often competing to see who could better express an idea or emotion. Roscius, in fact, wrote a treatise comparing acting and oratory. In an age when actors were held in contempt, his grace and eloquence were praised in poems, Sulla awarded him the gold ring signifying noble equestrian rank, and he amassed a great fortune, retiring from the stage when still a young man. More than two thousand years have passed, and his name is still a synonym for eminence or perfection in acting. *Roscian* means pertaining to or involving actors, and when we say someone gave a Roscian performance, we mean one of outstanding skill.

Roscius's only real competition on the stage was the actor Aesopus, who performed mainly in tragedies. Aesopus was noted for artful facial expressions and gestures that were said to be unrivaled. The old tale about Cleopatra dissolving an expensive pearl in vinegar to impress Caesar may have its origin in a story about Aesopus taking a pearl from the earring of a beautiful actress and dissolving it in vinegar, so that, according to one anonymous writer, "he might have the satisfaction of swallowing $5,000 in one gulp."

Histrionic Actors

Etruscan actors from the Roman province of Etruria who were called *istri* give us our word *histrionics*: of or relating to actors and acting; or excessively emotional, affected. The Romans called these provincial actors *istriones* and from this Latin word came the English *histrionics*.

The First Pantomime Actors—Naked and Not

Rome's only really original contribution to Western theater was the *pantomime*, a silent individual performance by a *pantomimus*, an actor who danced or acted in mask and cloak and did not speak a word, unlike the earlier Greek *mimi*, who spoke and sang when they performed. This purely Roman creation was a favorite of audiences in Rome, who idolized the *pantomimi* and often made them rich. Just one *pantomimus* played each of the roles in a play, wearing a different mask for each character, while all the words were sung by a choir.

Pantomime became so popular in Rome that it drove both tragedy and comedy from the stage. One of its most accomplished practitioners was Bathyllus, whose name came to be used for any pantomime actor. Paris was the name of two Roman pantomime performers. The first remained the emperor Nero's favorite until he was executed by Nero for beating him in an acting contest. The second took the first Paris's name and ironically met the same fate twenty years later in A.D. 87 when the emperor Domitian had him put to death.

Mimi players were also popular in Rome and were often naked actresses who performed in bawdy plays.

Sex on Stage: Roman Realism

Under the dissolute Roman emperor Elagabalus, in about A.D. 220, realism rose to new heights (or sank to new lows) that haven't been seen on the stage since. Actors actually performed the sex act before audiences, including scenes of rape. Though the Roman players, who were slaves or freedmen trained to the profession, drew the line at really dying, convicted criminals were often put to death on stage in execution scenes. In reaction to "plays" like these the Christian church excommunicated all players in the fifth century A.D., and all theaters were finally closed in the reign of Justinian. For over ten centuries there were no more public plays except for religious dramas performed mainly in churches.

Modern Nude Mimes

Commenting on *Oh! Calcutta*, the once controversial erotic revue featuring a naked cast, critic Sir Robert Helpmann observed, "The trouble with nude dancing is that not everything stops when the music stops."

Contrary to popular belief, Kenneth Tynan's 1969 revue has nothing to do with Calcutta, India. The title of the play is from the French "*Oh, quel cul t'as*," which translates roughly as "Oh, what an ass you have."

Shakespeare and Other Great Actor-Authors

It is often forgotten that perhaps the greatest writer of all time could not make a living from writing. William Shakespeare was paid no more than eight pounds apiece for his plays (which was the highest price any playwright got at the time), and since he wrote fewer than forty plays, his income from writing during his twenty years in the theater was less than twenty pounds a year. He was not unusual in this regard (Ben Jonson estimated that he made less than two hundred pounds from his own plays), but the Swan of Avon probably had to support himself as a working actor all his life. However, according to one biographer, his income from all sources may have been the equivalent of about $50,000 a year after 1599, a fortune for his day. The Bard probably ghost-wrote plays to make ends meet, and there is a theatrical tradition that he often played the ghost in his *Hamlet*.

Other great acting authors include the immortal Molière, who surpassed any actor of his time as a comedic player and was considered as good an actor as he was a playwright. The French dramatist was especially good in his own masterpiece, *Le Misanthrope*, in which he played Alceste, who is desperately in love with Célimène, played by his wife. In real life Mrs. Molière was as flighty and unfaithful as his fictional character, lending great authenticity to Molière's performances. He, however, didn't go so far as French dramatist Etienne Jodelle. Jodelle's play *Cleopatre Captive* (1552) tried to establish classical drama on the French stage. In it Jodelle himself played the role of Cleopatra.

English greats Ben Jonson and Samuel Foote acted in many plays in their times. So did the German playwright-actor Karl Eduard von Holtei (1798–1880), who is also remembered for introducing vaudeville into Germany. As for English dramatist George Farquhar (1678–1707), he became a playwright after vowing never to act again when he almost fatally wounded another actor in a fencing scene he played in John Dryden's *Indian Emperor* (1665).

Few great novelists could claim to be actors, but in 1860 Fyodor Dostoyevsky played (of all things) the comic role of the postmaster in Nikolai Gogol's *The Inspector General*. His theater director in St. Petersburg called him a fine actor "who knew how to evoke real Gogolian laughter."

Eugene O'Neill tried acting, among other occupations, before he turned to playwriting. In 1916 he made his only appearance in an O'Neill play, appearing in his one-act drama *Before Breakfast* as the offstage husband whose only "speech" is a death cry when he cuts his throat with a razor.

Today Harold Pinter and Sam Shepard are among several playwrights who have appeared in their own plays and the plays of others.

Shakespeare on Acting Fundamentals

"Speak the speech, I pray you . . . trippingly on the tongue, but if you mouth it, as many of our players do, I had as lief the town-crier spoke my lines. Nor do not saw the air too much with your hand, thus, but use all gently, for in the very torrent, tempest, and, as I may say, whirlwind of your passion, you must acquire and beget a temperance that may give it smoothness. Oh, it offends me to the soul to hear a robustious periwig-pated fellow tear a passion to totters, to very rags, to spleet the ears of the groundlings who for the most part are capable of nothing but inexplicable dumb shows and noise. I would have such a fellow whipt for o'erdoing Termagant; it out-Herods Herod, pray you avoid it. . . .

"Be not too tame, neither, but let your own discretion be your tutor. Suit the action to the word, the word to the action."
—*Hamlet to his players in* Hamlet

Shakespeare and Burbage in Bed

With the passing of time there have been many variations, one more risqué than the other, on the old joke about Shakespeare, prominent actor Richard Burbage, and their lady friend. The incident may or may not have occurred, but here is the original story from the diary of seventeenth-century English author John Manningham:

> *Upon a time when Burbage played Richard the Third there was a citizen grew so far in liking him, that before she went from the play she appointed him to come that night unto her by the name of Richard the Third. Shakespeare, overhearing their conversation, went before, was entertained and at his game ere Burbage came. Then, message being brought that Richard the Third was at the door, Shakespeare caused return to be made that William the Conquerer was before Richard the Third.*

Shakespeare's Grandnephew

Probably the only one of Shakespeare's relatives to be active in the theater, Charles Hart (d. 1683) was the grandson of the Bard's sister Joan. He first played women's parts, but after serving in the English Civil War as a lieutenant of horse, won leading roles in John Dryden's plays. Samuel Pepys mentions him frequently in his famous diary, and he was especially praised for his acting of such Shakespearean parts as Othello, Brutus, and Hotspur. Legend has it that Hart was former orangeseller Nell Gwyn's first lover and trained her for the stage. The voluptuous Nell went on to attract Charles II's attention and became his mistress. The king's last words, in fact, were "Let not poor Nelly starve."

The World's First Actresses

As far as is known, the first actress on the French stage was an eighteen-year-old girl who played the part of the saint in the *Mystère de Sainte Catherine* at Metz in 1468. It is said that she played the part so charmingly and convincingly that a nobleman fell in love with her and took her as his wife. But this French player was hardly the first married by a man smitten with her performance. Saintliness had nothing to do with Justinian changing Roman laws against senators marrying actresses and taking the beautiful Theodora as his bride in the sixth century A.D. Theodora, whom he made empress when he became ruler of the Roman world, had been an early striptease artist and courtesan as well as an actress. The daughter of the bear-keeper at the Constantinople amphitheater, she had appeared on the stage while still a child.

It was in Shakespeare's *Othello*, on December 8, 1660, that the first woman appeared on the English stage. Prince Rupert's mistress, Margaret Hughes, played Desdemona that night at a new theater in Clare Market,

London. Before then boys had always played women's roles, and they kept doing so, for the most part, until the early eighteenth century. One Edward Kynaston, who died in 1706, seems to have been the last male to play a woman's part in a serious drama.

Lovely Mrs. Bracegirdle

A boy killed for her, lords fought for her, and playwright William Congreve had a lifelong liaison with her. This noted actress was Mrs. Anne Bracegirdle (1673–1748), who played Portia, Desdemona, Ophelia, and Cordelia, among many roles on the English stage. Mrs. Bracegirdle, as she was called at the time, was an orphan raised by Thomas Betterton, the greatest actor of the Restoration, and his wife, Mary, who acted under the name Mrs. Saunderson and was the first actress of any consequence on the English stage. Appropriately enough, Anne made her premier appearance in Thomas Otway's *The Orphan* (1680) when only six years old. From the time she reached maturity until the end of her acting days, the beautiful actress was desired by many men besides Congreve. The popular actor William Mountfort was murdered by fifteen-year-old Lord Charles Mohun because the boy regarded him as a rival of his friend Colonel Richard Hill for Mrs. Bracegirdle's affections, although Mohun was acquitted in a sensational, highly controversial trial. Mrs. Bracegirdle contributed greatly to the success of many Congreve comedies and was regarded as the best comic actress in England until challenged by the much younger Mrs. Anne Oldfield. It was decided to let the audience at the Haymarket Theatre determine who was the better actress, the test being the applause for the role of Mrs. Buttle in Betterton's *Amorous Widow*, which was played alternately by the two rivals on successive nights. When Mrs. Oldfield proved the winner, the lovely and gracious Mrs. Bracegirdle retired from the stage. On her death in 1748 she was buried in the cloisters of Westminster Abbey.

Joe Miller and His Jokes

Joe Miller didn't write the famous joke book that bears his name. The comic actor and barfly Josias Miller (1684–1738), a favorite at London's Drury Lane Theatre in parts such as *Hamlet*'s first gravedigger, was an illiterate. He married his wife, in fact, only so that she could read his parts for him. When Miller died leaving his family in poverty, his friend playwright

John Mottley gathered a collection of jokes attributed to him—and there were many, either because he was famed for his wit, or because it was something of a joke to credit this "grave and taciturn" actor with any joke making the rounds of the pubs. The proceeds of the seventy-two-page book went to Miller's family, and since it was the only joke book extant for many years, it went into numerous editions over the next two centuries. Eventually the original 272 jokes increased to well over 1,500. Because the jokes were widely quoted and imitated on the stage so long, any stale joke began to be called a "Joe Miller." The full title of the joke book was *Joe Miller's Jests: or, The Wit's Vade-Mecum, being a collection of the most brilliant jests, the polite repartees, the most eloquent bon mots, the most pleasant short stories in the English language. First carefully collected in the company, and many of them transcribed from the mouth of the facetious gentleman whose the most name they bear.* Some writers have gone so far as to say that the book is the basis for all stage and screen humor, and professional comedians such as Fred Allen have acknowledged their indebtedness to the collection. But poor starving Joe Miller probably had very little to do with it at all.

Garrick the Great

Many theater historians consider David Garrick (1717–79) the greatest English actor of all. A very versatile actor who excelled in both comic and tragic parts, he played characters ranging from Sir John Brute in *The Provok'd Wife* to Richard III and Lear. Garrick changed the course of English acting with his natural style, eschewing the mannered and pompous performances of his day. "That young man never had his equal as an actor, and he will never have a rival," Alexander Pope said of him. Garrick wrote a number of plays, too, and produced and directed everything from popular farces to Shakespeare.

Garrick's success as an actor was unequaled in his century, and he greatly influenced English drama as part owner of London's Drury Lane Theatre for thirty years. Still honoring him today is London's Garrick Club, founded in 1831, which has an extensive collection of theatrical memorabilia.

Garrick was a pupil of the legendary wit Dr. Samuel Johnson before he turned to the stage in 1740. He remained lifelong friends with Johnson. Once, after a performance of *Irene*, Garrick took his mother backstage to the dressing rooms of the actors. When asked to go backstage another time, Johnson replied, "No, David, I will never come back. For the white bubbies and the silk stockings of your actresses excite my genitals."

The Original Star

No modern-day press agent invented the term *star* for an actor or actress of exceptional talent or popularity, as is often believed. *Star* used in this sense is first recorded in a 1779 book on the theater in an appraisal of English actor David Garrick (see above): "The little stars, who hid their diminished rays in his [Garrick's] presence, began to abuse him." *Stardom* seems to have been coined by the American writer O. Henry in a 1911 short story.

Young Roscius

There were riots for seats and standing room at Covent Garden when boy-actor William Henry West Betty, often called Master Betty, played Richard III and Macbeth in 1804. Critics said the thirteen-year-old played Shakespearean roles better than the renowned David Garrick ever had and dubbed him the "Young Roscius" after the legendary Roman actor (*see* "Rome's Greatest Actors"). Master Betty was presented to the Royal Family; the House of Commons canceled a sitting so that its members could see his Hamlet; huge crowds waited in the cold to catch a glimpse of him when he left his dressing room. The Young Roscius had begun his phenomenal career in Belfast at the age of twelve, playing four roles in four nights. He was successful throughout the British Isles before ending his career in 1808 and going on to study at Cambridge. Master Betty returned to the stage four years later, when he was twenty-one, but was at best mediocre as an adult actor. He finally retired in 1824, a very rich man, living another fifty years with his memories of being the best child actor of all time.

Roscius has been a favorite honorary name for actors over the years. There have been, among others, the American Roscius (Ira Aldridge), the Young American Roscius (Samuel Cowell), the Ohio Roscius (Louis Aldrich), and the Scottish Roscius (H. E. Johnston).

The First Professional American Actor

We only know his last name—Greville—and have no idea of how old he was or when he died. He was a student at Princeton and abandoned his books to become a member of David Douglas's British acting company in New York. Greville seems to have played in several minor roles and left the company after a year.

The first American to make a career of professional acting was John Martin (1770–1807), a handsome actor who appeared in many New York productions. Aspiring players should know that, in the words of a theater historian, "He labored hard, lived poor, and died young."

"America's First Matinee Idol"

Though he was an Irishman with "an incurable Irish brogue" and had played in Dublin and London before sailing for America, the handsome actor John Henry (1738–94) has often been called "America's First Matinee Idol" (despite the fact that there were no matinees in his day). Henry did so well acting and producing that he could afford his own coach, a rarity among thespians of his time, but he tried to avoid ostentation by having the words THIS OR THESE painted on the coach under a picture of two crutches. The coach was necessary, he explained to detractors, because the gout had crippled him and he would have to walk on crutches if he didn't ride. Henry was possibly the first American actor involved in a sex scandal. After his first wife was lost at sea he lived for some time with her sister, by whom he had a child, but abandoned her to marry still another of his departed wife's sisters. When his star faded in America he sailed back to Ireland but died of a heart attack in passage; his new wife went insane over her loss and died herself a year later.

Traveling with the American Company and Other Troupes

It is said that during its long history every important actor in America appeared with the American Company, the longest-lived troupe of traveling American actors. Founded in 1758 by British actor David Douglas, a better businessman than performer, the company built its own theater on John Street in New York and encouraged the building of many more playhouses in other cities where it played. Overcoming financial hardship and a puritanical opposition to the theater, the American Company introduced a large repertoire of plays to the American public, including the tragedy *The Prince of Parthia* by Thomas Godfrey, which on April 24, 1767, at Philadelphia's Southwark Theatre became the first play by an American author to be professionally produced. The troupe lasted until its owners went bankrupt in 1805.

Troupes of actors go back even before the Roman *grex*, but the world's oldest still performing acting troupe, dating back to 1680, is the Comédie-

Française, which played for the first time in America in 1955, close to three centuries after its founding.

In Shakespeare's day, acting companies or troupes developed in large part because of a 1572 law by which common players were declared rogues or vagabonds unless they served a lord. Many companies arose bearing the name of a prominent nobleman, such as the Lord Chamberlain's Company, in which Richard Burbage and Shakespeare himself played.

Shakespeare by Flashes of Lightning: The Immortal Tragedian—or Horrid Little Man

The great but ill-starred English actor Edmund Kean (1789–1833) came into the limelight in the early nineteenth century after an unstable but adventuresome childhood. Kean had run away from boarding school to become a cabin boy aboard a merchant ship. Hating life at sea even more than school, he first demonstrated his ability to act by faking both deafness and lameness, thus securing his release. The remainder of his childhood was spent in the homes of several relatives and family friends, including his uncle Moses Kean, a mimic and ventriloquist who introduced him to the study of Shakespeare. Kean's only disadvantage as an actor was his short stature, but he made up for it with his matchless range of facial expressions, his deep, powerful voice, and his complete passionate penetration of the character he was playing: "I could not feel the stage under me," he remarked on one occasion. "Seeing him act," the poet Samuel Coleridge wrote of Kean, "was like reading Shakespeare by flashes of lightning."

But Kean, who had begun his stage career when only fourteen, was a "magnificent uncut gem" whose eccentricities and hard drinking wasted his talent away and marked him for an early grave. Once he was involved in an adultery suit that almost banished him from the stage; backstage in his dressing room he kept a pet lion someone had given him; he often rode his horse, Shylock, wildly through the night streets of London. Even the great actor's last performance was in character. While playing Othello to his son Charles's Iago at Covent Garden in 1833, Kean broke down and fell into his son's arms. "O God, I am dying. Speak to them, Charles," were his last words on the stage and the "immortal tragedian," or "horrid little man," died less than two months later, only forty-four.

Alexandre Dumas *père* later wrote a play entitled *Kean*, which was adapted by Jean-Paul Sartre in 1954 for modern audiences.

The Actor Who Became Hamlet

George Jones, a British actor who emigrated to the United States in 1838 and changed his name to Count Johannes, for some reason became obsessed with the role of Hamlet. As the years passed he played the role more and more, until it was the only part he would accept. But the Count unfortunately got worse, not better, with each performance. Soon audiences began booing him; he was hooted and jeered off the stage. Jones, probably insane to begin with, grew so mad that he took to gibbering insanely on the stage. Finally, no producer would have him, even as a curiosity, and he was forced to retire. The mad actor, one early critic said, had become too mad to play the Mad Prince.

Our First Modern Clown

An infant of one year when he made his debut at London's Drury Lane Theatre, the actor Joseph Grimaldi (1779–1837) performed for almost half a century in England. Starting as a dancer, he became internationally famous as the first modern clown, a great pantomimist so well known and beloved that *Joey* for a circus clown was coined by American circus performers in his honor. Grimaldi, the London-born son of an Italian actor, had no equal in pantomime; his much-acclaimed portrayal of a clown in *Mother Goose* has been revived many times. The first Joey's memoirs (1838) were edited by Charles Dickens, and his son Joseph Grimaldi (d. 1863) succeeded him on the London stage.

Grimaldi was the modern heir of such legendary figures as Harlequin, Pierrot, and even Merry Andrew, a figure possibly based on the nickname of Andrew Borde, a former monk who wrote a humorous book published in 1547.

Rachel the Immortal

Discovered singing for pennies in the streets by famous voice teacher Alexandre Choron, Elisa Félix, the daughter of poor Parisian peddlers, was trained for the stage and made her debut at the Comédie-Française just before her seventeenth birthday. Elisa took the stage name Rachel; her genius as a tragic actress, especially in the plays of Racine and Corneille, was acclaimed throughout Europe. Her brother and four sisters were also actors but came nowhere near equaling her. Rachel the Immortal ranks second only to Sarah Bernhardt among French actresses. While at the height of her career in such roles as Phèdre in Racine's play of that name, the fawn-colored "Rachel face powder," sometimes called *rachel* for short, was named in her honor by a Parisian cosmetic specialist. On a visit to America Rachel contracted tuberculosis, which led to her death three years later, in 1858. She was only thirty-eight, her tragic last illness and death the theme of a poem by Matthew Arnold.

America's Greatest Tragedian

Though the insane crime of his younger brother, John Wilkes Booth, who assassinated President Lincoln, threw a black shadow over his life, Edwin Booth is still remembered as the greatest American actor of his century. Booth made his debut in 1846, when only thirteen, touring with his father, Junius Brutus Booth, a brilliant tragedian whose periodic fits and drunken sprees ruined his own career. At the age of fifteen Edwin played Richard III when his father couldn't go on. After that came a great variety of roles, including a record one hundred consecutive performances as Hamlet. The small and slightly built Booth was celebrated in America and Europe for his dark good looks, magnificent voice, and natural, unaffected style of acting.

But terrible guilt descended upon Edwin Booth when his wife, Mary, died in 1863, at a time when he was in a drunken stupor and unable to be at her side. Two years later his brother assassinated Lincoln, and Edwin retired from the stage, only to experience more tragedy, equal to anything he had ever played upon the stage. In 1870 his son Edgar died shortly after birth, which caused the insanity of Booth's second wife. Then he went bankrupt, losing all his fortune, including the celebrated Booth Theater. Amazingly, however, the great tragedian recovered and returned to the stage, acting in many roles until his death in 1893 at the age of sixty. Booth left behind unparalleled critical praise for his acting genius, and there are even a few recordings of his magnificent voice, but he was proudest of something he did off the stage. In 1862, three years before his brother's infamous deed, Edwin saved Lincoln's oldest son, Robert, from falling into the path of a Pennsylvania Railroad train.

Whatever Lola Wanted, Lola Got: The Actress Who Became "King"

She had "a face full of expression, fine eyes, and golden hair that a mermaid might envy," according to a contemporary admirer. Lola Montez, "the international bad girl of the mid-Victorians," was the pseudonym of Irish-born actress Maria Dolores Eliza Rosanna Gilbert. Lola began acting before she turned thirteen, and after a scandalous divorce from an army officer she began touring the continent as a dancer, sleeping with every man she wanted, if he had money. She was very particular though, refusing the favors of the viceroy of Poland because he had false teeth. After taking three husbands and innumerable lovers (including composer Franz Liszt and dramatist Alexandre Dumas *père*), Lola became the mistress of Ludwig I of Bavaria in 1847. He made her Baroness of Rosenthal and Countess of Lansfeld. One story claims that the king confided she could "perform miracles of love with parts of her body" and that he indeed "gave her his kingdom" after a twenty-four-hour love session. In any case, Lola virtually ruled Bavaria, and her liberal sympathies during the revolution of 1848 caused the abdication of Ludwig and her banishment. She fled to England and then America, touring the country as an actress and ballet dancer. Not much of an actress, she was famed for her beauty and her scarlet past and present. She became the mistress of several wealthy Americans and was particularly successful performing in a sketch of her own life called *Lola Montez in Bavaria*. Toward the end of her short life—she was only forty or so when she died on Long Island in 1861—she devoted much of her fortune and energy to helping fallen women.

The Swedish Nightingale

One of the less sensational P. T. Barnum attractions was Jenny Lind. The incomparable showman brought his "Swedish Nightingale" to America in 1850 for a concert tour, and the golden-voiced operatic soprano gave ninety-five concerts in nineteen cities and grossed some $712,000—over half a million being Barnum's share. Jenny Lind, at the height of her powers, became the most famous singer of her time, due in large part to Barnum's hoopla. Her name and nickname are only rarely heard today but were once commonly used to describe any gifted singer, and many fashions of the day, including a carriage, were named after her. There were rumors that Barnum and the singer were romantically involved, but she married composer Otto Goldschmidt in 1852, and the couple lived in England until she died thirty-five years later, aged sixty-seven.

Barnum's Siamese Twins

They are perhaps the most famous of all sideshow performers, their names still remembered today. In fact, the impresario P. T. Barnum coined the descriptive name *Siamese twins* for Chang and Eng Bunker, Chinese joined twins born in Siam. Their name soon became generic, describing all twins joined at birth by musculofibrous tissue, either side by side or back to back. Siamese twins probably arise by the almost complete separation of a single egg into two parts, human identical twins representing the extreme of the same process—a complete separation. Always the same sex, with one usually left-handed and the other right-handed, conjoined twins make common use of one or more parts of their bodies, and the organs of one twin are usually a mirror image of those of the other—the heart of one, for example, being normally placed and that of the other in inverse position, what is known scientifically as *situs-inversus*. Siamese twins can easily be severed at birth where the union is superficial, but deeply united pairs like Chang and Eng seldom survive, and only a few have lived joined together.

Chang and Eng Bunker were born in Bangesau, Siam, on April 15, 1811, and were discovered at Mekong when they were sixteen. After Barnum brought these world-renowned "Chinese Double-Boys" to America he had considerable trouble with them, claiming that they were the only show business people he couldn't get along with. But then Chang and Eng hated everybody, even each other, Barnum said. At any rate, the two often quarreled with the impresario over his methods and only exhibited when they needed the money. In April 1846, they married two English sisters, Sarah and Adelaide Yates, and later fathered twenty-two children between them—Chang ten and Eng twelve, according to the records. They died on January 17, 1874, within two or three hours of each other, on their farm in New Hampshire. The last twin to die did not die of a broken heart, as the old story goes. Fatal illness in one Siamese twin dooms the other unless they can be separated, which was impossible in Chang and Eng's case.

Those Daring Young Men on the Flying Trapeze

A baby who has to be hung upside down from a trapeze bar to stop his crying would suggest to any parent a fledgling star aerialist. Such was the case with Jules Léotard, at least according to his *Memoirs*, a small volume swollen with windy conceit. In any event, Léotard, who inspired the song "The Daring Young Man on the Flying Trapeze," did become one of France's most famous aerialists in the nineteenth century, perfecting the aerial somersault, among other acrobatics, and starring in Paris and London circuses. Léotard died of tuberculosis in 1870 when only forty, but his name is remembered by the costume he invented, which is still worn by circus performers. That vanity played a large role as the handmaiden of his invention is witnessed by the plug the performer gave the *leotard* at the end of his *Memoirs*. "Do you want to be adored by the ladies?" he exhorts his male readers. "[Then] put on a more natural garb, which does not hide your best features." So far nobody earthbound has followed his advice. But the *leotard* is more popular for athletics today than ever. Originally the costume was a one-piece elastic garment, snug-fitting, low at the neck and sleeveless, but it became a garment covering the arms as well.

Blondin was the stage name of another great French aerialist, Jean François Gravelet (1824–97). The inimitable Blondin, whose name became a synonym for a star acrobat or tightrope walker, began his career at a mere five years of age and performed many great feats thereafter. The first man to cross Niagara Falls on a tightrope, on June 30, 1859, he later made the crossing while pushing a wheelbarrow, twirling an umbrella, and with another man on his back. The rope was 1,100 feet long, only 3 inches thick, and was suspended 160 feet above the falls. Later that day he walked on stilts part of the way across and went a distance with both feet tied in a burlap sack. He finally fried and ate an egg on a stove he had carried with him.

Oofty Goofty: The Wild Man of Borneo

History does not record Oofty Goofty's real name, nor a detailed physical description of him, but the shadowy, thin little man is remembered as one of the oddest thespians ever to set foot on a stage.

Oofty Goofty began his career as "the Wild Man of Borneo" in a San Francisco freak show late in the nineteenth century. After covering himself with tar from head to heel, he stuck large quantities of horsehair in the tar, which lent him a ferocious appearance. Locked in a cage on stage, he ate large chunks of raw meat thrown to him by attendants, growling and shaking the bars whenever a paying customer approached, yelping "Oofty goofty! Oofty goofty!"—a cry that soon became the only name he was known by.

Oofty Goofty's reign as "the wildest wild man in the history of wild men" ended when he became seriously ill because he could not perspire through his thick covering of tar and hair. But he had always considered himself a great performer and launched a career as a song and dance man in vaudeville. Unfortunately, his career only lasted for one song and dance—he was vehemently booed from the stage and thrown out of the theater.

When he landed on his back on the sidewalk Oofty Goofty discovered the great gift that would support him for the next fifteen years. He found that he was insensitive to pain. For the rest of his life he made a living by letting himself be kicked and pommeled for a price. It cost ten cents to kick the wild man as hard as one pleased, a quarter to hit him with a walking stick, and fifty cents to smack him with a baseball bat. In fact, Oofty carried a baseball bat with him wherever he went, approaching men in the street and inquiring, "Hit me with a bat for four bits, gents? Only four bits to hit me with this bat!"

It is said that Oofty Goofty's strange vocation—surely the cruelest act in show business—came to an end when heavyweight champion John L. Sullivan hit him with his bat, delivering a blow from which he never recovered. From that time on, his one claim to fame gone, he became a nonentity—no one even called him Oofty Goofty anymore—and within a few years he was buried in a lonely potter's field.

"Airy Fairy Lillian": The Toast of the Town

Beautiful and flamboyant Lillian Russell (1861–1922) was the toast of the town almost from the night she made her debut at New York's Tony Pastor's Opera House in burlesques of Gilbert and Sullivan comic operas. Only eighteen at the time, the singer and actress was fresh from Clinton, Iowa, where she had been born Helen Louise Leonard in 1861. For the next thirty years Lillian Russell's beauty and talent for light opera brought her fame and fortune unsurpassed by any contemporary performer, making her the first great prima donna of the American stage. The press called her "Airy Fairy Lillian." Success included her own company, a collection of male admirers that has probably never been matched since, several husbands whom she walked out on, and a number of sumptuous apartments and houses, like her summer home in then fashionable Far Rockaway, where she entertained lavishly and often failed to pay the bills. Among several things named for her was the Lillian Russell dessert, a half cantaloupe filled with a scoop of ice cream. Miss Russell ate like a longshoreman and never weighed less than two hundred pounds, which did not prevent Diamond Jim Brady from offering her a million dollars in cash for her hand in marriage. She even had a bicycle with a custom-fitted seat molded to her "every peculiarity of pose and shape." She will always be the toast of the town to the town of Lillian Russell, Kansas, which was named for her at the height of her fame.

Casey on the Stage

*Oh! somewhere in this favored land the
   sun is shining bright,
The band is playing somewhere, and
   somewhere hearts are light;
But there is no joy in Mudville—mighty
   Casey has struck out.*

This dramatic poem by Ernest Laurence Thayer (1863–1940) was first published in the *San Francisco Examiner* on June 3, 1888, and "Casey at the Bat" has been popular ever since. Its initial popularity was due as much to the actor De Wolf Hopper, who included the thirteen-stanza poem in his repertory, as it was to the poet, a former editor of the *Harvard Lampoon*. Everyone knows that there was no joy in Mudville when the mighty Casey struck out, but few are aware that Thayer patterned his fabled slugger on a real player, Daniel Maurice Casey, who was still posing for newspaper photographers fifty years after the poem's initial publication. As for Thayer, he was paid only five dollars for his poem, which the exceedingly tall, thin De Wolf Hopper recited more than ten thousand times, and which made a fortune for him—a fortune he desperately needed to pay alimony to six former wives.

America's Aphrodisiac: The "Won't You Come Play with Me" Girl

Few remember her today, but wasp-waisted Anna Held drove audiences wild in the Gay Nineties and the early years of the twentieth century. Miss Held, famous for her milk baths on stage and her renditions of "Won't You Come Play with Me?" and "I Just Can't Make My Eyes Behave," began her stage career as a street singer in her native Paris when only eight years old. She was a renowned musical comedy star by the time she turned sixteen. Showman Flo Ziegfeld discovered her during a European visit, married the siren, and starred her in many of his lavish productions. Anna, with her "hips that flowed like wine," easily pulled in more than $1,000 a week in Ziegfeld productions and went on to earn $5,000 a week in early silent films. After divorcing Ziegfeld, "America's Aphrodisiac" brought her "veiled naughtiness," "smallest waist in the world," and "sly teasing delivery" to vaudeville, finding a new stardom. The coquettish performer was courted for a time by the early chewing gum king William White, who is said to have spent up to $100,000 a month helping promote her stage career, completely backing at least one of her plays. White became so enchanted by his little Lorelei that he gave her a string of matched pearls worth $100,000. No one can say what went on in private, but Anna certainly chewed his gum vigorously in public. She also endorsed his Yucatan Gum as a way of keeping teeth bright, breath kissing-sweet, and strengthening sagging chin and drooping breast muscles. Even better for your health than naked milk baths.

Chicken Soup for the Soul

The great actor Jacob P. Adler performed mainly in the early Yiddish-American theater, noted for its avid, unreserved audiences. Adler was especially noted for his role of the main character, David Moishele, in *The Yiddish King Lear* (1892). One evening, right after the worst of Moishele's selfish daughters refused to give the hungry man a bowl of chicken soup, a voice cried out from the audience: "Leave those rotten children of yours and come home with me. My wife is a good cook. She'll fix you up!"

The Divine Sarah

French drama critic Francisque Sarcey, whose judgments (right or wrong) could make or break a play or actor, had no doubts about Sarah Bernhardt. He called her "She whose movements are disciplined, she who is a living harmony, a lyric in flesh and blood." Another critic of the day rhapsodized: "She has a voice like the silver sound of running water." Still another said: "In depicting human suffering she seems to absolutely control every organ of her body—her cheek blanches, tears come at her bidding." Though she was no great beauty, "the divine Sarah Bernhardt," as Oscar Wilde called her, is regarded by many as the greatest actress of all time. Born Rosine Bernhard, the illegitimate daughter of Jewish parents who converted to Catholicism, she was brought up in a convent until she entered the Paris Conservatoire at thirteen. After making her debut at the Comédie-Française in 1862, the sharp-eyed, frizzy-haired redhead played internationally, winning her great fame in tragic roles largely because of her "voice of gold" and magnetic personality. Sarah was probably the tallest, thinnest woman ever to star on the stage (Arthur "Bugs" Baer once wrote, "An empty cab drove up, and Sarah Bernhardt got out"), and her nickname "Sally Bee" became the sobriquet for any tall, lean woman. Sarah's great talents enabled her to play almost equally well in English as in French, and she toured America, among many other countries, earning and spending more than $25 million. One woman actually killed herself because she couldn't get tickets to a Sarah Bernhardt play.

The queen of the French stage, Sarah even performed the title role in *Hamlet* successfully and the loss of a leg in an accident late in her career did not diminish her talent or activity at all. She never lost her sense of humor, even about her amputated leg. When a boorish promoter offered her $100,000 to exhibit her leg at the Pan-American Exposition, she cabled back, "Which leg?"

"Energy creates energy," Sarah once said, explaining her remarkable vitality. "It is by spending oneself that one becomes rich." In 1912, Sarah Bernhardt made two motion pictures, *Queen Elizabeth* and *La Dame aux Camélias*, which remain as evidence of the incomparable talent that makes her name a synonym for a great actress. She died in 1923, aged seventy-nine, but had prepared herself for death long before then. During her adolescence, Sarah had conquered a morbid fear of death by persuading her mother to buy her a rosewood coffin, which she kept in her bedroom for the rest of her life and often slept in, as she said, "to get used to her final resting place" (a practice of the English poet John Dryden many years before her). The coffin was lined with letters from many of the more than one thousand lovers she is said to have had over her long, controversial career.

Sarah as Cleopatra

Playing Cleopatra, Sarah Bernhardt stabbed the slave who brought her the news of Marc Antony's defeat at Actium. According to one writer "she stormed, raved, wrecked the scenery in her frenzy and finally, as the curtain fell, dropped in a shuddering, convulsive heap." At this point, after the applause died, a proper Victorian lady was heard to say, "How different, how very different from the home life of our own dear Queen."

Duse the God

Though many critics consider her the greatest actress of all time, the Italian actress Eleonora Duse's personal life was filled with unhappiness. Born in 1859, the child of two traveling actors, she played her first part when only three years old, becoming an accomplished actress by the time she turned twelve. She was a small, dark, sad-eyed woman who had "a kind of physical eloquence, a beauty in motion" equaled by no other actress, according to one critic. Duse, as her adoring fans most often called her, always performed in Italian and never wore makeup ("I only make up my soul," she once said), but she managed to attract audiences all over the world with her total immersion in the characters she played, truly becoming Juliet in *Romeo and Juliet* and Marguerite in Dumas *fils*'s *La Dame aux Camélias*, among many other roles. She could make even the props she used perform for her—according to one legend, the rose she held in her hand as Marguerite opened when the character found hope and wilted when she despaired. Victor Hugo called Eleonora "Duse the God" and many admirers pronounced her even greater than Sarah Bernhardt, but all her numerous romances were ill-fated. The worst was her affair with the braggart Italian author Gabriele D'Annunzio, who boasted that a thousand husbands hated him and would show visitors pillows that he claimed were filled with the soft locks of women who were virgins before the Great One (meaning himself) met them. True to form, D'Annunzio played her for a fool in financial affairs and went so far as to detail their sexual relationship in his novel *Il Fuoco*. The loss of a lung from tuberculosis forced Duse to retire from the stage, but she made a comeback after ten years. Her weakened condition, however, caused her to die of pneumonia after she was caught in a rainstorm while performing in America in 1924. Parts of her silent film *Ceneré* (1916) remain as a testament to her acting skills, though she disliked the film and ordered it destroyed.

Duse vs. Bernhardt

On two successive nights in 1895 the two greatest actresses of the nineteenth century and perhaps all time played the title role in German playwright Hermann Sudermann's *Magda*, a romantic melodrama. The famous contest pitted the legendary Italian actress Eleonora Duse against her arch rival, French actress Sarah Bernhardt. All London was talking about this duel of giants: Duse, thirty-seven, with her "physical eloquence, a beauty in motion," against Bernhardt, thirteen years older, with her "voice like a golden bell." Many, including respected British drama critic Clement Scott, preferred the more florid Bernhardt, but the majority, like George Bernard Shaw, then drama critic of the *Saturday Review*, opted for Duse's more restrained and subtle style. Later Shaw would write of her performance:

> *When it is remembered that the majority of tragic actors excell only in explosions of those passions which are common to man and brute, there will be no difficulty in understanding the indescribable distinction which Duse's acting acquires from the fact that behind every stroke of it is a distinctly*

human idea. In nothing is this more apparent than in the vigilance in her of that high human instinct which seeks to awaken the deepest responsive feeling without giving pain.

Arguably, the Best Stage Players of All

Ancient Times—Thespis (sixth century B.C.). The legendary Greek poet and actor who first used actors in his plays and whose name gives us the word *thespian*.

Roman Times—Roscius (d. 62 B.C.). The Roman comic actor whose name has become synonymous with *actor*.

Sixteenth Century—James Burbage (c.1530–97). He was known as much for his heading an important acting company and for his building of London's first theater as for his acting. He was the great Richard Burbage's father.

Seventeenth Century—Richard Burbage (1567–1619). Rising from a boy actor to chief parts, Richard Burbage became Shakespeare's good friend and was praised as a painter as well as a thespian. His chief rival was Edward Alleyn (1566–1626), who, according to a traditional tale, quit the stage after seeing the devil one night while playing Dr. Faustus.

Eighteenth Century—David Garrick (1717–79). He is said to have "raised acting to an art." A sentimental favorite is old Charles Macklin (1697–1797), if only because the English actor, famed for his Shakespearean roles, retired from the stage when his memory failed at the age of ninety-three! After his retirement, it was his pleasure to go to the theater to heckle other actors.

Nineteenth Century—Edmund Kean (1787–1833). The great English tragic actor wins despite his weakness in playing romantic parts (his Romeo was a laughingstock). He has strong competition, however, from the great French actress Rachel and the Italian actress Eleonora Duse.

Twentieth Century—Sir Laurence Olivier (1907–89). The English actor who transformed himself into every character he played has many challengers, barely beating out Sarah Bernhardt (1844–1923), whose career spanned two centuries.

Of course not everyone would agree with this ranking. Famed director Joshua Logan, for example, picked the following twelve actors, in this order, as the best stage actors of all time: Edwin Booth, Tommaso Salvino, Coquelin,

Eleonora Duse, David Garrick, Ivan Moskvin, Sokolov, Alexander Moissi, Laurence Olivier, William Gillette, Rex Harrison, and Marlon Brando.

White Rats, Lambs, and Other Theatrical Clubs

The strangely named *White Rats* was a fraternal organization for vaudevillians founded at the turn of the twentieth century by actor George Fuller Golden. Golden named it after the similar British Water Rats, a society that had come to his aid when he was stranded in London. Several attempts were made to make a militant actors' union out of the White Rats, and it attracted a number of headliners, but all such efforts failed when theater owners blacklisted its members. By 1917 the White Rats went bankrupt and was dissolved.

A longer-lasting actors' club is the *Lambs Club*, founded in 1874 and also named after a similar British group. For many years it had its own theater on 44th Street east of Broadway in New York City, its building designed by noted architect Stanford White. The Lambs' president was called the *Shepherd* and every year the club held a show called the Lambs' Gambol, all the proceeds going to charity. In days past "a Lambs Club actor" was the name for any pretentious ham.

The *Friars Club*, a theatrical fraternity founded in 1904, has been headed by such prominent *Abbots* as George M. Cohan, Georgie Jessel, Milton Berle, Joe E. Lewis, and Frank Sinatra. The Friars, based in a clubhouse on East 55th Street, is noted for its "roasts" of celebrities—facetious tributes at a banquet in which the celebrity is both praised and good-naturedly insulted in speeches by friends.

It is said that the *Players Club* was modeled after London's Garrick Club in 1888 as a meeting place for both actors and others interested in the theater. It had as its charter members such notables as Edwin Booth, John Drew, Mark Twain, and Civil War general William Tecumseh Sherman.

The oldest American theatrical social club, and perhaps the best known, is Harvard's *Hasty Pudding Club*, founded in 1795 and named after Joel Barlow's mock-epic poem "The Hasty Pudding." Over the years its theatricals have featured as performers and writers such notables as Oliver Wendell Holmes, William Randolph Hearst, Franklin Delano Roosevelt, and Robert Sherwood.

The World's Worst Actor: Ronald "the Inept" Coates

Shakespearean actor Ronald Coates has been nominated by several writers as the worst actor in the history of the legitimate theater. Coates, however, had supreme—or absurd—confidence, calling himself "a second David Garrick."

On- and offstage he paraded himself about clad in billowing pantaloons, a star-spangled coat, and a huge feathered hat. Coates had the audacity to rewrite Shakespeare's plays to suit his own purpose. Once when playing Romeo, he tried to pry open Juliet's coffin with a crowbar. His performances were invariably ridiculous and he was frequently booed off the stage for his overblown interpretations; indeed, his British audiences often became so violent that they threatened him with lynching, forcing his fellow actors to demand police protection before agreeing to go on with him. Some people came to laugh at Coates, however; in fact, at one performance several members of the audience were so convulsed by laughter that they had to be treated by a doctor. Coates got so bad that he eventually had to bribe theater managers to obtain a role, but he kept on acting. Only death removed him from the stage. It did not come at the hands of an angry theater mob but in a traffic accident in 1848 at the ripe old age of seventy-four. He remains known to history by the name British audiences gave him: Ronald "the Inept" Coates.

"The World's Best Bad Actor"

Iowa-born Corse Payton (1867–1934) was proud to be as "corny" as his home state, actually billing himself as the "World's Best Bad American Actor." Corse left home at the age of sixteen for an acting career, but he took most of his family with him, organizing a traveling company that toured the Midwest and West for many years. The trouping trail ended in Brooklyn, New York, of all places, when Payton had saved enough money to open Corse Payton's Theater there. For some twenty years his stock company offered a great variety of plays ranging from melodramas to Shakespeare, seats priced at ten cents, twenty cents, and thirty cents. Lillian and Dorothy Gish, Ernest Truex, Richard Bennett, and Fay Bainter were just a few of the actors who served apprenticeships with the self-advertised ham over his long career. In his last years he lived in Brooklyn and built a charming Dutch-Colonial house in the then fashionable seaside town of Far Rockaway, New York, where he entertained such luminaries as Lillian Russell, Enrico Caruso, and Governor Al Smith.

The World's Worst Act

The Cherry Sisters—Lizzie, Effie, Jessie, and Addie—began their singing career in 1893 when they appeared in an amateur night at a Grand Rapids, Michigan, theater. From then on it was all downhill. The Cherry Sisters, ranging in age from seventeen to twenty-two, were so bad that people came to see them for the laughs, and they were soon playing to packed houses, though they were forced to perform behind a wire-mesh screen to protect them from the rotten tomatoes and garbage audiences invariably threw at them. The sisters managed to make only a meager living and were considering retirement when the great impresario Oscar Hammerstein discovered them. Hammerstein, in deep financial trouble, decided to try a new gimmick. "I've been putting on the best talent recently and it hasn't gone over," he advised reporters. "Now I'm going to try the worst."

Hammerstein signed the Cherry Sisters to a contract guaranteeing them $1,000 a week and on November 16, 1896, they opened at New York's Olympia Theater. They wore cherry red dresses, hats, and mittens and for their first number sang the immortal

> *Cherries ripe boom-de-ay!*
> *Cherries ripe boom-de-ay!*
> *The Cherry Sisters*
> *Have come to stay!*

This was followed by numbers like "Don't You Remember Sweet Alice, Ben Bolt?," "I'm Out upon the Mash, Boys," and "Curfew Must Not Ring Tonight." The sophisticated New York audiences sat shaking their heads, but the critics weren't so merciful. About the best review the Cherry Sisters got was in the *New York Times*: "It is sincerely hoped that nothing like them will ever be seen again."

But the Cherry Sisters *were* seen again—and again and again. Even sophisticated New Yorkers, however, took to carrying overripe tomatoes, eggs, and beer bottles to the theater, and the girls soon had to bring their wire-mesh screen back into service. Nevertheless, the Cherry Sisters—billed as "The World's Worst Act"—played to standing room only crowds for over seven years. When they retired to the family farm in 1903 they had amassed a fortune of more than $200,000, the equivalent of millions today.

Great Affectations

- An affected actress annoyed composer-playwright Jerome Kern throughout rehearsals with her rolled *r*s. "Tell me, Mr. Kern," she finally said, "you want me to c-rr-ross the stage, but I'm behind a table. How shall I get acr-rr-ross?"

    "Why, my dear," Kern replied, "just r-r-roll over on your *r*s."

- A young actor was entertaining a circle of admirers at a party and kept telling them how busy he was, continually referring to his crowded schedule, which he pronounced *shedshoole* in the British manner. "If you don't mind my saying so," annoyed playwright Dorothy Parker finally said, "I think you are full of *skit*."
- An actress full of herself asked director Alfred Hitchcock, "What do you think is my very best feature?" "You're sitting on it," Hitchcock replied.

The Most Tasteless Performers of All Time

Hadji Ali, billed as "The Amazing Regurgitator," in the late nineteenth century, had one of the most tasteless acts in vaudeville history. Ali would swallow a variety of things, including objects supplied by his audiences, and regurgitate them at will. But it must be said that upchucking coins, jewels, watches, watermelon seeds, peach pits, and the like wasn't the exciting part of his act. For a grand finale Hadji swallowed a gallon of water and a pint of kerosene. He'd first throw up the kerosene, spewing it five feet across the stage, where it set a small heated metal castle on fire. He then vomited the gallon of water to extinguish the flaming castle while the audience cheered. There are records of his performances on film.

Even more tasteless was French vaudevillian Joseph Pujol (1851–1945), known by the stage name Le Petomane. Pujol had only one talent: he could make musical notes by bending over and expelling gas from his well-tempered derriere, which was, mercifully, not exposed. Le Petomane was so popular that he constantly outdrew Sarah Bernhardt with his flatulent "songs" and impressions of musical instruments and noted opera singers. He would also, in the same manner, blow out a candle from a distance of one foot and play "The Marseillaise" for an encore.

"Wake Me Up When Kirby Dies"

What player would really want such words to be his living memorial in the language? Charles Hemstreet told the unfortunate thespian's story in *When Old New York Was Young* (1902):

> *Something more than sixty years ago (1841) the attention of theatre-goers was directed to a young actor who appeared at intervals in the Chatham Theatre. He was J. Hudson Kirby. His acting had not much merit, but he persisted in a theory that made him famous. It was his idea that an actor should reserve all his strength for scenes of carnage and death. The earlier*

acts of a play he passed through carelessly, but when he came to death scenes he threw himself into them with such force and fury that they came to be the talk of the town. Some of the spectators found the earlier acts so dull and tiresome that they went to sleep, taking the precaution, however, to nudge their neighbor, with the request to wake them up for the death scene. And for long years after Kirby's time, the catchphrase applied to any supreme effort was "Wake me up when Kirby dies."

More Bad Acting

- Richard Brinsley Sheridan's classic comedy *The Rivals* was badly received on its first night at the Covent Garden on January 17, 1775, due to a poor performance by John Lee, who played Sir Lucius O'Trigger. Lee was so incensed when an apple hit him in the head after one scene that he strode to the edge of the stage and cried out: "By the powers, is it *personal*?—is it me or the matter [the character he was playing]?"

- In *The Critic* Sheridan cast the role of Lord Burleigh with a Mr. Moody, a "very stupid actor" who "looked profound." The actor couldn't possibly blunder, Sheridan bet a friend, for his directions clearly said: "Mr. Moody as Lord Burleigh will advance from the prompter's side—proceed to the front of the stage—fall back to where Mr. Waldron stands as Sir Christopher Hatton—shake his head, and exit." Sheridan lost. On opening night, instead of shaking his own head, Moody walked over to Waldron-Hatton, took the actor's head in two hands, and slowly shook it from side to side before making his exit.

- Many critics found Thomas Sheridan, the father of playwright Richard Brinsley Sheridan, an outstanding actor, but Dr. Johnson thought him rather obtuse. "Sherry is dull," he once told Boswell, "naturally dull; but it must have taken him a great deal of pain to become what we now see him as. Such an excess of stupidity, sir, is not in nature."

- Colley Cibber (1671–1757), who would later become famous as a much-ridiculed dramatist, had a bit part in a Thomas Betterton play. Suffering from stage fright, he ruined the scene he was in. "Fine him for that!" Betterton told an assistant. "Why, sir, he has no salary," he was advised. "No?" Betterton said. "Why then, put him down for ten shillings a week and fine him five shillings."

- Gunnar Heiberg (1857–1929), a brilliant dramatist who had the misfortune to follow too closely on the footsteps of Ibsen, was even unluckier in the looks nature willed him. He was among the ugliest men in theater history. In fact, his repulsive physical appearance led to his becoming a writer. He wanted to be an actor but no one in Germany or all Europe would even give him an audition, and so he turned to writing plays instead.

- The American humorist, poet, and cartoonist Oliver Herford (1863–1935) was talking to an actor noted for his vanity. "Why, I'm a smash hit!" the man declared. "Only yesterday, during the last act, I had the audience glued to their seats!"

    "Wonderful! Wonderful!" exclaimed Herford. "Clever of you to think of it!"

- In a production of *Carmen* at New York's Metropolitan Opera House real horses were used to pull Carmen's coach across the stage. One of the horses, responding to a call of nature, left a large mess center stage. The pile was still there in the climactic scene when Enrico Caruso, playing Escamillo, was supposed to stab Maria Jeritza, playing Carmen. But the diva refused to fall and die when Caruso stabbed her. An angry Caruso stabbed her again, shouting, "Die! Fall, will you!" Madame Jeritza screamed back, "I'll die if you can find me a clean place!"

- When serving as drama critic for the *New York Tribune* in 1915, Heywood Broun's most memorable review began with his description of a performance by actor Geoffrey Steyne as "the worst to be seen in the contemporary theatre." Steyne sued for damages to his professional reputation. While the suit was pending he chanced to appear in another play that Broun reviewed. Broun noted this time that "Mr. Steyne's performance was not up to his usual standard." (The suit was eventually dismissed.)

- Eugene O'Neill's father, James, gave up a promising career as an actor for the financial security of playing the leading role in *The Count of Monte Cristo*, which he played more than five thousand times. "A chip off the old block, eh?" Eugene said to him soon after he, too, had chosen the theater as a career. "Say, rather, a slice off the old ham," James O'Neill replied.

- At a benefit performance in New York the widely disliked Alexander Woollcott played Henry VIII and Madge Kennedy portrayed Anne Boleyn. The audience booed and hissed for a full five minutes when Woollcott made his entrance, but he was incapable of getting the message. "I can't understand why Madge should be so unpopular," he remarked as he came offstage.

- "What's my motivation for doing it?" a young method actor asked his director when told to make a certain stage movement. "Your job," the director replied.
- Wrote director George S. Kaufman in a telegram sent between acts to actor William Gaxton, who played the president in *Of Thee I Sing*: I AM WATCHING YOUR PERFORMANCE FROM THE REAR OF THE HOUSE. WISH YOU WERE HERE. Another time Kaufman reviewed the performance of a young Italian operatic tenor. "Guido Nazzo is nazzo guido," he wrote. The wisecrack was so widely repeated that it nearly ruined the singer's career. Kaufman was so truly sorry that he apologized to Nazzo and offered him a part in one of his plays.

Performers with the Best New York Accents

1. Leo Gorcey, Huntz Hall, and the rest of the Dead End Kids
2. Bugs Bunny
3. Betty Boop
4. Popeye
5. Henry Winkler ("The Fonz")

The Hardest Speech Ever Given an Actor (Try It!)

In 1755 young actor and playwright Samuel Foote (1720–77) composed the following speech after pompous fellow player Charles Macklin boasted that he could repeat anything after hearing it once: "So she went into the garden to cut a cabbage leaf to make an apple pie; and at the same time, a great she-bear coming up the street pops its head into the shop—What no soap? So he died; and she very impudently married the barber; and there were present the picaninnies and the Jobilies, and the Garyulies, and the great Panjandrum himself, with the little round button at top."

"Old Macklin" (he lived to be a hundred) gave up in disgust, unable to memorize this nonsense, but the mnemonic exercise gave the language both the phrase *no soap*, for the failure of some mission or plea, and *great Panjandrum*, the big boss, or someone who imagines himself to be the big boss.

Actor Foote, who was disliked by Dr. Johnson, once announced that he was going to do an imitation of the Great Cham on the stage. Johnson sent word that he had ordered a new oak cudgel and would be present that evening to correct any faults in the impersonation with it. Foote canceled the show.

Say What?: The Longest Words Ever Delivered on Stage

Any actor who can remember words like these deserves an Oscar. Start with "Aldiborontiphoscophornio! Where left you Chrononhotonthologos?," which begins Henry Carey's farce *Chrononhotonthologos, the Most Tragical Tragedy That Ever Was Tragedized by Any Company of Tragedians* (1734). Chrononhotonthologos was the King of Queerummania, and his name is now used (by anyone who can pronounce it) for any bombastic person delivering an inflated address. Aldiborontiphoscophornio was a courier in the play. Carey is better remembered for writing the popular song "Sally in My Alley"; he may also have written the words and music to the British anthem "God Save the King."

Longer than any stage word is this Greek monstrosity of fully 170 letters that occurs in Aristophanes' comedy *The Ecclesiazusae* and describes a fricassee of hash made of seventeen sweet-and-sour ingredients. The goulash transliterates into English as the 182-letter *lopadotemachoselachogaleokranioleipsanodrimhypotrimmatosilphioparaomelitokatakechymenokichlepikossyphophattoperisteralektryonoptekephalliokigklopeleiolagoiosiraiobaphetraganopterug*. Translated it means "limpets, slices of saltfish, thorn-backs, whistle-fishes, cournelberries, a remoulade of leftover brains seasoned with silphium and cheese, thrushes basted with honey, blackbirds, ringdoves, squabs, chickens, fried mullets, wagtails, rock pigeons, and wings ground up in wine that has been boiled down."

The most commonly used long stage word is certainly the thirty-four-letter word meaning "superb" featured in the film *Mary Poppins*: *supercalifragilisticexpialidocious*.

Mesopotamia

David Garrick wrote that actor George Whitefield's voice was so masterful that "he could make men either laugh or cry by pronouncing the word Mesopotamia."

"Two-a-Dayers": American Vaudeville Performers

In its heyday from about 1885 to 1928 there were as many as 20,000 acts playing American vaudeville. Vaudeville takes its name from the village of Vire in fifteenth-century Normandy, where a group of performers was called the Compagnons du Vau de Vire (the Companions of the Vire Valley). Their popularity spread and soon the word *ville* (town) was substituted for Vire, the name of the original village. *Vaudeville* came to mean "valley town songs" and then the acts that featured them. Much later, in the mid-nineteenth century, Americans borrowed the French word to describe variety shows offering musical and comedy acts on the same bill—also called *olios*. Such shows, often coarse at first, initially played in saloons and honky-tonks around the country but did not become tremendously popular until the establishment of the B. F. Keith national circuit in 1883.

Vaudeville featured many famous stars of musical comedy and the legitimate theater, including the Barrymores and Sarah Bernhardt, but relied mainly on its own star comics and song and dance acts, such as Weber and Fields, Gallagher and Shean, Harry Lauder, Harrigan and Hart, the Marx Brothers, Will Rogers, the Seven Little Foys, Fanny Brice, Al Jolson, Eddie Cantor, and Jimmy Durante, many of whom later left vaudeville for the theater or movies. The most prestigious theater a vaudevillian could play was New York's Palace Theater, built by Martin Beck on Broadway between 46th and 47th Streets in 1913; "playing the Palace" became the dream of every "two-a-dayer." The Palace was converted to a movie theater and later a legitimate theater after vaudeville's demise, which came in the early 1930s with the perfection of radio and sound films.

Sober Sue

Impresario Oscar Hammerstein offered $1,000 to anyone who could make Sober Sue laugh when she performed in her vaudeville act at New York's Victoria Theater in 1908. Sue's ten-minute act attracted the best comedians in America, but their best jokes and funniest faces failed to evoke even the faintest smile on her stone face. Only Hammerstein and Sober Sue (her last name is forgotten) knew that she couldn't lose, for Sue wasn't, strictly speaking, an actress—she was totally unable to smile; her facial muscles were paralyzed. Hammerstein never paid out a cent and got the best comedy acts in the business for nothing.

A Music-Hall Shakespeare

British music-hall star Wilkie Bard (whose real name was Billie Smith), named himself after Shakespeare, the immortal Bard, and even modeled his high, domed forehead after the playwright's. Wilkie Bard (1870–1944) was famous for his impersonations and pantomimes, as well as his decidedly un-Shakespearean tongue-twisting song "She Sells Sea Shells on the Seashore," which was all the rage at the turn of the twentieth century.

Mr. Gallagher and Mr. Shean

Their trademark song "Mr. Gallagher and Mr. Shean" with its recurring line "Positively, Mr. Gallagher—Absolutely, Mr. Shean" helped make Edward Gallagher (1873–1929) and Al Shean (1868–1949) one of the most famous and best-remembered vaudeville teams, equaled only by Harrigan and Hart, who worked more often in musical comedy, and the famed Weber and Fields act ("Who vas dat lady I saw you with last night?" "Dat vas no lady, dat vas my wife."). Gallagher, tall, thin, and bespectacled, played straight man to the stocky Shean, Gallagher wearing a straw hat and Shean an Egyptian fez. The act broke up in 1912, after only two years, but the comedians reconciled in 1920 thanks to the efforts of Shean's sister, Minnie Marx, mother of the Marx Brothers. Gallagher and Shean split again five years later for reasons unknown, and Gallagher died in 1930 after a nervous breakdown. Shean continued to play in vaudeville and movies until the end of his life.

Harrigan and Hart

> "Vaudevillians Harrigan and Hart are still an unforgettable memory in the minds of old-time New Yorkers. Their sketches were humorous pictures of those phases of local life that they all understood so well.... All their plays were marvels in the way of local detail and rich in homely wit. I remember one scene in which the members of the Board of Aldermen visited Dan Mulligan's house and were so well entertained, that they all fell asleep in the dining room.
>
> "'Whatever will I do?' demanded Mrs. Mulligan of her husband, 'The aldermen are all sound asleep. Will I wake them?'
>
> "'Leave them be,' said Mulligan. 'While they sleep the city's safe.'"
> —*from James L. Ford,*
> Forty-Odd Years in the Literary Shop, *1921*

The Top Banana

An old joke in a popular burlesque and vaudeville act featured three comics dividing two bananas. The comedian who got left out of the distribution was told "You got the third banana." From this saying the lowest buffoon in any act came to be called *the third banana* and the title *top banana* was used to describe the head comic in any act or musical comedy. Much later, in the 1950s, the expression began to be applied to the head of any group.

Stripteasing

Stripteaser Georgia Sothern (or her press agent), wrote H. L. Mencken in 1940 asking him to coin a "more palatable word" to describe her profession. The Sage of Baltimore, who had hatched other neologisms (for instance, *bootician* for a bootlegger), gallantly responded, suggesting that stripteasing be related "in some way or other to the zoological phenomenon of molting." Among his specific recommendations were *moltician* (too close to *mortician*); *gecko*, after a family of molting lizards called the Geckonidae (not very appetizing, either); and *ecdysiast*, which comes from *ecdysis*, the scientific term for molting. Miss Sothern adopted the last and it was publicized universally; a new word was born to the world and a new union called the Society of Ecdysiasts, Parade, and Specialty Dancers appeared. But not every artfully unclad body was happy with Mencken's invention. Said the Queen of Strippers, Gypsy Rose Lee: "'Ecdysiast,' he calls me! Why the man is an intellectual Slob. He had been reading *books. Dictionaries.* We don't wear feathers and molt them off.... What does he know about stripping?" Most would agree that *stripteaser* is far more revealing.

The American burlesque in which Miss Sothern and Gypsy Rose Lee performed their striptease acts owes something to traditional burlesque, which is comedy employing satire or caricature (the word *burlesque* in fact deriving from the Italian *burla*, ridicule). But burlesque derived more directly from the minstrel show and variety theater. American burlesque, rarely produced today, featured often raunchy dialect and slapstick comedians, song and dance acts, and scantily dressed chorus girls as well as bump-and-grind strippers. It operated in circuits distinct from vaudeville after the turn of the twentieth century, mainly in the Columbia and Empire Circuits, and grew more daring until police raids inspired by laws proposed by New York Mayor LaGuardia led to the closing of the famed Minsky burlesque houses and others during the Great Depression. The best-known and most artistic stripper of the golden era was Gypsy Rose Lee (born Rose Louise Hovick), who began her show business career as a child song and dance act and wrote mystery novels after her burlesque days ended. Fanny Brice, Bobby Clark, Phil Silvers, and Abbott and Costello were among the many great comedic talents who worked in burlesque.

Hootchie-Kootchie Dancers

The hootchie-kootchie is the Turkish belly dance that many of us "have no stomach for," as comedian Beatrice Lillie once said. The name for the "mildly lascivious" dance—"not as sensuous as actual bumps and grinds since the hips are swayed rather than the pelvis rotated," we're told—has no source in an oriental name, unless it comes from the Bengal state of Cooch Behar. The best guess is that *hootchie-kootchie* derives from the English dialect words *hotch*, "to shake," and *couch* (pronounced *cooche*), "to protrude." Dancer Little Egypt (Catherine Deviene) made a fortune and got herself arrested several times by dancing the hootchie-kootchie in the nude at the 1893 Chicago World's Fair and a number of private parties. A low-down hootchie-kootcher, like Danny Kaye's famous Minnie the Moocher, is simply a hoochie-koochie dancer.

The Great Caruso

Enrico Caruso (1873–1921) was a depositor at the Fifth Avenue branch of the Bank of New York, which was close by the Metropolitan Opera House. One day a new teller did not recognize him. According to a bank history, "When an alert young paying teller sees a famous name like Caruso on a check, he instinctively becomes suspicious. . . . The more Caruso tried to convince the distracted teller that he *was* Caruso, the more convinced the latter became that he was a fraud. Then Caruso had an inspiration. Stepping back a few paces from the teller's window so that he would not blow the money around, he placed one hand on his breast and began to sing an aria, from *Tosca*. Long before he had finished, the teller began to count the money out in a panic. When he came to the end, Caruso bowed and took his money, while the customers and the clerks cheered."

The greatest of tenors, Enrico Caruso was born in Naples, Italy, of a poor family and had little musical training except in singing the sensuous Neapolitan ballads of his city. He first came into prominence with his appearance in Puccini's *La Bohème* in 1898. This performance in Milan was the beginning of a career never matched by an opera singer for riches and adulation; his appearances and recordings carried his "celestial golden voice" around the world. From 1903 on, Caruso was the leading tenor at New York's Metropolitan Opera House. A lighthearted man of boyish charm, he was something of a cutup. When he pinched a girl's derrière in a Paris park, the resulting publicity gave rise to the nautical expression *a touch of Caruso*, meaning the turn of a ship's engines astern. Caruso's great vocal range and power have never been equaled. His was a tragic death. He ruptured a blood vessel while singing in 1920 and died the following year. Better to remember him vacationing one summer in the then fashionable seaside suburb of Far Rockaway, New York, where, local legend has it, he used to walk along the beach mornings singing, calming the stormiest seas. There never was a more beautiful voice.

Judged by Her Work, Not Her Weight or Years

Luisa Tetrazzini, the Italian-born diva whose role of Lucia di Lammermoor made her famous to opera lovers throughout the world early in the twentieth century, counted as her favorite dish *chicken Tetrazzini*: diced chicken in cream sauce flavored with sherry, baked in a casserole with spaghetti, cheese, and mushrooms. According to those who saw her, Madame Tetrazzini shared a problem common to many opera stars; she looked as if she had often dined on the highly caloric dish. The coloratura soprano made her debut in Florence in 1895 and ended her concert career in 1931, after starring in Spain, Portugal, Russia, England, the United States, and many other countries. She died in 1941, aged sixty-nine. It is said that the great diva's children tried to have her declared incompetent in her late years. The judge dismissed the case after she sang an aria for him in court.

A Dieting Prima Donna

Melba toast, the traditional story goes, originated as several pieces of burnt toast served to the Australian opera star Dame Nellie Melba (1861–1931) at the Savoy in London. The prima donna had been on a diet, ordered toast, and enjoyed the crisp, crunchy, overtoasted slices that were served to her by mistake. The maître d' named them in her honor and put *melba toast* on the menu. Whether the story is true or not, thin, crispy melba toast honors Dame Nellie, as does the peach, ice-cream, and raspberry sauce dessert *peach melba*, which the French chef Escoffier concocted for her. Nellie Melba was the stage name adopted (from the city of Melbourne) by Helen Porter Mitchell, who became a Dame of the British Empire in 1918. The world-famous soprano made her debut in *Rigoletto* in Brussels (1887) and went on to star at London's Covent Garden, the Paris Opera, La Scala, and New York's Metropolitan, among numerous opera houses. Unlike many opera stars, Nellie Melba did not study singing until she was over twenty-one years old, although she had previously been trained as a pianist. Few equaled her before or since in pure vocalization and unsurpassed agility, her lyric soprano having bell-like clarity. It is said, however, that she nearly ruined her voice in 1896 when she sang Brunhild in *Siegfried*. The celebrated singer retired in 1926, becoming president of the Melbourne Conservatoire.

The Great Houdini

The magician Erih Weiss (1875–1926) adopted the stage name Harry Houdini early in his career. Strangely enough, he named himself after another magician he admired—Jean-Eugene-Robert Houdin (1850–71), a French magician celebrated for the fact that he did *not* attribute his feats to supernatural powers. Houdini, a magician's magician who invented many tricks, also exposed numerous spiritualists and other fraudulent performers. He wrote a number of books and left his extensive library to the Library of Congress, where there is now a Houdini Room. The supreme magician has become the object of almost cultlike worship among fellow illusionists. Once he claimed that if anyone could break the shackles of death and contact the living from the grave, he could. Since his death—"He was fifty-two when he died, his life like a deck of cards"—followers have periodically held séances at his grave in Glendale, New York, in the Machpelah Cemetery, where a granite bust of the magician stares down at them. "The Handcuff King" inspired a Houdini Hall of Fame at Niagara Falls, New York.

The Red Dancer of the Thousand Veils

Behind the patina of the pseudonym Mata Hari is a rather prosaic Dutch name. Margaretha Geertruida Zelle (1876–1917) used Mata Hari as both her stage name and her nom de guerre when she chose to become a spy for the Germans before World War I. Acclaimed throughout Europe for her interpretations of naked Indonesian dances, she met many men in high places, including German officials in Berlin, who recruited her as a spy in 1907. During World War I, her dancing was the rage of Paris, and she became intimate with top Allied officers, many of whom confided military secrets to her. Mata Hari, who slept with literally hundreds of men, thrived by deceiving the spies active in Paris, but she was eventually betrayed to the French secret service by another German agent, Captain Walter Wilhelm Canaris, later the head of Germany's secret service in World War II. Her trial was the most publicized of the many espionage trials held during the war, and her name became synonymous for a glamorous female spy and femme fatale. Mata Hari was convicted by a French court-martial and executed by a firing squad.

The Sheik

To say silent screen star Rudolph Valentino was a sex symbol is putting it mildly. Italian-born Rodolfo D'Antonguolla came to the United States in 1913, and after working as a gardener, a cabaret dancer–gigolo, and then a bit player in Hollywood, he zoomed to stardom under his stage name in *The Four Horsemen of the Apocalypse* (1921), which was followed by hits like *The Sheik, Blood and Sand, Monsieur Beaucaire,* and *The Son of the Sheik.* Valentino became the embodiment of romance and sex to women all over the world; after seventy-five years his name is still a synonym for a handsome lover. Women had always been attracted to Valentino—it is said that he left Italy to escape an enraged husband, and when he came to New York he was arrested when police found him in the apartment of a woman suspected of extorting money from fun-seeking businessmen. But after his movie successes, Valentino became an object of worship to thousands of females. Women ripped his clothes off him in the streets for souvenirs, exposed their bodies to him, climbed uninvited into his bed. The crowds were unbelievable wherever he went—once when he took a stroll aboard the *Leviathan* so many women rushed to his side that the captain feared the danger of a disastrous list. The antics of individuals were even more unbelievable—one woman broke her leg climbing into his dressing room, others paid his valet twenty dollars for a vial of his used bathwater. Yet despite his dark good looks, this star of stars was a timorous lover, a superstitious man who tried to bolster his sexual powers with aphrodisiacs and magic amulets, who always preferred food to women, and who found his neurotic, clamorous admirers completely undesirable. Valentino died of peritonitis caused by a bleeding ulcer, when he was only thirty-one years old. More than fifty thousand people, overwhelmingly women, attended his funeral in New York in 1926, and even today admirers come to mourn at his crypt in the Los Angeles cemetery where he is buried. Some 250 women have claimed publicly that the "Sheik" fathered their love children, many of whom were born years after Valentino's death.

Not-So-Tall, Dark, and Handsome

The cliché "tall, dark, and handsome" as the description of an attractive man can be traced to newspaper descriptions of movie idol Rudolph Valentino in the 1920s, though Valentino was only of average height. Mae West undoubtedly popularized the expression in her 1933 film *She Done Him Wrong,* in which Cary Grant was the object of her desire.

The First Cheesecake

Cheesecake means, of course, photographs of delectable female models. The old story is that in 1912 *New York Journal* photographer James Kane was developing a picture of an actress that included "more of herself than either he or she expected." As he looked at it, he searched for the greatest superlative he knew of to express his delight and exclaimed, "That's real cheesecake!"

"It" Girls and "Oomph" Girls

Silent movie star Clara Bow (1905–65) was Hollywood's *It* girl, although Rudyard Kipling first used *It* to represent sex appeal in his short story "Mrs. Bathurst" (1904): "Tisn't beauty, so to speak, nor good talk necessarily. It's just It. Some women will stay in a man's memory if they once walked down a street." The expression became very popular in the late 1920s when Clara Bow starred in the 1926 film version of Elinor Glyn's novel *IT*. As the It girl Miss Bow was one of a long line of types admired by American men, including the *Gibson girl*, the *Ziegfeld girl*, the *Vamp* (actress Theda Bara), the *Screen's Bad Girl* (Mae West), the *flapper*, the *oomph girl* (Ann Sheridan), the *sweater girl*, the *pinup girl*, the *peekaboo girl* (Veronica Lake), the *Threat* (Lizbeth Scott), and the *Playmate* or *Bunny*. Clara Bow lived up to her reputation both on- and offscreen. She had affairs with scores of celebrities ranging from Gary Cooper to "Banjo Eyes" Eddie Cantor and "Count Dracula" Bela Lugosi, and there is a persistent though unsubstantiated story that on one occasion she played with the entire University of Southern California football team (the "Thundering Herd").

Nicknames of Ten Great Silver Screen Sex Symbols

Rudolph Valentino (the Sheik)

Mae West (the Screen's Bad Girl)

Clara Bow (the It girl)

Theda Bara (the Vamp); her stage name Theda Bara was an anagram for *Arab death*

Marlene Dietrich (Lili Marlene)

Greta Garbo (the Mystery Woman)

Marilyn Monroe (Marilyn)

John Barrymore (the Great Profile)

Francis X. Bushman (the World's Handsomest Man)
John Gilbert (the World's Greatest Lover)

The Screen's Bad Girl

"Come up and see me sometime!" is what the apocryphal soldier, sailor, or airman who invented the term *Mae West* is supposed to have said when he tried on his lifejacket and noticed that he bulged prominently where the famous movie star did. Anyway, we do know that the inflatable life jacket was introduced at the beginning of World War II and named for the world's oldest sex symbol because it "bulged in the right places." Mae West (1892–1980), who starred in films until she died at age eighty-seven, was a phenomenon of our time. She starred on Broadway until the police closed two of her plays, *Sex* and *Pleasure Man*, in 1928, migrating to Hollywood, where she won far greater fame as "Diamond Lil," the "Screen's Bad Girl," and the "Siren of the Screen." Her buxom bosom used to be honored in Cockney rhyming slang; breasts were *Mae Wests*. Her name, *Webster's* advises, is also given to a twin-turreted tank, a malfunctioning parachute with a *two-lobed* appearance, and a bulging sail. At one time a figure eight–shaped cruller was named for her, too. That's a total of at least six words or phrases—which is a better record than Pompadour or any other woman. It is said that Mae West acquired the nickname "Baby Vamp" when she was only five and played a vamp at a church social; she repeated the performance in a stage play the same year, perfecting her famous walk at that time. "I do all of my best work in bed," she once replied when a reporter asked her how she went about writing her memoirs. Another of her great lines was her order to her maid in one picture: "Peel me a grape, Beulah." She claimed to be sexually active well into her eighties and once claimed (*not* in her eighties) to have made love with one of her paramours for fifteen consecutive hours.

Ribald Responses

- "You're Mar-got Asquith, aren't you?" screen siren Jean Harlow asked Lady Margot Asquith at a party.
    "No," responded the peeress archly. "The *t* is silent, as in *Harlow*."
- "How many husbands have you had?" a reporter asked actress Zsa Zsa Gabor.
    "You mean apart from my own?" Zsa Zsa replied.

- "Goodness, where did you get that necklace?" a friend asked Mae West.

    "Never mind," Miss West responded, "but you can take it from me that goodness had nothing to do with it." This became the title of her autobiography.

- "How did you get to know so much about men?" gossip columnist Hedda Hopper once asked the irrepressible Miss West.

    "Baby," Mae replied, "I went to night school."

- Told about a certain promiscuous actress, Dorothy Parker observed, "That woman speaks eighteen languages and she can't say 'no' in any of them."

- "What do you wear when you go to bed?" a reporter asked Marilyn Monroe.

    "Chanel No. 5," she answered. (Another version has her saying she put on nothing but the radio.)

I Vant to Be Alone: Greta Garbo

Aside from some Goldwynisms (*see* Chapter 4) "I vant to be alone" may well be the single most famous quotation to come out of Hollywood, and the most unusual—because it is a sentiment uncharacteristic of most movie stars. It's too bad that the reclusive Swedish-born American actress Greta Garbo didn't say it in real life, though she did in one of her films. The legendary actress made it clear for history that what she really said to prying reporters was "I want to be let alone."

Greta Garbo, born Greta Gustafsson, endured a hard childhood before she began the acting career that made her the fabled "mystery woman" of Hollywood. Raised in a Stockholm slum, Greta was forced to leave school at thirteen, working a variety of jobs until she became a model for a department store catalog. Her first break came when director Mauritz Stiller noticed her and took her under his wing. It was Stiller who changed her name to Garbo, made her over into a svelte version of her former self, and starred her in his first film, *Gösta Berlings Saga* (1924). Yet it was her beautiful, high-cheekboned face with sad expressive eyes that made Greta a natural for silent films. Soon Louis B. Mayer, the head of MGM, noticed her in another movie and signed her for $350 a week, a good salary at the time. But Garbo quickly tired of both the salary and the extremely popular "vamp" roles in which she was usually cast. She held out for $5,000 a week and lead parts, winning a new contract after MGM banned her for seven months.

Many silver screen stars couldn't make the transition from the silents to the talkies, but Garbo's sexy voice made her more popular than ever after her first sound film *Anna Christie* in 1930, a picture widely promoted with the slogan "Garbo Talks!" Though she always disdained movies, despite her brilliant performances in films like *Anna Karenina*, *Queen Christina*, and *Camille*, she kept working until she retired in 1941 with a tidy fortune.

All her acting career, Garbo remained a mystery woman, this image adding to her allure. Never marrying, she carried on long affairs with her frequent costar, John Gilbert, billed as "The World's Greatest Lover"; conductor Leopold Stokowoski; and many others. Retiring to her New York apartment, she continued her reclusive ways until her death in 1990, age eighty-five, often traveling under aliases like "Miss Brown" and wearing the big slouch hats that became her trademark. Her ashes are buried in a secret location.

Garbo Speaks

"A deep, husky throaty contralto," wrote the *New York Herald Tribune*'s critic in describing the sultry Swedish star Greta Garbo's voice when she spoke in a film for the first time in *Anna Christie* (1930). The movie had been widely advertised under the headline "Garbo Talks." Garbo's first film words, spoken in a bar, were "Gif me a viskey . . . and dawn't be stingy, baby."

John Gilbert's Voice

> "You've probably heard the old story about John Gilbert—they said his voice was too high and therefore he couldn't be a talking-film star. That was not true at all. His voice was not high; he had a good voice. But you see, his image was the passionate lover, like Valentino. And you can't put that into words. In the beginning they tried putting it into words—such as 'I love you, I adore you, I must have you'—and they became funny; they're very funny. But if they're left out, then the audience puts in their own words or no words and he was all right. The studio didn't know anything else but to say his voice was too high."
> —Director King Vidor interviewed by *Time* magazine film critic Richard Schickel

An actor who *did* have a bad voice for sound films was leading man John Bowers. Bowers's death, in fact, was the model for Norman Maine's suicide in *A Star Is Born*. Despondent because he couldn't make the transition to talkies, Bowers took off his shoes and bathrobe and swam out into the Pacific, never to be seen again.

Sex Before Acting?

Charlie Chaplin wrote in his autobiography: "Like Balzac, who believed that a night of sex meant the loss of a good page of his novel, so I believed that it meant the loss of a good day's work at the studio." Chaplin was right about Balzac, though Balzac may not have been right about sex and writing. The French novelist did believe that the two acts of love were incompatible and that his writing prowess depended on how much sperm he retained in his body while writing. He once "suffered" an uncontrollable nocturnal emission and claimed that it cost him a masterpiece the following day.

The Making of a Star

William Randolph Hearst made his mistress Marion Davies a silent film star by hiring the best drama coaches and directors to teach her, setting up his own film company to produce her films, and lavishing her with gifts such as a house on the MGM lot. Hearst, then fifty-five, met the seventeen-year-old when she was a dancer in the Ziegfeld Follies, and they became lovers and companions until he died thirty-five years later; his wife steadfastly refused to give him the divorce that would enable them to marry. The publishing tycoon Hearst, the prototype for Kane in *Citizen Kane*, spent some $10 million furthering his lover's career, not including the publicity he gave her in his ten newspapers—each of which had strict orders to mention Marion Davies's name at least one time in every edition. Davies never became a star of the first magnitude, although she did demonstrate a considerable comedic talent. Her pronounced stutter prevented her from making the transition to the talkies. She died in 1961, age sixty-three, ten years after her great benefactor.

The King

"Frankly, my dear, I don't give a damn." This was of course Rhett Butler's farewell line to Scarlet O'Hara in *Gone with the Wind* (1939), but contrary to popular opinion these words and the film did not make Clark Gable a movie legend overnight. Gable was a star long before his famous farewell—almost a decade before. After acting with stock companies, taking Broadway bit parts, and appearing in grade B Hollywood films, the boy from Cadiz, Ohio, had costarred with Greta Garbo and Joan Crawford by 1931, becoming one of the movies' top ten box-office attractions within a year.

Gable won an Oscar for best actor in Frank Capra's *It Happened One Night* (1934), much to the dismay of the underwear industry, whose sales of undershirts dropped drastically when he appeared bare-chested in the film. His name was a household word by the time Judy Garland sang "You Made Me Love You" to his photograph in *Broadway Melody of 1938* and soon someone wrote a song *about* him, "Please, Mr. Gable."

Gable's best pictures were *Mutiny on the Bounty* (1935), *Gone with the Wind*, and his last film, *The Misfits* (1960), in which he starred opposite Marilyn Monroe. "The King," as columnist Ed Sullivan dubbed him, generally played himself, a tough but sensitive soul with rugged good looks and a twinkle in his eye; he never considered himself a great actor. He married five times but the great love of his life was actress Carole Lombard, his costar in the early *No Man of Her Own* (1932). The two were habitual practical jokers. One time Lombard secretly had her hospital room switched while recuperating from an operation. Gable went into her former room in the dark to kiss her goodnight and wound up in the embrace of an eighty-year-old woman.

Lombard died long before her time in an airplane crash while returning from a trip to sell war bonds in 1942, and Gable all but withdrew from making movies. He served as a tail-gunner in the Air Force and married Kay Spreckels after the war, but a lot of the sparkle left his eyes. He himself died too young, in 1960 when he was only fifty-nine, his heart failing four months before the birth of his only child.

Good-Bye, Norma Jean, Sweet Angel of Sex

> "We think of Marilyn who was every man's love affair with America, Marilyn Monroe who was blonde and beautiful, and had a sweet little rinky-dink of a voice and all the cleanliness of American backyards. She was our angel, the sweet angel of sex, and the sugar of sex came up from her like a resonance of sound in the clearest grain of a violin." —*Norman Mailer,* Marilyn: A Biography *(1973)*

Charlie Chaplin: The Little Tramp

If any one actor's name has become synonymous with movies, it is Charlie Chaplin's. Charlie Chaplin, always pictured in our minds as his beloved character the Little Tramp, has to both critics and moviegoers been far and away the world's greatest movie star over the hundred-year history of the cinema.

After a vaudeville career in England and America, Charles Spencer Chaplin, child of a London slum, brought his brilliant pantomime to pictures when he was hired in 1913 by Mack Sennett's Keystone Company. His wistful Little Tramp was serendipitously created soon thereafter. Sennett had asked him to find a costume for a "comedy" they were shooting that day, and Charlie selected from a Keystone storeroom the baggy pants, tight jacket, oversize shoes, and derby hat that were to become the Little Tramp's trademark. His improvisations in the costume made the whole crew laugh, and the immortal character was born. Chaplin refined him after he broke with Keystone and made such films as *The Kid* (1920), with Jackie Coogan as a foundling the Tramp rescues from a garbage can.

In all his films the Tramp was a little guy trying to cope with the world around him, "trying to get along," as Chaplin put it once. He became the best-known and most loved character in the history of the movies; his fans included Albert Einstein and Winston Churchill, among many other notables. People loved to imitate his funny walk; even his dab of a mustache became popular. After he founded the film company United Artists with Douglas Fairbanks, Mary Pickford, and D. W. Griffith, Chaplin made millions on films like *City Lights* (1931) and *The Gold Rush* (1925), which contains the unforgettable scene in which the starving Little Tramp boils his shoe and eats it, twirling the laces on his fork as if they were spaghetti.

Chaplin continued making great films into the 1930s; his last silent movie, *Modern Times* (1936), was made almost ten years after the advent of sound. "A good silent film is superior to a good stage play," he insisted, "while a good sound film is inferior to a good stage play." But he bowed to the public's taste and made his next picture, *The Great Dictator* (1940), in sound. Then came *Monsieur Verdoux* (1947) and *Limelight* (1952). All of these films were well received critically for the most part, but did poorly at the box office. *Modern Times*, in fact, might have summed up Chaplin's feelings at the time, with its ending showing the Little Tramp and a young girl walking down a long road escaping "civilization" like Huck Finn and so many other American heroes had before them. The last silent title on the silver screen read: "Buck up. Never say die. WE'LL GET ALONG."

The Little Tramp, of course, did much better than just get along, achieving immortality, but for a while Chaplin himself barely managed to get along. For the remainder of his film career in Hollywood he experienced little but trouble. Chaplin was attacked in the press for his liberal political views and publicly humiliated by a paternity suit brought against him by actress Joan Barry, during which the press spotlighted his involvement with teenage girls—two of his wives had been sixteen when he married them and Barry herself was nineteen when he first met her. Acquitted of violating the Mann Act, he was judged the father of Joan Barry's child in the paternity case (though later blood tests proved he could not have been the father). He left the United States in 1952, settling permanently in Switzerland with Oona O'Neill, Eugene O'Neill's daughter, whom he had married during the Barry trial when he was fifty-four and she was eighteen. Unable to travel to the United States because his passport was rescinded (he was a British subject), Chaplin did not return until 1972, when public opinion had changed and Hollywood, courageous as ever, finally gave him an honorary award for his immeasureable part in making pictures "the art form of this century." Charlie Chaplin died in 1977, age eighty-eight.

Cinema's First Great Clown

"I owe him everything," Charlie Chaplin once said of Max Linder (1882–1925), who introduced the intelligent style of comedy Chaplin adopted. The urbane, handsome Linder forsook the slapstick knockabout comedy of the time when he starred with the French Pathé studio, which also boasted the world's first comic star, André Deed (1884–1933). Linder rarely indulged in slapstick, his gags brilliant variations on simple themes. Chaplin followed in his footsteps.

There were outstanding cinema comedians before him, but Linder was the world's first great film clown, bringing a new subletly to the screen. The inventive Linder's principal subject was the chaotic world around him, but that same chaos brought about his downfall after his career peaked in 1914. At that time World War I caused the severe decline of the French film industry, and Linder's career went into eclipse. He failed in several comebacks, including a try in Hollywood, and in 1925, when he was only forty-three, he and his young wife committed suicide. It is said that almost every visual or sight gag in movies originated in his films.

More than Slapstick

The slapstick used in early low comedies was "a large paddling implement consisting of two boards hinged at one end but loose at the other." Clowns in late-nineteenth-century American variety shows used this slapstick to give other performers laugh-getting light but loud whacks on the rear end. The slapsticks were so widely used that they gave their name to any broad, loud knockabout comedy.

All of the early film comedians specialized in slapstick comedy. But the greatest among them, including Harold Lloyd, and Laurel and Hardy, brought something more to the cinema. As Robert Sherwood put it when writing of Buster Keaton: "Keaton's motto seems to be 'Fall and the world laughs at you. . . .' [He] is a distinct asset to the movies. He can attract people who would never think of going to a picture palace to see anyone else. Moreover, he can impress a weary world with the vitally important fact that life, after all, is a foolishly inconsequential affair."

W.C.

Croaky-voiced, bulbous-nosed W. C. Fields, with his bored deadpan delivery and cynical, misanthropic air, somehow became one of the most endearing of American comedians—no small miracle for a comic who (onstage) hated children, dogs, and mankind in general, drank to excess, and never gave a sucker an even break. The portly Fields (born William Claude Dunkenfield in Philadelphia) began his working life, appropriately enough, as a "drowner"—as a young man, he was hired by concessionaires to pretend that he was drowning so that crowds would gather and they would sell more food and drink. Fields went on to become a tramp juggler in vaudeville, performing all over the world before landing in Hollywood where he made some of the most famous films of the 1930s. Anecdotes about him are legion. "May I fix you a Bromo-Seltzer?" a waiter asked him when he was suffering from one of his famous hangovers. "Ye gods, no!" Fields moaned. "I couldn't stand the noise."

But many lines attributed to the comedian are apocryphal. For example, at a Friars Club banquet to honor Fields's fortieth year in show business, Leo Rosten, the author of *The Joys of Yiddish*, among many other humorous books, rose to introduce the comedian. In the course of his remarks Rosten ad-libbed, "Any man who hates dogs and children can't be all bad," inventing the famous line that is persistently attributed to Fields. Neither is it true that, when found on his deathbed reading a Bible, Fields quipped, "I'm looking for a loophole."

After his death on Christmas Day 1946, it was discovered that Fields, who had trusted no one ever since associates swindled him early in his career, had established over two hundred bank accounts under various pseudonyms all over the world. According to one story, only forty-five of these account were ever found. In any case, he did leave his wife and son $10,000 each in his will—but left his mistress, Carlotta Monti, $25,000. His will also provided funds for a "W. C. Fields College" for orphans "where no religion of any sort is to be preached," his will explaining that "Harmony is the purpose of this thought."

Finally, it should be noted that only his name and vital dates—W. C. FIELDS 1880–1946—appear on the comedian's gravestone in Glendale, California, where he is buried in the Great Mausoleum, Forest Lawn Memorial Park.

Nowhere to be found is the famous epitaph attributed to him: "On the whole I would rather be living in Philadelphia."

A Marx Brothers Quiz

1. What were the real names of these five riotous comics who played in vaudeville, musicals, movies, radio, and television?
2. Who was the oldest Marx Brother?
3. What was the name of their famous stage mother?
4. What was the name of their first act in vaudeville?
5. Which brother left the act early on?
6. Describe each of the brothers.

Answers:

1. Chico—born Leonard Marx; Harpo—Adolph; Groucho—Julius; Gummo—Milton; Zeppo—Herbert.
2. Chico (1887–1961). Next, in order, came Harpo (1888–1964), Groucho (1890–1977), Gummo (1895–1977), and Zeppo (1901–79).
3. Minnie Marx, whose grandparents had been performers in Germany and whose brother was Al Shean of vaudeville's famous Gallagher and Shean team. Shean wrote a few routines for his nephews.
4. "The Four Nightingales."
5. Gummo; Zeppo joined the act to take his place.
6. Zeppo was the straight man; Chico, who played the piano, portrayed a fast-talking Italian; Groucho was the bushy browed wisecracker, who walked from a deep crouch, flourishing his cigar

and often leering; Harpo, always mute, wore a red wig and tattered clothes, often playing the harp and frequently chasing girls and stealing everything in sight.

Radio Days

Often ranked as the top radio comedian of all time, Fred Allen, the stage name of John Florence Sullivan (1894–1956), was a morose-looking man with a nasal delivery who believed that "the world is a grindstone and life is your nose." Allen once saved a little boy from being hit by a truck. Pulling the boy to safety, he shouted, "What's the matter, son! Don't you want to grow up and have troubles?" Another time he told a friend, "Hollywood is a great place to live—if you're an orange."

All of the scripts for Allen's long-running radio show—thirty-nine a year—were bound by the comedian and stacked on ten feet of shelves beside a one-volume copy of the collected works of Shakespeare, which occupied a mere three and a half inches of space. "I did that as a corrective," Allen explained, "just in case I start thinking a ton of cobblestone is worth as much as a few diamonds."

James Thurber said that one of Allen's off-the-cuff remarks was among the funniest he had ever heard. It was made in the early days when Allen earned his living as a vaudeville comic juggler. Night after night Allen noticed a musician in the pit who never smiled and always wore a blank expression. Finally, one evening, he stopped his act, leaned over the pit, and asked the man, "How much would you charge to haunt a house?"

Called "vaudeville's Voltaire" when he appeared as a juggler-comic, Allen played under a sign that read: MR. ALLEN IS QUITE DEAF—IF YOU CARE TO LAUGH AND APPLAUD PLEASE DO SO LOUDLY.

The Movies' Youngest Millionaire

Jackie Coogan (1914–84) made his film debut in *Skinners Baby* (1916), when he was only sixteen months old. He later starred with Charlie Chaplin in *The Kid* (1918); he was by that time history's youngest self-made millionaire, in the movies or any other profession, a title he still retains. Charlie Chaplin, Coogan's costar in *The Kid*, signed Hollywood's first million-dollar contract in 1917. The contract, with the First National Exhibitor's Circuit, called for Chaplain to star in eight movies.

Shirley Temple made her first movie million before she was six years old and her later fame exceeded Coogan's. "I stopped believing in Santa Claus when I was six," she once said. "Mother took me to see him in a department store and he asked for my autograph."

Hollywood's Top Ten Moneymaking Stars

The results of the *International Motion Picture Almanac*'s 1997 Top Moneymaking Stars poll ranks Hollywood's most bankable stars as follows:

1. Harrison Ford
2. Julia Roberts
3. Leonardo DiCaprio
4. Will Smith
5. Tom Cruise
6. Jack Nicholson
7. Jim Carey
8. John Travolta
9. Robin Williams
10. Tommy Lee Jones

In 1996 Tom Cruise (5th) was number one, tied with Mel Gibson; his last four films have grossed over $100 million each. John Travolta (8th) was number three. Only two of the top moneymakers—Jack Nicholson and Robin Williams—received Academy Award nominations in 1997; both of them won Oscars.

Since 1932 the poll has asked several hundred U.S. and Canadian theater owners to name the actors who brought in the most box office revenue the preceeding year. The first star to be ranked number one was Marie Dressler.

In a similar 1994 poll the National Association of Theater Owners voted Harrison Ford the Star of the Century. Ford, fifty-six, has appeared in four of the top ten highest-grossing films of all time—*Star Wars* (1977), *The Empire Strikes Back* (1980), *Raiders of the Lost Ark* (1981), and *Return of the Jedi* (1983). The Star Wars trilogy alone has thus far grossed over $6 *billion*.

Selling Out?

> "I believe that God felt sorry for actors, so He created Hollywood to give them a place in the sun and a swimming pool. The price they had to pay was to surrender their talent."
> —*Sir Cedric Hardwicke,* A Victorian in Orbit, *1961*

Seven Rich and Famous Show People Who Didn't Finish Grammar School (8th Grade)

1. Buffalo Bill Cody—American impresario and performer
2. Charlie Chaplin—British movie actor
3. Isadora Duncan—American dancer
4. Maksim Gorky—Russian dramatist
5. Sean O'Casey—Irish dramatist
6. Noël Coward—British actor and playwright
7. John Philip Sousa—American composer and band conductor

The Uplifting Down-at-the-Heels Actor

In his long career as an actor, mostly playing bit parts at a salary of no more than $55 a week, Conrad Cantzen begged for food, slept in empty dressing rooms, and lived in barely furnished rooms where his bed was several layers of newspaper. But his worst memory was of wearing run-down shoes. "Many times I have been on my uppers," he recalled, "and the thinner the soles of my shoes were, the less courage I had to face the manager looking for a job." That is why he left his entire fortune to what he called the Conrad Cantzen Shoe Fund for Needy Actors when he died in 1945. This was no surprise to his friends, who knew how he felt about poorly shod players. What surprised them was that Cantzen, who had $11.85 in his pockets when he died, had somehow squirreled away nearly $250,000 in eighteen different bank accounts around New York City. No one has ever discovered how he did it.

Too True to Life

After a rehearsal of Eugene O'Neill's *The Iceman Cometh* (1946), the playwright and the cast walked along Eighth Avenue in New York toward Gilhuly's, where they were to lunch. The actors in their costumes and makeup looked like the bums they were playing and soon half a dozen or so real bums began following them. Once everybody got inside Gilhuly's the bouncer began throwing the real bums out, but O'Neill spoke to the owner and asked him to let them stay. The actors playing bums ate side by side with the real bums as O'Neill's guests.

Best Modern-Day Actor

Star of stage and screen, nominated for ten Oscars and winner of one (for the lead role in *Hamlet*, 1948), Sir Laurence Kerr Olivier is regarded by many critics and movie fans as the greatest actor of his day. Certainly he was one of the most versatile, starring in everything from typical dark, handsome leading-man roles to appearances as Hamlet, Oedipus, Hotspur, and Justice Swallow with the Old Vic. One of his best performances was as Archie Rice, the old has-been or never-was song and dance man in *The Entertainer* (1958). He played Othello and Richard III as well as both Caesar and Marc Antony to his wife Vivien Leigh's Cleopatra. Olivier was sometimes criticized for his mannerisms, but his perfect characterizations and versatility made him the most acclaimed actor of his generation, which included such great English actors as Ralph Richardson, John Gielgud, and Richard Burton. He died in 1989 at age eighty-one.

Today's "Best" Movie Actors and Actresses

Four living film actors (Dustin Hoffman, Jack Nicholson, Marlon Brando, and Tom Hanks) share the honor of winning the most Oscars for best actor awarded by the Academy of Motion Picture Arts and Sciences. Each has won two times. Jack Nicholson was nominated twelve times for best actor, holding the record there, and also won an Oscar for best supporting actor. Katharine Hepburn won the Oscar for best actress four times, having been nominated a record twelve times.

Of course no one can say who is the "best" actor of the thousands working today. Marlon Brando, Robert De Niro, Anthony Hopkins, Jack Nicholson, and Robert Duvall are names frequently mentioned. But he or she could just as well be relatively unknown, or a character actor like U.S. player Jan Leighton, who has portrayed some 3,400 different roles since 1951. Only time will tell. (*See also* Chapter 8.)

What's His/Her Real Name?

Who would think that John Wayne was originally Marion Morrison, or that Cary Grant was born Archibald Leach, or that Roy Rogers was Leonard Slye? Anyway, a score of more than twelve right on this quiz is excellent (including the answers we've given you).

1. Judy Garland
2. Boris Karloff
3. Marilyn Monroe
4. Roy Rogers
5. John Wayne
6. Pola Negri
7. Edward G. Robinson
8. W. C. Fields
9. Eddie Cantor
10. Mary Pickford
11. Richard Burton
12. Marlene Dietrich
13. Ava Gardner
14. Jack Benny
15. Cary Grant
16. Lucille Ball
17. Fred Astaire
18. Tony Curtis
19. Claudette Colbert
20. Lauren Bacall
21. Rita Hayworth
22. Jerry Lewis
23. Theda Bara
24. Greta Garbo
25. Sophia Loren
26. Paul Muni

Answers:

1. Frances Gumm
2. William Henry Pratt
3. Norma Jean Baker
4. Leonard Slye
5. Marion Morrison (he was called Little Duke by his father, Big Duke)
6. Barbara Apollonia Chalupiec
7. Emanuel Goldenberg
8. William Claude Dukenfield
9. Edward Israel Iskowitz
10. Gladys Smith
11. Richard Jenkins
12. Marie Magdalene Dietrich
13. Ava Lavinia Gardner
14. Benjamin Kubelsky
15. Archibald Leach
16. Lucille Desiree Ball
17. Frederick Austerlitz
18. Bernard Schwartz
19. Lily Chauchoin
20. Betty Perske
21. Margarita Cansino
22. Joseph Levitch
23. Theodosia Goodman
24. Greta Gustafsson
25. Sofia Scicolone
26. Friedrich Muni Weisenfreund

From Othello to Othello: Black Actors in America

Though there are many African American players on the stage and screen today, blacks were rarely the subject of early American plays and black actors seldom appeared in American productions—even the part of Othello was played by a white man in blackface. James Hewlett, only a modestly gifted actor, is probably America's first black professional actor and starred in America's first black play, *The Drama of King Shotaway* (1823), which was about a West Indian slave revolt. "Shakespeare's Proud Representative," as he was called, might have accomplished much more if it had not been for white roughnecks who harassed him on the stage and streets.

Ira Aldridge, considered the first great black actor in America, suffered the same heartless, brainless prejudice. Aldridge left the United States early in his career, however, unable to get enough roles here, and played for nearly forty years in Europe until he died in 1867.

Bert Williams, among the best of comedians of any race, appeared in at least five Broadway plays, his genius always shining through the blackface he was required to wear in an age of extreme prejudice. Williams also performed in vaudeville and in eight Ziegfeld Follies. He is said to have died of a weary heart and overwork, in 1922, when only forty-six. "He was the funniest man I ever saw, and the saddest man I ever met," W. C. Fields said of him.

All the excellent black actors on the American stage and screen since the 1920s can't be listed here, but they include Eddie Anderson, Pearl Bailey, Angela Bassett, Bill Cosby, Ossie Davis, Sammy Davis Jr., Vivica A. Fox, Morgan Freeman, Cuba Gooding Jr., Lou Gossett Jr., Irma Hall, Ellen Holly, James Earl Jones, Canada Lee, Hattie McDaniel, Sidney Poitier, Richard Pryor, Paul Robeson, Richard Roundtree, Wesley Snipes, Denzel Washington, Forest Whitaker, Lynn Whitfield, Vanessa Williams, Oprah Winfrey, and Alfre Woodard, among many others. Charles Gilpen, despite his drinking problem, was called "the greatest actor of his race," by Moss Hart. He died in 1930, barely forty-two. Paul Robeson (1898–1976), truly a Renaissance man, was the outstanding black actor of his time and the best known, due in part to his political activism. His most acclaimed role was as Othello in a 1943 production that ran longer than any other Shakespearean revival in history.

Following in Royal Family Footsteps: Acting Dynasties

There are scores of actors and actresses whose children and even grandchildren have acted on the stage or screen—Henry Fonda, Jane and Peter Fonda, and Bridget Fonda are notable recent-day examples, as were the three generations of Tyrone Powers. Indeed, there were many family vaudeville acts like the "Seven Little Foys." But America's major acting dynasties were the Drews, Barrymores, and Booths.

The Irish-born American actor John Drew (1827–62) was the father of John Drew (1853–1927), who specialized in Shakespearean comedy, and actress Georgiana Drew (1856–93), who married the handsome and brilliant actor Maurice Barrymore (1848–1905). The children of Georgiana and Maurice were matinee idol John Barrymore (1882–1942) and stage and screen actors Ethel Barrymore (1879–1959) and Lionel Barrymore (1878–1954). John Barrymore, known as "The Great Profile," often appeared on the stage as Hamlet and Richard III, and also starred in many movies. Ethel won an Academy Award for *None but the Lonely Heart* (1944). Lionel Barrymore, in his last years confined to acting in a wheelchair due to severe arthritis, won an Oscar for *Free Soul* (1931). George S. Kaufman and Edna Ferber's play *The Royal Family* (1927) is said to be a satire of the Barrymore family. Today actress Drew Barrymore continues the family tradition.

Most renowned of all American acting families is the dynasty founded by Junius Brutus Booth (1796–1852). The British-born Booth was considered the only rival of the great Edmund Kean when he acted in England. When Booth emigrated to the United States in 1821 his reputation as a great tragedian increased, despite frequent periods of insanity and drunkenness. His first son, Edwin Booth, treated elsewhere in these pages, also achieved great fame, as did his son John Wilkes Booth, who became the most famous—or infamous—actor in American history after he assassinated Abraham Lincoln.

The world record for a family acting dynasty—four generations so far—is held by the Barrymore family and by England's Redgrave family. Actor Roy Redgrave started it all when he made his film acting debut in 1911. His son Michael Redgrave and Sir Michael's two daughters Vanessa and Lynn and son Corin, came next. They were followed by Vanessa's two daughters, Joely and Natasha Richardson, and Corin's daughter, Jemma.

Among today's young actors who have followed in family footsteps are:

- Tony Goldwyn (producer Sam Goldwyn's grandson)
- Jennifer Grant (Cary Grant's daughter)
- Angelina Jolie (Jon Voight's daughter)
- Chiara Mastroianni (Marcello Mastroianni's daughter)
- Brawley Nolte (Nick Nolte's son)
- Tracee Ross and Rhonda Ross Kendrick (Diana Ross's daughters)
- Natasha Wagner (Natalie Wood and Robert Wagner's daughter)

Top Schools for Actors

The oldest of the many American schools for acting is the American Academy of Dramatic Arts, founded in 1884, as the Lyceum Theatre School for Acting. Its famous graduates include Lauren Bacall, Anne Bancroft, Hume Cronyn, Ruth Gordon, Jason Robards Jr., Edward G. Robinson, Rosalind Russell, Robert Redford, and Spencer Tracy.

The Actors Studio, Inc., was founded in 1947 by Elia Kazan, Cheryl Crawford, and Robert Lewis. While not nearly as old as the Academy, it has probably exerted more influence on the American theater, especially after 1948, when Lee Strasberg became its guiding light with his "method school" of acting inspired by Stanislavsky's theories. Noted graduates include Julie Harris, Geraldine Page, Kim Stanley, and Maureen Stapleton. Marilyn Monroe, Paul Newman, Joanne Woodward, and other Hollywood stars also studied there.

Great Lost Parts

- Georgie Jessel was hired by Warner Brothers to play the lead in the first talking feature, *The Jazz Singer* (1928), a role Jessel created on the Broadway stage. The studio reneged and gave Al Jolson the part instead.
- Laurence Olivier was signed as Greta Garbo's leading man in her classic *Queen Christina* (1932). Garbo insisted that she had to have her lover, John Gilbert, who got the part.
- Though "Beverly Hillbillies" star Buddy Ebsen was under contract to play the Tin Woodman role in *The Wizard of Oz* (1939), he had to withdraw when he proved allergic to the aluminum makeup the role required. Jack Haley got the part.
- Bette Davis lost her chance to play Scarlett O'Hara in *Gone with the Wind* (1939) when she balked at playing opposite Errol Flynn as Rhett Butler. Warner Brothers had agreed to loan producer David O. Selznick both of them in a package deal and withdrew their offer when Bette expressed her disapproval.
- Burt Lancaster refused the lead role in *Ben-Hur* (1959), which won Charlton Heston an Oscar.
- A Hollywood studio promised to finance Vittorio De Sica's landmark film *The Bicycle Thief* (1947) if Cary Grant got the starring role. Luckily, De Sica refused and later hired a nonprofessional at a casting call in which no professional actors were considered.

- W. C. Fields turned down the role of the Wizard in *The Wizard of Oz* (1939).
- The roles of Rick and Ilsa in *Casablanca* (1943) were originally meant for Ronald Reagan and Ann Sheridan, not Humphrey Bogart and Ingrid Bergman—in fact, the story was bought as a vehicle for Reagan. Before Bogey got the Rick role, George Raft turned it down, just as he had turned down what came to be classic Bogart roles in *High Sierra* and *The Maltese Falcon*!
- Eva Marie Saint turned down the key role in *The Three Faces of Eve* (1957). The part went to Joanne Woodward for whom it won an Oscar.
- Frank Sinatra had a verbal agreement with director Elia Kazan to play the Terry Malloy character in *On the Waterfront* (1954), but Kazan broke the agreement when Marlon Brando unexpectedly became available. The role earned Brando his first Oscar.
- On the other hand, Brando turned down the title role in *The Man with the Golden Arm* (1955), enabling Sinatra to get the part.

Casting Problems

British actor Ernest Thesiger's favorite pastime was embroidery; in fact, he shared the interests of most of his woman friends, from sewing to cooking and housekeeping. One time Thesiger complained to Somerset Maugham that the playwright never wrote any parts for him. "But I am always writing parts for you, Ernest," Maugham replied. "The trouble is that somebody called Gladys Cooper *will* insist on playing them!"

Odd Ways to Get a Part

- German dramatist Bertolt Brecht created the famous role of the dumb girl in his *Mother Courage* for his wife, Helene Weigel, solely because the play was first performed in Sweden and she didn't speak Swedish.
- During a long American writers' strike against television producers in 1981, producers, actors, and even secretaries and stagehands churned out scripts for the voracious daytime soap operas. One actor on a popular soap knew his character would soon be killed off and volunteered to be the show's head writer during the strike. Not only did his character live, he also became the lead—and any actor who protested this sudden turn of events saw his or her character quickly killed off.

- British actor Michael Caine told about how he got his first part from a casting agency in his autobiography *What's It All About?* (1995): "[The casting agent] asked the three of us, 'What size is your chest?' Each of us thought he was addressing us alone, so we answered in unison with our chest sizes. 'Who said forty?' he asked, and I put my hand up. Now I knew how Marilyn Monroe felt. 'What's your inside leg measurement?' he demanded. 'Thirty-two,' I replied. His eyes lit up. 'Perfect. Come in,' he said, beckoning me into his small office.

  "When I got inside he explained that I would be playing a policeman in a small film the next day. I had been cast because I fitted the uniform that the company already had in their wardrobe."

- Moss Hart got the idea for *The Man Who Came to Dinner* (1939) after author-actor Alexander Woollcott spent a weekend at his house. After Woollcott left, Hart remarked to George S. Kaufman, "Can you imagine what would have happened if the old monster had fractured his hip and had to stay?" When Woollcott learned of his subsequent caricature as Sheridan Whiteside in the Kaufman-Hart play, he quipped, knowing a good thing when he had one, "The thing's a terrible insult and I've decided to swallow it." Later he toured in the part.

II

THE SUPPORTING CAST: FROM STAGE MOTHERS TO COMPUTERS

Stage Mothers and Stage Fathers

Stage parents have too often supported their own bank accounts and egos rather than the child actors they dragged by the collar to stardom. "My mother was the stage mother of all time," Judy Garland told Barbara Walters in one of her last television interviews. "She really was a witch. If I had a stomachache and didn't want to go on, she'd say, 'Get out on that stage or I'll wrap you around a bedpost!'" But there were many stage mothers even worse. Jackie Coogan's mother, Lillian, was the most historically important among them, along with his stage father, Arthur Bernstein. Jackie was one of the most popular child stars of all time—best known for his starring role in Charlie Chaplin's *The Kid* (1921) when he was only seven. He earned as much as $1 million a picture (making him the youngest self-made millionaire in history). But he was never given more than a $6.50 weekly allowance in all the time before he legally came of age. In 1935, Coogan sued his parents for the millions he had earned, but though he won in court, there was apparently only about $125,000 left for him to retrieve—barely enough to pay his legal expenses. Coogan died in 1984. His outrageous fleecing resulted in the passage of the 1939 Coogan Act, which protects child performers by empowering the courts to put in trust a large percentage of their earnings while they are minors.

The Applauders

The best "supporting cast" for a theatrical production can be the audience itself, as performers have known since earliest times. The Roman emperor Nero, for example, had over five thousand "clappers" whom he brought along with him to provide applause on his concert tours; he also took the precaution of locking all of his audiences into the theater. Since then performers and playwrights over the years have often used applauders, sometimes called a *claque*, to applaud their work and offset the opinions of critics. The French, who originated this system in 1820 or so, had the strategy down to a science. Claquers were divided into

- *commissaires*—who memorized the play and pointed out its literary merits
- *rieurs*—hired to laugh at the jokes
- *pleureurs*—women hired to cry when appropriate
- *chatouilleurs*—kept the audience in good spirits
- *bisseurs*—hired to cry *bis!* ("encore!")

The French had an agency called *Assurance des succès dramatiques* from which claquers could be hired. One French claque leader, or *chef de claque*, was nicknamed Monsieur Claque; according to journalist Pierre Joseph Proudhon, he had "the enormous hands of a washerwoman (all the better to clap with) and is paid thirty-six pounds for his attendance if the play succeeds and twelve pounds if it fails."

Claques could be hired to cheer for one's play or destroy a rival's play. In the latter case trumpets, rattles, whistles, and other noisemakers accompanied the boos and hisses. Often the claque leaders attended rehearsals of the play they were hired to praise or damn, so that they could synchronize their actions with those of the plot and players.

One time the illustrious French actress Rachel hired a claque to applaud her performance in a new play. She was pleased with the applause the first night, but disappointed the second, and she told the group's leader. Replied the offended *chef de claque*: "I cannot remain under the obloquy of a reproach from lips such as yours. At the first performance I led the attack in person thirty-three times. We had three acclamations, four hilarities, two thrilling moments, four renewals of applause, and two indefinite explosions." His troops were so exhausted from the opening night, he explained, that they had to rest a little the second night!

The Most Applauded Performer of All Time

Of all performers past and present, so far as history records, opera tenor Placido Domingo won the most applause from an audience. He needed no help from a claque. After his performance of *Otello* at the Vienna Staatsoper on July 20, 1991, Domingo was applauded for a full one hour and twenty minutes. However, Italian tenor Luciano Pavorotti received more curtain calls than Domingo—165 to Domingo's 101—for his performance in *L'Elisir d'amore* at the Deutsche Oper in Berlin on February 24, 1998. Pavorotti was "only" applauded for one hour and seven minutes.

Claptrap

Claptrap initially meant a playwright's trick or device to catch applause, "a trap to catch a clap by way of applause from the spectators at a play," as the first person to define the term put it. The word finally came to mean any pretentious, insincere, or empty language.

Applause!

The practice of asking radio and television studio audiences to applaud at various points during a show isn't an annoying modern-day invention. It dates back at least to Roman times, when in Plautus's comedies a character called the Epilogue summed up the play after its conclusion and finally asked the audience for applause. In Plautus's *Amphitryon*, for example, the actor implores the audience: "Now, spectators, for the sake of Jove almighty, give us some loud applause!"

Killed by Applause

The Athenian lawmaker Draco was an avid theatergoer. According to one story, the official, popular despite his draconian laws, was killed by applause there. While he was sitting in the theater at Aegina in about 590 B.C., other spectators hailed him by applauding wildly and throwing their cloaks and caps in tribute. So many landed on Draco that he was smothered.

What Is Applause?

> "Applause is but a fart, the crude
> Blast of the fickle multitude."
> —*Anonymous actor, 1645*

Supreme Applause of Silence

The two and a half minute solo dance of the incomparable Russian ballerina Anna Pavlova in *The Dying Swan* is doubtless the best known in all ballet. Pavlova treasured it above all her other roles; in fact, the ballerina's dying words, spoken in a delirium of fever, were "get my Swan costume ready." Many ballet critics also cherished the dance. English critic C. W. Beaumont praised her performance best, writing, "The emotion transferred was so overpowering that it seemed a mockery to applaud when the dance came to an end, our souls had soared into empyrean with the passing of the swan; only when the silence was broken could we feel that they had returned to our bodies."

Extras! Extras!

As early as 1912 the Italian film *Quo Vadis* had "a cast of thousands"—most of them extras—for verisimilitude. Extras have been around since the earliest days of movies, but never so many as played in Richard Attenborough's epic *Gandhi*, which won the Academy Award as best picture in 1982, winning Attenborough the best director Oscar and Ben Kingsley the best actor Oscar as well. In the funeral scene of *Gandhi* alone over 300,000 extras appeared.

Of all the stories telling of extras who rose from obscurity to stardom, one of the most interesting and least known is that of James Murray. In 1928 director King Vidor began looking for a lead for what was to become his realistic film *The Crowd*, which many consider to be among the best movies ever made. Vidor wanted to use an unknown actor and noticed an extra on the lot whom he thought would be ideal for the part. Vidor asked the man to audition the next day, but he didn't show up. Remembering his name as only "Something-or-other Murray," the director found his address from the studio "Extra Book" and tested him, and James Murray went on to give an extraordinary performance; *The Crowd* was subsequently nominated for an Academy Award. Vidor offered him the lead in his next picture, but once more Murray failed to show up. This time he couldn't be found. Several years later a drunken panhandler approached Vidor on Hollywood Boulevard. It was Murray. Vidor got him sobered up and offered him a part in his latest film, but Murray refused, again vanished into the crowd, and was never seen by him again.

"George Spelvin" and "Walter Plinge" and Co.

Playwright Winchell Smith's 1906 dramatization of George Barr McCutcheon's *Brewster's Millions*, a perennial favorite, included among its cast members a "George Spelvin." This was a second, fictitious name given in the playbill to a member of the cast who played two parts. Since that day "George Spelvin" has had the same theatrical use. Though Smith's play widely popularized the name, it had been used in this way as early as 1886 in Charles A. Gardiner's *Karl the Peddler*. It has since been given to dolls substituted for infants, to animals, and even to dead bodies in movies and play credits, having been used well over ten thousand times in Broadway productions alone. At one time, a club of Broadway actors was called the Spelvin Club. "Harry Selby" is another fictitious name used in the same way, but far less frequently. In England "Walter Plinge" is similarly employed. One version of this story claims that the fictitious Walter Plinge came from a real Walter Plinge who was a genial bartender working at a pub near the Lyceum Theatre in about 1900. His policy of easy credit endeared him to the players, who immortalized his name in print. (*See also* "Alan Smithee," Chapter 4.)

The Daredevils: Stuntmen and Stuntwomen

One early Hollywood stuntman recalled that he earned twenty-two dollars a week and had broken twenty-two bones one week. "That's a dollar a bone, not bad," he laughed.

The pay is much better today, but there are just as many broken bones and hardly a year goes by without several stuntmen being killed or badly injured performing difficult stunts.

Among the best known of the almost anonymous but indispensable Hollywood stuntmen was Yakima Canutt, who was awarded an honorary Oscar in 1966 "for achievement as a stuntman and for developing safety devices to protect stuntmen everywhere." The legendary stuntman, born Enos Canutt in 1895, was called Yakima because as a rodeo star he had been headlined as "The Cowboy from Yakima." He died in 1986, age ninety. His son, Joe, followed in "Yak's" footsteps.

The stunt safety devices used today are often as ingenious as the dangerous stunts themselves. In *The Towering Inferno*, for example, a female character had to be set on fire and then jump out of a high window. The stuntman doubling for the actress—there are still few stuntwomen—was suited in three layers of protective clothing, including fire-resistant underwear, an aluminum-base "silver suit," and asbestos gloves. A fireproof ski mask protected his face, and over that he wore a mask that resembled the starlet's face. At the last possible moment in the scene the stuntman's back—coated with a flammable paste that burns brightly, giving off little heat—was set aflame and he took his fiery leap. Exactly twenty seconds were allotted to shoot this dangerous stunt before other stuntmen rushed in with fire extinguishers to put out the blaze, no damage done.

Stuntmen are rarely honored except in the credits at the end of the picture, which only a handful of people in each theater stay to read. One of the few films made about them is *The Stunt Man* (1980), which earned Oscar nominations (but no wins) for actor Peter O'Toole, director Richard Rich, and screenwriters Lawrence B. Marcus and Richard Rich. It won no awards or nominations for stunts or visual effects.

Sometimes stuntmen are "discovered" working on the sets of movies and go on to become stars. A notable example is Gary Cooper, whom director Henry King discovered doing dangerous stunts on the set of *The Winning of Barbara Worth* in 1926.

A million-dollar reward was offered by actor Burt Lancaster to anyone who could prove that he (a former acrobat) did not perform all his own stunts in his film *The Flame and the Arrow*.

Greasepaints

As these examples show, makeup has been used to enhance dramatic productions since earliest times:

- In their ritual ceremonies Australian Aborigines traditionally wear wreaths, flowers, and feathers over greased bodies and faces daubed with white clay.
- Chinese theater still makes use of masks, and grotesquely painted faces of blue, green, vermilion, and white are used to depict demons and spirits. So does Kabuki drama in Japan.
- The god Dionysus was represented in Greek drama with long hair and beard, and two small horns projecting from his forehead, while his reveling bacchants had their faces smeared with wine dregs or mulberry juice.
- The French farce actor known as Gros Guillaume during the reign of Henri IV wore face makeup consisting of a thick covering of

flour which, at comic moments in a play, he sent flying into the eyes of other actors by puffing out his cheeks.
- The famous white face of today's circus clowns came directly from the mask worn by the actor playing Pierrot in the Italian commedia dell'arte. Sometime in the early eighteenth century the first circus clown used makeup to simulate Pierrot's mask.
- By Elizabethan times the mask had been discarded as a means of facial makeup in the English theater, but makeup remained crude until the nineteenth century, when improved stage lighting—which had first consisted of candles and then smoking oil lamps—prompted the scientific study of the subject.
- Greasepaint, often a synonym for the thespian life, was invented more than a century ago and is basically a composition of oil, spermaceti, and wax, running in color schemes from white to black. It replaced the charred cork or *minstrel black* that was used to depict black stage characters and was even used for the face of Othello.

Men of a Million Faces: Movie Makeup Artists

Great movie makeup artists have been the stuff of legends since early Hollywood days, when actor Lon Chaney Sr. was known as the "Man of a Thousand Faces." Since then creations such as the Hunchback of Notre Dame and a hundred monsters worse than Dr. Frankenstein's have become part of American folklore. This is not to mention dramatic makeup jobs on actors like Dustin Hoffman, who passed from youth to great age in *Little Big Man*, or the deterioration of the main character in *The Picture of Dorian Gray*. Yet the names of Hollywood makeup artists are little known outside Hollywood. Among the exceptions are the Westmore family, which has been represented by three generations in the art, and Jack Pierce, whose accomplishments are covered in Chapter 5. In fact, makeup was not an Academy Award category until 1982. Here, at least, are the winners since then, plus a few honorary Oscars awarded previously. The Oscars are listed here in the years in which they were received.

- William Tuttle won an honorary Oscar "for his outstanding makeup achievement for *The Seven Faces of Dr. Lao*" (1964).
- John Chambers won an honorary Oscar for *Planet of the Apes* (1968).
- Rick Baker—*An American Werewolf in London* (1981)
- Sarah Monzani and Michèle Burke—*Quest for Fire* (1982)

- No award (1983)
- Rick Baker and Paul Engelen—*Greystoke: The Legend of Tarzan, Lord of the Apes* (1984)
- Michael Westmore and Zoltan Elek—*Mask* (1985)
- Chris Wales and Stephan Dupuis—*The Fly* (1986)
- Rick Baker—*Harry and the Hendersons* (1987)
- Ve Neill, Steve La Porte, and Robert Short—*Beetlejuice* (1988)
- Manlio Rocchetti, Lynn Barber, and Kevin Haney—*Driving Miss Daisy* (1989)
- John Caglione Jr. and Doug Drexler—*Dick Tracy* (1990)
- Stan Winston and Jeff Dawn—*Terminator 2* (1991)
- Greg Cannom, Michèle Burke, and Matthew W. Mungle—*Bram Stoker's Dracula* (1992)
- Greg Cannom, Ve Neill, and Yolander Toussieng—*Mrs. Doubtfire* (1993)
- Rick Baker, Ve Neill, and Yolander Toussieng—*Ed Wood* (1994)
- Peter Frampton, Paul Pattison, and Lois Burwell—*Braveheart* (1995)
- Rick Baker and David LeRoy Anderson—*The Nutty Professor* (1996)
- Rick Baker and David LeRoy Anderson—*Men in Black* (1997)
- Jenny Shircore—*Elizabeth* (1998)

The Protean Player: Lon Chaney, The Man of a Thousand Faces

"Don't step on that spider, it might be Lon Chaney!" went a popular joke of silent-film days. Chaney had already appeared in more than 125 films before producer Irving Thalberg signed him to the contract under which he played the title roles in *The Hunchback of Notre Dame* (1923) and *The Phantom of the Opera* (1925). Victor Hugo's *Hunchback* had been filmed before, as early as 1906, but it was Chaney who made it a movie masterpiece. This superb mime actor, the son of deaf and dumb parents, was among the first film actors to wear elaborate special-effects makeup of his own creation. It took three painful hours every day for him to prepare himself for the cameras, the hardest part of which was squeezing into a metal breastplate that weighed a total of about thirty pounds. The heavy rubber hump on his back and shoulder weighed more than forty pounds.

In his role as the disfigured Erik in *The Phantom of the Opera* Chaney suffered even more. Celluloid discs stuffed in his mouth exaggerated his cheekbones, while a wire device fixed his mouth in a deathlike grin and jagged false teeth encircled it. His nostrils were stretched out by a spreader he had invented, and even his eyes were forced wide open by wires.

In these two silent films alone Chaney set a makeup standard for years to come, and his work certainly still ranks as the greatest makeup artistry created by an actor himself. Chaney never won an Oscar—there were none at the time—but years later he was honored with the greatest tribute an actor can receive from the industry—a movie based on his life (*Man of a Thousand Faces*, 1957).

"Clown White" and Other Dangerous Makeup

It is said that Thespis himself painted his face with white lead before he invented the unpainted linen mask of the Greeks. From earliest times actors used such dangerous substances for makeup. In the religious dramas of medieval times, for example, white lead and gold paint were applied to the face and hands of actors portraying Christ, even though they were known to be poisonous. In 1513, "a naked gilded child," who was supposed to represent the golden age, died after being painted gold.

From as far back as Nero's time—when men and women of his court used white lead to blanch their skin—lead-based makeups have brought actors pain, suffering, and often death. The victims included Belgian opera singer Charles Zelger, who died in 1864 after a long, painful illness caused by blood poisoning that he contracted three years previously by whitening his beard while playing in a London production of *William Tell*. White lead also used to be the basis for "clown white," the white used for clowns' faces. It was replaced by zinc oxide because the lead was found to be extremely dangerous, so much so that it caused the death of George Washington Lafayette Fox (1825–77), America's most famous circus clown, "the peer of pantomimists." Fox suffered for many years and his illness caused extremely erratic behavior—one time he leaped off the stage without provocation to attack people in the audience.

The True Actor's Face: No Makeup Necessary

The unexcelled Eleonora Duse was the most prominent of a number of actors who have refused to wear any makeup at all in any performance. "Genius, of course, makes its own laws," one critic wrote of Duse in a role she was playing. "Every emotion that stirred within her was reflected in her face, her whole bearing and figure were equally expressive. No living person has ever looked so like a corpse as Mme. Duse in the character of Fedora feeling the effects of the poison in her body and in her soul. For these transformations she needs no external artifice of paint, which she seems to despise. She achieves them solely through the force of her imagination."

English comedian Joseph Munden (1758–1832), regarded by some as the greatest actor of his day, rivaled Duse in this respect. Essayist Charles Lamb had this to say of Munden:

> *He has no face . . . that you can properly pin down and call his. . . . If his name could be multiplied like his countenance, it might fill a playbill. He and he alone literally* makes faces: *applied to any other person, the phrase is a mere figure [of speech] denoting certain modifications of the human countenance. Out of some invisible wardrobe he dips for faces, as his friend Suett used to for wigs, and fetches them out as easily. In the grand grotesque of farce, Munden stands out as single and unaccompanied as Hogarth.*

The Elephant Man (1980) was nominated for six Academy Awards, including best picture, best actor (John Hurt), and best director (David Lynch), though it did not win an Oscar. This true story of John Merrick, an extremely deformed, disabled, and courageous man of Victorian times, has its counterpart in the story of Rondo Hattan, a Hollywood actor of the 1940s. Hattan suffered from acromegaly, a chronic disease caused by overactivity of the pituitary gland, which is marked by enlargement of the face, jaw, and extremities. He made a living by playing in monster and horror films, never using makeup in his roles.

Dressing and Undressing the Stars: Edith Head and Co.

As the following list shows, Edith Head has won far and away more Oscars for costume design than any other Hollywood designer. In addition to her nine Oscars, she has been nominated for another dozen and would have garnered even more if the Academy had awarded Oscars for her category before 1948. In fact, Edith Head, who began her career before there were any Oscars, has won and been nominated for more Academy Awards (thirty-five) than any other individual in movie history, in any category. These include four Oscar wins in a row (from 1948 to 1951) and two Oscars won in one year (1950, when she won both the black-and-white and color pictures costume awards). No one else has even come close, despite all her fabulous competitors. Director John Huston once said of her, "They say about Edith that getting the Oscar is written into her contract."

Because there was no Academy Award category for costume design before 1948, many outstanding costume designers are not included in the list below. Adrian—who worked closely with Greta Garbo—is the greatest who comes to mind. Neither does the list reflect the impact that the dressing and undressing of Hollywood stars has had on worldwide fashion. When Gable wore no undershirt in *It Happened One Night,* for example, undershirt sales in the country plunged by 75 percent almost overnight. Audrey Hepburn's "little black dress" and big hat from *Breakfast at Tiffany's* are still popular. When Katharine Hepburn and Marlene Dietrich started wearing slacks, so did droves of American women. The jeans, T-shirts, and black leather jackets Marlon Brando, Peter Fonda, and James Dean wore on the screen made these articles of clothing common attire. Harrison Ford's battered leather jacket in *Raiders of the Lost Ark* set a fashion trend, and when Ray-Ban sunglasses were worn by Will Smith and Tommy Lee Jones in *Men in Black,* Ray-Ban sales tripled.

- Roger K. Furse won the costume Oscar for *Hamlet* (1948).
- Edith Head and Gile Steele—*The Heiress* (1949)
- Leah Rhodes, Travilla, and Marjorie Best—*The Adventures of Don Juan* (1949 color)
- Edith Head and Charles Le Maire—*All About Eve* (1950)
- Edith Head, Dorothy Jeakins, Eloise Jensson, Gile Steele, and Gwen Wakeling—*Samson and Delilah* (1950 color)
- Edith Head—*A Place in the Sun* (1951)
- Orry-Kelly, Walter Plunkett, and Irene Sharaff—*An American in Paris* (1951 color)
- Helen Rose—*The Bad and the Beautiful* (1952)
- Clave, Mary Wills, and Madame Karinska—*Hans Christian Andersen* (1952 color)
- Edith Head—*Roman Holiday* (1953)
- Charles Le Maire and Emile Santiago—*The Robe* (1953 color)
- Edith Head—*Sabrina* (1954)
- Sanzo Wada—*Gate of Hell* (1954 color)

- Helen Rose—*I'll Cry Tomorrow* (1955)
- Charles Le Maire—*Love Is a Many Splendored Thing* (1955 color)
- Jean Louis—*The Solid Gold Cadillac* (1956)
- Irene Sharaff—*The King and I* (1956 color)
- Orry-Kelly—*Les Girls* (1957 color)
- Cecil Beaton—*Gigi* (1958 color)
- Orry-Kelly—*Some Like It Hot* (1959)
- Elizabeth Haffenden—*Ben-Hur* (1959 color)
- Edith Head and Edward Stevenson—*The Facts of Life* (1960)
- Bill Thomas and Valles—*Spartacus* (1960 color)
- Piero Gherardi—*La Dolce Vita* (1961)
- Irene Sharaff—*West Side Story* (1961 color)
- Norma Koch—*Whatever Happened to Baby Jane?* (1962)
- Mary Wills—*The Wonderful World of the Brothers Grimm* (1962 color)
- Piero Gherardi—*Federico Fellini's 8½* (1963)
- Irene Sharaff, Vittorio Nino Novarese, and Renie—*Cleopatra* (1963 color)
- Dorothy Jeakins—*The Night of the Iguana* (1964)
- Cecil Beaton, *My Fair Lady* (1964 color)
- Julie Harris—*Darling* (1965)
- Peggy Dalton—*Doctor Zhivago* (1965 color)
- Irene Sharaff—*Who's Afraid of Virginia Woolf?* (1966)
- Elizabeth Haffenden and Joan Bridge—*A Man for All Seasons* (1966 color)
- John Trusbott—*Camelot* (1967) (all awards for this year and after are for films in color)
- Danilo Donati—*Romeo and Juliet* (1968)
- Margaret Furse—*Anne of the Thousand Days* (1969)
- Nino Novarese—*Cromwell* (1970)
- Yvonne Blake and Antonio Castillo—*Nicholas and Alexandra* (1971)
- Anthony Powell—*Travels with My Aunt* (1972)
- Edith Head—*The Sting* (1973)

- Theoni V. Aldridge—*The Great Gatsby* (1974)
- Ulla-Britt Söderlund and Milena Canonero—*Barry Lyndon* (1975)
- Danilo Donati—*Fellini's Casanova* (1976)
- John Mollo—*Star Wars* (1977)
- Anthony Powell—*Death on the Nile* (1978)
- Albert Wolsky—*All That Jazz* (1979)
- Anthony Powell—*Tess* (1980)
- Milena Canonero—*Chariots of Fire* (1981)
- John Mollo and Bhanu Athaiya—*Gandhi* (1982)
- Marik Vos—*Fanny and Alexander* (1983)
- Theodor Pistek—*Amadeus* (1984)
- Emi Wada—*Ran* (1985)
- Jenny Beavan and John Bright—*A Room with a View* (1986)
- James Acheson—*The Last Emperor* (1987)
- James Acheson—*Dangerous Liaisons* (1988)
- Phyllis Dalton—*Henry V* (1989)
- Franca Squarciapino—*Cyrano de Bergerac* (1990)
- Albert Wolsky—*Bugsy* (1991)
- Eiko Ishioka—*Bram Stoker's Dracula* (1992)
- Gabriella Pescucci—*The Age of Innocence* (1993)
- Lizzy Gardiner and Tim Chappel—*The Adventures of Priscilla, Queen of the Desert* (1994)
- James Acheson—*Restoration* (1995)
- Ann Roth—*The English Patient* (1996)
- Deborah L. Scott—*Titanic* (1997)
- Sandy Powell—*Shakespeare in Love* (1998)

Gowns by Jean Louis

He designed the legendary black satin gown Rita Hayworth wore in *Gilda* when she sang "Put the Blame on Mame," and the equally sexy "beads and skin" formfitting dress Marilyn Monroe had to be sewn into when she sang "Happy Birthday" to President John F. Kennedy at his 1962 celebration in

Madison Square Garden. But these were only two of the hundreds of famous costumes and fashions the French-born designer Jean Louis Berthault (1907–97) created over a prolific forty-year career in Hollywood, where he served as head designer at Columbia Pictures. In that time, he designed clothes for over two hundred stars, almost every star in Hollywood, one source says. All his sixty films carried the credit "Gowns by Jean Louis."

Jean Louis won an Oscar for his designs in *The Solid Gold Cadillac* (1956) and was nominated for thirteen more Academy Awards for his work in such films as *A Star Is Born, Born Yesterday,* and *From Here to Eternity.* His many private clients included the Duchess of Windsor, Nancy Reagan, and Irene Dunne. In his later years, after his first wife's death, he married Loretta Young, a friend for more than half a century. In the 1950s he had designed the gowns for all fifty-two episodes of Miss Young's "Loretta Young Show," a popular TV series that began each week with Miss Young making a grand entrance wearing one of his creations.

Hairdresser to the Stars

Few moviegoers know his name and he never won an Oscar—there being no category for "Best Hairstyling"—but Sydney Guilaroff was among the most celebrated artists in Hollywood. He created Judy Garland's braids in *The Wizard of Oz,* made Lucille Ball a redhead, did Grace Kelly's hair for her wedding to Prince Rainier, gave Claudette Colbert her distinctive bangs. Other stars whose hair he styled include Greta Garbo, Ava Gardner, Elizabeth Taylor, Marilyn Monroe, Joan Crawford, Lana Turner, Lena Horne, Kathryn Grayson, Ginger Rogers, Norma Shearer, and Ann-Margret.

The hairdresser to the stars created hairdos in over a thousand movies while serving as chief stylist at MGM from 1934 to the early 1980s. His crowning glory was *Marie Antoinette* (1938), starring Norma Shearer, for which he fashioned fully five thousand wigs, some so elaborate that they featured live songbirds in cages.

Guilaroff (pronounced *gil-er-ahf*) was a Canadian who left home at age thirteen and drifted to New York, where he apprenticed as a stylist. A few years later, he created the 1920s hairstyle fad called "the shingle" while still only a teenager—for a walk-in customer who happened to be movie star Louise Brooks. Later, MGM's Louis B. Mayer brought him to Hollywood at actress Claudette Colbert's insistence.

The "wizard with scissors," who had an unerring eye for what type of cut went with what type of face, was a lifelong bachelor who counted Grace

Kelly, Joan Crawford, Elizabeth Taylor, and Marilyn Monroe among his close friends. According to his memoir, *Crowning Glory* (1996), written a year before his death at age eighty-nine, he was also among Hollywood's great lovers, having had long affairs with Greta Garbo and Ava Gardner, to name just two of his many romances.

The Most Expensive Haircut in History

No Hollywood hairstylist inspired these words. Some anonymous critic used them to describe the haircut given by Delilah (Hedy Lamarr) to Samson (Victor Mature) in Cecil B. DeMille's *Samson and Delilah* (1949). The epic cost over $3 million to make.

The Peekaboo Wave

Veronica Lake's famous "peekaboo wave," her hair partially covering one side of her face, was possibly the best-known hairstyle of the early 1940s. But the peekaboo caused trouble when America went to war and women began working in defense plants in large numbers. Serious injuries became common because women often caught their long hair in the machines they were operating. The U.S. government asked Paramount to help by changing Lake's hairstyle, which the studio was glad to do for the war effort.

Special Effects: Creating the Great Kong

King Kong of Skull Island was not fifty feet tall and sixty feet broad, as RKO publicists claimed. Kong was created by genius model maker Willis H. O'Brien, who used six different models of the gorilla in the 1933 movie *King Kong*, which was first called *The Beast* and *The Eighth Wonder*. Each of these miniature models, eighteen inches high, had moving parts that enabled the gorilla to be filmed performing various scenes. In the famous scene where Kong scales the Empire State Building with actress Fay Wray in hand, for example, an eighteen-inch model of the beast holds a six-inch model of Miss Wray in his hand as he ascends the clearly phallic symbol.

Many other special effects by special effects master Linwood G. Dunn were employed to make scenes in the picture realistic. When King Kong tore off Fay Wray's clothes, for instance, her clothes were actually removed by wires while one of the King Kong models was painstakingly animated so that its movements matched the removal of the clothes.

For closeups, however, O'Brien did create a giant King Kong head eighteen feet high, which was covered with hair from the skins of eighty bears, according to a studio PR release. Its eyes were about a foot long, its nose two feet long, and its six-foot-long mouth was big enough to hide several men inside. These hidden technicians operated controls that could move Kong's eyes, mouth, and neck. Later, in 1976, a remake of *King Kong* featured a forty-foot-high model of Kong (built at a cost of $24 million) that required twenty technicians to operate. But the film was a financial flop, even though it won an Academy Award for visual effects.

Yak Hair

It has, thus far, taken 2,706 pounds of yak hair to make the fur for the cast of the musical *Cats*, which opened in London on May 12, 1981, and is still playing there and on Broadway.

Most Disgusting Special Effect

Mercedes McCambridge, whose voice was used for fourteen-year-old Linda Blair's scary "devil voice" in *The Exorcist* (1973) had many demanding roles on the stage and screen over her career, including an Oscar award–winning, best supporting actress performance in *All The King's Men* (1949). But she described her work in *The Exorcist* as among the physically hardest she had ever done. "One of the hardest sequences," she wrote in *The Quality of Mercy* (1981),

> was the invention of the sound for the bilious green vomit that spewed in projectile surges from the child's [Linda Blair's] mouth. . . . When I felt I was ready to go for a take I would load my mouth with apple sections, munching them to a not-quite-mealy consistency and then, from a paper cup I would add, in my distended mouth, two eggs—yolk and gluey stuff. At the instant before the pea soup and cornflakes (special effects) erupted on the screen, I would swallow the glob I'd been holding, down to mid-gullet, flex my diaphragm muscles, and gag it up onto the nest of microphones. I had to do it many times before it was absolutely right. It made me so dizzy and weak that I would have to lie down for an hour between throw-ups, and then I'd go back and have another go at it.

Those Leeches

Those famous leeches that were all over Humphrey Bogart in *The African Queen* (1951) were only rubber and were stuck to Bogart with waterproof glue. Each leech contained a small "blood sac" that broke when peeled off.

Computerized Special Effects

Computers may someday take the place of directors, actors, and cameras in the making of movies, but now they are limited to helping create special effects. Among the first films to use computers in this way was *Westworld* (1973), in which Yul Brynner played a robot gunslinger, alternating in the part with a specially constructed robot (really a sophisticated computer) that looked exactly like him. John Whitney Jr., who devised the computer techniques that made it possible to show the audience how the world looked through the eyes of a robot, did not win an Academy Award for his brilliant innovative work, but he did pave the way for many films to come.

Spielberg Has His Hand in a Lot of Things

Director Steven Spielberg doesn't appear in every one of his pictures as Alfred Hitchcock did, but Spielberg's hand does perform in one of his films. In the director's *Poltergeist* one of the characters seems to be pulling off chunks of his face to reveal gruesome flesh beneath the skin. Actually the face doesn't belong to an actor but is a dummy head made with two layers of latex, the second of which resembles flesh. The hand that the camera captures reaching up and tearing off chunks of the face is Spielberg's.

Stage Realism

House on Fire, a Roman play presented under Nero, who so loved fires that he burned down Rome, featured a house actually burning on the stage. To give the play even more realism, the actors earned their pay by rushing into the violent flames and salvaging whatever of the rich furnishings they could. They were allowed to keep all they could save.

Although there were many exceptions—Leonardo da Vinci, for example, invented a revolving stage carrying scenery in the 1490s—stage scenery in early times was usually very crude and sometimes left entirely to the imagination. It was common practice in Shakespeare's day to place a sign on the stage reading THIS IS THE FOREST OF ARDEN. But in modern times the great stage designer Gordon Craig, and many of his followers, introduced the idea that the dominant images of a play should be used to create a realistic setting that symbolizes the whole. "Take *Macbeth*," Craig once explained. "In what kind of place is that play laid? I see two things. I see a lofty and steep rock. That is to say, a place for fierce and warlike men to inhabit, a place for phantoms to nest in. Ultimately, this moisture will destroy the rock; ultimately these spirits will destroy the men."

Making Waves

One early way to depict sea waves in a stage play was to assemble dozens of extras on hands and knees under a large blue or green cloth. The extras (or the human wave machine) would then move about under the cloth, heaving backward and forward to suggest the movement of the sea.

Occupational Hazards

Prompters in most European countries except England furnished actors with words from their parts while hidden in an open hole in the middle of the front of the stage, near the footlights. There the prompter sat with his book and candle, popping up with the appropriate lines when an actor went dumb. Prompting was much more necessary in centuries past because actors played many more parts than their modern-day counterparts. In England during the 1870s a certain Squire Bancroft is said to have played four different parts a week for a little under five years (over a thousand different parts). Because the prompters in their holes spoke while inhaling dust from the stage floor, according to the Russian director Stanislavsky, "it is a well-known fact that three quarters [of them] end with tuberculosis."

Prompters have usually been appreciated by actors, but old Charles Macklin, while acting at the Drury Lane in the 1770s, had occasion to take one to task. Macklin had honed to perfection several pauses for effect between lines. These he called his short pause, his long pause, and his grand pause. One evening he was working on a presentation of the latter when the prompter tried to feed his next lines, thinking he had forgotten them. Macklin stormed into the wings and threw the prompter out. "This fellow interrupted me in my grand pause!" he exclaimed to the audience.

They Steal My Thunder: Early Sound Effects

Our author, for the advantage of his play, had invented a species of thunder . . . the very sort that is presently used in the theater. The tragedy itself was coldly received, not withstanding such assistance, and was acted but a short time. Some nights after, Mr. Dennis, being in the pit at the representation of Macbeth, *heard his own thunder made use of; upon which he rose in a violent passion and exclaimed, "See how the rascals use me! They will not let my play run, and yet they steal my thunder!"*

This early account, from the *Biographia Britannica*, is accurate in all respects, according to most authorities. Restoration playwright John Dennis had invented a new and more effective way of simulating thunder on the stage (by shaking a sheet of tin) for his play *Appius and Virginia* (1709). The play soon closed, but a rival company stole his thunder, inspiring his outburst and giving us the expression.

An earlier way to make thunder was described by the Italian designer Nicole Sabbattini in about 1650. An inclined wooden trough with shallow steps in it was placed high over the stage and at the appropriate moment cannonballs were rolled along it. To make accompanying lightning a plank was cut in two along a zig-zag line. Then another plank, "covered in tinsel and carrying a row of candles," was placed in back of it. "When the lightning was needed, the two halves of the front plank were quickly parted and then re-joined."

Other clever backstage sound effects over the years have included glass poured from one pail to another to suggest the smashing of glass; rice flung up into the air to suggest a body falling into water when it hits the floor; and the wind machine, which is a ribbed drum revolved against a silk sheet to make a sound resembling howling wind.

Seeing Things in a Different Light

In Peter Bogdanovich's oral history *Who the Devil Made It* (1997), silent-film director Allen Dwan (b. 1885) tells of how he invented the mercury vapor lamps that proved such a great improvement over the early klieg lights, which gave off clouds of carbon dust. Dwan also recalls how when he was on film location his rival directors and producers "sent snipers out with long-range rifles" to shoot out his lights and cameras.

But klieg lights themselves had been a great improvement upon previous lighting used for the stage and movies. These bright incandescent lights were the invention of the German-born brothers Kliegl, John H. (1867–1959) and Anton T. (1872–1927) who emigrated to the United States and in 1897 established the firm of Kliegl Brothers, pioneering in the development of lighting equipment and scenic effects. The light they invented was first called the *Kliegl light*, which proved too difficult to pronounce, so the lights' real name was modified like those of many of the actors who worked under them. It is said that Hollywood movie stars adopted the dark glasses that became their trademark because of the intense klieg light. The bright lights in ultraviolet rays caused a form of conjunctivitis marked by burning of the eyeballs, redness, tearing, and photophobia that was common to all who worked under the arcs. In order to conceal and protect their "klieg eyes," the stars and lesser galaxies took to wearing "shades," and have traditionally done so ever since.

Even before klieg lights were used, theater stages were lighted with *Drummond light* or *limelight*. British Royal Engineer Thomas Drummond (1797–1840), a Scottish inventor, devised the Drummond light, as an aid in murky weather while assisting in a land survey of Great Britain, and soon after adapted it for use in lighthouses. Drummond, who later became secretary of state for Ireland, utilized calcium oxide, or lime, which gives an intense white light when heated. The Drummond light wasn't used on the stage as a spotlight or called limelight until after the inventor's death in 1840, when the expression *in the limelight*, "in full glare of public attention," naturally arose from it. Limelights have long since been replaced, but the phrase still survives.

Since about 1965 tungsten-halogen lamps or quartz-iodine lamps have provided movie cameramen and directors with a vastly improved lighting source, ensuring high light output that is consistent in color.

Bizarre Belasco, High Priest of Props

The colorful producer, director, and actor David Belasco (1859–1931) who is said to have worn a clerical collar, so much did he want to be known as the high priest of American drama, probably staged the most realistic settings in theater history. One of his plays at the Belasco Theatre featured an exact duplication of Childs' Restaurant on stage, complete with fresh coffee being brewed and pancakes being made while the play was in progress. Earlier in his career he had produced a passion play featuring a herd of sheep. For another play he bought an old theatrical boardinghouse and had it reconstructed on stage, wallpaper and all; in *The Auctioneer* (1901) he duplicated a real auction shop down to the last detail, cluttering the stage with over ten thousand props.

Belasco was a strange man who always seemed to be onstage. One of his favorite tricks was to fake a temper tantrum in which he would jump up and down stomping his watch to pieces. The watch was really one of a dozen cheap watches kept for such performances. The bizarre producer spent his last years in private rooms above his theater, where he lived surrounded by peculiar objets d'art jumbled up with theatrical props.

Most Expensive Prop

The most expensive prop in film history was the forty-foot-high model of King Kong built at a cost $24 million for the movie *King Kong* (1976).

The full-scale replica of a Spanish galleon, constructed for Roman Polanski's *Pirates* in 1986, cost $10.2 million to build, making it the second most expensive prop in movie history.

Lights, Camera, Action!: Consummate Cameramen

Cameramen or cinematographers usually don't get the credit they deserve from the moviegoing public. Not many people can name two or three cameramen offhand, not even a relative star like James Wong Howe or Sven Nykvist, who has long worked in collaboration with the Swedish director Ingmar Bergman. Yet camera work can make or break a film and some otherwise poor films are a joy to watch almost solely because of their cinematography. Here are the cameramen who have won Oscars since the Academy Awards originated in 1927–28. This unique listing of course ignores many brilliant early cinematographers, especially those from other countries, but these are often covered in other chapters. Among the Academy Award winners here, Joseph Ruttenberg and Leon Shamroy have won the most Oscars—four each. Ruttenberg won for *The Great Waltz* (1938), *Mrs. Miniver* (1942), *Somebody Up There Likes Me* (1956), and *Gigi* (1958), while Shamroy won for *The Black Swan* (1942), *Wilson* (1944), *Leave Her to Heaven* (1945), and *Cleopatra* (1963). Arthur C. Miller, Freddie Young, and Vittorio Storaro have each won three Oscars. The annual winners, along with their often stunning pictures, follow:

- Charles Rosher and Karl Struss—*Sunrise* (1927–28)
- Clyde De Vinna—*White Shadows in the South Seas* (1928–29)

- Joseph T. Rucker and Willard Van der Veer—*With Byrd at the South Pole* (1929)
- Floyd Crosby—*Tabu* (1930–31)
- Lee Garmes—*Shanghai Express* (1931–32)
- Charles Lang—*A Farewell to Arms* (1932–33)
- Victor Milner—*Cleopatra* (1934)
- Hal Mohr—*A Midsummer Night's Dream* (1935)
- Gaetano Gaudio—*Anthony Adverse* (1936)
- Karl Freund—*The Good Earth* (1937)
- Joseph Ruttenberg—*The Great Waltz* (1938)
- Gregg Toland—*Wuthering Heights* (1939)
- Ernest Haller and Ray Rennahan—*Gone with the Wind* (1939 color)
- George Barnes—*Rebecca* (1940)
- Georges Périnal—*The Thief of Bagdad* (1940 color)
- Arthur C. Miller—*How Green Was My Valley* (1941)
- Ernest Palmer and Ray Rennahan—*Blood and Sand* (1941 color)
- Joseph Ruttenberg—*Mrs. Miniver* (1942)
- Leon Shamroy—*The Black Swan* (1942 color)
- Arthur C. Miller—*The Song of Bernadette* (1943)
- Hal Mohr and W. Howard Green—*Phantom of the Opera* (1943 color)
- Joseph LaShelle—*Laura* (1944)
- Leon Shamroy—*Wilson* (1944 color)
- Harry Stradling—*The Picture of Dorian Gray* (1945)
- Leon Shamroy—*Leave Her to Heaven* (1945 color)
- Arthur C. Miller—*Anna and the King of Siam* (1946)
- Charles Rosher, Leonard Smith, and Arthur E. Arling—*The Yearling* (1946 color)
- Guy Green—*Great Expectations* (1947)
- Jack Cardiff—*Black Narcissus* (1947 color)
- William H. Daniels—*The Naked City* (1948)
- Joseph A. Valentine, William V. Skall, and Winton C. Hoch—*Joan of Arc* (1948 color)

The Supporting Cast: From Stage Mothers to Computers

- Paul C. Vogel—*Battleground* (1949)
- Winton C. Hoch—*She Wore a Yellow Ribbon* (1949)
- Robert Krasker—*The Third Man* (1950)
- Robert Surtees—*King Solomon's Mines* (1950 color)
- William C. Mellor—*A Place in the Sun* (1951)
- Alfred Gilks and John Alton—*An American in Paris* (1951 color)
- Robert Surtees—*The Bad and the Beautiful* (1952)
- Winton C. Hoch and Archie Stout—*The Quiet Man* (1952 color)
- Burnett Guffey—*From Here to Eternity* (1953)
- Loyal Greggs—*Shane* (1953 color)
- Boris Kaufman—*On the Waterfront* (1954)
- Milton R. Krasner—*Three Coins in the Fountain* (1954 color)
- James Wong Howe—*The Rose Tattoo* (1955)
- Robert Burks—*To Catch a Thief* (1955 color)
- Joseph Ruttenberg—*Somebody Up There Likes Me* (1956)
- Lionel Lindon—*Around the World in 80 Days* (1956 color)
- Jack Hildyard—*The Bridge on the River Kwai* (1957)
- Sam Leavitt—*The Defiant Ones* (1958)
- Joseph Ruttenberg—*Gigi* (1958 color)
- William C. Mellor—*The Diary of Anne Frank* (1959)
- Robert L. Surtees—*Ben-Hur* (1959 color)
- Freddie Francis—*Sons and Lovers* (1960)
- Russell Metty—*Spartacus* (1960 color)
- Eugen Schüfftan—*The Hustler* (1961)
- Daniel L. Fapp—*West Side Story* (1961 color)
- Jean Bourgoin and Walter Wottitz—*The Longest Day* (1962)
- Freddie A. Young—*Lawrence of Arabia* (1962 color)
- James Wong Howe—*Hud* (1963)
- Leon Shamroy—*Cleopatra* (1963 color)
- Walter Lassally—*Zorba the Greek* (1964)
- Harry Stradling—*My Fair Lady* (1964 color)

- Ernest Laszlo—*Ship of Fools* (1965)
- Freddie Young—*Doctor Zhivago* (1965 color)
- Haskell Wexler—*Who's Afraid of Virginia Woolf?* (1966)
- Ted Moore—*A Man for All Seasons* (1966 color)
- Burnett Guffey—*Bonnie and Clyde* (1967) (awards for this year and after are for films in color)
- Pasqualino De Santis—*Romeo and Juliet* (1968)
- Conrad L. Hall—*Butch Cassidy and the Sundance Kid* (1969)
- Freddie Young—*Ryan's Daughter* (1970)
- Oswald Morris—*Fiddler on the Roof* (1971)
- Geoffrey Unsworth—*Cabaret* (1972)
- Sven Nykvist—*Cries and Whispers* (1973)
- Fred J. Koenekamp and Joseph F. Biroc—*The Towering Inferno* (1974)
- John Alcott—*Barry Lyndon* (1975)
- Haskell Wexler—*Bound for Glory* (1976)
- Vilmos Zsigmond—*Close Encounters of the Third Kind* (1977)
- Néstor Almendros—*Days of Heaven* (1978)
- Vittorio Storaro—*Apocalypse Now* (1979)
- Geoffrey Unsworth and Ghislain Cloquet—*Tess* (1980)
- Vittorio Storaro—*Reds* (1981)
- Billy Williams and Ronnie Taylor—*Gandhi* (1982)
- Sven Nykvist—*Fanny and Alexander* (1983)
- Chris Menges—*The Killing Fields* (1984)
- David Watkin—*Out of Africa* (1985)
- Chris Menges—*The Mission* (1986)
- Vittorio Storaro—*The Last Emperor* (1987)
- Peter Biziou—*Mississippi Burning* (1988)
- Freddie Francis—*Glory* (1989)
- Dean Semler—*Dances with Wolves* (1990)
- Robert Richardson—*JFK* (1991)
- Philippe Rousselot—*A River Runs Through It* (1992)
- Janusz Kaminski—*Schindler's List* (1993)

- John Toll—*Legends of the Fall* (1994)
- John Toll—*Braveheart* (1995)
- John Seale—*The English Patient* (1996)
- Russell Carpenter—*Titanic* (1997)
- Janusz Kaminski—*Saving Private Ryan* (1998)

The Two-Mile Movie

It takes one and a half feet of 35-millimeter film to make one second of screen time. A two-hour movie thus uses about two miles of film—not counting the film that has been cut.

Digital Film Restoration

By one estimate, almost half the movies made before 1950 have been lost because they were improperly stored, and many more have deteriorated to some degree. Digital film restoration can do nothing about the former films but can vastly improve those that are flawed. The process involves converting each frame of a movie into a digital image, which is then displayed on a computer screen and repaired by an artist using a digital pen and tablet; the repaired frame is finally recorded back onto the film. The process can also be used to correct mistakes made in the original filming; for example, the artists restoring Walt Disney's *Fantasia* added an animal's foot missing in the original, and director George Lucas added new creatures to scenes of the rereleased *Star Wars* trilogy. "With digital, if you can think it, you can do it," one restoration expert says. "If you want to take Humphrey Bogart out and put Brad Pitt in you can do it." Entire pictures can be virtually made over. The biggest, if not the only, problem in this complicated process is the $1 million to $5 million it costs to digitally restore a film.

III

Playwrights and Their Muses and Mates

Aeschylus the Hero: Founder of Greek Drama

Aeschylus, one of the two or three greatest playwrights the world has known, was also a famous war hero. The founder of Greek drama fought as a soldier in his country's war against Persia. He saw action at Marathon, Artemisium, Salamis, and Plataea, and his brother Cynaegirus was killed fighting beside him at Marathon while attempting a conspicuously gallant act. The Athenians revered Aeschylus as a war hero as well as a great tragedian, placing portraits of the brothers in the picture that served as the national memorial of the battle. In his epitaph, probably written by himself, the dramatist is represented not writing but fighting at Marathon.

Aeschylus is said to have been acting in one of his own plays when a reference to Demeter, the goddess of agriculture, was made and the audience accused him of revealing the secrets of that "Earth Mother," who had the power to make the earth barren. The audience rose up in fury, cursing the playwright and charging toward him. Aeschylus saved himself by fleeing to the altar of Dionysus in the orchestra, which even the angry crowd respected as an inviolable sanctuary. Later, when tried for his crime, he pleaded that "he did not know that what he said was secret" and was freed, probably largely because of his heroism as a soldier.

Aeschylus is considered the world's greatest dramatist by some; others believe he is second only to Shakespeare, mainly because he lacked Shakespeare's sense of humor. Though he came from a noble family, bravely fought for his country, and was noted for his dignity, sublimity, and eloquence, he suffered a quite undignified death far removed from the themes of utmost grandeur that he chose for his plays. Aeschylus died in 456 B.C., when he was sixty-nine. According to legend, at least, he was killed when an eagle dropped a tortoise on his bald head, mistaking it for a rock to break its meal upon.

The Founder of Tragedy

Some ancient writers regard Phrynichus (c. 512–476 B.C.) as the real founder of tragedy, and the Greek tragedian was probably the first dramatist to introduce a separate actor, distinct from the chorus leader, which laid the foundation for stage dialogue. Phrynichus was also the first to introduce women characters on stage (they were played by men in masks). His most famous play was *The Capture of Meletus* (c. 493), which dealt with the fall of Athens's sister city to the Persians. The audience was moved to tears by this work, but in an age when playwrights were expected to write only about the accepted myths and legends of the early Greeks, Phrynichus was fined a thousand drachmas for his innovation and forbidden ever to present the play again. One theory has it that the Athenian statesman and commander Themistocles secretly arranged to have the author write *Capture* to stir up the Athenians to go to war against the Persians.

Greece's Grand Old Man of Drama

Few if any other writers have dominated a national literature for as long as Sophocles did in his day. Of his 118 plays, 20 won the esteemed first prizes at the Greek Dionysian and Lenaean festivals. He won his first prize when only twenty-five and his last sixty years later when an old man of eighty-five. Among the earliest writers to be honored as an athlete as well as an author, this sword maker's son (born in 496 B.C.) was renowned as a ballplayer and won a prize as a wrestler. After the battle of Salamis, the handsome Sophocles was chosen to lead the youths of Athens in a nude victory dance.

Sophocles' sons are said to have summoned him to court in his old age (he lived to be ninety) so that a jury might find him incompetent to manage his estate on the grounds of senility. After he read them the play he had just finished, *Oedipus at Colonus*, the jury sided with him, reasoning that no man in his dotage could write such a work. They even escorted him home as an honor. "If I am Sophocles I am no dotard," he told his accusers at his trial, "and if I dote I am not Sophocles."

An old, possibly apocryphal, story holds that the playwright died when his breath failed him because he had no time to pause while reading a long passage from his tragedy *Antigone*.

The Frozen Words of Antiphanes

Some 365 comedies, one for every day of the year, are attributed to Antiphanes (c. 408–334 B.C.), apparently a foreigner who settled in Athens. Plutarch credits him for originating an anecdote that has been repeated by many writers, including Rabelais, and is even told in recent times of the Texas Panhandle. "Antiphanes said merrily," Plutarch assures us, "that in a certain city the cold was so intense that words were congealed as soon as spoken, but that after some time they thawed and became audible; so that the words spoken in winter were articulated next summer."

The Revered Euripides

Legend has it that a group of Athenians held captive at Syracuse passed the time by enacting scenes from the great Attic dramatist's plays. So impressed were their hardened captors by these beautiful passages that they freed their prisoners and asked them to continue their playacting for a while as honored guests. When the former captives returned to Athens they honored the dramatist as a daring war hero who had liberated them.

Euripides' works were so revered in ancient Greece that prisoners were sometimes allowed to go free if they could recite passages from the poet. One time a vessel pursued by pirates wasn't allowed to enter a Sicilian harbor until some of the voyagers could recite a few lines from Euripides. And when Athens was conquered in 404 B.C. and about to be destroyed, the Spartan generals were moved to mercy by an Athenian singing the first chorus of Euripides' *Electra*. Another tradition holds that when the Athenian expedition to Syracuse failed in 415 B.C., the captured Athenians were chained and put to work in the stone quarries—all except those who could recite passages from the plays of Euripides.

Still another ancient story—stemming perhaps from the legend that the dramatist lived alone with his books, hating society in general and women in particular—has it that a group of women at a secret festival plotted to murder Euripides because he had satirized them on the stage. This may not be true, but it is the plot of Aristophanes' play *Thesmophoriazusae*. Though his last years, in the words of a biographer, were spent staring out at the sea "all day long, thinking to himself and writing, for he simply despised anything that was not great and high," in his youth Euripides had been a well-rounded, active man. In addition to being a dramatist and accomplished painter, he was an excellent athlete who won prizes at the games in Athens and Eleusis.

The Greek tragedian is thought to have been "of a morose disposition," as might well be expected of a man who lost his wife, two sons, and a daughter when they partook of a deadly but deceiving *Amanita* mushroom species. (*Amanita verna*, the destroying angel, is easily confused with several edible mushroom species.) Euripides himself possibly had an even more terrible death by natural forces. In 406 B.C., when he was seventy-four, he is said to have been torn to death by the hunting dogs of King Archelaus of Macedonia, whom he served as court poet, or to have been ripped apart by a mob of women who objected to one of his plays.

"Menander the Writer"

Though the Greek dramatist Menander is now considered his era's greatest master of comedy, he wasn't a very successful writer in his lifetime. He certainly was successful at love. A rich, handsome man, he loved the beautiful courtesan Glycera. When Ptolemy I invited Menander to his court at Alexandria, the poet sent the playwright Philemon in his place, explaining, "Philemon has no Glycera."

An ancient writer tells us how Demetrius, governor of Athens, came to meet the dramatist: "Menander, famous for his comedies—whom Demetrius had not known personally though he had read him and admired his genius—came, perfumed and in flowing robe, with languid step and slow. Seeing him at the end of the line the tyrant asked, 'What effeminate is that who dares enter my presence?' Those nearest replied, 'This is Menander the writer.'"

Said Aristophanes in tribute to the master playwright: "O Menander, O Life, which of you imitated the other?" Menander originated many popular proverbial sayings, including "Conscience makes cowards of us all" ("Conscience makes cowards of the bravest men"), "Evil communications corrupt good manners," and perhaps "I am a man and consider nothing human alien to me." Possibly the most famous of these proverbs is "the good die young"—in his original far more poetic words:

> *Whom the gods love, die young; that man is blest*
> *who, having viewed at ease this solemn show*
> *Of sun, star, ocean, fire, doth quickly go*
> *Back to his home with calm uninjured breast.*

Menander died relatively young himself, in 292 B.C. at the age of fifty, drowning after a seizure of cramps while swimming in the harbor at Piraeus.

The Ultimate Tribute

One old story, which may not be true, says that the Roman playwright Terence died of a broken heart after he lost the translations he had made over the years of the plays of his idol, the Greek playwright Menander.

Philemon and His Fans

In ancient Greece, Menander alone was more highly regarded than Philemon as a comic dramatist, but just fragments of Philemon's plays remain today. Plutarch says that Philemon journeyed to Egypt and on the way fell into the hands of King Magas of Cyrene, whom he once satirized. Magas frightened him and treated him with much contempt, finally freeing the poet and insulting him with a contemptuous present of toys fit only for a child.

Philemon won more prizes than his rival Menander, who is much favored by critics today, but this was probably because he was the first playwright to raise to an art form the use of a personal claque that applauded and cheered him. Living to be one hundred or so, the playwright worshiped the work of his great predecessor Euripides, who had lived a century before him. "If I could be sure that the dead have consciousness," he once said, "I would hang myself to see Euripides."

There are several accounts of Philemon's death in about 263 B.C., but the most popular one has him dying of laughter over a joke he had just made.

A Muse, Anyone?

It was traditional for the ancient Greek dramatists to invoke a particular Muse to help in the act of creation; the appeal for inspiration usually came toward the start of work. The Nine Muses were the children of the gods Zeus and Mnemosyne. Few playwrights or screenwriters would admit to employing them today, but many could use their help. As Shakespeare wrote in the Prologue to *Henry V*, "O for a Muse of fire that would ascend / The brightest heaven of invention." Here they are to choose from for any kind of play you might begin:

> *Calliope* (her name, pronounced *ka-LIE-o-pee*, does not rhyme with rope, although the musical instrument named after her can; the name means "beautiful voice"). The chief Muse, usually associated with

epic poetry, poetic inspiration, and eloquence, she has as her emblems a pen and a scroll of parchment.

Clio (*KLIE-o*; means "to tell of"). Muse of history and heroic exploits, she is often represented like Calliope.

Euterpe (*yoo-TER-pee*; means "to delight well"). Muse of music and lyric poetry, patron of flute players, joy, and pleasure, she invented the double flute, which is her symbol.

Thalia (*tha-LIE-uh*; means "blooming"). Muse of gaiety, comedy, and pastoral life, she is depicted wearing a comic mask and garland of ivy while holding a shepherd's crook and a tambourine.

Melpomene (*mel-POM-i-nee*; means "to sing"). Muse of tragedy, song, and harmony, "the mournfullest Muse" is shown wearing a tragic mask and garland of grape leaves.

Terpsichore (*terp-SIK-o-ree*; means "dance-liking"). Muse of dancing, choral song, and lyric poetry, usually depicted seated and holding a lyre.

Erato (*ER-a-to*; from the Greek *eros*, "love"). Muse of erotic and love poetry and miming, she is shown holding a stringed instrument such as a lyre.

Polyhymnia (*POL-ee-HYM-nee-uh*; means "many hymns"). Muse of the chant and inspired hymn and said to be the inventor of the lyre, she is depicted as grave in countenance and wrapped in long, flowing robes.

Urania (*yoo-RAY-nee-uh*; from *uranus*, "sky"). Muse of celestial phenomena, whose name means "the heavenly one" and whom Milton made the spirit of the loftiest poetry, she is often shown pointing with a wand or staff at a celestial globe she holds in her hand.

Proverbial Playwrights

The words of the ancient Greek and Roman playwrights have lasted for thousands of years, many of them becoming proverbial in English and other languages. Here are just a few.

- "By suffering comes wisdom."   —Aeschylus, *Agamemnon*
- "God loves to help him who strives to help himself."   —Aeschylus, *Seven Against Thebes*

- "None love the messenger who brings bad news."   —Sophocles, *Antigone*
- "Though a man be wise it is no shame for him to live and learn." —Sophocles, *Antigone*
- "For money you would sell your soul."   —Sophocles, *Antigone*
- "The very hair on my head / Stands up for dread."   —Sophocles, *Oedipus at Colonus*
- "Leave no stone unturned."   —Euripides, *Heracleidae*
- "I laughed till I cried."   —Aristophanes, *The Frogs*
- "Old age is but a second childhood."   —Aristophanes, *The Frogs*
- "When shall I see those halcyon days?"   —Aristophanes, *The Clouds*
- "He works and blows the coals and has plenty of other irons in the fire."   —Aristophanes, *Acharnians*
- "You knew not how to live in clover."   —Menander, *The Girl from Samos*
- "I call a fig a fig, a spade a spade."   —Menander, an unidentified fragment of his work
- "What is yours is mine, and all mine is yours." ("What's mine is yours, and what is yours is mine," as Shakespeare put it in *Measure for Measure*.)   —Plautus, *Trinummus*
- "He whom the gods favor dies in youth."   —Plautus, *Baccides*
- "Nothing is there more friendly to a man than a friend in need." ("A friend in need is a friend indeed.")   —Plautus, *Epidicus*
- "Nothing in excess."   —Terence, *Andria*
- "In the bloom of youth."   —Terence, *Andria*
- "Nothing is said now that has not been said before."   —Terence, *Andria*
- "I did not care one straw."   —Terence, *Eunuchus*

The Bridegroom of Poetry

The ancient Hindus so admired the playwright Kalidasa that they called him the "Bridegroom of Poetry." His long drama *Shakuntala* is considered the greatest Hindu classic play. This fourth-century Sanskrit drama won the admiration of the great German author Goethe 1,300 years later.

Alliterative Playwrights

In 1556, English playwright, poet, printer, and preacher William Baldwin (d.1563) wrote a verse play featuring fully sixty-two characters, each of whose names began with the letter *L*. English playwright John Heywood (1497–1580) comes in a distant second in such eccentric namings. His play *The Four Ps*, "a merry interlude," has four principal characters, "a Palmer, a Pardoner, a Poticary [apothecary], and a Peddler." Baldwin, who died of the plague in 1563, is better known for his religious satire *The Black Cat*, which some consider the first English novel, while Heywood is best known for collections of English proverbs.

The First Opera

Italian poet Ottavio Rinuccini (1562–1621) has the distinction of having written the lyrics for the first true opera known to history. *Dafne*, music by Jacopo Peri, was performed in 1597 before a group of music lovers called the *camerata* at the home of the wealthy Jacopo Corsi in Florence.

A Modern Early-English Opera

Edna St. Vincent Millay's libretto for Deems Taylor's romantic Wagnerian opera *The King's Henchman* (1927), set in tenth-century England, contains only words of Anglo-Saxon origin. The popular work was commissioned by the Metropolitan Opera.

Not for an Age but for All Time: Will Shakespeare, or Shagspere

> "And thou, who didst the stars and sunbeams know,
>   Self-schooled, self-scanned, self-honored, self-secure,
>   Didst tread on earth unguessed at."
>   —Matthew Arnold, "Shakespeare"

Though legends abound about him, little is really known about the private life of the greatest English poet and dramatist. William Shakespeare, or Shagspere, was born on April 23, 1564 (St. George's Day), at Stratford-upon-Avon of substantial, middle-class parents—his father was a glover and served as an alderman—and received a solid grammar school education, well above the standards for the time. There is evidence that the

"Sweet Swan of Avon," as Ben Jonson called him, left Stratford for London to avoid a charge of poaching. He probably acted in the earl of Leicester's company and by 1592 had achieved some fame as a dramatist and actor. By this time Shakespeare had acquired property and he lived like a gentleman with his wife, Anne Hathaway, whom he had married ten years previously, raising three children, Susanna and the twins Hamnet and Judith. Shakespeare was one of the few writers in his day to win fame and wealth. The Bard of Avon died on his own birthday in 1616, age fifty-two, in Stratford, where he had retired three years or so before. That is the bare bones of it, but countless stories and speculations have tried to flesh out the dramatist's life, ranging from the spelling of his name to the alleged infidelity of his wife, the identity of the dark lady of the sonnets, and the fantastic theories that Francis Bacon, Christopher Marlowe, and others actually wrote his plays. It is not even certain that Shakespeare wrote the famous epitaph on his gravestone at Holy Trinity Church in Stratford. (*See* Chapter 11.)

Shakespeare's plays and poems have appropriately evoked even more speculation than his personal life. Thirty-seven plays in all have been attributed in whole or part to him, beginning possibly with *Henry VI* (1589) to *Henry VIII* (1613). It would be impossible to even try to show in how many ways the 814,780 words in his plays or the 1,277 speaking characters he created have enriched English—Hamlet, the irrepressible Falstaff, and all Shakespeare's characters come so alive in the dramas that they have stepped off the stage and into the language forever. Despite his "borrowings," his assimilative temperament, and his "lack of education," the "myriad minded" Shakespeare remains "great above rule," "not for an age but for all time," "not England's poet, but the world's."

Shakespeare was not the inspired, uneducated writer he has often been made out to be. He possessed a large vocabulary, having used 29,066 different words in his plays, as compared to the 6,000 different words used in the entire Bible. Today the average English-speaking person uses something like 2,000 words in everyday speech. It has been pointed out that one out of every ten words Shakespeare employed in his plays and poems is used for the first time anywhere. A sample of his word inventions include *aerial, auspicious, assassination, barefaced, bump, clangor, critic, countless, laughable, hurry, eventful,* and *road.*

The Bard was known in his day as a very rapid writer. "His mind and hand went together," his publishers Heminges and Condell reported, "and what he thought, he uttered with that easiness that we have scarce received from him a blot in his papers." (Even if he should have blotted out a thousand lines, as his friend Ben Jonson quipped.) But it is often forgotten that despite his prolific mind the greatest writer of all time could not make a living solely from writing. (*See* Chapter 1.)

Shakespeare's Death

Shakespeare left London in 1613 to retire in Stratford-upon-Avon, where he died three years later. If we are to believe the diary of a Mr. Ward, the vicar of Stratford, "Shakespeare, [Michael] Drayton and Ben Jonson had a merry meeting, and, it seems, drank too hard, for Shakespeare died of a fever then contracted."

The Bard's Dramatic Temperament

In his *Brief Lives*, John Aubrey claims that Shakespeare's father was a butcher, not a glover. "I have been told by some of the neighbors," he goes on to say, "that when he was a boy he exercised his father's Trade, but when he kill'd a Calfe he would do it in a high style, and make a speech."

Shakespeare the Poacher

Legend holds that as a young man of nineteen Shakespeare was prosecuted by justice of the peace Sir Thomas Lucy for deer poaching from Charlecotte Park. Lucy's family owned the village of Charlecotte and though the village did not have a deer park, it did have a warren that was a preserve for deer and other animals. Additionally, Lucy was well known as a preserver of game and had introduced into Parliament a bill for game preservation. According to an unsubstantiated story, told by Nicholas Rowe in 1710, but mentioned by Archdeacon Davies of Sapperton, Gloucestershire, who died in 1708, and others before him, Shakespeare aggravated his troubles with Lucy by writing a derogatory ballad about him. The trouble arising from the incident is important because he is said to have later caricatured Lucy as Justice Shallow in *The Merry Wives of Windsor*, though many critics deny this. Nicholas Rowe gave the Lucy ballad, perhaps Shakespeare's first published poetry, as follows:

> *A parliemente member, a justice of peace,*
> *At home a poor scare-crowe, at London an asse,*
> *If Lowsie is Lucy, as some Folke miscalle it,*

Then Lucy is lowsie whatever befall it:
　He thinks himself greate,
　Yet an asse in his state,
We allowe by his ears but with asses to mate.
　If Lucy is lowsie, as some Folke miscalle it,
　Sing lowsie Lucy, whatever befall it.

Shakespeare's Son

Another old story has it that Shakespeare was the father of a child born to Mrs. Davenant, the proprietress of an inn at Oxford where the playwright often stopped during his frequent travels from London to Stratford-upon-Avon. One day Shakespeare, who had been made the child's godfather, arrived at the inn and the boy was called from school to see him. Running home, he encountered an old gentleman quite familiar with the affairs of the family, who asked where he was going in such a rush. "To my godfather, Shakespeare," the boy said. "Fie, child," replied the old man, "why are you so superfluous? Have you not learned yet that you should not use the name of God in vain?"

The boy, later Sir William D'Avenant, became England's unofficial poet laureate in 1638. Credited as the founder of English opera with his *Siege of Rhodes*, he also is noted for adapting Shakespeare's *Tempest*.

After the poet laureate contracted syphilis and lost his nose to the disease, those he encountered either sympathized with his impairment or laughed at him. D'Avenant was surprised then when an old woman he met commiserated with him and blessed his *eyesight*. On being questioned, she explained that he would really be in trouble if his eyes failed because he had nowhere to prop a pair of eyeglasses.

During his final illness D'Avenant apologized for not having finished his romantic epic *Gondibert*, which already totaled about 1,700 quatrains. "I shall ask leave to desist," he said, "when I am interrupted by so great an experiment as dying."

Shakespeare and Ben Jonson

Shakespeare's contemporary Thomas Fuller (1608–61) compared the Bard and his friend playwright Ben Jonson: "Many were the wit-combats betwixt him and Ben Jonson, which two I behold like a Spanish great galleon, and an English man of war. Master Jonson (like the former) was built far higher in learning; solid, but slow, in his performances. Shakespeare, with the English man of war, lesser in bulk, but lighter in sailing, could turn with all the tides, tack about, and take advantage of all winds, by the quickness of his wit and invention."

Four Thousand Ways to Spell "Shakespeare"

If one of the seven known signatures of William Shakespeare came on the market or a new one was discovered, it would sell for about $1.5 million—second only to a "Julius Caesar," which would be worth $2 million, according to experts. As it now stands, no one really knows how Shakespeare spelled his name. The seven unquestionably genuine signatures are very difficult to decipher. The name is spelled *Shakspeare* on the Bard's own monument, but *Shakespeare* on the tombs of his wife and daughter. Other early variations are *Shakspere* and *Shagspere* (on his marriage license). In 1869 a Philadelphian named J. R. Wise published a book called *Autograph of William Shakespeare . . . Together with 4,000 Ways of Spelling the Name.*

Was Bacon Shakespeare?

- Ohio-born schoolteacher Delia Salter Bacon (1811–59) is remembered for her theory, expounded in *The Philosophy of the Plays of Shakespeare Unfolded* (1857), that Shakespeare's plays were written by a group of men headed by the brilliant Sir Francis Bacon and including Sir Walter Raleigh and Edmund Spenser. They had, she said, concealed a great philosophic system within the plays by the use of ciphers, which she had discovered. Her contemporary Nathaniel Hawthorne said that her devotion to this single idea "had thrown her off balance" and when she traveled to England to research her theory more she went entirely out of her mind. For the last two years of her life she was violently insane.

- The making of long words was a popular game in Elizabethan England and *honorificabilitudinity*, meaning "honorableness," was one of the most absurd ones made. Shakespeare parodied this word by stretching it out still longer in *Love's Labor's Lost*, using the original Latin ablative plural when he has Costard the clown say to the servant Moth: "I marvel thy master hath not eaten thee for a word, for thou art not so long by the head as honorificabilitudinitatibus." This is the word that "proves" to some people that Bacon was the author of all plays attributed to Shakespeare. For it rearranges letters from the Latin sentence *Hi ludi F. Baconis nati tuiti orbi*, which says, translated, "These plays, F. Bacon's offspring, are preserved for the world."

- In a mock trial held in Washington, D.C., in 1987, three United States Supreme Court justices unanimously ruled that the works of Shakespeare were written by William Shakespeare and no one else. The next year, at a mock trial in England, three Law Lords, the British equivalent of U.S. Supreme Court justices, came to the same conclusion.

Did Shakespeare Write the Bible?

According to some numerologists, yes—or at least he helped to write the King James Version of the Bible. Their "evidence":

1. The King James Version of the Bible was published in 1610, when Shakespeare was forty-six. (Actually, it was published in 1611.)
2. *Shake* is the forty-sixth word of the Psalm 46.
3. *Spear* is the forty-sixth word from the end in the Psalm 46.

Shakespeare's Birds

In *Henry IV* Shakespeare mentions a starling "taught to speak nothing but 'Mortimer.'" His sentence inspired a group of literary enthusiasts who wished to introduce all the birds in Shakespeare's plays to America. These bardologists brought a score of starlings across the Atlantic in 1890 and released them in New York's Central Park. The starling has since become the most numerous of all American birds and a pest that preys on gardens—including the many public Shakespeare gardens in which are planted all the flowers and vegetables mentioned in Shakespeare's work.

The Shakespeare of Japan

Japanese dramatist Sugimori Nobunori (1653–1724), widely regarded as the "Shakespeare of Japan," probably took his pen name, Chikamatsu Monzaemon, because his prominent samurai family objected to his writing for the plebian *joruri*, or puppet theater, of Japan. Chikamatsu himself liked to write for puppets because they could not distort the meaning of his work, as he felt actors did in the plays he wrote for Kabuki theater. In any case, this one dramatist alone for three-quarters of a century made puppet theater more popular than any theater of living actors in Japan, something unique in theatrical history.

"Audiences nowadays will not accept plays unless they are realistic and logical," someone once told Chikamatsu. "The old plots are full of nonsense that nobody will tolerate anymore. The reputation of Kabuki actors depends on just how realistic their acting seems."

"What you say seems plausible," he replied, "but it does not take into account the true methods of art. Art is something that lies in between reality and unreality. Of course it seems desirable, in view of the current taste for realism, for the actor playing retainer to copy the gestures and speech of a real retainer, but would a real retainer rouge and powder his face the way actors do? Or would the audiences like it if an actor, on the grounds that real retainers pay no attention to how they look, were to perform unshaven or display a bald head? The theatre is unreal, and yet not real. Entertainment lies between the two."

Strangest Playwright Collaborators

Apart from authors of modern musical comedies like Gilbert and Sullivan (*see* "Gilbert and Sullivan") or Rodgers and Hammerstein, there seem to be few collaborating playwrights in the history of the theater who existed and thrived on a permanent basis. The French brothers Goncourt (Edmond and Jules) come to mind, as does the French team Emile Erckmann and Alexander Chatrain, who wrote plays under the pen name Erckmann Chatrain in the mid-to-late nineteenth century. But the greatest and oddest of the lot were Shakespeare's contemporaries Francis Beaumont and John Fletcher, good friends who collaborated on about fifteen plays between 1606 and 1616, when Beaumont died of the plague.

Beaumont and Fletcher not only shared in the writing of their plays, they shared clothes, a bed, and a mistress. Of their partnership John Aubrey said: "There was a wonderful consimility of fancy. They lived together not far from the playhouses, had one wench in the house between them, the same clothes and cloak, &C." John Dryden wrote that Beaumont was "so accurate a judge of plays that Ben Jonson, while he lived, submitted all his writings to his censure and 'tis thought used his judgement in correcting if not contriving all his plots." Fletcher is thought to have collaborated with Shakespeare on *Henry VIII*, among other plays.

One time the "twin stars of our stage," as Algernon Swinburne called them, were sitting in a tavern apportioning the work involved in a tragedy they were writing. Fletcher wanted to work on one scene, Beaumont another, and they finally divided the work equally. During their conversation, however, one of them was overheard saying, "I'll kill the king." Both men were accused of treason, arrested, and held until the authorities were satisfied they were not assassins.

On a blank page of his copy of Beaumont and Fletcher's (or more likely Fletcher and Massinger's) *Fair Maid of the Inn*, Keats wrote two centuries later:

Bards of Passion and of Mirth,
Ye have left your souls on earth!
Have ye souls in heaven too?

"The Last of the Elizabethans"

British poet and playwright Thomas Lovell Beddoes (1803–49) once hired a theater for a night so that his lover, a baker named John Degen, could play Hotspur in *Henry IV*. Thinking himself "the last of the Elizabethans," Beddoes even tried to grow a beard and dress like Shakespeare. The writer attempted suicide after an argument with his lover. He cut an artery in his leg, but only succeeded in losing the leg—it had to be amputated after infection set in. Six months later he made another attempt, with curare, and succeeded.

A Prolific "Monster of Nature"

Spanish dramatist Lope Félix de Vega Carpio (1562–1635) wrote more than 2,200 plays in his seventy-three-year lifetime, far more than any other known playwright in history. Several of his plays were written overnight and one hundred of them in a day each—these records no author has come close to equaling. Some five hundred of Vega's plays survive. The playwright did not print his plays, for fear that fewer people would then come to the theater. But publishers regularly sent men with amazing memories to his performances. After sitting through two or three hearings, these men committed the plays to memory and dictated them to the publishers' printers. Though known "memorizers" were sometimes barred from the theater—at one performance Lope's cast refused to go on until one such man was ejected—the publishers were always quick to find replacements.

A child prodigy who read Latin at five and wrote his first play at twelve, Lope de Vega's life was as passionate and prolific as his literary productions. His many love poems are dedicated to several of his many mistresses. The Spaniard was married twice and fathered at least four children out of wedlock, including three born to Spanish actress Micaela de Lujan, who starred in several of his plays.

The Spanish playwright and his great contemporary Cervantes were sworn enemies, probably because Lope de Vega smarted over the satire of himself and his plays in *Don Quixote*, which he probably read in manuscript. A former friend of Cervantes, he wrote in a letter to a prominent physician on August 4, 1604, that his own plays were odious to Cervantes and that "no poet is as bad as Cervantes, nor so foolish as to praise *Don Quixote*." This is the first recorded mention anywhere of Cervantes's novel. Cervantes began his career trying to keep up with Lope's output, but he gave up when he learned that the playwright had in one week written ten plays, one of them tossed off before breakfast. "There is no competing with 'a monster of nature,'" he remarked.

The idol of Spain, Vega was so beloved that one reviewer who dared criticize him lived in constant fear of assassination. Wherever Lope went he was engulfed by crowds of admirers. No other playwright in history has known such adulation. In his own day his name indeed came to mean anything superlative of a kind, such as Lope cigars, Lope melons, and Lope horses.

Vega's last days were sad ones, especially because of the death of his son Lope and the elopement of his daughter Antonia; both events are said to have "wounded him to the soul." A contemporary wrote that every Friday he "scourged himself so severely that the walls of his room were sprinkled with his blood."

An old story claims that on his deathbed in 1635 Vega asked how much time he had remaining. His death was imminent, he was told. "All right then, I'll say it," he declared. "Dante makes me sick."

"Es de Lope"

Perhaps only Eugene O'Neill, Samuel Beckett, and a few other contemporary playwrights could claim styles so unique that their work is easily recognized without being identified. None of them, however, had a style so recognizable and beloved that a popular expression was dedicated to it. Only Lope Félix de Vega Carpio can claim this honor. The prolific author wrote in a graceful, flowing style at once so elegant, earthy, and effortless—so perfect, most people thought—that it gave rise to the common expression *Es de Lope* ("It is Lope's"), said whenever a line or two of his were heard.

More Prolific Playwrights

- Thomas Heywood (1574?–1641), called a "prose Shakespeare" by Charles Lamb, was "a model of light and rapid talent." One of the most prolific writers in English literary history, he once said he had "an entire hand or at least a finger in 220 plays," and this was seven years before death ended his writing career. Heywood always insisted that he wrote for the stage, not the press; he was one of those few dramatists who protested against the printing of his work because he claimed he had no time to polish it for publication.

- Alexandre Hardy (1569–1631) was also among the most prolific of playwrights. The French dramatist claimed to have written more than six hundred plays, though only thirty-four survive. All his plays were written for the same troupe of actors, with whom he toured the country.
- Mystery author Edgar Wallace (1875–1932) was incredibly quick and prolific. Wallace wrote his play *On the Spot* in just two and a half days, and not a word of it was changed when it appeared on stage.

Bad Deal for Cervantes

At a time when he was so poor that he had to borrow money to buy a suit of clothes, Miguel Cervantes (1547–1616) signed one of the worst contracts in theatrical history. In September 1592, the author of *Don Quixote* contracted with a producer to write six plays at fifty ducats each—but no payment was to be made unless the producers considered that each of these plays "was one of the best ever produced in Spain." If any of these plays were ever written or Cervantes was ever paid for one, it has gone unrecorded. Perhaps Cervantes had second thoughts about the deal. Incidentally, Cervantes did not die on the same day as Shakespeare (April 23, 1616), as the traditional story holds. When Shakespeare died, England was still using the Julian calendar; Spain had already adopted the Gregorian calendar, by which Shakespeare died on May 3, 1616, not April 23, 1616.

"A Condensation of Human Misery"

Born terribly deformed and almost completely crippled, with quack remedies for syphilis later destroying his nervous system, the French poet and dramatist Paul Scarron (1610–60) once described himself for his readers:

> *I am going to tell you as nearly as possible what I am like. My figure was well made, though small. My malady has shortened it by a good foot. My head is rather large for my body—my face is full, while my body is that of a skeleton. My sight is fairly good, but my eyes protrude, and one of them is lower than the other. My legs and thighs formed at first an obtuse,*

next a right, and finally an acute, angle; my thighs and body form another; and with my head bent down on my stomach I resemble not badly the letter Z. My arms have shrunk as well as my legs, and my fingers as well as my arms. To sum it up, I am a condensation of human misery.

Scarron became an abbé when nineteen years old. A possibly apocryphal story says that when he was about thirty, serving his canonry at Le Mans, he tarred and feathered himself like a carnival freak for a lark. On discovering this the people of Le Mans chased him into a swamp where he had to hide until their rage subsided and where he contracted rheumatism that made his pain even worse. In any event, from the age of thirty on, Scarron lived in a state of pain so severe that he was able to endure life only with the aid of opium. Yet he still wrote comedies. Despite his misery, he also presided over the most famous salon in Paris, his body enclosed by a box from which only his head and arms protruded. His wit was so treasured that people continued to come even when his mounting debts forced him to charge his guests for dinner.

"For my sister's bitch," ran the dedication to a collection of Scarron's plays and poems, which he had dedicated to his sister's dog. Scarron and his sister had a falling-out while the book was being printed. The playwright could not eliminate the dedication as he wanted to, so in the book's errata he noted: "For 'my sister's bitch' read 'my bitch of a sister.'" (*See* "Poor Scarron's Epitaph," Chapter 11.)

Molière the Immortal

France's greatest dramatist and actor, the immortal Molière (Jean-Baptiste Poquelin), lived as a child in a house on a Paris street that was decorated with sculptures representing a group of monkeys playing. This was a prophetic beginning, for the monkey had long been the traditional emblem of comic drama. Voltaire tells us that Molière was so good as an actor in comic roles because he suffered "from a kind of hiccup which was quite unsuited to serious roles . . . [but] which served to make his acting in comedy the more enjoyable."

Though only passable as a tragedian, Molière invented the French comedy of manners with *Les Précieuses Ridicules* (*The Pretentious Young Ladies*) in 1659. His *Tartuffe* (1664), which has to this date been performed more often than any other French play, is an exposure of the hypocritically pious. These apparently included a great number of real-life clergymen, considering their reaction to the play. The archbishop of Paris, for example, threatened with excommunication anyone who read, heard, or performed it, and another clerygman cried that "[Molière] should be burned at the stake as a foretaste of the fires of hell."

Though he distrusted and satirized doctors, Molière got along well with his own physician, Monsieur de Maurvilan. Asked why, he replied: "We reason with one another; he prescribes remedies; I omit to take them and I recover." On February 10, 1673, the playwright-actor appeared in his last play, *Le Malade Imaginaire* (*The Imaginary Invalid*), playing the part of Argan, a hypochondriac who had twice pretended death. Just as he uttered the word "*Juro*" ("I swear") when Argan took the Hippocratic oath as a physician, he began coughing convulsively. Hiding his pain, he completed the play, but once he got home he began coughing more violently, burst a blood vessel in his throat, and choked to death on his own blood. He was only fifty-one. Though he is said to have renounced his profession before he died, he could not be buried in a consecrated grave because he was connected with the theater, which was thought to be an evil institution at the time. Tradition has it that his patron, Louis XIV, let him be buried in a churchyard anyway, but fourteen feet down—just beyond the depth that the church considered consecrated ground. His grave has never been found.

Molière's Moron

Moron, as a designation for a feebleminded person, is said to be one of the few words ever voted into the language. It was adopted in 1910 by the American Association for the Study of the Feebleminded from the name of a foolish character in Molière's play *La Princesse d'Élide*, which Molière had written for the amusement of his king.

Kings and Queen of the Playwrights

Pierre Corneille (1606–84), the creator of French classical tragedy, was accorded what may be the highest praise ever given a dramatist. When Napoléon saw his play *Andromède*, he exclaimed, "If Corneille were alive I would make him king!" Corneille, however, began to fail in his later years, and his masterpieces were replaced by rather mediocre plays. When his *Agésilas* (1666) was followed by *Attila* the next year, the critic Nicolas Boileau-Despréaux cruelly remarked, "After *Agésilas*, alas! But after *Attila*, stop!" ("*Après L'Agésilas, helas! Mais après L'Attila, hola!*")

Tradition holds that Corneille and his younger brother, Thomas, lived in attached houses with a panel that could be opened between them. Thomas was better at versification than Pierre, who often opened the panel and asked him to supply a rhyme.

Another kingly playwright was Polish dramatist Juliusz Slowacki (1809–49), who lived in political exile from 1831 until his death, during which time he wrote over thirty plays. Considered the founder of Polish tragedy today, he never saw any of his best plays performed in his lifetime. It wasn't until 1927, seventy-eight years after his death, that his body was removed from Paris to Kraków, where he was buried in the royal vault, because, it was said, "he was the equal of kings."

Though more noted for her sexual accomplishments, the Russian empress Catherine the Great (1729–96), a friend of Voltaire, was an accomplished playwright whose historical tragedies and comedies usually pleased her audiences, even if they were not masterpieces. Catherine often rose at five and worked twenty hours a day. She wrote her work under pseudonyms so as not to influence critical opinion. Catherine also edited a satirical magazine and wrote poems, librettos, historical articles, and a fairy tale, *Prince Khlor*, that became a Russian classic. She did have secretaries to correct her poor spelling and grammar, but still one wonders when she found time for all her fabled lovemaking.

Murdering the Language

Novelist Henry Fielding, also a British justice of the peace, wrote an article for the satirical journal *The Champion* demanding that English poet laureate and playwright Colley Cibber (1671–1757) be tried for murder of the English language. Fielding was apparently getting even with Cibber, who called him "a broken wit." Cibber, however, was also ridiculed by Alexander Pope, who made him the hero of the *Dunciad*, and William Congreve said his play *Love's Last Shift* "has only in it a great many things that were like wit, that in reality were not wit." Cibber, a rude and vain man, who showed modesty only in the title of his autobiography (*An Apology for the Life of Mr. Colley Cibber, Comedian*, 1740), made many enemies, but he did make a valuable contribution to the sentimental comedy genre with plays like *The Careless Husband*. An actor and theatrical manager as well as a playwright, he had a stock answer whenever an aspiring dramatist asked him to explain why he had rejected a play submitted to him. "Sir," he would say, pausing to take a pinch of snuff, "there is nothing in it to coerce my passions."

No Muse Was Wycherley's Mate

In William "Manly" Wycherley's prologue to *The Country Wife* (1673), which was attacked for obscenity in its time but is actually a satiric attack on sexual hypocrisy, the author invites anyone in the audience who dislikes the play to come at the end to the actors' dressing room where the players would "patiently . . . give up to you / Our poets, virgins, nay, our mistresses too."

Wycherley might have thrown in his wife, too, had he been married at the time. Theirs was a marriage made in hell. The courtship began in a Bath bookshop, where Wycherley was pleased to hear a woman ask for a copy of his play *The Plain Dealer* (1676). "Here's the plain dealer, madam, if you want him," a friend said, pushing him into her arms. After Wycherley apologized, the woman assured him, "I love plain dealing best." She turned out to be the wealthy countess of Drogheda, and Wycherley courted and secretly married her, losing all King Charles's patronage when he found out. To make matters worse, the countess proved pathologically jealous and followed the playwright everywhere. When she did allow him to meet alone with his friends, it was in a tavern next to their house, where in summer or winter he was made to sit with the window open and the blinds up so that she could see that no women were present. When his wife suddenly died a year or so after their marriage, Wycherley thought his problems were over since he would inherit her fortune. He ran up huge debts that he could not repay when he found that creditors claimed all of the countess's money. Wycherley spent a full seven years in jail before James II, pleased with a manly character thought to resemble him in *The Plain Dealer*, paid off his debts and settled a pension on him. This playwright died in 1716, age seventy-five. (*See also* Chapter 11.)

First Woman to Make a Living Writing Plays

The first woman to earn her living as a playwright seems to have been Mrs. Aphra Behn (1640–89), a widow who wrote some fourteen popular plays, as well as poems and novels, including such tales of love and adventure as *The Fair Jilt*, *The Rover*, and *The Amours of Philander and Sylvia*. Mrs. Behn's novel *Oroonoko* may have suggested the "noble savage" philosophy to Rousseau. Also a spy for England's Charles II, she is buried in the east cloister of Westminster Abbey. A woman of supreme self-confidence, she called herself the "Incomparable Astraea"; others called her "a scandal in a scandalous age."

"To Write Like a Madman"

English dramatist Nathaniel Lee (1643?–92) began his career as an actor but couldn't earn a living due to acute stage fright. Lee wrote a number of popular tragedies with passages of great beauty despite their mad extravagances. He eventually lost his mind; he was committed to Bedlam twice in his short life, the second time escaping from his keepers and later dying in a drunken fit. Once the English journalist Sir Roger L'Estrange visited Lee in the madhouse. L'Estrange couldn't conceal the sorrow he felt for the gifted writer, but Lee sensed and spurned his pity, improvising:

> *Faces may alter, names can't change,*
> *I am strange Lee altered, you are still Le-Strange.*

During his first Bedlam stay, Lee asked a visitor to jump off the building's roof with him. "Let us immortalize ourselves; let us leap down this moment!" he urged his friend. "Any man could leap down," his friend replied, thinking quickly, "so we could not immortalize ourselves that way. But let us go down and see if we can leap up." Lee immediately forgot about jumping off the building and ran downstairs and began trying to leap up to the roof.

"'Tis very difficult to write like a madman," Lee told a friend while confined in Bedlam, "but 'tis a very easy matter to write like a fool."

Bribed Playwright

Probably the first major French writer to live entirely by his pen, Alain-René Lesage (1668–1747) followed in the footsteps of Molière, producing over sixty farces and librettos in addition to his masterpiece *Gil Blas*, one of the greatest foreign influences on English comedy. Lesage's comedy *Turcaret* satirized French financiers so scathingly that several Parisian moneylenders offered him 100,000 francs if he would refuse to let the play go onstage. Though the shrewd Lesage valued money as much as any writer, to his credit he turned down the offer and the play went on as scheduled. The moneylenders next tried the cast, but they refused the bribe, too.

"Recanting Settle"

Bombastic Elkanah Settle (1648–1724), a dramatic rival of Dryden in his early days, switched so often from one political side to another that he was known as "Recanting Settle." He was appointed poet of the city of London in 1691, but for all his maneuvering, he "is chiefly remembered today for the elaborate bindings on the presentation copies of his poems." In his old age, when stage plays were forbidden, Settle helped make his living by keeping a booth at Bartholomew Fair where he presented what he called a "droll humor," playing the part of the dragon in his farce while wearing a green leather suit he designed.

It's Not Funny

His early tragedies often had great dramatic and poetic power, but British dramatist and poet laureate Nicholas Rowe (1674–1718) had no comedic talent. The author usually confined himself to what he called "she-tragedies," about victimized women, yet he once tried his hand at writing something funny: *The Biter* (1704). He sat in the theater laughing hilariously throughout the premiere of his play, but no one else in the audience uttered a single laugh or smiled a smile all evening. Rowe never again wrote a comedy.

The Cook Did It

Antiquarian John Warburton (1682–1759) collected fifty or sixty Jacobean plays, three of which now survive as the priceless Lansdowne manuscripts at the British Museum. Most of the often unique plays were destroyed when Warburton left them in the care of his cook, Betsy Baker, who burned them for fuel or used them as linings for her pans.

Most Beloved Playwright

The founder of modern Italian comedy, Carlo Goldoni (1707–93), once bet a friend that he could write sixteen comedies for the stage within a year. Not only did he win his bet, but the sixteen plays included some of his best work. Though this prolific author wrote some 250 plays over his long life, he died a pauper. Nevertheless, he has been called one of the "most cheerful and lovable men in literary history." He himself explained his personality this way: "My mother brought me into the world with little pain, and this increased her love for me. My first appearance was not, as is usual, announced by cries and this gentleness seemed then an indication of the pacific character which from that day forward I have preserved."

Voltaire's Revenge

French critic Elie Catherine Fréron (1719–76) made the mistake of attacking Voltaire and the Encyclopedists. Voltaire, not a man to be tampered with, attacked him in a barrage of wicked epigrams, in his tragedies, in the virulent satire *Le Pauvre Diable*, and in an anonymous work called *Anecdotes sur Fréron* (1760). What hurt the critic most was Voltaire's making him the principal character in his comedy *L'Escossaise*. In this comedy Fréron's magazine *L'Année Litteraire* (*The Literary Year*) is called "*L'Ane Litteraire*" ("*The Literary Ass*"). The play also depicts Fréron as a scoundrel, spy, toad, hound, snake, lizard, and a man with a heart of filth, among other things. Voltaire later circulated a quatrain about the critic:

> *The other day, down in a valley,*
> *A serpent stung Fréron.*
> *What think you happened then?*
> *It was the serpent that died.*

The Absentminded Professor

One of the greatest intellects of the eighteenth century, the German dramatist and academic Gotthold Ephraim Lessing (1729–81) grew very absentminded toward the end of his life. One night he came home and found his house locked. As he had forgotten the key, he knocked on the door, but the servant called out, "The professor is not at home."

"Very well," Lessing replied. "Tell him I'll call another time."

Sherry

Second only to Molière as a writer of comedies, and probably the theater's greatest wit, Richard Brinsley Sheridan (1751–1816) hated the theater and never even saw a play until after he finished his own second effort, *The Duenna*. He avoided going to the theater whenever he could and, excepting his own pieces at rehearsal, never saw a play from beginning to end. The dilatory Sheridan was so relieved when he finished writing *The School for Scandal* at the last possible moment on opening night that he wrote on the final page of the manuscript, "Finished at last, Thank God!" Yet *Scandal* was a great success. Sheridan's old fencing master, Angelo, told how a friend of his was passing a block away from the Theatre Royal in Drury Lane on May 8, 1777, when he heard a sudden noise like an explosion. Wondering what it might be, he made his way toward the playhouse. He soon realized that the loud sudden noise which had startled him and still continued was the prolonged applause when the curtain fell after the fourth act of *The School for Scandal*.

Sheridan's farce *The Critic* (1779), in which he created Sneer the critic and Puff the unscrupulous literary advertiser, among other lifelike literary characters, had no last scene up until two days before its first night's performance at Drury Lane. The actors rehearsed what they could but were afraid the play would never go on. Finally, Sheridan's father-in-law, Thomas Linley, stepped in. Sheridan was invited to a rehearsal at the theater and when he got there was asked to step into the greenroom for a moment to discuss a matter of some concern. As soon as Sheridan stepped in the room, the door was locked behind him. Inside he found a roaring fire, a comfortable chair, a large table, a platter of anchovies, two bottles of claret—and pen, ink, and paper. Through the door his father-in-law told him that he would be locked in the room until he wrote the last scene. Sheridan sat down, ate the anchovies, drank the claret, and finished his play.

Despite his theatrical successes, Sheridan valued politics over playwriting and considered his finest accomplishment not *The School for Scandal* or *The Rivals*, but his famous speech as an M.P. during the impeachment trial of Warren Hastings; two hours after he made that speech he was offered a thousand pounds, a great sum at the time, for the copyright.

Forever in debt despite the vast amounts of money his plays made, Sheridan and his wife, Elizabeth, moved from one place to another, a step ahead of their creditors. At one time they rented twelve places in London alone. Once Sheridan told his son, Thomas, that they were descended from the kings of Ireland and that their rightful name was O'Sheridan. "That is true," Tom said, "for we owe everybody."

Lord Byron was a great admirer of Sheridan's brilliant wit and once recalled a night when "*he* talked and we listened, without one yawn, from six till one in the morning." Another time Byron told a group of friends, "Whatever Sheridan has done or chosen to do has been par excellence the best of its kind. He has written the best comedy, the best opera [*The Duenna*], the best farce [*The Critic*], the best address [the *Monologue on Garrick*], and, to crown all, delivered the best Oration [the famous Begum speech in Parliament] ever conceived in this country." The next day word got back to Sheridan of this extravagant compliment and he burst into tears.

Sherry, as he was called, was always joking, even to the point of masquerading as a policeman one time in Bath and arresting people. His last joke was made on the day of his painful death, July 7, 1816, at about noon. He looked up at a woman friend several hours before he died and spoke words he had put in the mouth of his creation Mrs. Justice Credulous: "I won't die, Bridget, I don't like death." (*See also* Chapter 11.)

Sheridan's Mrs. Malaprop

Then, sir, she should have a supercilious knowledge in accounts;—and as she grew up, I would have her instructed in geometry, that she might know something of the contagious countries . . . and likewise that she might reprehend the true meaning of what she is saying. This, Sir Anthony, is what I would have a woman know;—and I don't think there is a superstitious article in it.

The above is a speech of Mrs. Malaprop in the first act of Richard Brinsley Sheridan's *The Rivals*. Mrs. Malaprop is the name of an affected, talkative woman in the play, the aunt of the heroine, Lydia Languish. Sheridan coined the name of his most famous character from the French *mal a propos*, "unsuitable, out of place," for he had her ludicrously misuse many "high-sounding" words out of her ignorance and vanity, just as Shakespeare had Dogberry do in *Much Ado About Nothing* and Mistress Quickly do in *1* and *2 Henry IV.* Sheridan's *The Rivals* was produced in London in 1775, and Mrs. Malaprop's name soon became a synonym for the misuse of words, especially by those who are trying to sound important. Here are more of Mrs. Malaprop's malapropisms from the play, words she always delivered with great aplomb:

- "She's as headstrong as an allegory [for "alligator"] on the banks of the Nile."
- "I would by no means wish a daughter of mine to be a progeny [prodigy] of learning."
- "Don't attempt to extirpate [extricate] yourself from the matter."
- "He is the very pineapple [pinnacle] of politeness."

(*See also* "Mr. Malaprop," Chapter 4.)

A Malapropian Playwright

Long after Sheridan created his Mrs. Malaprop, the playwright Clemence Dane (Winifred Ashton; 1888–1965) on whom Noël Coward based Madame Arcati in *Blithe Spirit*, became well known for her unintentional double entendres. One time a friend asked about the condition of her goldfish, which when last seen were ailing in a shadeless pool. "Oh, they're all right now!" she replied. "They've got a vast erection covered with everlasting pea!"

Mrs. Grundy

They eat, and drink, and scheme, and plod,
And go to sleep on Sunday
And many are afraid of God—
And many more of Mrs. Grundy.

These lines from Frederick Locker-Lampson's poem "The Jester" (1857) were inspired by a character in playwright Thomas Morton's comedy *Speed the Plough*, first staged at London's Covent Garden in 1800. Actually Mrs. Grundy is something less than a character, for she never appears on stage and is never described physically. She is the epitome of propriety, the narrow-minded neighbor of Farmer Ashfield and Dame Ashfield, his wife, who is obsessed with Mrs. Grundy's opinion of things. "What will Mrs. Grundy say? What will Mrs. Grundy think?" is on Dame Ashfield's lips so often that the words became proverbial for "What will that straitlaced neighbor say? What will the neighbors think?" Mrs. Grundy herself became a symbol of prudish propriety or social convention.

The First Professional American Playwright

His name is little known today, despite the establishment of a Dunlap Society, but William Dunlap (1766–1839) deserves recognition as the first American to make a serious business of writing plays. The New Jersey–born Dunlap trained as a portrait painter before turning to the stage; when only sixteen he painted famous portraits of George and Martha Washington, and later in life he worked as an intinerent painter of miniature portraits, a kind of painter-peddler traveling around the country and accepting commissions from anyone who could pay. By the time he was twenty-three Dunlap wrote his first play, *The Father*, a comedy of manners, and by 1796 he was sole owner of New York's Old American Company. His company produced some thirty of his own plays and thirty-five of his translations before it went bankrupt nine years later. These productions included Dunlap's original blank verse tragedy *André*, about British major John André, hanged as a spy for the secret negotiations he carried on with Benedict Arnold when the

American officer tried to betray West Point. The versatile Dunlap turned back to painting later in life, published a magazine, and wrote several scholarly books, including the first history of the American theater.

America's First Playwriting Contest

In 1828 famed actor Edwin Forrest (*see* Chapter 7) announced the first prize contest for a new American play, specifically "a tragedy of five acts, of which the hero . . . shall be an aboriginal of this country." John Augustus Stone's *Metamora; or The Last of the Wampanoags* was the winner, its title perhaps suggested by James Fenimore Cooper's *Last of the Mohicans* (1826). Stone's play proved immensely popular for many years in Forrest's repertory and a grateful Forrest erected a monument to him in Philadelphia after Stone, despondent over his ill health, drowned himself there in the Schuykill River in 1834 when he was only thirty-four years old.

Since this first playwriting contest there have of course been hundreds more, many of which encouraged budding professional playwrights. Arthur Miller, for example, while still in college, won the 1936 Avery Hopwood Prize for a promising young playwright.

The Playwright Who Invented a Language

Norwegian philologist, playwright, and poet Ivar Andreas Aasen (1813–96) is the only person known to have created a national language. The author had collected all of his country's difficult regional speech for the books he had written on Norwegian dialects. Out of these he fashioned a popular language, or *folk-maal*, which replaced the Dano-Norwegian his countrymen had previously used, to enable all the nation's different dialect users to understand each other. Aasen has been hailed as having "an isolated place in history as the one man who has invented or at least selected and constructed a [national] language." In order to do this, he not only constructed the new composite language but also wrote many poems and plays in the *folk-maal* to help popularize it.

A Playwright Who Posed as a Woman

The frontispiece portrait of "Clara Gazul," in the slim volume *Le Théâtre de Clara Gazul* (1825) was actually a faked portrait of the twenty-two-year-old French author Prosper Mérimée wearing a mantilla! Mérimée had written six short plays he attributed to "Spanish actress Clara Gazul," because he thought that his first published work would be more successful if people thought a celebrity had written it. Before his hoax was exposed, *Le Théâtre de Clara Gazul* was widely acclaimed.

The First Chauvinist on the Stage

Nicolas Chauvin of Rochefort was a genuine hero, wounded seventeen times in service of the French Grand Armée, who retired only when so scarred that he could no longer lift a sword. How then did his name become associated with excessive nationalism or superpatriotism? Chauvin actually was left with little after his war service. For his wounds and valor he received a medal, a ceremonial saber, and a pension of about forty dollars a year. Instead of growing bitter, the old soldier turned in the opposite direction, for after all his sacrifices had to mean something. Chauvin became an idolator of the Little Corporal; even after Waterloo and Napoléon's exile, he spoke of nothing but his hero's infallibility and the glory of France. The veteran became a laughingstock in his village, but he would have escaped national attention if dramatists Charles Cogniard and his brother Jean hadn't heard of him and used him as a character in their comedy *La Cocarde Tricolor* (1831). The play truthfully represented Chauvin as an almost idolatrous worshiper of Napoléon and was followed by at least four more comedies by other authors caricaturing the old soldier. As a result the French word *chauvinisme*, or chauvinism, became synonymous with fanatical, unreasoning patriotism and all that such blind, bellicose worship of national prowess implies.

Verdi! Verdi!

Within the space of little more than a year, from 1838 to 1840, Guiseppe Verdi, the Italian composer and interpreter of Shakespeare, lost his infant daughter, Virginia; his son, Ichilio; and his first wife, Margherita. Yet, all alone, his young family wiped out, living in a state of despair bordering on a mental breakdown, he worked on the words and lyrics of the comic opera *Un Giorno di Regno*, commissioned by the director of La Scala.

Verdi's opera *Rigoletto*, containing the famous melody "*La donna e mobile*" ("The woman is flighty"), was abused by many critics as "uninspired" and "puerile and queer" for some ten years before being generally recognized as a masterpiece, though the public loved it from the first time it was performed in 1851 at the Venice Theater in Venice, Italy. One newspaper critic went so far as to say that to even discuss it "would be a loss of time and space."

The Austrians occupying northern Italy in the nineteenth century couldn't understand why the chant *Verdi! Verdi!* at the end of operas written by the composer frequently inspired anti-Austrian riots. They finally learned that *Verdi* was also an acronym for the name of the man Garibaldi was advocating as head of a united Italy: *Vittorio Emanuele, Re d'Italia* ("Victor Emmanuel, King of Italy"). After the Austrians were expelled in 1857, Victor Emmanuel was crowned king.

So beloved was Verdi by his countrymen that when he lay dying in a Milan hotel room in 1901, at the age of eighty-eight, officials ordered that all wagons in the city have their wheels covered with straw so that they would not disturb him when passing by his window.

History's Greatest Histrionic Hypochondriac

German poet and dramatist Oscar von Redwitz (1823–91) may not have written of suffering as well as Goethe or Rilke, but he certainly suffered more—at least in his mind. Probably history's greatest hypochondriac, the baron is said to have visited a doctor *every day* of his life from the time he was forty, complaining of fully ten thousand different ailments or symptoms. For all his ailments, he lived until he was sixty-eight, a ripe old age for his time.

A Plot Too Improbable for the Stage

When French playwright Victorien Sardou (1831–1908), a nervous man, knocked over his wine glass at a literary dinner party, he blushed from embarrassment. But this was nothing compared with the embarrassing chain of events to come, which wouldn't have been believed in one of his plays:

The woman at Sardou's side sprinkled salt on the stained tablecloth where Sardou had spilled the wine.

Sardou tossed some of the salt over his shoulder to ward off bad luck.

The salt hit the butler in the eyes.

The butler, rubbing his eyes, dropped a platter of chicken on the floor.

The family dog began devouring the chicken and then choked on a chicken bone.

The young son of Sardou's host tried to loosen the chicken bone from the dog's throat.

The dog bit the boy's finger.

The boy's finger had to be amputated.

Dr. Chekhov

"All things considered, I'm a mediocre playwright," Anton Chekhov (1860–1904) wrote to a friend after finishing *The Seagull* in less than a month. On opening night, the audience more than agreed with his assessment. Most had come expecting a farce and booed and hissed when the final curtain came down, after having laughed and whistled through the entire performance. Chekhov put his collar up, bent over, and hurried out of the theater, unable to leave fast enough. However, the play's second performance several days later, which Chekhov did not attend, was a resounding success, with encores after each act and cries of "Author! Author!" This was mainly because the audience had not come expecting a comedy.

The image of the seagull brought down by a thoughtless hunter, so central to Chekhov's *The Seagull*, was suggested by a woodcock winged by the author's friend Isaak Levitan while they were hunting together. Levitan could not finish off the bird staring at them with bright black eyes and begged Chekhov to do so. Chekhov finally agreed and smashed its head with the butt of his rifle. Later he wrote to a friend: "And while two idiots went home and sat down to dinner, there was one less beautiful, infatuated creature in the world."

That the realism of Ibsen and Strindberg wasn't intentionally emulated by Chekhov, despite all the naturalistic Stanislavskian interpretations of his plays, is evidenced by a letter the author sent to a friend in 1888. "The modern theatre is a skin disease," Dr. Chekhov wrote, "a sinful disease of the critics. It must be swept away with a broom; it is unwholesome to love it." Yet he did love the theater, to a certain extent. When a friend implored him to drop medicine and give all his time to writing, Chekhov piquantly replied, "Medicine is my lawful wife and literature is my mistress. When I get tired of one, I spend the night with the other."

Chekhov's worst words for his afflictions weren't for his heart trouble or the tuberculosis that eventually killed him when he was only forty-four, but for the "vile, loathsome hemorrhoids" that plagued him as they had another great Russian author, Nikolai Gogol. (Gogol had written his mother in 1831 that "no one man in St. Petersburg is free from this nuisance.")

Wrote Chekhov to a friend early in 1893: "It's not syphilis, it's worse—hemorrhoids . . . pain, itching, tension. I can't sit, can't walk; my whole body is so sore I feel like hanging myself."

As Chekhov lay dying in 1904, his doctor sent for a bottle of champagne. It was hopeless; there was no chance he would live. The doctor poured him a glass and Chekhov took it, turning to his wife, Olga, and smiling. His last words were "It's been so long since I've had champagne." After slowly draining the glass, he rolled over on his left side and in a few moments stopped breathing. It was a week before his body reached Moscow from Germany. The group of friends led by Maksim Gorky who met the train were furious that his coffin had been carried in a filthy green van with the words FOR OYSTERS on it.

The Master of Modern Drama

A storm of conservative outrage greeted Henrik Ibsen's *Hedda Gabler* (1890) and *The Master Builder* (1892), one critic coining the word *Ibsenity* as a synonym for obscenity. Yet the founder of modern prose drama and the first major playwright to write prose tragedy about ordinary people, Henrik Ibsen, considered himself more a poet than a reformer, despite the themes of many of his plays. The Norwegian, among the world's greatest dramatists, had some odd working habits. He got himself started writing every morning by first feeding a pet scorpion that he kept in a jar on his desk. Then he would glance at the picture of his rival August Strindberg that he had hung over his desk. "He is my mortal enemy and shall hang there and watch while I write," he told a friend.

Ibsen made enemies easily and wasn't a forgiving man. When, for example, author John Paulson protested that he had meant no harm by portraying the Norwegian playwright as Pehrsen in *The Pehrsen Family* (1882), Ibsen sent him a card with one word written on it: *Scoundrel*.

Ibsen was all his life a very lonely person who always remembered the poverty he suffered when his wealthy father, Knud Henriksen Ibsen (Henrik was named for him), failed in business. One of his closest relationships was with a woman forty-four years younger than himself. The eponymous heroine of Ibsen's *Hedda Gabler* was suggested to him by the beautiful Emilie Bardach, a Viennese woman he fell in love with in 1889, when he was sixty-one and she only seventeen. Although her bold, loose ways frightened him and he never met her again after that summer, he thought of her as the "May-day of my September" and wrote to her years later that the few months he spent with her were the happiest and most beautiful in his life.

He was a contentious man until the end, never accommodating his own thought to the ideas of others, rarely discussing the idea of a play with anyone until he completed it. "You seem to be improving," his attending nurse told him during his final illness in 1906, when he was seventy-eight.

"On the contrary," Ibsen countered.

These were his last words, winning him his last argument with the world.

A Dream Dreamt by Ibsen

While wandering on a high mountain range, myself and some friends, we became tired and then despondent, and were suddenly surprised by night. Like Jacob, we lay down to sleep and rested our heads on stones. . . . In a dream an angel appeared before me, saying, "Arise, and follow me." "Wither will you lead me in this darkness?" I asked, and received the reply: "Come, I will reveal to you human existence in its true reality." Full of foreboding, I followed my guide and we descended a number of steep steps; and rocks towered above us like gigantic arches, while spread before us lay a vast city of death with horrible remnants and tokens of mortality and transient existence—a perished grandeur, an immense, sunken world of corpses, death's silent subjects. Over all hovered a withered, ghastly twilight that enveloped churchyards, graves, and sepulchers. In a stronger light, row upon row of white skeletons reflected a phosphorescent glow. A fear seized me as I stood by the angel's side.

"Here, you see, all is vanity," he said.

Then came a roar like that which heralds a storm, which grew to a raging hurricane so that the dead moved and stretched their arms toward me, and with a cry I awoke wet from the cold night-dew.

"Smiles" Strindberg

The never-resting genius August Strindberg (1849–1912) wrote more than fifty plays, many of them masterpieces of structual virtuosity, but gloom often pervaded them. The Swedish playwright's misogyny and often oppressive pessimism (Robert Benchley once called him "Smiles" Strindberg) had no single cause. It was certainly motivated by the fact that his father married the Strindberg family's housekeeper after she had given him three sons. (Strindberg's 1886 autobiography was entitled *The Son of a Servant*.) Each of the playwright's three wives was at least as mentally troubled as he was, which probably also contributed to his hatred of women. His second wife, Frida, was an Austrian who for a time ran an illicit nightclub in London. Ezra Pound once recalled the notorious Madame Strindberg dismissing a customer from her table at the club. "Sleep with you, I will," she cried, waving him away, "but talk to you—never! One must draw a line *somewhere*."

When his first marriage failed and his wife, Siri, left him, Strindberg imagined that feminists were persecuting him and had won his wife over to their side. Seeking to dispel an imaginary rumor that his marriage ended because he was less than a man, he hired a doctor to come with him to a bordello and measure his erect penis, which proved to be of a perfectly normal length.

Gilbert and Sullivan

Librettist Sir William Schwenck Gilbert (1836–1911) and composer Sir Arthur Seymour Sullivan (1842–1900) collaborated on their immortal comic operas for twenty-five years before a quarrel ended a perfect partnership that peerlessly combined social satire with grand opera. Gilbert was the wittier of the two. The lyricist half of Gilbert and Sullivan once outraged fellow members of London's Garrick Club by making fun of Shakespeare. "All right then," he said when they strongly protested, "what do you make of this passage then: 'I would just as lief be thrust through a quickset hedge, as cry, "Plosh," to a callow thistle.'"

"Why, that's perfectly clear," one club member said, defending the Bard. "It just means that the bird-lover would rather get himself all scratched up in the thorny bush than disturb the bird's song. What play is the passage from?"

"No play," said Gilbert. "I made it up—and jolly good Shakespeare, too."

- After enduring a terrible performance by an actor in his company, Gilbert hurried from his seat and burst into the man's dressing room, crying, "My dear chap! Good isn't the word!"
- Unaware of the recent death of a famous composer, a friend asked Gilbert what the man was doing.
  "Nothing," Gilbert replied.
  "Surely he is composing," the friend persisted.
  "On the contrary," Gilbert said, "he is *decomposing*."
- "No good play is a success," he once confided. "Fine writing and high morals are useless on the stage. I have been scribbling twaddle for thirty-five years to suit the public taste, and I should know."

In addition to his lyrics for comic operas like *The Mikado*, *The Pirates of Penzance*, and *H.M.S. Pinafore*, Gilbert was the author of many shows without Sullivan. He died a hero's death, suffering a heart attack while trying to save a girl who had fallen into a lake in Middlesex, an effort all the braver because he was seventy-five at the time.

A Gilbert and Sullivan Quiz

Name the thirteen comic operas written by Gilbert and Sullivan.

Answers:

1. *Trial by Jury* (1875)
2. *The Sorcerer* (1877)
3. *H.M.S. Pinafore* (1878)
4. *The Pirates of Penzance* (1879)
5. *Patience* (1881)
6. *Iolanthe* (1882)
7. *Princess Ida* (1884)
8. *The Mikado* (1885)
9. *Ruddigore* (1887)
10. *The Yeomen of the Guard* (1888)
11. *The Gondoliers* (1889)
12. *Utopia, Limited* (1893)
13. *The Grand Duke* (1896)

The Supreme Buffoon

Alfred Jarry (1873–1907), French dramatist of the theater of the absurd, has been called "the supreme buffoon." His actions were often inexplicable; once, for example, he pointed his revolver at a man who presumed to stop him on a corner in Paris and ask for street directions. Jarry wrote what is considered by many the first avant-garde play, *Ubu Roi*, when he was only fifteen. In his literary gossip column, "Ja Vie Anecdotique," which appeared in the magazine *Mercare de France*, the poet Guillaume Apollinaire, a Jarry admirer, once described a visit he made to the absurdist's weird apartment in the Rue Casette:

"Monsieur Alfred Jarry?"
   "Second floor and a half."

I was somewhat puzzled by that answer from the concierge. I climbed up to where Alfred Jarry lived—second and a half turned out to be correct. The stories of the house had seemed too high-ceilinged to the owner, so he had cut each of them in two. In this way the house, which still exists, has fifteen stories, but since it is actually no higher than the houses around it, it is but a reduction of a skyscraper. For that matter, reductions abounded in Alfred Jarry's abode. His second and a half was but the reduction of a story: Jarry was quite comfortable standing up, but I was taller than he, and had to bend. The bed was but a reduction of a bed—a pallet: Low beds were the fashion, Jarry told me. The writing table was but the reduction of a table: Jarry wrote on the floor, stretched out on his stomach. The furnishing was but the reduction of furnishing, consisting solely of a bed. On the wall hung the reduction of a picture. It was a portrait of Jarry, most of which he had burned, leaving only the head. . . . The library was but the reduction of a library, to put it mildly. It consisted of a cheap edition of Rabelais and two or three volumes of the Bibliothèque Rose. *On the mantelpiece stood a large stone phallus, made in Japan, a gift to Jarry from Felicien Rops. This virile member, larger than life, Jarry had kept covered with a purple velvet sheath ever since the day when the exotic monolith had frightened a literary lady. She had arrived breathless from climbing up to the second floor and a half, and was bewildered at finding herself in this furnitureless "Great Chamber." "Is it a cast?" she inquired.*

"No," answered Jarry. "It's a reduction."

G.B.S.

Few are the humans who have the talent or will to impose their own names on the language, but George Bernard Shaw, no ordinary mortal, did just that. Shaw did not like the way *Shawian* sounded and so Latinized his name to *Shavius* and coined the word *Shavian* from it. *Shavian,* meaning characteristic of the work or style of George Bernard Shaw, soon bred the phrases *Shavian wit* or *Shavian humor* referring to the dramatist's brilliant written or impromptu lines. Shaw, who began as a music reviewer and novelist, went on to write *Arms and the Man* (1898), *Man and Superman* (1903), and *Pygmalion* (1912), among many far-famed plays. His plays are marked by large social themes and brilliant rhetoric that is often found in their controversial prefaces. But the personal life of this self-confessed genius became almost as famous as his plays. Shaw's Fabian socialism, his vegetarianism, his phonetic spelling, reform ideas, and not least of all, his love affairs, fascinated the public right up until his death in 1950, age ninety-four. The cantankerous iconoclast was probably too brilliant for the good of his plays, but his rich humor and mastery of dialogue make up for his inability to create living characters. As for the Shavian wit, Shaw was as celebrated for it in real life as in his plays. The portly author G. K. Chesterton, for example, once thought he had scored when he told the stringy Shaw, "Looking at you, one would think there was a famine in England." But not after Shaw replied, "Looking at you, one would think you caused it." Then there was the time Shaw received an invitation from a celebrity hunter: *Lady Blank will be home Thursday between four and six.* He returned the card with the message *Mr. Bernard Shaw likewise* written underneath. Or take his advice to William Douglas Home: "Go on writing plays, my boy. One of these days a London producer will go into his office, and say to his secretary, 'Is there a play from Shaw this morning?' and when she says 'No,' he will say, 'Well, then we'll have to start on the rubbish.' And that's your chance, my boy." But for all his sharp wit, the bearded Irishman could be bested; he was an immense target. "Bernard Shaw had discovered himself and gave ungrudgingly of his discovery to the world," wrote Saki (H. H. Munro). "Shaw isn't prominent enough to have enemies and none of his friends like him," Oscar Wilde quipped. The actress Cornelia Otis Skinner got the best of Shaw in the following exchange of telegrams after a revival of *Candida*—Shaw: EXCELLENT. GREATEST. Skinner: UNDESERVING SUCH PRAISE. Shaw: I MEANT THE PLAY. Skinner: SO DID I. And even Mrs. Shaw occasionally bested the master. "Isn't it true, my dear, that male judgment is superior to female judgment?" Shaw once asked his wife. "Of course, dear," she replied. "After all, you married me and I you."

You Never Can Tell

George Bernard Shaw earned about three dollars a year for ten years from writing during the 1886–96 period when he began his literary career in London. Shaw, mainly supported by his mother at the time, published only one article, three poems, and a patent-medicine advertisement. Much of his work rejected during this decade—including five novels—was published when he became recognized as one of the greatest dramatists of his or any other era.

The Real 'enry 'iggins

David Jones (1881–1967), head of the Phonetics Department at University College, London, always claimed that he was the prototype of George Bernard Shaw's Henry Higgins in *Pygmalion* (though, in fact, Shaw probably didn't base the character on him). Jones claimed that Shaw in gratitude had a free box reserved for him for any production of the play as long as the author lived. He said Shaw chose the name Higgins after glimpsing a sign reading Jones and Higgins over a London shop; Shaw calling the character Higgins because he obviously couldn't use Jones.

Born to Write, Not to Talk

Some playwrights can't talk about their plays; others hardly make sense when they talk about anything—they were born to *write*. In his *Essays Critical and Historical* (1834), the British historian Lord Macaulay described such a playwright and his thought processes—Oliver Goldsmith (1730–74), author of the immortal *She Stoops to Conquer*:

> *Minds differ as rivers differ. There are transparent and sparkling wines from which it is delightful to drink as they flow; to such rivers the minds of Burke and Johnson may be compared. But there are rivers of which the water when first drawn is turbid and noisome, but becomes pellucid as crystals and delicious to the taste if it be suffered to stand still till it has deposited a sediment; and such a river is a type of mind of Goldsmith. His first thoughts on every subject were confused even to absurdity, but they required only a little time to work themselves clear. When he wrote they had that time, and therefore his readers pronounced him a man of genius; but when he talked he talked nonsense and made himself the laughingstock of his hearers. He was painfully conscious of his inferiority in conversation; he felt every failure keenly; yet he had not sufficient judgement and self-command to hold his tongue. His animal spirits and vanity were always impelling him to try to do the one thing which he could not do. After every attempt he felt that he had exposed himself, and withered with shame and vexation; yet the next moment he began again.*

Actor David Garrick wrote a mock epitaph on Goldsmith.

Here lies Nolly Goldsmith
For shortness called Noll,
Who wrote like an Angel
But talked like poor Poll.

Another stuttering playwright was Henry Guy Carlton (1856–1910). Producer John Golden wrote that the popular playwright insisted on reading his plays in their entirety at first rehearsals, despite his terrible stammer, which wasted many hours. Carlton was a stutterer who liked to joke about his affliction. Meeting a friend one day, he asked, "N-N-Nat, c-c-an you g-g-give m-m-me f-f-fifteen m-m-minutes?"

"Why certainly," his friend said. "What is it?"

"I w-w-want to have a f-f-five-minute c-c-conversation with you," Carlton advised.

America's Only Nobel Prize–Winning Playwright

Eugene O'Neill's father, James O'Neill, was a noted popular actor of the day. After he saw his son's play *Beyond the Horizon*, he said: "It's all right, Gene, if that's what you want to do, but people come to the theater to forget their troubles, not to be reminded of them. What are you trying to do—send the audience home to commit suicide?"

Eugene O'Neill himself, though probably the greatest dramatist of the twentieth century, was on the verge of suicide several times in his career and more than once suffered complete physical breakdowns before his death in 1953, age sixty-five. It is said that his first marriage in 1909 resulted from one of his drinking blackouts, begun after he returned with a case of malaria from a gold prospecting adventure in Honduras. He awoke one morning in a flophouse with a girl beside him. "Who the hell are you?" he demanded. "You married me last night," she said.

O'Neill's artistic integrity was legendary. Russel Crouse once asked him if he would shorten the script of *Ah, Wilderness!* so that the curtain would fall earlier. Finally, O'Neill, always adamant about cutting a word from his plays, reluctantly agreed. The next day he called Crouse and told him, "You'll be happy to learn I cut fifteen minutes."

"How?" Crouse replied ecstatically. "Where did you do it? I'll be right over to get the changes."

"Oh, there aren't any changes in the text," O'Neill explained, "but you know we've been playing this thing in four acts. I've decided to cut out the third intermission."

Yet O'Neill's stage directions left much to be desired, hardly matching the brilliance of his dialogue. In his play *Where the Cross Is Made*, for example, the playwright gives stage directions describing a man with one arm who must sit at a table "resting his elbows, his chin in his hands."

On the days when he worked on *Long Day's Journey into Night*, the family tragedy that is the most personal of his plays, O'Neill was tortured by his own words. "He would come out of his studio at the end of a day gaunt and sometimes weeping," recalled his wife, Carlotta. "His eyes would be all red, and he looked ten years older than when he went in in the morning."

In 1949, O'Neill gave up hope of ever writing again, and two years later he and his wife moved into the Boston residential hotel where he met his end. "I knew it," he said one day to Carlotta. "Born in a goddam hotel room and dying in a hotel room." Knowing his life was drawing to a close, O'Neill asked Carlotta to help him destroy his nine-play cycle, *A Tale of Possessors Self-Dispossessed*, which he had been working on for more than twenty years. "Go and get the unfinished manuscripts and let's sit in front of the fireplace and burn them," he told her. Later she recalled: "And so we sat, feeding the flames, through the long dusk. When the darkness came O'Neill had passed into unequivocal silence. You don't know how horrible it was. It was like tearing up children."

But Carlotta had seen him like this many times. She once told of the night at Marblehead, Massachusetts, when she and her husband, very ill with a disease resembling Parkinson's, argued violently and she "almost pushed him out of the house," only to save him later when she called the doctor. O'Neill stumbled in the snow without his cane. "He left without his coat and hat," she recalled. "I stood by the window, where I could see him trying to make his way out of the driveway. Suddenly, before he reached the road, he slipped and fell heavily into a ditch. It had begun to snow again. I don't know how long I stood by that window, watching the tiny white flakes hide his entire body from view."

In the early 1920s a depressed O'Neill had written the following mock epitaph for himself:

> EUGENE O'NEILL
> *There is something*
> *To be said*
> *For being dead.*

O'Neill won four Pulitzer Prizes. In 1936 he was awarded the Nobel Prize for literature, the only American writer so honored who was exclusively a playwright.

Just Plain Folks

In his acceptance speech for the gold drama medal of the National Institute of Arts and Letters, American playwright Tennessee Williams (1911–83) told the following story:

> *One time, [actress] Maureen Stapleton received a phone call from a friend who said that so-and-so was getting married, and the caller said, "Why is she marrying that man? You know he is a homosexual," and Maureen said, "Well, what about the bride?" And the caller said, "Well, of course we know she's a lesbian. And you know they're not even getting married by a real minister, but by one who's been defrocked!" And Maureen said, "Will you do me one favor? Will you please invite Tennessee Williams? Because he'll say, 'Oh, they're just plain folks!'"*

Gayest of the Gay

Playwright and actor Noël Coward (1899–1973) tried to keep his homosexuality a secret, lest receipts from his plays should diminish. In the 1960s a biographer tried to convince him that he could reveal his sexual nature in that much more tolerant era, citing the example of drama critic T. C. Worsley, who had done so with no trouble. "There is one essential difference between me and Cuthbert Worsley," Coward replied. "The British public at large would not care if Cuthbert Worsley had slept with mice."

Coward, the author of *Blithe Spirit*, *Private Lives*, and many other smart, sophisticated comedies was among the fastest and most facile of modern wits. "I write at high speed," he once said, "because boredom is bad for my health."

- It is said that when his childhood friend actress Gertrude Lawrence married Robert Aldrich, Coward cabled her this poem: "Dear Mrs. A. / Hooray, hooray / At last you are deflowered / I love you this and every day / Yours truly, Noël Coward."
- "I've always thought I'd be particularly good in *Romeo*," he once remarked to a friend. "As the Nurse."
- One time Coward was mistaken for actor Rex Harrison. He replied, rather indignantly, "Do I look as if I sold Bentleys in Great Portland Street?"
- Coward corrected singer Elaine Stritch when she pronounced the name of the city of Babel to rhyme with *scrabble*.

  "It's *bayble*, Stritch," he advised.

  "I've always said *babble*," she countered. "Everyone says *babble*. It means mixed-up language, doesn't it? Gibberish. It's where we get *babble* from."

  "That's a *fabble*," Coward said.

- The playwright had a six-month-old elephant delivered to songwriter Cole Porter's Beverly Hills house with an attached note reading *This trunk call says it all. To Coley from Noely.* Not one to be bettered, Porter soon sent a live alligator to Coward's house with the attached note: *Here are some teeth to match your tongue. To Noely from Coley.*
- Coward heard that a rather obtuse actor had "blown his brains out." "He must have been a marvelously good shot," the playwright observed.

Five Famous Play Prototypes

- Not much is known about Romeo and Juliet, but they were real lovers who lived in Verona, Italy, and died for each other in the year 1303. The Capulets and Montagues were among the inhabitants of the town at that time, and, as in Shakespeare's play, Romeo and Juliet were victims of their parents' senseless rivalry. Their story was told in many versions before the Bard of Avon wrote of his "star-crossed lovers," and similar tales date as far back as the play *Ephesiaca* by the pseudonymous third- or fourth-century writer Xenophon of Ephesus. But Shakespeare found the tale in Arthur Brooke's poem *The Tragicall Historye of Romeus and Juliet, containing a rare example of loves constancie . . .* (1562). Romeo alone means a male lover today and has a derisive ring, but Romeo and Juliet still means a pair of youthful, often helpless, lovers.
- In his famous *La Dame aux Camélias* (1848), better known on the stage and screen as *Camille*, Alexandre Dumas *fils* wrote about Marguerite Gautier, one of the world's most endearing fictional creations, a courtesan who wore no flower other than the camellia—a white camellia for twenty-five days of the month and a red one the other five days. Marguerite was based on a real-life Parisian courtesan, Marie Duplessis, the mistress of many wealthy aristocrats and Dumas's lover for a time. Marie, who used the camellia as a trademark, died of tuberculosis at the age of twenty-three, and Dumas immortalized her in his book.
- Anyone with a prodigious nose is likely to be called a Cyrano de Bergerac after the eponymous hero of Edmond Rostand's play (1897). Rostand's hero was based on the very real Savinien de Cyrano de Bergerac (1619–55), who had a nose every bit as long as his fictional counterpart's and whose exploits were even more remarkable. The historical Cyrano was a brave soldier, great lover, and eloquently influential writer of comedies and tragedies whose works are said to have inspired Molière,

as well as Swift's *Gulliver's Travels.* This swaggering swordsman fought countless duels with those foolish enough to insult or even mention his nose, and his single-handed duel against one hundred enemies while serving as an officer in the Guards is a well-documented fact. Cyrano's exploits became legend long before Rostand fictionalized him. Surprisingly, he did not perish on the wrong end of a sword but far more prosaically. Cyrano died as a result of a wound caused by a falling beam or stone while staying at the home of a friend.

- The butler hero of Sir James M. Barrie's play *The Admirable Crichton* (1902) is based on an actual prototype. But no butler was the model for Barrie's resourceful hero, though the historic figure did personify the same admirable qualities as Lord Loam's man. The real Crichton, a son of Scotland's lord advocate, was born in 1560 and while still in his teens was acknowledged as the leading mental and physical prodigy of his day. James Crichton earned his Master of Arts degree when only fifteen. By the time he turned twenty he had mastered over a dozen languages, as well as all the sciences, in addition to being a poet and theologian of some note. The fabled prodigy was also said to be handsome—"all perfect, finish'd to the fingernail," wrote Tennyson—and without peer in his ability as a swordsman. He served with the French army, then tutored the scions of royalty. Unfortunately, this ideal gentleman proved unwise or human enough to steal the heart of a prince's lady while traveling in Italy. He was in all probability assassinated, run through from behind by three masked men in the prince's hire. Another version has it that Crichton met his end at the hands of a pupil in a street quarrel, but in any event he died when only about twenty-five. The epithet "Admirable Crichton" first came into use in 1603, but all record of the man's genius might have died had it not been for Barrie's genius.

- Peter Pan, the boy who refused to grow up, has been familiar to theatergoers for several generations, and we now use his name to describe a person who retains in mature years the naturalness of spirit and charm associated with childhood, or one who absolutely refuses to escape from the comfortable irresponsibility of childhood. Sir James Barrie introduced his immortal character to the stage in the play *Peter Pan* (1904), although the fantastic world of Peter Pan had previously been presented in his *The Little White Bird* (1902). *Peter Pan*, a poetical pantomime, as it has been called, charmed audiences from the night it first appeared. Peter has since been played by many great stars, ranging from Maude Adams to Mary Martin, and a statue of him stands in Kensington

Gardens, London. Barrie, who described his business as "playing hide and seek with angels," named Peter for one of his nephews, for whom he wrote the story, giving the character his last name from the god Pan, "goat-footed," patron of forests, meadows, flocks, and shepherds. Wendy, Peter's girlfriend, also borrowed her name from a real person. This was Barrie's own nickname, bestowed upon him by the daughter of his friend, poet W. E. Henley. Little Margaret Henley called him Friendly, then Friendly-Wendy, and then ultimately Wendy, the name he dubbed his character.

"Sir James," an editor once asked the famous author, "I suppose some of your plays do better than others. They are not all successes, I imagine?"

"No," the playwright confided, smiling, "some Peter out and some Pan out."

Magnanimous Playwrights

Agatha Christie's play *The Mousetrap*, which had the longest run of any play in history, with more than ten thousand performances when it closed, has brought millions to the author's nephew, to whom she gave the royalties as a gift.

Less remunerative but much odder was the royalty playwright Sir James Barrie gave to the child of one of his friends. The boy had been told he would be sick the next day if he ate any more chocolates. "I shall be sick *tonight*," he replied laconically, and helped himself to another piece. Delighted with the epigram, Barrie decided to use it as the basis for lines spoken in *Peter Pan* (1904) and gave his friend's son a royalty of a halfpenny a performance for the copyright.

A Patronizing Playwright Above the Law

Prolific German dramatist George Kaiser (1878–1945), the author of some seventy plays, decided in his first years as a writer to let the world support his art. After being supported for a while by his family, he married a rich woman in 1908, and lived comfortably for a time. When her money ran out a decade or so later, he sold her estate without her permission. Not stopping there, he rented a villa and proceeded to sell all the furniture in it. Tried for theft, he made a notorious, impassioned speech before the court claiming that the artist had the privilege of immunity from the common laws of life, and was above the law in this respect. Unfortunately for Kaiser, the court thought otherwise and he was sentenced to a long jail term.

An Unpatronized Patron of the Arts

Peggy Guggenheim (1898–1979), a patron of the arts in many ways, told the story of the time she was traveling back to Paris with Irish playwright Samuel Beckett and they had to stop in Dijon for a night. Beckett asked for a double room and a delighted Peggy assumed he wanted to sleep with her. But when she climbed naked into his bed that night he said no, he certainly didn't want to make love. "Then why did you take the double room?" she demanded. "It was cheaper," Beckett said.

Expensive Working Habits and No Habits at All

Popular New York playwright, composer, and actor George M. Cohan (1878–1942), who wrote such hits as *Forty-Five Minutes from Broadway* and the song standards "Over There," "It's a Grand Old Flag," and "Yankee Doodle Dandy," had the most expensive working habit of any dramatist trying to find inspiration. Cohan would often rent an entire Pullman car drawing room and keep traveling until he finished what he was working on. He could turn out 140 pages a night this way. Much more than Edmond Rostand, author of the poetic drama *Cyrano de Bergerac* (1897), whose method was, however, much cheaper. Rostand simply worked in the bathtub so he wouldn't be interrupted by his many friends.

Buying In

Aspiring composer McNair Ilgenfritz thought that by leaving the Metropolitan Opera $150,000 he could accomplish in death what he could not in life: having one of his operas produced by the Met. He failed once again, for the sorely tempted Metropolitan had to refuse his bequest in 1953 when accused by critics of prostituting the arts.

The Shortest Plays Ever

The little theater pieces called *dramaticules* were so named by Samuel Beckett, who wrote one called *Come and Go* that had three female characters and a text of just 120 words.

But this dramatist was bested by French author Tristan Bernard, whose play *Exiles* is world's shortest with dialogue. The complete seventeen-word text:

Exile: Whoever you are have pity on a hunted man. There is a price on my head.
Mountaineer: How much?

Beckett, however, won back the title with *Breath*, a thirty-second play that consists of a pile of rubbish on stage, a breath, and a cry.

Winner Take Nothing

Richard Walton Tully's play *The Bird of Paradise* (1906), about an American man's love for a Hawaiian girl, was challenged as plagiarism by a mysterious woman who was awarded a judgment of more than $780,000 when she finally brought the case to court in 1924. Tully, a popular playwright who had collaborated with David Belasco, spent all his savings fighting this decision, and it was finally overturned on appeal in 1930. *The Bird of Paradise* was made into a musical that year, but Tully, financially and psychologically exhausted, was never able to write again.

Wrong Diagnosis

Terence Rattigan's play *In Praise of Love* (1973) is about a woman dying of leukemia whose husband tries to keep her illness a secret from her. Rattigan himself had been advised that he had leukemia ten years before he wrote the play. He decided to live to the fullest the two or three years he thought he had left and went on a world cruise. When he got back to England, a year later, he was told that there had been a mistake and he didn't have leukemia at all.

A Playwright's Playwright

In Lillian Hellman's last days a nurse told a friend of Hellman's that the American playwright was "half-paralyzed and almost totally blind: she couldn't eat, couldn't walk; couldn't find a comfortable spot in her bed, couldn't stand up . . . was probably dying." Thanking the nurse for the information, the friend visited the writer's room, asking her how she felt.

"Not good," she answered, and he asked why. "This is the worst case of writer's block I ever had in my life," she replied. "The worst case."

The World's Worst Playwright

On the basis of his one and only play, many would agree that the world's worst playwright was, of all people, the great artist Pablo Picasso. The legendary Spanish painter wrote the fortunately little known play *Desire Caught by the Tail* (1941). One of its stage directions instructed that the character Tart, played by a blond stripper, "go to the front, face the audience and urinate and syphilize for a full five minutes." What *syphilize* means no one knows, but Tart urinated on stage for a while in what was the dramatic highlight of the play, which is supposed to be about food, money, and sex. Amazingly enough, Albert Camus directed this avant-garde piece, which featured Jean-Paul Sartre and Simone de Beauvoir, among numerous Parisian notables. Other characters included Fat Anxiety, Thin Anguish, and Big Foot. Slides of Picasso's paintings flashed on a screen while Tart stripped, the artwork redeeming her act somewhat. At the play's conclusion come two good lines from Big Foot, which seem to speak of the impending doom of Europe at the time: "We sprinkle the rice powder of angels on the soiled bed sheets and turn the mattresses through blackberry bushes. And with all power the pigeon flocks dash into the rifle bullets! And in all bombed houses, the keys turn twice around in the locks!"

A Nobel Prize Quiz

Name eleven playwrights who were awarded the Nobel Prize for Literature.

Answers:
1. José Echegary y Eizaguirre, Spanish dramatist (1904)
2. Maurice Maeterlinck, Belgian poetic dramatist and essayist (1911)
3. Gerhart Hauptmann, German dramatist (1912)
4. Rabindranath Tagore, Indian poet and playwright (1913)
5. William Butler Yeats, Irish poet and playwright (1923)
6. George Bernard Shaw, Irish playwright (1925)
7. John Galsworthy, English novelist and playwright (1932)
8. Luigi Pirandello, Italian playwright (1934)

9. Eugene O'Neill, American playwright (1936)
10. Jean-Paul Sartre, French philosopher and playwright (1964)
    (He declined the award.)
11. Samuel Beckett, Irish playwright (1969)

The great dramatists Ibsen, Strindberg, and Chekhov were nominated but never won the Nobel. Likewise Bertolt Brecht and Sean O'Casey.

Note that Irish playwrights outnumber all other nationalities with three winners (Yeats, Shaw, and Beckett).

Wrote Sartre in declining the prize: "It is not the same thing if I sign Jean-Paul Sartre, or if I sign Jean-Paul Sartre, Nobel Prize winner. A writer must refuse to allow himself to be transformed into an institution, even if it takes place in the most honorable form."

IV

Moguls, Mavens, and Momzers (Including Producers, Directors, and Screenwriters, et al)

Monsters and Pirates and Bastards, But . . .

"I'll tell you about these men [early Hollywood producers]. They were monsters and pirates and bastards right down to the bottom of their feet, but they *loved movies.* They loved *making* movies, they loved *seeing* movies, and they protected the people who worked for them. Some of the jerks running the business now don't even have faces. Not one of them has ever been on the back lot or rummaged through the vaults or walked through their stockpiles to see what they *bought!* I listen to them talk and don't know what they're saying. All they want to know is how much did it cost and what will it gross and how much can they dump it for. When we previewed *Key Largo* back in 1948, Jack Warner stood in the lobby talking to everybody who came out and said 'Great picture!' and 'How did you like it, little lady, it's a powerful picture, don't you think?' before they even got their preview cards filled out. These guys today should be running gas stations."

—Richard Brooks (*director of* Crossfire, Blackboard Jungle, Cat on a Hot Tin Roof, In Cold Blood, *and other films*) in the New York Times, *January 18, 1970*

The Greatest Show on Earth

Phineas Taylor Barnum, American impresario and forerunner of all the Mike Todds and Sol Huroskes of Broadway and movie history, was born in 1810, the son of a storekeeper and farmer. At twelve he became a successful lottery operator, but he failed in business and publishing before beginning his career as a showman in 1835. Barnum began by exhibiting Aunt Joice Heth, an aged black woman he fraudulently claimed had been George Washington's nurse. Thousands paid to see the "162-year-old" woman, who wasn't more than eighty when she died, illustrating the saying, probably falsely attributed to him, that "there's a sucker born every minute." The showman soon founded the American Museum in New York, embarking on a career that included exhibitions of the dwarf General Tom Thumb (Charles Stratton), reputedly thirty-one inches tall; singer Jenny Lind, the famous "Swedish Nightingale"; and the first bearded lady, among countless other attractions. Among his many frauds or "poetic licenses" were a sign labeled TO THE EGRESS, implying a mysterious monster but actually a fancy word for exit, which helped empty his museum so more paying customers could fit in; a "genuine preserved mermaid," which in reality was a monkey's torso expertly sewed to a tail of a fish; dancing turkeys that danced because the floor of their cage was heated; an animal "of a horse's size, a deer's haunches, an elephant's tail, a camel's color, and the curly wool of sheep, with some resemblance to a young buffalo"; a cherry-colored cat (black-cherry-colored); and "Swiss" bell ringers who were really British. Barnum opened his circus in Brooklyn in 1871, proceeding to tour the world with "The Greatest Show on Earth." The African elephant, Jumbo, purchased from the London Zoo, was one of the show's stars, as were the famous Siamese twins, Chang and Eng. Barnum had not only a great flair for showmanship, but was master or inventor of every method known for fleecing the public, from unscrupulous advertising to inflated attendance figures. "The Prince of Humbugs" became mayor of Bridgeport, Connecticut, and a member of the state legislature, but his name is rightfully remembered as a synonym for pretentious ballyhoo and boastful exaggeration, as well as for a great showman. He died in 1891 without ever publicly regretting his past, and that he was something of an American folk hero is illustrated by the fact that at least six towns in the United States are named after him. Ringling Brothers, Barnum & Bailey Circus also bears his name.

The Great Ziegfeld and His Zaftig Girls

The most famous of American theatrical producers, Chicago-born Florenz Ziegfeld first found fame in 1893 as the manager of Eugene Sandow, the "World's Strongest Man." But within three years he was producing a Broadway series of light musical farces featuring his first wife, wasp-waisted Anna Held, America's aphrodisiac at the time. In these seven early plays—vehicles like *A Parlor Match* (1896) and *A Parisian Model* (1906)—Ziegfeld perfected the techniques that enabled him to produce the extravagant musical revues to which his name became irrevocably linked: the Ziegfeld Follies. Though there were to be many other plays, the Follies became the best and longest-lasting series of musical revues ever produced, running from 1907 to 1925. The Ziegfeld Follies featured beautiful chorines in scanty but dazzling costumes designed by Joseph Urban (among the greatest of set designers) who were ballyhooed as "the glorification of the American girl." The opulent costly productions starred such acts as Fanny Brice (Ziegfeld's second wife), banjo-eyed Eddie Cantor, W. C. Fields, Will Rogers, Bert Williams, and Marilyn Miller, many of whom Ziegfeld discovered. "Unfailing Urban" designed elaborate sets for them, and the perennial song favorites introduced in the revues included "A Pretty Girl Is Like a Melody," "By the Light of the Silvery Moon," "Shine on Harvest Moon," "Row, Row, Row Your Boat," and "Second Hand Rose," to name just a few.

"Out of the regular leg show," wrote eminent critic George Jean Nathan, "Ziegfeld has fashioned a thing of grace and beauty, of loveliness and charm; he knows quality and mood. He has lifted, with sensitive skill, a thing that was mere food for smirking baldheads and downy college boys, out of low estate and into a thing of symmetry and bloom."

Ziegfeld, a legend in his own time, was also hailed for his Ziegfeld Theatre, one of Broadway's most beautiful. Designed by Urban, the egg-shaped boxless auditorium had a gilt proscenium and stage, its walls and ceiling were covered with richly colored murals. Opened in 1927, it was the home of the Ziegfeld Follies of 1931, but all other Follies produced by Ziegfeld himself were played at the legendary New Amsterdam Theatre on 42nd Street. After Ziegfeld died in 1932, age sixty-five, the Ziegfeld Theatre housed a few more Follies staged there by the Shuberts, but they never matched the magnificent originals. Despite many protests, the theater itself was demolished in 1966 to make room for an office building.

Ziegfeld's last words were said to be "Curtain! Fast music! Lights! Ready for the last finale! Great! The show looks good! The show looks good!"

Buffalo Bill's Wild West Show

Colonel William Frederick Cody (1846–1917), the peerless horseman and sharpshooter who became the original Buffalo Bill, earned his nickname as a market hunter for buffalo (bison) hides and as a contractor supplying buffalo meat to workers building the Union Pacific Railroad in 1867. To his glory then, and shame now, he killed 4,280 buffalo in one year, mostly for their hides and tongues. It is hard to separate truth from fiction in Cody's life, since his fame owes much to the dime novels that made him a celebrity in the late nineteenth century. Buffalo Bill was a herder, a Pony Express rider, a scout and cavalryman for the Union Army in the Civil War, and an Indian fighter who is said to have killed the Cheyenne chief Yellowhand singlehandedly. He was also a member of the Nebraska state legislature. Buffalo Bill, with his white mustache and goatee, toured the country as an actor for ten years in dramas exaggerating his exploits. His Wild West Show, which he organized in 1883, toured the United States and Europe with outdoor performances, bringing him great personal fame, yet financial problems caused this legendary American hero and showman to die in poverty and relative obscurity. Today his name conjures up visions of "sportsmen" picking off buffalo from the platforms of moving trains, abundant buffalo meat rotting on the plains, and the destruction of the great herds.

Three Generations of Hammersteins

One evening German-born impresario Oscar Hammerstein (1847–1919) was buttonholed by a desperate, wild-eyed man who proposed a bizarre plan.

"Mr. Hammerstein, I will perform an act on your stage that will be the talk of the world," he promised. "You can advertise it in advance and you can charge $100 a ticket. Here is my proposition: if you'll put $50,000 in escrow for my wife, I'll go on your stage, and in full view of your audience, commit suicide."

"Marvelous," Hammerstein replied, "but what will you do for an encore?"

Such ripostes were typical of the hardened Hammerstein, who ran away from home as a boy and emigrated to America, making a fortune as a cigar manufacturer before building his first theater in New York. Although his poor management as a theater owner caused him to lose more than half a dozen playhouses, he won fame as a producer of vaudeville acts and plays, especially for his productions of Victor Herbert's opera *Naughty Marietta* (1910). Hammerstein also wrote a number of musicals. His sons William and Arthur were successful producers in their own right, but it was his grandson Oscar Hammerstein II (1895–1960) who won everlasting fame as a lyricist and producer.

Collaborating with composers Richard Rodgers, Jerome Kern, and Sigmund Romberg over the years, the younger Hammerstein became the most successful lyricist of his day, writing the words for such masterpieces as *Show Boat* (1927), *Oklahoma!* (1943), *Carousel* (1945), *South Pacific* (1949), *The King and I* (1951), and *The Sound of Music* (1959), the first show written with Kern and the last five written with Rogers. The classic lyrics he wrote for songs have become part of the language, including "Old Man River," "Make Believe," "Can't Help Lovin' Dat Man," "Lover Come Back to Me," "Stouthearted Men," "Why Was I Born," "I've Told Every Little Star," "All the Things You Are," "Oklahoma!," "Oh, What a Beautiful Morning," "People Will Say We're in Love," "If I Loved You," "June Is Bustin' Out All Over," "You'll Never Walk Alone," "Bali Ha'i," "I'm Gonna Wash That Man Right Outta My Hair," "Some Enchanted Evening," "There Is Nothin' Like a Dame," "Younger Than Springtime," "A Wonderful Guy," "Getting to Know You," "Hello, Young Lovers," "I Whistle a Happy Tune," "The Sound of Music," "My Favorite Things," "Climb Every Mountain," and "Do-Re-Me"—among many, many others. As if this were not enough, he and Rodgers directed and produced many of their own shows and produced such hits as *I Remember Mama* (1944) and *Annie Get Your Gun* (1946).

The First Movie Moguls

December 28, 1895, is often celebrated as the birthday of the movies. On that day, at the Grand Café in Paris, the Lumière brothers (Louis and Auguste), who invented the movie projector, showed their movies to paying customers for the first time. The show included the short farce *L'Arroseur Arrosé*, the world's first fiction movie, and several very brief documentaries such as a train pulling into a station and quitting time at a factory.

Actually the term *moving picture* for a movie, film, flick, picture show, motion picture, etc., has a longer history than one would think. *Moving picture* dates back to the early eighteenth century, when it was used to describe picture books or *flip books* flipped quickly to give the effect of motion. The term was finally applied to the cinema two centuries later. Before then the closest thing to moving pictures were *magic lanterns*, rude optical instruments employing a lens to cast a magnified image of a transparent picture drawn on glass onto a wall in a dark room. Such devices were known in

Europe by the mid-seventeenth century, but the first one called by that name was the brainchild of a Danish inventor who exhibited it in France in 1665, the French dubbing the machine a *lanterne magique*.

The Great Train Robbery

For many years it was thought that the oldest full-length American movie was *The Great Train Robbery* (1903), but this very important film was a ten-minute one-reeler, which while longer than most shorts of the day wasn't a complete full-length feature film. Though foreign feature films like the Italian *Quo Vadis* (1912) ran as long as two hours, the first American movie to qualify as a complete feature film was the 1912 silent-movie version of Shakespeare's *Richard III*, starring British-born stage actor Frederick Barkham Warde (1851–1935), who had played opposite such greats as Edwin Booth and had his own American touring company. The historic film was found in 1997 in the basement of a Portland, Oregon, home.

As for the more important *The Great Train Robbery*, it was made by Edwin S. Porter, production director for Thomas Edison's New Jersey movie company. In an earlier movie made that same year, *The Life of an American Fireman*, Porter devised many of the techniques he would use in *The Great Train Robbery*, including the editing of his scenes to make a story with a beginning, middle, and end. But it was *The Great Train Robbery*, the first film to have a preliminary scenario, that captured the public imagination. Porter filmed it in a continuity of fourteen individual shots, cutting back and forth as the action unfolded. What he created was the classic Western, even though it was filmed mainly in Paterson, New Jersey, using a train loaned to Porter by the Delaware, Lackawanna Railroad. In fact, Max Aronson, one of the actors, later became famous as Bronco Billy, filmdom's first Western hero.

Audiences flocked to see *The Great Train Robbery* after its New York opening in late 1903, and the film was soon playing all over the country. More than any other film up to that time, it inspired an interest in movies among the public—and an interest in opening more theaters among businessmen. Thanks in large part to this ten-minute film, the movies were finally more than a novelty, so this "picture play" was far more important than the following review in the *Philadelphia Inquirer* (June 26, 1904) gave it credit for:

> The Great Train Robbery *has proved a thriller in nearly all the larger cities of the United States. . . . The picture play begins with a view in a lonesome telegraph station, in which an operator, receiving train orders, is*

overcome, bound hand and foot, gagged and left unconscious on the floor by the desperadoes; proceeds with the capture of the train, murder of the fireman, killing of the express messenger, blowing open the safe, holdup of the passengers, and shooting of one who attempts to escape; and winds up with a horseback ride through the mountains with the bags of booty, a wild weird dance in a log cabin, pursuit by the sheriff's posse and the death of all the robbers. There is a great amount of shooting. The smoke of the pistols is plainly seen, and men drop dead right and left, but no sound is heard. Nevertheless, while witnessing the exhibition, women put their fingers in their ears to shut out the noise of firing.

A Realistic Unbelievable Plot

According to author Irving Wallace, in 1914 a now defunct Hollywood silent-movie studio hired the army of Mexican revolutionary Pancho Villa to fight a real battle in his revolution according to studio specifications. A contract was signed with a cash-hungry Villa for $25,000, and a Hollywood camera crew joined his Division of the North. The script dictated how the battle should be fought, and the crew's director told Villa when to fight—only in daylight between the hours of 9 A.M. and 4 P.M. Cease-fires were called to allow the camera to be moved to new angles. The proud director brought the footage back to Hollywood after Villa won the battle, but most of it was never used—it was found too unbelievable for release. The film eventually had to be shot on the studio lot.

Edison's Pioneer Film Studio

The world's first film stars were music hall and circus performers like Annie Oakley and Buffalo Bill Cody, who were filmed performing their acts at the world's first film studio, the so-called Black Maria (named jokingly after police paddy wagons) on the grounds of Thomas Edison's laboratories in West Orange, New Jersey. The Black Maria was a revolving hut covered with tarpaper and had a roof that opened to let in sunlight. Edison's giant Kinetograph at one end of the hut photographed the performers on a little stage at the other end. The short films were shown in Kinetoscopes—penny-in-the-slot peepshows through which one viewer at a time could watch them. Kinetoscope parlors sprang up all over the world after Edison introduced his films in 1893, demonstrating how popular movies could be and inspiring inventors to invent systems that enabled large audiences to watch movies.

You Ain't Heard Nothin' Yet: The First "Talkie"

Movie myth insists that Al Jolson's *The Jazz Singer* (1927) was the first sound film ever made, but in truth sound had been used in movies long before this, ever since Edison's first Kinetoscopes in the late nineteenth century. Many short sound films at the time featured great actors and actresses speaking their parts, as when Sarah Bernhardt spoke in the duel scene from a 1900 version of *Hamlet*.

What held back talking pictures was the huge investment needed to convert Hollywood studios and movie theaters across the country to sound systems. Toward the middle of the 1920s Warner Bros. realized that they had fallen far behind the other major studios and decided as a last-chance gamble to produce synchronized sound movies. Warners built its own huge Hollywood theater, bought the old Vitagraph company with its fifteen houses, and converted its studio stages to sound. On August 6, 1926, it premiered its first synchronized sound film, a lavish Vitaphone production of *Don Juan* starring John Barrymore.

But *Don Juan* failed to capture the large audience Warners had hoped for. Still gambling and deeply in debt, the studio decided to make a sound film of the Broadway hit musical *The Jazz Singer*. When Georgie Jessel, star of the Broadway production, insisted on too high a fee, Warners engaged Al Jolson for the title role, using the same director, Alan Crosland, who had made *Don Juan*. The result exceeded their wildest expectations. The film premiered at Warners Theater in New York on October 6, 1927, and audience and critics alike thrilled to Jolson's renditions of songs like "Mammy" and "Toot Toot Tootsie Goodbye." Jolson's familiar line from the film "You ain't heard nothin' yet!" became a prophetic catchphrase. Within a mere three years sound films were legion; the silent film and most silent film stars were extinct—though not the thousands of techniques that had made silent films so immensely popular.

Born on the Fourth of July?

Louis B. Mayer of Metro-Goldwyn-Mayer may have been born on Independence Day, but no one knows for sure. Mayer always claimed he didn't know, that his birth certificate was lost when he emigrated to America from Russia. But he chose the birthday of his adopted country as his own and held a big picnic for MGM employees every year on the Fourth of July. Mayer died in 1957, age seventy-two.

George M. Cohan, the "Man Who Owned Broadway" in his day, was definitely born on the Fourth of July, as he made clear in his song "Yankee Doodle Boy." The American actor, writer, and producer was an intensely patriotic man. When his song "You're a Grand Old Rag" was criticized for its title, he changed it to "You're a Grand Old Flag."

Both Cohan and Mayer were unpopular producers. When Cohan tried to mediate the Actor's Equity strike in 1919, he was rebuffed and never forgave the union. To say the production head of Paramount Pictures, B. P. Schulberg, did not get along with producer Mayer is putting it mildly. Before he died Ben Schulberg told his son, novelist Budd Schulberg: "Put my ashes in a box and tell the messenger to bring them to Mayer's office with a farewell message from me. Then, when the messenger goes to Louis' desk, I want him to open the box and blow the ashes in the bastard's face."

Mr. Malaprop: The World's Longest Collection of Goldwynisms

> "Don't tell me about Goldwynisms. You want to hear Goldwynisms go talk to Jesse Lasky."
>
> —*Samuel Goldwyn*

The film pioneer Samuel Goldwyn (1882–1974) was a modern-day "Mr. Malaprop" unrivaled for his fractured English. Goldwyn, born in Warsaw, Poland, came to America when only thirteen; immigration officials gave him the name Goldfish as the closest equivalent to his Polish name. Later, he legally changed this to Goldwyn—from the Goldwyn Pictures Corporation, which had been named for himself and his partners, the Selwyn brothers. Of this coinage Judge Learned Hand said years later, "A self-made man may prefer a self-made name." A self-made man Goldwyn was. Even before forming Goldwyn Pictures he had produced Hollywood's first full-length feature, *The Squaw Man*. After Goldwyn Pictures became part of Metro-Goldwyn-Mayer in 1924, he struck out on his own as an independent producer, his eighty-odd movies including *Dodsworth*, *Wuthering Heights*, *The Little Foxes*, *Pride of the Yankees*, *The Best Years of Our Lives*, *Porgy and Bess*, *The Secret Life of Walter Mitty*, and *Guys and Dolls*. Goldwyn received the Medal of Freedom in 1971 for "proving that clean movies could be good box office." No doubt many of the thousands of Goldwynisms attributed to him—word manglings, mixed metaphors, malapropisms, grammatical blunders, and the like—were invented by press agents, writers, friends, and enemies. But, genuine or not, they became part of the legend surrounding the man. Of Goldwyn's peculiar language F. Scott Fitzgerald observed: "You always knew where you were with him—nowhere."

- One of Mr. Malaprop's first Goldwynisms came when as a young producer facing severe financial problems he declared himself "on the brink of an abscess" [for "abyss"].
- "Tell me, how did you love [for "like"] the picture?" he once asked a reviewer.
- Another time he accused Metro-Goldwyn-Mayer director George Cukor of "biting the hand of the goose that laid the golden egg."
- "But Mr. Goldwyn," a colleague asked at a script conference, "what is the *message* of this film?"

    "I am just planning a movie," he replied. "I am not interested in messages. Messages are for Western Union."
- "I want a movie," he instructed one director, "that starts with an earthquake and works up to a climax."
- "This is a perfect scenario," he told a new screenwriter. "It is the first time in my life that I've seen a perfect scenario. There's absolutely nothing wrong with it. I want you to have a hundred copies made so I can distribute them to all the other writers so that everybody should see a really perfect script. And hurry," he called as the thrilled writer hastened from his office, "before I start rewriting it."
- "This is the mucus [for "nucleus"] of an idea," he told a studio writer.
- He constantly referred to his great film *Wuthering Heights* as "*Withering Heights.*"
- "I'm sorry you thought our film of *The Secret Life of Walter Mitty* was too blood and thirsty," he told James Thurber, the story's author. "Not only did I think so," said Thurber, "but I was horror and struck."
- Someone at a story conference suggested making a movie about Bismarck. "Who the hell wants to see a picture about a herring?" he demanded.
- "You're going to call him 'William'?" he demanded of a scriptwriter on one of his films. "What kind of a name is that? Every Tom, Dick, and Harry is called William. Why not call him Bill?"

- "The most important thing in acting is honesty," he observed. "Once you've learned to fake that, you're in."
- Rejecting one novel for a film, he observed, "Take away the essentials and what have you got?"
- "At least let me destroy all letters that are ten years old or more," his secretary suggested in an effort to restore some order to his cluttered files. "OK," he agreed, "but don't forget to make copies."
- Of one film he said, "It's greater than a masterpiece—it's mediocre."
- On reading the title of the book *The Making of Yesterday: The Diaries of Raoul de Roussy de Sales, 1938–1942*, he commented: "How do you like that? Four years old and already the kid keeps a diary!"
- "Gentlemen, do not underestimate the danger of the atom bomb," he warned associates after Hiroshima. "It's dynamite!"

There must be at least several hundred more Goldwynisms attributed to the Prince of Malaprops. Here's another long selection, some of them doubtless spurious:

- "It rolls like a duck off my back." (Probably invented by a screenwriter.)
- In a toast to Britain's Field Marshal Montgomery: "Here's to Marshall Field Montgomery Ward."
- "An oral contract isn't worth the paper it's written on."
- "Include me out."
- "In two words: im-possible!" (Goldwyn categorically denied this one.)
- "We have passed a lot of water since this." (For "a lot of water has passed under the bridge.")
- "A man who goes to a psychiatrist should have his head examined." (Also attributed to Lillian Hellman.)
- "We have to get some fresh platitudes."
- "It's dog eat dog in this business and nobody's going to eat me."
- After a director changed a night scene to a daytime shot: "Nobody can change night into day, or vice versa, without asking me first!"
- "You've got to take the bull by the teeth."
- "It's spreading like wildflowers."

- Of a sagging film: "Let's bring it up to date with some snappy nineteenth-century dialogue."
- "I've got a great slogan for the company: 'Goldwyn pictures griddle [for "girdle"] the Earth!'"
- Of an actress he had ballyhooed who didn't pass muster with the public: "Well, she's colossal in a small way."
- On being told that a film script was "too caustic": "Never mind the cost. If it's a good picture, we'll make it."
- "Our comedies are not to be laughed at."
- To rival producer Darryl F. Zanuck: "We're in terrible trouble. You've got Gable and I want him."
- To Garson Kanin: "Sidney Howard tells me you're a real clever genius."
- To a bridge partner who protested that she hadn't overbid and asked how she could know he had nothing: "Didn't you hear me keeping still?"
- To the husband of an actress who withdrew from a Goldwyn film because she was pregnant: "You not only screwed her, you screwed me!"
- "If you won't give me your word of honor, will you give me your promise?"
- "I got this beautiful new Picasso in Paris. Somewhere over there on the Left Wing."
- "Modern dance is so old-fashioned."
- "What's that?"
    "A sundial. It tells time by the sun."
    "My God, what'll they think of next?"
- "I've been laid up with intentional flu."
- "He worked his way up from nothing, that kid. In fact, he was born in an orphan asylum."
- "We can get all the Indians we need at the reservoir."
- On his deathbed: "I never thought I'd live to see the day." (Said to have been invented by author Clifton Fadiman.)

(*See also* "Mrs. Malaprop," Chapter 3.)

A Bee Hero

"I know you don't understand picture technique," Sam Goldwyn told the Belgian dramatist Maurice Maeterlinck. "You don't have to. Just go home and write your greatest book over in the form of a scenario." Several weeks passed and Maeterlinck returned with a script of his earlier *Vie des Abeilles* (1901). "Now we'll see something," Goldwyn crooned, taking the scenario into his office. Not long after he came rushing out, highly agitated. "My God," he cried, "the hero is a bee!"

Hollywoodese

> "Hollywood talks and thinks in superlatives. Movie people do not 'like' things; they are 'mad about' them. They do not dislike things; they loathe or detest them. . . . The revealing story is told of two movie producers meeting on the street; 'How's your picture doing?' asked the first. 'Excellent.' 'Only excellent? That's too bad!' "
> —Leo Rosten, The Movie Colony, The Movie Makers, 1941

King Cohn

Until his death in 1958 Harry Cohn was indisputably in charge of Columbia Pictures and was noted for picking winners like Frank Capra and Rita Hayworth. Cohn did have some friends, contrary to all the stories about him. Capra, for example, resented working at the old Columbia Studios, which he called "Poverty Row" and "a riff-raff of a place," but he respected Cohn, considering him a "very very strange, odd, powerful, forceful, and controversial man" who would "give you a yes or no right now, and mean it and not go back on it," who "ran his own place." Director William Wellman was another admirer. "I'm one of the few guys that was crazy about him," he said. "He was a rough, tough guy, but he was a hell of a producer. . . ." Wellman made the six-reel silent film *When Husbands Flirt* for Cohn in three and a half days, using long shots from other Columbia pictures.

Nevertheless, Harry Cohn's reputation in Hollywood usually ranged somewhere between rat and fink, and there were few mourners among the directors, actors, and writers who turned out in force for his funeral. Noting the unusually large attendance, comedian Red Skelton remarked, "Well, it only proves what they always say—give the public something they want to see, and they'll come out for it."

The Marx Brothers vs. Warner Brothers

When Warner Bros. warned the Marx Brothers not to use the name Casablanca in their film *A Night in Casablanca* because (the studio claimed) this would infringe upon the title of Warners's movie *Casablanca*, Groucho Marx wrote them the following letter now in the Groucho collection of the Library of Congress. Jack Warner, who regarded actors as "bums" and writers as "schmucks with Underwoods," was not amused.

"Apparently there is more than one way of conquering a city and holding it as your own," Groucho wrote. "For example, up to the time that we contemplated making a picture, I had no idea that the city of Casablanca belonged to Warner Brothers.

"However, it was only a few days after our announcement appeared that we received a long, ominous legal document warning us not to use the name 'Casablanca.'

"It seems that in 1471, Ferdinand Balboa Warner, the great-great-grandfather of Harry and Jack, while looking for a shortcut to the city of Burbank, had stumbled on the shores of Africa and, raising his alpenstock, which he later turned in for a hundred shares of the common, he named it Casablanca.

"I just can't understand your attitude. Even if they plan on rereleasing the picture, I am sure that the average movie fan could learn to distinguish between Ingrid Bergman and Harpo. I don't know whether I could, but I certainly would like to try.

"You claim you own Casablanca and that no one else can use that name without your permission. What about Warner Brothers—do you own that, too? You probably have the right to use the name Warner, but what about Brothers? Professionally, we were brothers long before you were.

"Even before us, there had been other brothers—the Smith Brothers, the Brothers Karamazov; Dan Brothers, an outfielder with Detroit and 'Brother, can you spare a dime?' This was originally 'Brothers, can you spare a dime,' but this was spreading a dime pretty thin.

"The younger Warner Brother calls himself Jack. Does he claim that, too? It's not an original name—it was used long before he was born. Offhand, I can think of two Jacks—there was Jack of 'Jack and the Beanstalk' and Jack the Ripper, who cut quite a figure in his day. . . ."

And so the letter went on, à la Groucho. Needless to say, *A Night in Casablanca* remained *A Night in Casablanca*.

Warner's Biggest Blunder

Literary agent Laurie Williams offered producer Jack Warner the film rights to a new bestselling book. Warner replied: "I wouldn't pay $50,000 for any damn book anytime!" He had turned down *Gone with the Wind*.

Jack Warner generally did have a good eye for properties, though, as is illustrated by an observation made later in his career. Told that Ronald Reagan had been nominated to run for governor of California, the studio head voiced his objection. "No, no," he said. "Jimmy Stewart for governor; Reagan for his best friend."

MGM *Rejections*

Writers Herman Mankiewicz, Samuel Hoffenstein, and Louis Weitzenkorn wrote many successful screenplays for MGM. Knowing this, a beginning, unagented writer mailed MGM a script with the following note attached:

> *Don't be too hasty in tossing this story into the waste basket. You will notice that its envelope is postmarked Wilkes-Barre, Pennsylvania. Let me remind you that Wilkes-Barre breeds writers. It gave MGM Herman J. Mankiewicz, Samuel Hoffenstein, and Louis Weitzenkorn.*

The author soon received MGM's reply:

> *Thank you for your note about Wilkes-Barre. We are sending back your script, which we cannot use. We are also returning Herman J. Mankiewicz, Samuel Hoffenstein, and Louis Weitzenkorn.*

G.B.S. vs. Hollywood

George Bernard Shaw was a shrewd literary negotiator. He was once overheard saying to a motion picture producer, "There's no use in our talking about it [anymore] because, obviously, you're a great artist and I'm just a businessman." Another time Sam Goldwyn telephoned Shaw, trying to drive down his price for the film rights to several of his plays. Goldwyn argued, "Think of the millions of people who would get a chance to see your plays who would otherwise never see them. Think of the contribution to art."

"The trouble is, Mr. Goldwyn," said Shaw, "that you think of nothing but art and I think of nothing but money."

Mounting Production Costs

- Cecil B. DeMille was advised by the front office that he was spending too much money on *The Ten Commandments*. "What do you want me to do?" the great director snapped back. "Stop now and release it as *The Five Commandments*?"

- Production costs of *The Captain Hates the Sea*, starring John Gilbert, mounted due to the major league drinking of its star and much of the rest of the cast. Producer Harry Cohn had no idea why the picture was taking so long, because the location was on a ship out at sea, but he fired off a telegram to director Lewis Milestone: HURRY UP, THE COST IS STAGGERING.
  Milestone cabled back in reply: SO IS THE CAST.

- The long-running hit *Abie's Irish Rose* (1922) was financed in large part by gangster-gambler Arnold Rothstein, the man who fixed the 1919 World Series. It made him millions, becoming for its time the longest-running Broadway play, despite horrific reviews.

- In a 1962 speech at Edinburgh the brilliant playwright Arthur Adamov (1908–70) of the theater of the absurd advised: "The reason why most Absurdist plays take place in No Man's Land with only two characters is mainly financial."

- While *Titanic* cost more than $200 million to make, the typical Hollywood film costs $10 to $50 million. Some lower-budget films can be more profitable than the giants. *Titanic* is the highest-grossing picture of all time, but even if it makes two times what it cost, it will not come near rivaling the records of low-budget films that make ten times or more than their cost. Hollywood's biggest loser so far is MGM's *Cutthroat Island* (1995), a pirate picture that cost $100 million and has only earned about $12 million.

Hollywood's Golden Rule

"Whoever has the gold makes the rules." —*Anonymous*

Radio and TV Firsts

Radio broadcasting became technically possible by 1906 and was used by ships at sea and by military forces during World War I, but it wasn't available as a medium of information and entertainment until about 1920, when experimental stations began broadcasting music and news.

The world's first radio play was written by novelist Richard Hughes (1900–76), later the author of the bestseller *High Wind in Jamaica*. Hughes's

Danger, commissioned by the BBC in 1924, concerned three English visitors trapped in a Welsh coal mine. The play also introduced the first radio sound effects, calling for the echoes occurring underground in the tunnel to be simulated by the actors speaking into a large bucket.

The world's first crude television system was built in 1923 by Russian American scientist Vladimir Zworykin, who based his work upon that of British scientist Campbell Swinton and Russian inventor Boris Rosing. Three years later Scottish inventor John L. Baird improved Zworykin's invention, and in 1927 television was demonstrated publicly for the first time by American Telephone and Telegraph. The first image shown in the demonstration was Secretary of Commerce Herbert Hoover, a speech he was making in Washington, D.C., being transmitted to a group of bankers and investors in New York City on April 27.

Inventing the Soaps

Newsweek magazine seems to have used the term *soap opera* first in a November 13, 1939, article, putting the expression in quotes as if it were new. Earlier a writer in the *Christian Century* (August 24, 1939) came very close to coining the term, however: "These fifteen minute tragedies . . . I call them 'soap tragedies' because it is by the grace of soap I am allowed to shed tears for these characters who suffer so much from life." He was referring, of course, to the soap manufacturers who sponsored many of the early radio serials characterized by melodrama and sentimentality that are now called *soap operas* or simply *soaps* (an abbreviated form that is twenty years or so old).

The first radio soap opera was a short-lived 1930 nighttime series called "Painted Lives" by Irna Phillips. At the time it was believed that housewives couldn't spare even an hour or so for radio listening during the day, but Chicago advertising executives Anne and E. Frank Hummert thought differently and moved their soap opera "Just Plain Bill" to daytime radio in 1933, a year after they created it. "Just Plain Bill," about a small-town barber who married above his station, won the attention of housewives throughout America and they made time for listening. Soon Hummert Productions moved to New York, turning out eighteen different serials that ran a total of ninety fifteen-minute episodes a week and drew fan mail of over five million letters a year. The brilliant Anne Hummert—who had started as Frank's assistant at the Blackett, Sample, and Hummert ad agency—created most of these, farming out the actual writing but keeping track of every twist of plot and characterization in each with her fabled photographic memory.

By the end of the 1930s, Hummert soap operas were garnering over half the ad revenues of daytime radio and the Hummerts were well on their way to becoming multimillionaires. They had created a new entertainment form and all over America millions were listening to programs like "John's Other Wife," "Young Widow Brown," "Stella Dallas," "Ma Perkins," "Lorenzo Jones," "Helen Trent," "The Goldbergs," and "Mary Noble, Backstage Wife."

The Hummerts did not follow the soaps into television, retiring when radio began to be displaced. Frank Hummert died in 1966 but Anne lived another thirty years until the ripe old age of ninety-one.

"The First Movie That Stinks on Purpose"

One reviewer called producer Mike Todd's *The Scent of Mystery* (1960), starring Peter Lorre, "the first movie that stinks on purpose," although this Smell-O-Vision film wasn't the first theatrical production to do so.

Smell-O-Vision was invented by one Hans Laube, who called himself an *osmologist* and believed that his process would make people desert their home television sets and come stampeding back into the empty movie theaters of the era. Unlike its rival process Aroma-Rama, which released a variety of confusing scents one after another through a theater's ventilation system, Smell-O-Vision's scents were discharged at the proper time from fifty tiny "scent vents" attached to the back of every seat. The scents were often overwhelming and even gross, as when the bulls were running in the Festival of Pamplona. But a *New York Times* critic wrote: "The odor squirters are mildly and randomly used, and patrons sit there sniffing and snuffling like a bunch of bird dogs trying to catch the scent." Needless to say, the film had a short run as a novelty, and the process never caught on.

As noted, Smell-O-Vision was hardly an original idea. In the popular play *Alabama* (1891), for example, magnolia perfume was released in New York's Madison Square Theatre during a scene that took place in a magnolia grove.

Thackeray's Hollywood Agents

When Thackeray's masterpiece *The History of Henry Esmond* (1852) was reprinted in Random House's Modern Library series, the editors received this letter from a Hollywood agency addressed to William Makepeace Thackeray, Esq.:

Dear sir:

We have read your recent book The History of Henry Esmond, *and believe it possesses material adaptable for motion pictures.*

We are recognized agents for writers at all studios and as such would like to represent you in the sale of both your own personal services and your literary products.

In the event you have already made a commitment to some agent for the above book, we nevertheless are impressed with your potential possibilities as a screen writer and would be interested in both your services and future stories.

We would appreciate your advising us by return mail whether or not you are represented here in Hollywood; and in the event that you are not and desire us to represent you, we would be happy to forward to you a copy of our agency agreement with writers for your information and guidance. . . .

The Random House editors decided to have a little fun, writing back:

Thank you for your letter telling me that you believe that my recent book, The History of Henry Esmond, *possesses material adaptable for motion pictures. This effort is a rather crude attempt, I fear, but I am now working on a new novel which I think will be a natural for pictures. I am thinking of calling the new book* Vanity Fair.

I will be interested in hearing what you think of this title.

Sincerely yours,
William Makepeace Thackeray

The agency immediately replied:

Acknowledging receipt of your letter of December 28, in reply to our previous communication, we feel that the title which you are thinking of giving your new book, namely Vanity Fair, *is a good one. We would greatly appreciate receiving a manuscript on this story. Perhaps you could also send us a manuscript at this time, or if not, a copy of the book,* The History of Henry Esmond. *We would like to submit this, if we are authorized to do so by you, to the studios for their consideration. . . .*

"We Nail a Lie"

Among the earliest studio publicity stunts to promote a star was a crude effort by Carl Laemmle, head of the Imp company, when he enticed Florence Lawrence, the "Biograph Girl," from Biograph to his production company.

To trumpet his triumph, Laemmle took out ads in newspapers under the heading WE NAIL A LIE, pretending to squash a rumor (planted by himself) that Florence Lawrence had died. The ads denied the "black, silly lie" that Miss Lawrence [the "Impgirl," formerly known as the Biograph Girl] had been killed by a streetcar . . . "[on the contrary] Miss Lawrence was not even in a streetcar accident, is in the best of health, will continue to appear in 'Imp' films, and very shortly some of the best work in her career is to be released."

The Anatomy of Ballyhoo: *Promoting* Tarzan of the Apes

Peerless press agent Harry Reichenbach counted his publicizing of the film *Tarzan of the Apes* (1917) as his greatest triumph. Reichenbach took the job from a Hollywood producer on a commission basis. Since no theater would show the film, he rented New York's Broadway Theatre for its premiere and proceeded to decorate the lobby with jungle trees and foliage to give the effect of an African wilderness. As he wrote in *Phantom Fame: The Anatomy of Ballyhoo* (1931): "Between two palms loomed the shaggy mane of a ferocious, stuffed lion and in the boxes, chattering, gibbering monkeys were swinging from coconut trees. I turned loose another troupe of four live apes in the lobby forest."

Soon after *Tarzan of the Apes* opened, Reichenbach later wrote, a feature story appeared on the front page of all the New York newspapers, under headlines like SIMIAN ROYALTY STEPS OUT and JUNGLE PRINCE MAKES SOCIETY DEBUT. According to Reichenbach:

> *The story told of a certain Prince Charley, a giant ourang-outang, who, dressed in a neat-fitting tuxedo and high silk hat, entered the fashionable Knickerbocker Hotel on Saturday night while the lobby was aglitter with New York's elite. Prince Charley, timid and embarrassed, was about to introduce himself to this brilliant assemblage when he noticed a revolving door on the Forty-second Street side and began to spin wildly around in it. Exhilarated by this turn in his social life, the big ape leaped back into the lobby with greater confidence and cordially screeched to the other high hats to try his new sport, but they had all made a clearance in record time.*

According to the story, New York City's finest had to capture Prince Charley and after a series of misadventures, "return him to his jungle in the lobby of the Broadway Theatre," where the Tarzan picture was playing. But in truth there was really no Prince Charley—Reichenbach had invented the whole story, which made *Tarzan of the Apes* a worldwide triumph. As Reichenbach put it:

> *The fact that I had planted this episode [in the papers] and used it to promote the Tarzan picture established more firmly in my mind that the whole difference between the things one dreamed about and reality was simply a matter of projection. Many publicity stunts that occurred later on in my work took on this magic-lantern effect. An idea that would seem at first flush extravagant and impossible became, by the proper projection into life, a big item of commanding news value.*

Ars Gratia Artis

These words are the Latin for "art for art's sake." The expression is famous as the slogan for the Hollywood Metro-Goldwyn-Mayer studio since 1916, when publicist Howard Dietz introduced it along with the Metro-Goldwyn-Mayer lion. Dietz also invented the MGM slogan "More Stars Than There Are in Heaven." Neither slogan is entirely accurate.

Name Changes

A Hollywood producer urged director Elia Kazan to change his last name to Cézanne when he first came to Hollywood from Broadway. "But Cézanne is the name of a French artist," Kazan protested. "Never mind," said the producer. "You make just one good picture and nobody will ever remember the other guy."

Another time actor Peter Lorre tried to convince producer Harry Cohn to make Dostoyevsky's *Crime and Punishment* into a film. He had the difficult story condensed into an outrageous page and a half synopsis and had Cohn read it while he waited. "Why, this is fine, fine," Cohn said when he finished. "We can change the title. But tell me one thing. Has this story got a publisher yet?"

Eugene O'Neill's play *Ah, Wilderness!* (1933) was originally entitled *Oh, Wilderness!* by the author, who took his title from a line in the *Rubaiyat* of Omar Khayyám. But O'Neill's only comedy, which featured George M. Cohan as the father and which critic George Jean Nathan called "the tenderest and most amusing comedy of boyhood in American drama," saw its name changed before it went on the boards. Its producers changed the title to *Ah, Wilderness!* so that it would be placed at the top of the alphabetical play listings in the newspapers of the day.

The Mink-Lined Rut: Writing for Hollywood

- Hollywood screenwriter Nunnally Johnson (1897–1977), whose films include the classic *The Three Faces of Eve* (1957), was asked how he'd manage writing for the new wide screen. "Very simple," he replied. "I'll just put the paper in sideways."

- Herman J. Mankiewicz's (1897–1953) drinking problem and sharp, irreverent tongue—which cost him several Hollywood jobs—caused his wife much trouble. One time a friend who hadn't seen the couple in several months asked the screenwriter, "How's Sara?"
  "Sara who?" Mankiewicz replied, acting puzzled.
  "Sara. Your wife, Sara."
  "Ah, you mean Poor Sara."

- Anita Loos (1893–1981) wrote her famous *Gentlemen Prefer Blondes* in 1925 as a spoof of her good friend H. L. Mencken's taste for "dumb blondes." Loos wrote over one hundred silent-movie scripts for D. W. Griffith's Biograph Company and wrote the titles for Griffith's masterpiece, *Intolerance* (1916). She got her start as a screenwriter by mailing an unsolicited script to Griffith. One time on returning to Hollywood and scriptwriting from New York, Loos quipped, "Well, back to the mink-lined rut."

- Poet and humorist Samuel Gordon Hoffenstein (1890–1947) worked for years as a Hollywood scenarist, moving from New York to Los Angeles and doing the screen adaptations of *An American Tragedy* and *Sentimental Journey*, among other novels. Once an interviewer inquired about his lot in Hollywood, expecting a self-pitying reply. "In the movies we writers work our brains to the bone and what do we get for it?" Hoffenstein asked. Then he answered his own question: "A lousy fortune."

Screenwriter's Pay

Writers were usually paid five dollars for a movie story idea throughout the first decade of the century. The story was then improvised from the idea by the director, who never used a written script. By 1913, however, writers were being paid ten times as much for an idea, writers were given credits, and at least three technical scriptwriting or "photoplay" manuals had been published. That year, one Italian film company offered an international prize of about $5,000 for any original screen idea. Soon established authors like Jack London were sought out and rewarded handsomely for their work, but a problem had already emerged that may never be resolved to the satisfaction of writers. As one screenwriting manual put it: "All authority has been given to the director . . . all manuscripts are subject to his interpretation, alteration, and elimination . . . often actors en masse have had no further intimation of what they were doing than the vociferous bellowings of a director beyond the camera. Thus was the writer deprived of his most necessary ally in the interpretation of his finer dramatic ideas."

Highest Paid "Screenwriter"

There are still thousands of Americanisms that are different from British English expressions, though these have dwindled with the spread of movies, television, and increased foreign travel. A good example of such differences is found in a story about plain old tunafish. The highest word rate ever paid to a screenwriter is the $15,000 producer Darryl F. Zanuck gave American author James Jones for correcting a line of dialogue in the film *The Longest Day*. Jones and his wife, Gloria, were sitting on the beach when they changed the line "I can't eat this bloody old box of tunny fish," to "I can't stand this damned old tunafish." That works out to three word changes at $5,000 a word.

Thomas Dixon's novel *The Clansman*, used by D. W. Griffith as the basis for *The Birth of a Nation*, earned several million dollars when Dixon accepted a 25 percent interest in the film instead of the $7,500 that Griffith owed him for the story and was unable to pay.

The One and Only

Though he was bored by Hollywood, author and drama critic Robert Benchley (1889–1945) is the only writer ever to win an Academy Award for a film he starred in. His *How to Sleep*, which he wrote and performed alone, won the 1936 Academy Award for the best live-action short subject.

Hollywood Holdouts

Among the thousands of writers who have written for the movies are such giants as William Faulkner, F. Scott Fitzgerald, George Bernard Shaw, Theodore Dreiser, Aldous Huxley, Thornton Wilder, John Steinbeck, Maxwell Anderson, Clifford Odets, George S. Kaufman, Nathanael West, John O'Hara, Dorothy Parker, and Lillian Hellman. But though Hollywood lured great writers with the promise of gold, many resisted the temptation for various reasons. Willa Cather, for example, was so incensed about the Hollywood film made from her novel *A Lost Lady* (1923) that she stipulated in her will that her work could never again "be adapted for the screen, stage, radio, television, or any new medium which hereafter may be discovered or perfected."

Playwright George S. Kaufman was so outraged at Paramount Picture's offer of $30,000 for the film rights to one of his plays that he countered by offering $40,000 for *Paramount*.

Eugene O'Neill's response to a request for him to write a screenplay as a vehicle for sex symbol Jean Harlow is perhaps the most unequivocal refusal in the history of the movies. A cable had been sent to him requesting his services and asking for a collect reply in no more than twenty words. The playwright cabled back:

No No No No No No No
No No No No No No No
No No No No No O'Neill

With Faulkner in Hollywood

Director Howard Hawks bet Ernest Hemingway that he could make a film out of what he considered the author's worst book, "That goddamned piece of junk . . . *To Have and Have Not*."

"You can't make a picture out of that," Hemingway replied.

"OK," Hawks said, "I'll get Faulkner to do it. He can write better than you anyway."

William Faulkner took the screenplay assignment and the film was completed in 1945, though neither he nor the picture was nominated for Academy Awards.

The most famous screenwriter story about Faulkner has him asking his producers one day if he could leave the office and finish his work at home. Several days passed and Faulkner was nowhere to be found in Hollywood. Finally his agent located him in Oxford, Mississippi, and demanded to know why he was there. "Well, Ah asked mah producer if Ah could work at home," he explained, "and he said fine, so heah Ah am."

Cleaning out Faulkner's desk soon after he left the Warner Brothers writing factory, coworkers found the fruits of his labor: an empty whiskey bottle and a piece of paper on which he had written, more than five hundred times, *Boy meets girl.*

Famous Novelists Nominated for Screenwriting Oscars

Many excellent screenwriters, playwrights (George Bernard Shaw, Robert Sherwood, Tennessee Williams, William Saroyan), and even one songwriter (Irving Berlin) have been nominated for screenwriting Oscars. But can you name the ten Oscar nominations that have gone to writers primarily known as novelists? Only one novelist actually won the Oscar.

Answers:

1. John Steinbeck (*Lifeboat*, 1944)
2. Raymond Chandler (*Double Indemnity*, 1944)
3. John Steinbeck (*A Medal for Benny*, 1945)
4. Raymond Chandler (*The Blue Dahlia*, 1947)
5. John Steinbeck (*Viva Zapata!*, 1953)
6. Eric Ambler (*The Cruel Sea*, 1953)
7. Vladimir Nabokov (*Lolita*, 1962)
8. Mario Puzo (*The Godfather*, 1972)
9. Mario Puzo (*The Godfather: Part II*, 1974)
10. Pat Conroy (*The Prince of Tides*, 1991)

Mario Puzo was the only novelist to win an Oscar, and he won for both his nominations, sharing both prizes with director Francis Ford Coppola.

Not That Big

A Hollywood screenwriter, cornering Thomas Mann at a party, continually put himself down in comparison to the Nobel Prize–winning German writer. He was nothing compared to Mann, the screenwriter went on; his scripts were feeble, he was a mere hack, a zero, a nonentity. Mann, the epitome of politeness, listened until the writer left and then turned to his host. "That man has no right to make himself so small," he said. "He is not that big."

Out There with Dorothy Parker

American author, critic, and screenwriter Dorothy Parker (1893–1967) surely ranks with Oscar Wilde, George Bernard Shaw, Richard Brinsley Sheridan, and several others as one of the ten greatest literary wits in history. Born

Dorothy Rothschild in what is now Long Branch, New Jersey, she married Eddie Parker in 1917, kept her married name after their divorce, and was commonly called Miss Parker. It is often forgotten that Dorothy Parker was nominated for original screenplay Oscars for *Smash-Up: The Story of a Woman* (1947), losing to Valentine Davies's *Miracle on 34th Street*, and for *A Star Is Born* (1937). She certainly had the sharpest tongue in Hollywood, a town she was forced to work in but always hated.

- One bright afternoon, as a notoriously stupid Hollywood producer swaggered by on the street, Dorothy Parker commented to a companion, "He hasn't got enough sense to bore assholes in wooden hobbyhorses."

- For a time Miss Parker worked as a writer for Metro-Goldwyn-Mayer, a Hollywood studio not then noted for its kind treatment of writers. One afternoon she threw open a window in the little cottage Metro provided her and screamed to passersby, "Let me out of here! Let me out of here! I'm as sane as you are!"

- "Don't you think she ought to wear a brassiere in this scene?" a producer asked her, pointing at his leading lady.
   "God, no," Miss Parker replied. "You've got to have something in this movie that moves."

- Miss Parker was asked to leave William Randolph Hearst's palatial San Simeon estate, either for drinking or for sleeping with another guest. Thinking this hypocritical, since Hearst drank and loved there with his mistress, actress Marion Davies, she wrote the following in the visitors' book on leaving:

   Upon my honor,
   I saw a Madonna
   Standing in a niche,
   Above the door
   Of the famous whore
   Of a prominent son of a bitch.

- She took one of her dogs to a Hollywood party that she found "dreadfully boring." When the dog upchucked on the carpet, she turned to her hostess and explained, "It's the company."

- Summoned to appear before the House of Representatives Un-American Activities Committee in 1952, she spent the evening before the dreaded day in a Washington, D.C., bar. There a loudmouth annoyed her, voicing his approval of Hollywood producers who worked "against the Reds." Miss Parker rose and stared at him icily. "With the crown of thorns I'm wearing," she said as she turned and left, "why should I be bothered with a prick like you?"

Hollywood's Hardest Critic

Among the greatest of hard-boiled American wits, Wilson Mizner (1876–1933), who had been a carnival barker, cardsharp, and boxer, wrote Broadway plays and at least one screenplay. But he is best remembered for his trenchant one-liners about Hollywood:

- "Working for Warner Brothers is like fucking a porcupine—it's one hundred pricks against one."
- To a sneaky movie producer: "You're just a mouse studying to be a rat."
- To another movie producer: "A demitasse cup would fit over your brain like a sunbonnet."
- On Hollywood in general: "It's a trip through a sewer in a glass-bottomed boat."
- "I've spent years in Hollywood and still think all the movie heroes are in the audience."
- "Some of the greatest love affairs I've known involved one actor, unassisted."
- Of a larcenous studio mogul: "He's the only man I ever knew who has rubber pockets so he can steal soup."
- To a Hollywood gossip columnist on the radio: "If you don't get off the air, I'll stop breathing it."
- To a much-married actress who finally married into royalty: "You're nothing but a parlayed chambermaid; you've compromised so many gentlemen that you think you're a lady."
- And in uncharacteristic charity: "Be nice to people on your way up because you'll meet 'em on your way down."

More Hollywood Put-Downs

"It's hard to tell where Hollywood ends and the DTs begin."
—*W. C. Fields*

After Jimmy Stewart made *The Spirit of St. Louis* (1957), a reporter asked if he had minded talking to a fly in the scenes where Charles Lindberg was making his historic flight over the Atlantic. A spokesman for the actor forwarded this answer to the reporter:

> "Mr. Stewart does not mind speaking to insects. After all, he has been dealing with agents and producers all his life."

> "Don't be surprised if you get a wire from me that I have broken my contract, bombed the studio, or been arrested for public gibbering. Don't be surprised at all." —*from a Hollywood letter to a friend by the author Stephen Vincent Benét*

> "Hollywood impresses me as being ten million dollars worth of intricate and highly ingenious machinery functioning elaborately to put skin on baloney." —*drama critic George Jean Nathan*

> "All the sincerity in Hollywood can be put into a gnat's navel and you'd still have room for three caraway seeds and an agent's heart." —*Fred Allen*

"The Poor Son of a Bitch": The Movie Career of F. Scott Fitzgerald

His great work was certainly his novels and short stories, several of which were made into movies, but F. Scott Fitzgerald (1896–1940) spent many years as a screenwriter in Hollywood, especially toward the end of his tragically short life when he was battling poverty and the bottle. Fitzgerald's early Hollywood years were glittering, zany, crazy ones. Bathing naked in a public fountain, chewing up banknotes and spitting them out a cab window, turning cartwheels and somersaults down crowded streets, stealing all the women's purses at a party and boiling them together in a large pot—there was no end to the often juvenile antics of Scott and his wife, Zelda Fitzgerald. Among the craziest was their drunken pursuit one night of the handsome author John Mark Saunders, considered by Zelda to be too much of a ladies' man. Finally finding Saunders's Hollywood home, the pair, accompanied by two friends, knocked on the door and the hospitable Saunders let them in, getting everybody drinks. Zelda proceeded to sit down beside him on the couch, pull open his robe, sniff deeply, and invite Scott over to do the same because "John smells lovely!" Both of them sat on opposite sides of Saunders, noses sunk in his chest hair, sniffing. Zelda next took up a pair of scissors and urged Saunders to let her castrate him, explaining that then all his women problems would be over. Saunders, with patience deserving an Oscar, merely smiled and politely refused.

Years later Fitzgerald preserved this true Hollywood success story in his notebook. A famous producer was asked a favor by a man he hardly knew: he had only to call the man by his first name and slap him on the back while they stood in the studio commissary. Having the man's record traced and finding nothing amiss, the producer obliged him. "The man ascended into Heaven," Fitzgerald noted. "Almost literally, for he was taken into one of the best agencies—which is what George Gershwin referred to when he said, 'It's nice work if you can get it.' He sits there today, with a picture of his wife and children on the wall, and has his nails manicured at the Beverly Hills Hotel. His life is one long happy dream."

Among the unused notes for Fitzgerald's *The Last Tycoon*, his novel about Hollywood and brilliant producer Irving Thalberg, is the true story of "a really appalling woman" and how she failed in her attempt to give damaging court testimony against "X," a Hollywood producer. A day before his case came to trial X rounded up a dwarf and two nondescript performers and sent them to the woman—each of them delivering outlandish messages to her about the case. The next day X had his attorney open his defense by stating that the woman was mentally unbalanced. Sure enough, when she was called to the stand she quickly launched into the story of her strange visitors and their messages. X won his case. As Fitzgerald put it, "the jury shook their heads, winked at each other and acquitted."

In the last two years of his life Fitzgerald was a ghost of his former ebullient self. Drinking Coca-Cola by the case instead of alcohol, he tried to conserve all his energy in order to finish his work. He wrote *The Last Tycoon* in bed for this reason, though a fatal heart attack prevented him from finishing it. During these last terrible years in Tinseltown a Hollywood director put a pudgy finger in his face and remarked, "Pay *you*. Why, you ought to pay *us*."

Paying her respects as Fitzgerald lay in a Hollywood funeral parlor, Dorothy Parker remembered the words of the anonymous mourner at Jay Gatsby's funeral in *The Great Gatsby*. "The poor son of a bitch!" was all she said as she filed by the coffin.

Blacklisted

During the Hollywood blacklist years, when some screenwriters lost their jobs because of their political beliefs or codes of honor, writer Walter Bernstein used the pseudonym "Bob Rogers" for a script he did for one studio. The studio, dissatisfied with the script, turned it over to screenwriter Dick Jones for rewriting. "Dick Jones" was still another pseudonym Bernstein used.

Down to the Folds of Their Clothes: The First Directors

Ancient Greece's great tragic playwrights—Aeschylus, Sophocles, Euripides—could be said to be directors in a rough sense of the word. These immortal playwrights not only conceived their dramas, they taught the actors the poetry, originated costumes and scenery, and invented the choral dances. But Greek drama was still largely collective. The first director in the modern sense of the word is said to have been George II, duke of Saxe-Meiningen, who in 1874 organized an amateur troupe in his small German duchy and brought it to Berlin, fashioning realistic productions out of disciplined coordinated ensemble acting. The first true master of the art of production, the duke designed all his sets, costumes, and every movement and gesture of every play he directed. As one critic put it: "He dictated the very folds of every costume. Every member of the small troupe had to sacrifice his individuality to the total production; those who refused were dismissed from the company." Later, Konstantin Stanislavsky, who became the greatest of naturalistic directors, began his career by emulating the style and methods of the duke of Saxe-Meiningen, though Stanislavsky branched out in new directions.

The Most Sadistic Director

Physically, at least, the marquis de Sade (Comte Donatien-Alphonse-François de Sade) seems to have been one of the beautiful people, a handsome little man. Actually, various descriptions of the miniature aristocrat exist. One writer gives him "blue eyes and blonde well-kept hair," another "a delicate pale face from which two great black eyes glared," and a third tells us that he was "of such startling beauty that even in his early youth all the ladies that saw him stood stock still in rapt admiration."

Unfortunately, there is no authentic portrait of de Sade, but one might expect the probable descendant of the Laura made famous in Petrarch's immortal love poems four centuries before to present a striking appearance.

However, from 1777 on, de Sade spent all but thirteen of his remaining thirty-seven years in prison or in the lunatic asylum at Charenton.

While imprisoned he began writing the novels and plays that give his name to the language. Among his works are *The 120 Days of Sodom* (1785), in which six hundred variations of the sex instinct are listed, *Justine, or Good Conduct Well Chastised* (1790), and *The Story of Juliette, or Vice Amply Rewarded* (1792), all replete with myriad descriptions of sexual cruelty. Never able or willing to reform, de Sade died in 1814 at the age of seventy-four, while still at Charenton, where he wrote and directed fashionable plays performed by the inmates.

Extremely Meticulous Research

The screenwriter who researched the film *De Sade* (1974) in Hamburg's notorious red-light district submitted an expense account including such items as "a party for 69 prostitutes, $430 . . . a farewell dinner for 21 masochists and 21 sadists, $300 . . . and rest cure in Garmisch-Partenkirchen, $1,850."

A Fallen King: America's Greatest Director

David Wark Griffith (1875–1948), later director of *The Birth of a Nation* (1915), was hired by Edwin S. Porter, head of Edison studio, to make his first film, *The Adventures of Dolly*, in 1908. Over the next five years D. W. Griffith directed more than five hundred nine-minute one-reelers for Biograph Studio, making every kind of movie from Westerns and thrillers to costume dramas and comedies while perfecting his craft. Even before he made *The Birth of a Nation* he was considered America's top director, introducing such devices as the close-up and fade-out.

The Birth of a Nation, a story of the South during and after the Civil War, was based on the novel *The Clansman* (1905) by Thomas Dixon, a Baptist minister whose writings favored the Ku Klux Klan. In fact, Dixon wrote the picture's screenplay. The film was the first American large-screen spectacle and a hit everywhere, becoming one of the most profitable movies of all time. "But Griffith's stylistic and technical innovations had even more influence upon the cinema's future," one critic wrote. Despite its offensive treatment of American blacks the film remains an authentic masterpiece.

Griffith's next masterpiece, the epic *Intolerance* (1916), told stories of intolerances in four different historical periods. But, too far ahead of its time, it failed at the box-office and ruined Griffith financially. Several great pictures followed, including *Hearts of the World* (1918) and *Orphans of the Storm* (1921), but his work deteriorated and by the early 1930s he was out of films forever, a broken and bitter man. He lived another eighteen years. Author James Salter described him living his last years alone in a faded Hollywood hotel: "He was a metaphor for the fabled life: staggering triumph, praise, Babylonian splendor, rejection, a fallen king."

Barrymore's Last Director

Raoul Walsh, who began his career as an actor and assistant director for D. W. Griffith, made such famous films as *What Price Glory* (1926), *Sadie Thompson* (1928), *They Died with Their Boots On* (1941), *Gentleman Jim* (1942), and *The Revolt of Mamie Stover* (1956). He directed Humphrey Bogart, Errol Flynn, Clark Gable, and Gary Cooper, among many great stars, and was close friends with all of them. Walsh wasn't above a practical joke, however. When John Barrymore died, Errol Flynn, a great admirer of his, took it very badly. Walsh drove over to the funeral home where Barrymore was laid out and found that one of the owners was an actor who used to work in his pictures. "What can I do for you, Mr. Walsh?" he asked, and Walsh said, "I'd like to borrow Barrymore's body for two hours, I want to take him somewhere to surprise somebody." The mortician, loaded to the gills, finally agreed and they both slid Barrymore, stiff as a board, into Walsh's station wagon. Walsh drove over to Flynn's house. Flynn wasn't home but his Russian valet, Alex, came out. Then, in Walsh's words:

> *I said, "Alex, Mr. Barrymore didn't die, he's drunk. Help me carry him in the house." Hell, the dumb Russian helped me carry him in and we sat him on the couch there. And he said, "He's terrible, isn't he?" "You bet your ass he's terrible." Sat him on the couch and we had a hard time putting his legs down. I said, "Push harder!" We finally propped Barrymore up. Alex said, "I never saw so drunk a man." A little while and Flynn comes in, walked up . . . EHHHH!!! And he dashed out of the house and went and hid in the bushes. I went out and called him and said, "Come on in." He said, "No, what the hell have you done?" I said, "Well you missed the old boy and I brought him up here. At least come in and say hello to him." "No, I'm not going in there," [he said]. I said, "All right, c'mon, Alex, let's get him back before he falls asleep." Got Alex to put the guy back in the station wagon and back to Malloy Brothers, and the guy was waiting. "Where the hell did you take him, Mr. Walsh?" [he said]. I said, "I took him up to Errol Flynn's." He said, "Why the hell didn't you tell me? I'd a put a better suit on him."*

When making the silent-movie classic *What Price Glory*, Walsh filmed a scene with the two main characters cursing at each other, using terms like "You dirty son of a bitch, you lousy bastard, you prick," etc. For the titles, of course, innocuous euphemisms like "You're not a pal of mine" were printed on the screen. But after the film premiered at New York's Roxy Theatre, the studio received hundreds of letters from lip-readers complaining about the "disgusting language" that was used. This apparently did the film no harm at the box office. In fact, word of mouth about the lipreading helped *What Price Glory* earn back its production cost in two weeks. As for the controversial "profanity," *What Price Glory*, written by Maxwell Anderson and Laurence Stallings, had been acclaimed as a landmark in the theater's battle for honesty and genuine speech when it first appeared as a play two years earlier. Critic Alexander Woollcott wrote, "No war play written in the English language . . . has been so true, so alive, so salty, and so richly satisfying."

Off the Cuff

The expression *off the cuff*, for "unrehearsed or extemporaneous," probably derives from impromptu notes early Hollywood directors jotted down on their shirt cuffs while shooting a difficult scene in a movie. These ideas, not in the script, were conveyed to the actors when the scene was reshot.

Longest-Lasting Director

American director King Vidor had the longest directorial career of any movie director. The Texas-born Vidor's career lasted sixty-seven years, from his first silent two-reeler, *Hurricane in Galveston* (1913)—which he and a friend made using a camera made out of cigar boxes and parts of a movie projector—to a short documentary called *The Metaphor* that he made in 1980, at the age of eighty-six. In between, the versatile Vidor made a score of films, including such powerful classics as *The Big Parade*, *The Crowd*, *The Champ*, *Our Daily Bread*, *Stella Dallas*, *The Fountainhead*, *Ruby Gentry*, *Duel in the Sun*, and epics like *War and Peace* and *Solomon and Sheba*. A master of melodrama, he successfully made the transition from silent to sound movies. Vidor even directed parts of *The Wizard of Oz* after his friend Victor Fleming left the film to take over direction of *Gone with the Wind*. Though his name isn't in the credits, he directed the "Somewhere over the Rainbow" and "We're off to See the Wizard" scenes, among others.

Vidor, who died at the age of eighty-eight in 1982, isn't the oldest director to make a film. This honor goes to the Dutch director Joris Ivens (1898–1989), who made the French movie *Une Histoire de Vent* in 1988 when eighty-nine. Hollywood's George Cukor (1900–83) should also be mentioned. Cukor, who directed fifty movies, made his last (*Rich and Famous*) in 1981 at age eighty-one.

Young Directors

A great number of actors made their stage and screen debuts as babes in arms or young children, but the youngest director of a professionally made film in theater history is Sydney Ling (b. 1959) who wrote, produced, and directed the feature-length movie *Lex the Wonderdog* in 1972 when he was only thirteen. The youngest director of a film featuring well-known stars was Steven Paul (b. 1960), who produced and directed *Falling in Love Again* starring Elliott Gould and Susannah York in 1980, when he was twenty years old.

Filmdom's Master of Suspense

A customs official once asked Alfred Hitchcock his occupation. "Producer," Hitchcock said. "What do you produce?" the official asked. "Gooseflesh," Hitchcock replied.

Producing goosebumps did indeed make the British-born American film director popular with movie and TV audiences everywhere. Hitchcock is one of the few film directors "whose movies are sold on his name alone" as his fellow director Peter Bogdanovich noted. Possibly only Charlie Chaplin, Orson Welles, and Steven Spielberg—whose films have grossed well over $5 billion by now, making him the world's most financially successful director—come close to him in this respect.

But if Hitchcock, with his trademark appearances on television and walk-ons in most of his fifty-odd films, remains even after his death the world's most popular director, he also ranks among the great masters of film. Born in London in 1897 and educated at a Jesuit prep school, he was trained as an engineer and worked in silent pictures as a scenario writer and production manager for several years before he made his first movie, *The Pleasure Garden* (1925). Nine more silent films followed, including *The Lodger* (1926) and *Blackmail* (1929), both accomplished works. Of his sound films in the next decade, *The Man Who Knew Too Much* (1934), *The Thirty-Nine Steps* (1935), and *The Secret Agent* (1936) are considered the best. Beginning in the 1940s came more than thirty years of notable films, including among many others *Rebecca* (1940), *Shadow of a Doubt* (1943), *Spellbound* (1945), *Notorious* (1946), *Strangers on a Train* (1951), *Rear Window* (1954), *Vertigo* (1958), *Psycho* (1960), and *The Birds* (1963)—the last three usually considered his greatest works.

At least ten or so of Hitchcock's films appear on many "100 Greatest Films" lists. His *Rebecca* won an Oscar for best picture, but though he was nominated five times (for *Rebecca, Lifeboat, Spellbound, Rear Window,* and *Psycho*) he never won an Oscar for best director. Nevertheless, he was far more than a jolly punning fat man with a taste for the macabre. He remains one of the greatest craftsmen in the history of cinema, a master of the psychology and mechanics of suspense. In fact, his name has given us the term *Hitchcock ending* for an often ironic, surprise ending characteristic of the films, plenteous television plays, short-story anthologies, and magazine stories he directed, sponsored, collected, and published over his long career. Hitchcock died in 1980, age eighty-one. Stories abound about the great director.

- Hitchcock confirmed the old story that his father, a London greengrocer, sent him with a note to the local chief of police when he was a child. After reading the note, the chief had him locked in a jail cell for five minutes, finally letting him out with the warning "That's what we do to naughty boys." This incident instilled in him a morbid fear of the police. The reason he never learned to drive, he revealed, is "the simple fact that if you don't drive a car you can't get a ticket." Such personal fears, apparent in his films, can also be attributed to the cruel punishments he suffered at the Jesuit school he attended.

- Hitchcock became a director "entirely because a particular cameraman had curried favor with the director and the director said he didn't want me on his next picture. It was then I was asked would I like to be a director, which hadn't occurred to me. I was maneuvered deliberately away from my job and I knew who it was and how it was done. It happens in our business all the time. I used to say, 'Well one thing they can't take away from me is my talent.'"

- He defined pure cinema as "complementary pieces of film put together like notes of music to make a melody."

- The plump director was said to be a prodigious trencherman. In any case, Hitchcock, as his famous profile attested, was fond of food. One time he was invited to a dinner where the fare was decidedly unsubstantial. While coffee was being served his hostess said, "I do hope that you will dine here again, Mr. Hitchcock."

"By all means," said the director. "Let's start right now."

- One time Hitchcock telephoned the prolific Belgian novelist Georges Simenon, who wrote his books at incredible speed, sometimes in as little as ten days. Simenon's wife took the call. "I'm sorry," she said, "but Georges is writing and I can't disturb him."

 "Let him finish his book," Hitchcock replied. "I'll hang on."

- He bought the movie rights to *Psycho* for a bargain $9,000, then proceeded to buy up all the copies of the book he could to keep the ending of the film a secret.

- "You've often been quoted as saying 'actors are cattle,'" a reporter once asked him. "Is this true?"

 "I never said that!" he replied indignantly. "What I said was 'Actors should be *treated like* cattle.'"

Directorial Assist

Robert Walker, the star of director Leo McCarey's *My Son John*, died before the film was completed. Walker had already recorded lines in which his character confesses his crime to the FBI. This enabled McCarey to fashion a picture-ending death scene for the Walker character, but he had no film of the character dead or dying. His friend Alfred Hitchcock came to his aid, supplying him film from his classic *Strangers on a Train*, in which the psychotic character Walker plays dies beneath a carousel. McCarey removed the carousel from the shot and worked the dead Walker character into a wrecked taxicab shot, finishing his movie.

The Macguffin

Hitchcock defined his famous *macguffin* while talking about his film *Notorious* (1946):

> So the question arose, in designing the story for the film, what were the Germans up to down in Rio, what were they doing there? And I thought of the idea that they were collecting samples of uranium 235 from which the future atom bomb would be made. So the producer said, "Oh, that's a bit far-fetched—what atom bomb?" I said, "Well, both sides are looking for it . . . [but] if you don't like uranium 235, let's make it industrial diamonds. But it makes no difference, it's what we call the "macguffin." . . . The

macguffin is the thing the spies are after, but the audience doesn't care. *It could be the plans of a fort, the secret plans of an airplane engine.*

The Countdown

In his early science-fiction film *Lady in the Moon* Vienna-born director Fritz Lang (1890–1976) invented the word *countdown* for a rocket launch. "[If] I count one, two, three, four," he later recalled, "an audience doesn't know when it will go off. But if I count down . . . five, four, three, two, one, ZERO—then they will know."

Lang made several brilliant movies distinguished by their use of wonderful special effects. His film *The Last Will of Dr. Mabuse* (1932) was confiscated by the Nazis because of its antigovernment content, and though Joseph Goebbels later offered him the post of head of the German film industry, he fled to America. He had a long and prolific career here, including his collaboration with Bertold Brecht on *Hangmen Also Die* (1943), but after *Beyond a Reasonable Doubt* (1956), he grew disgusted with the studio system and quit making films in the United States.

Awesome Orson

A prodigy of the theater and movies who acted as a child and was writing plays (never produced) at the age of nine or so, Orson Welles made his first film, the four-minute piece *The Hearts of Age*, in 1933 when only eighteen, but the *wunderkind* first came to public attention that same year when he performed with Katharine Cornell as the lively, cynical Mercutio in *Romeo and Juliet*. Welles directed many admired plays for the Depression-era Federal Theater Project, including *Dr. Faustus* and an all-black *Macbeth*, before founding the Mercury Theater with John Housman.

After precipitating panic throughout America with his realistic impression of a Martian landing on earth in a 1938 radio play based on H. G. Wells's *War of the Worlds*, Welles took his Mercury company to Hollywood, where he began making a dozen or so movies, including such masterpieces as *Citizen Kane* (1941), *The Magnificent Ambersons* (1942), *Macbeth* (1948), *Othello* (1952), *Touch of Evil* (1958), *The Trial* (1963), and *Chimes at Midnight* (1966). He also became well known for his imposing presence in popular films like *The Third Man*, in which he played the Harry Lime character.

Welles's fame rests mainly on *Citizen Kane*, which is almost invariably included, often in the top spot, on authoritative lists of the ten best films of all time. It is by far the best of Welles's movies, a mixture of extravagance, realism, and poetic purity like nothing that had been seen before, from its haunting opening depiction of Xanadu to the final close-up of Kane's hand holding the glass ball while he murmurs "Rosebud." As for Welles's technique in the picture, one critic called it "an instant treasury of new solutions to old problems."

But though *Citizen Kane* was an artistic triumph, it fared poorly at the box office, owing in large part to Kane's resemblance to William Randolph Hearst, whose newspapers caused so much trouble that RKO had to bypass the usual distribution channels. Never again did Hollywood give Welles the complete control that made *Kane* possible. Much of Welles's remaining work was done in Europe.

Welles could be dictator as well as director. It was his intention to "modernize" the Lord's Prayer for a religious movie in which he was to appear as the deity. "You can't do that," one of his writers said, "it's God's word." "Don't tell me about God's word," Welles insisted. "I am God." Another time he stared out at a tiny audience from a theater stage in Wisconsin. "What a pity it is," he said, "that there are so few of you and so many of me."

Welles often defended his early theatrical experiments against radio ad-agency executives. After one broadcast an account executive argued that background sound effects drowned out the dialogue. "You object to the fact that the background predominated in a certain scene," Welles countered. *"Well who told you it was the background?"*

Welles was particularly innovative in creating sound effects for his radio plays. In *The Count of Monte Cristo*, for example, to create the effect of a dank prison cell he had the scene played in the studio bathroom, "where the dripping toilet water created the desired ambience."

Orson George Welles died in 1985, age seventy, leaving behind a body of work rarely matched in the theater or cinema. It was thought at one time that he had wasted his talents or burned out early, like many prodigies, but his brilliant and diverse work remains as proof that this is far from true.

Action!

Superstar Clint Eastwood is one of many actors who have put on another hat and directed films. Eastwood never shouts "Action!" when he starts a scene, opening with a casual "OK" instead. "I learned years ago on [the TV series] 'Rawhide,'" he once told a reporter, "that when you say 'Action!'—it sends adrenaline through the actors. Even horses get very hip to the word. They know something's about to happen. Up in the saddle, the actor squeezes the horse, and the horse jumps out of the shot. Then you have to start over."

A Great Director's Quiz

Many directors are considered—or consider themselves—the all-important auteurs (or authors) of their films, but relatively few moviegoers can identify them with even their most famous works. Listed below are some of the best-known movies of fifty world-famous American and foreign directors. See how many you can match with their directors. A score of 50 percent is excellent; 100 percent is unbelieveable.

1. Lawrence of Arabia
2. The Servant
3. To Be or Not to Be
4. Star Wars
5. The Godfather
6. Psycho
7. What Price Glory? (silent film)
8. Meet Me in St. Louis
9. It's a Wonderful Life
10. Raging Bull
11. Jaws
12. L'Avventura
13. Last Tango in Paris
14. The Young and the Damned
15. Shadows
16. Z
17. Breathless (black and white)
18. A Star Is Born (with Judy Garland)
19. The Ten Commandments (silent film)
20. Dressed to Kill
21. La Strada
22. The Birth of a Nation
23. The Sting
24. The Treasure of the Sierra Madre
25. On the Waterfront
26. Paths of Glory
27. Rashomon
28. Hangmen Also Die
29. Bonnie and Clyde
30. The Wild Bunch
31. Chinatown
32. Laura
33. Pather Panchali
34. La Grande Illusion
35. Hiroshima Mon Amour
36. Rome—Open City
37. The Blue Angel
38. The 400 Blows
39. The Big Parade
40. Some Like It Hot
41. The Best Years of Our Lives
42. High Noon
43. The Quiet Man
44. The Grapes of Wrath
45. Wings
46. Citizen Kane
47. The Virgin Spring
48. The Pawnbroker
49. Odd Man Out
50. The Bicycle Thief

Answers:

1. David Lean
2. Joseph Losey
3. Ernst Lubitsch
4. George Lucas
5. Francis Ford Coppola
6. Alfred Hitchcock
7. Raoul Walsh
8. Vincente Minnelli
9. Frank Capra
10. Martin Scorsese
11. Steven Spielberg
12. Michelangelo Antonioni
13. Bernardo Bertolucci
14. Luis Buñuel
15. John Cassavetes
16. Costa-Gavras
17. Jean-Luc Godard
18. George Cukor
19. Cecil B. DeMille
20. Brian De Palma
21. Federico Fellini
22. D. W. Griffith
23. George Roy Hill
24. John Huston
25. Elia Kazan
26. Stanley Kubrick
27. Akira Kurosawa
28. Fritz Lang
29. Arthur Penn
30. Sam Peckinpah
31. Roman Polanski
32. Otto Preminger
33. Satyajit Ray
34. Jean Renoir
35. Alain Resnais
36. Roberto Rossellini
37. Josef von Sternberg
38. François Truffaut
39. King Vidor
40. Billy Wilder
41. William Wyler
42. Fred Zinnemann
43. John Ford
44. John Ford
45. William Wellman
46. Orson Welles
47. Ingmar Bergman
48. Sidney Lumet
49. Carol Reed
50. Vittorio De Sica

Directing the Feet

Labanotation is a little-known but important notation system that amounts to a graphic shorthand for dance, enabling a choreographer to delineate every possible movement of the human body individually or in ensemble. Introduced by its creator, Rudolf Laban, in his *Kinetographie Laban* (1928), labanotation was the first practical method capable of scoring the various complex movements and positions of an entire ballet or musical comedy. The Laban system amounts to a complete break with tradition from the old numbered-footprint dance plans familiar to us all. It dispenses entirely with the musical five-line horizontal staff, using a three-line vertical staff that is divided in the center. Code symbols on each side of the line indicate foot and leg movements, while symbols in parallel columns outside the lines pertain to all other body gestures. Every slight movement from toe to head can be noted, as well as their direction, timing, and force, and by grouping together the staffs for individual dancers an entire work can be "orchestrated."

Laban did for the dance what Guido d'Arezzo did for musical notation almost a thousand years before him. Prior to his system dancers had to rely on their memories of performers who had appeared in classical ballets, but now almost exact revivals can be given, and ballet composers can finally adequately copyright their creations.

Born in Pressburg (Bratislava) on December 15, 1879, the German dance teacher and choreographer had a great influence on modern dance, with Mary Wigman and Kurt Jooss among his pupils. Rejecting nineteenth-century traditionalism, he tried to express industrialized urban life in his work, even experimenting with group improvisations, using masses of German factory workers after World War I. Laban wrote many books, including *Principles of Dance and Movement Notation* (1956). He died in London on July 1, 1958.

Alan Smithee

Just as "George Spelvin" is used in play or movie credits as the name of an actor playing a part anonymously, "Alan Smithee" is sometimes used as the name for a director or producer who desires anonymity. A recent film jokingly used the pseudonym as part of its title: *An Alan Smithee Film: Burn Hollywood Burn* (1998). (*See also* "George Spelvin," Chapter 2.)

Movie Anachronisms

> *Cecil B. DeMille*
> *Was feeling ill*
> *Because he couldn't put Moses*
> *In the Wars of the Roses*

This famous clerihew by Nicholas Bentley comments on filmmakers who often don't care about anachronisms in their epics. The word derives from Greek *ana chronos*, "out of time," "to be late," or "back-timing," and means an error in chronology, putting a person, event, or thing in the wrong time period. Sometimes this is done intentionally by an author to achieve verisimilitude and timelessness, or for humorous purposes, as in Mark Twain's *A Connecticut Yankee in King Arthur's Court*. Anachronisms have been common from Virgil to George Bernard Shaw. Some classic examples are Shakespeare's references to a striking clock in *Julius Caesar*, 1,400 years before such clocks were invented; his reference to billiards in *Antony and Cleopatra*; to cannon in *King John*; and to turkeys in *1 Henry IV*.

Shakespeare did not blunder, as is so often asserted, when he wrote of a seacoast in (landlocked) Bohemia. According to one biographer, "Under King Premysl Ottocar II (1258–78) the Kingdom of Bohemia stretched to the Adriatic Sea, and in 1526, upon the accession of the first Hapsburg to the throne of Bohemia, the realm of the King of Bohemia comprised the Archduchy of Austria, which bordered the Adriatic Sea between the territories of the Venetian Republic."

In movies there have been Roman soldiers wearing tennis shoes and wristwatches (*Spartacus*, 1960), a 1945 scene in *The Godfather* (1972) in which the American flag has fifty stars though there were only forty-eight states at the time, and TV antennas on houses in Victorian England (*The Wrong Box*, 1966), among many other examples. These do not include thousands of movie mistakes, such as a dead body moving in *Shane* or the bachelor in *Double Indemnity* wearing a wedding ring.

What Film Can Be

After a preview of his last film, *The Dead* (1987) based on James Joyce's short story, the director and screenwriter John Huston (1906–87) was asked by an interviewer if the picture had done what he wanted it to do. "Yes," he said. "It opens—finally, it opens up another door—and I think that's what Joyce intended. You walk through a series of arches, so to speak, and then, presently, at the end of a corridor, a door opens and you see backward through time, and you feel the flow of time, and realize that you're only part of a great endless procession."

V

ANIMAL ACTORS, CARTOON CHARACTERS, AND MOVIE MONSTERS

Ancient Animal Actors

Animal performers have appeared in dramas since earliest times, often in the cruelest of circumstances. The Romans, of course, held fights between wild animals and human prisoners in the Colosseum. Lions, tigers, crocodiles, giraffes, rhinoceroses, and other animals were imported from all over the world to fight one another or gladiators. The Colosseum was in fact dedicated with shows lasting a hundred days that featured nearly ten thousand animals killed in hunting scenes. One grisly theatrical thrill featured a criminal dressed as Orpheus ripped apart by bears, while in another a woman dressed as Europa was strapped to the back of a bull that tried to shake her loose.

Even before this, imitation of animals perhaps marked the beginning of drama itself. "The most primitive traces of human mime are certainly connected with hunting games or rituals," one nineteenth-century scholar writes.

> *The earliest reason for imitating an animal may have been a direct means of communication: at a stage when language is very inadequate, the returning hunter wants to describe what he has seen or done, and so acts out his adventures. But the acting soon becomes part of the hunt itself. Hunters either imitate the animal they are pursuing in order to stalk closer unobserved—by dressing in seal skins and flopping along the ice, for example,*

Eskimos can move much nearer to the seals than they can without these props. Or else the hunters play the part of another animal whose skill is hunting, expecting that sympathetic magic will enable them to borrow this animal's talents.

Such animal imitations were common well into the Middle Ages.

Wild Animals on the Legitimate Stage

While in medieval days animals were usually imitated on stage by using props such as heads and skins (including even an ingenious dromedary prop that "moved its mouth, opened its mouth, and stuck out its tongue"), real animals were used frequently by the seventeenth century. Among them was a lion that amazed London audiences by turning a roasting ox on a spit. Another was a lion trained to appear with a company of dogs; the suspense here was wondering when the lion would turn on and devour one of the canines.

A large menagerie was woven into the plot of *Hyder Ali, or The Lions of Mysore*. Years later *Gulliver on His Travels* (1876) boasted one scene using "three hundred girls, two hundred men, two hundred children, thirteen elephants, nine camels, and fifty-two horses, in addition to ostriches, emus, pelicans, deer of all kinds, kangaroos, Indian buffalos, Brahmin bulls, and, to crown the picture, two living lions led by the collar and chain into the center of the group."

It's a Dog's Life

British author and sometime producer Richard Brinsley Sheridan, who was among the greatest wits of all time, could be especially tough on actors. One of the biggest hits Sheridan produced at London's Drury Lane Theatre was Frederick Reynolds's play *The Caravan, or The Driver and His Dog* (1809), in which the trained dog Carlos jumped nightly into a pool to save a drowning child. After opening night, an elated Sheridan, sure he had a hit that would save him from financial ruin, rushed backstage shouting, "Where is my Preserver?" Reynolds modestly stepped forward to receive the great man's plaudits. "Pooh, not you—*the dog*!" Sheridan said. Another evening during *The Caravan*'s long run a principal actor ran up to Sheridan indicating that something terrible had happened. "What is it?" Sheridan asked. "I've lost my voice, can't you tell!" the actor finally managed. "Oh, is that all?" Sheridan replied. "I thought something had happened to the dog."

Animal Actors, Cartoon Characters, and Movie Monsters

Dog drama, starring performing dogs, was popular throughout the world in the nineteenth century. These melodramas were largely inspired by the success of Sheridan's *The Caravan*, though there had been performing dogs long before that. Guilbert de Pixérecourt (1773–1844), called the "Corneille of the Melodrama," wrote the most popular canine play. His *The Dog of Montargis* (1814) was translated into many languages. The great German author Johann Wolfgang von Goethe hated this play. When the duke of Weimar insisted on launching a production of it starring a poodle, a disgusted Goethe quit the Weimar Court Theater. Nevertheless, *The Dog of Montargis* was as celebrated as *Hamlet* in its day and the melodramatic plots of Pixérecourt (he was the first author to use the word *melodrama* in its present sense) entertained and inspired giants like Dumas *père* and Hugo.

Horse Operas or Hippodramas

The Hollywood term *horse opera* for a Western had another meaning a century ago when horses acted in *Hippodramas* on the stage, just as they do in the opera *Aida* and movies today. Some of the most spectacular equestrian performances included:

- Horses that danced on stage in horse ballets (*balletto a cavallo*) or performed in elaborate battle scenes. One critic said they were "trampling Shakespeare" out of existence.
- A horse that played Richard's steed, White Surrey, in a stage presentation of *Richard III* and another horse that played in *Macbeth*.
- Equestrian actors in stage dramas that revolved around horses, such as *Dick Turpin's Ride to York*; *Mazeppa*; *Timour the Tartar*; and *The Blood-Red Knight*.
- A sturdy horse that in the German play *Die Rauber in den Abruzzen* (1830) carried the hero up a pile of rocks on stage to the window of a house, while a ferocious dog attacked the villain downstage.
- A talented horse in an 1833 French play that, according to a viewer, "fired a pistol and then walked all about as if it was lame—and at last it laid down . . . and died—with its four legs in the air!"
- An early horse method actor. In 1843 the owners of the horse that played Rosinante in a French production of *Don Quixote* told the press that their steed had given up eating in order to better fit the part and look more like Don Quixote's old emaciated steed. When the horse died later that year, critic Théophile Gautier called it "a sad victim of the theatrical art."

Jumbo

JUMBO THE ONLY MASTODON ON EARTH . . . THE GENTLE AND HISTORIC LORD OF BEASTS . . . THE TOWERING MONARCH OF HIS MIGHTY RACE . . . THE PRODIGIOUS PET OF BOTH ENGLAND AND AMERICA . . . STEADILY GROWING IN TREMENDOUS HEIGHT AND WEIGHT . . . JUMBO, THE UNIVERSAL SYNONYM FOR STUPENDOUS THINGS . . .

Thus did P. T. Barnum, all in one handbill, advertise the only show business animal whose name did indeed become "the universal synonym for stupendous things." Barnum had purchased the fabled elephant from the London Zoological Garden in 1881 for "The Barnum and Bailey Greatest Show on Earth." Jumbo, captured by a hunting party in 1869, was one of the largest elephants ever seen in West Africa, the natives naming the six and a half ton beast from the Swahili *jumbo*, meaning "chief." He had become a great favorite in the London Zoo, giving rides to thousands of children, and his sale to the American showman caused quite an uproar. Not that this deterred Barnum. When his agent excitedly cabled that Jumbo was lying in a London street blocking traffic, Barnum replied, "Let him lie as long as he likes. Great advertisement." Within six weeks the incomparable P.T. had reaped $336,000 from his $30,000 investment. He made Jumbo's name a synonym for "huge" throughout America and the world. Billing the animal as a star attraction in his circus, he even persuaded Philadelphia merchants to call a shade of cloth *Jumbo gray*. Within a year after his purchase the elephant's name had become a household word. When Jumbo was accidentally killed in an Ontario, Canada, railroad yard in 1885, Barnum cried and much of the world wept with him.

Animal Vaudevillians

Dog acts were the most popular animal acts in vaudeville, one of the most highly trained being Coen's Dogs, who acted out a village scene without human guidance on stage. But dogs often performed as partners with geese, cockatoos, and their archenemies, cats—and got along with all of them splendidly. Other famous animal acts on stage included cats, horses, birds, monkeys, mules, seals, goats, and even elephants.

Long after vaudeville died many animal acts appeared on television variety shows. A mongrel called Benjy, who died in 1978, performed as a singer on *The Ed Sullivan Show* and *The Tonight Show*, among other engagements, wowing (or bow-wowing) audiences with his rendition of "Raindrops Keep Fallin' on My Head."

Animal Actors, Cartoon Characters, and Movie Monsters

Money the Master

A monkey named Clarabelle appeared in a picture with the great John Barrymore, who grew fond of the monkey and asked her trainer if he could buy her.

"How much do you make, Mr. Barrymore?" asked the trainer.

"Three thousand a week," Barrymore replied.

"Well, Clarabelle likes you, too," said the monkey's trainer, "and *she* makes *five thousand dollars* a week. She'd like to buy *you*."

A Matter of Priorities

According to longtime screen favorite Jackie Cooper, during the shooting of one of the popular Lassie pictures the great star collie was being filmed on a raft with a small child actor. Suddenly, a swift current caught the raft and began sweeping it rapidly downstream. Lassie's trainer Rudd Weatherwax acted quickly. "He tore off his jacket," Cooper recalled, "leaped into the water, swam out to the raft, and pulled Lassie off! The kid he left to fend for himself!" (Fortunately, the kid survived.)

Great Comebacks

Rin Tin Tin, the famous German shepherd silent-movie star of the 1920s, was found badly wounded in a trench by an American soldier during World War I and nursed back to health. Another animal actor who won widespread fame after coming close to death was the finicky television commercial star Morris the cat (who only ate 9-Lives cat food). Morris was due to be gassed at a Chicago animal shelter in twenty minutes when a local cat lover adopted him and later started him on his profitable career. Both animals earned millions and had guards to protect them from dognappers and catnappers. (*See also* Chapter 11.)

More Acting Animals

Today animals acting in movies are very well paid and their use is regulated by the Animal Anti-Cruelty League. In most cases they are provided by animal rental companies like Animals R Us. Over the years many have won real fame as the headlines in pictures; some of them, like Gentle Ben, have starred in over a dozen pictures. These would include the well-known Lassie of movies and television, Rin Tin Tin, and President Ronald Reagan's Bonzo the chimp. More than three hundred dogs were auditioned for the part of Lassie, fifty for Our Gang's Pete the pup. Here's a list of additional animal stars whose names are well known:

- Cheetah (Tarzan's chimpanzee friend)
- Clyde (the orangutan in *Every Which Way but Loose*)
- Flipper (the dolphin, played by Mitzi and Susie)
- Willy (the orca in *Free Willy*)
- André (the seal)
- Arnold (the pig)
- Gentle Ben (the bear)
- Bart (the bear)
- Morris (the cat)
- Otis and Milo (the dog and cat)
- Judy (the chimp)
- Willard and Ben (the trained rats)
- Francis the Talking Mule
- Mr. Ed (the talking horse)
- Pete the Pup (in the Our Gang movies)
- Toto (Dorothy's dog in *The Wizard of Oz*)
- Astor (the dog from *The Thin Man* movies)
- Sandy (Little Orphan Annie's dog)
- Cujo (the dog)
- Beethoven (the dog)
- Air Bud (the dog)
- Benjy (the dog)

(*See also* "Hoofprints for Posterity.")

A Tribute to Bonzo

On the same day in 1954 when he was scheduled to help present the first annual Patsy Awards for animal achievement in films, the chimpanzee Bonzo was killed in a trailer fire. Four of his stand-ins died with him. Bonzo had starred in *Bedtime for Bonzo* (1951) opposite Ronald Reagan. When Reagan became president years later, interest was revived in the film, and Bonzo became one of the best-known animal actors.

Animal Actors, Cartoon Characters, and Movie Monsters

Gorilla Quiz

Everybody knows about filmdom's King Kong, Mighty Joe Young, White Bomba, and the gorillas in *Gorillas in the Mist* and *Congo*, among other films. But can you name the classic Broadway *stage play* in which a gorilla kills the protagonist?

Answer

Eugene O'Neill's *The Hairy Ape* (1922), in which the brutish Yank, misunderstood by everyone, senses some kinship with a gorilla in the zoo and tries to free him from his cage, only to be killed by the beast, who doesn't understand him either.

Hoofprints for Posterity

Thousands of horses have been used in outstanding Hollywood Westerns, "oaters," low-budget Westerns, and cheap Italian "spaghetti Westerns." The most famous among them are:

- Trigger (Roy Rogers's horse)
- Champion (Gene Autry's horse)
- Tarzan (Ken Maynard's horse)
- Tony (Tom Mix's horse)
- Topper (Bill Boyd's horse)
- Pinto Ben (William S. Hart's horse)

Trigger, Champion, Tony, and Pinto Ben have their hoofprints enshrined at Grauman's Chinese Theater along with the footprints of noted human actors. It should also be noted that Trigger, who costarred with Roy Rogers in eighty-eight films and one hundred TV shows, was stuffed and mounted when he died in 1965 at age thirty-three. He can be seen at the Roy Rogers Museum in Victorville, California, as can Buttermilk, the horse of Rogers's wife and costar, Dale Evans.

Human Animal Actors

In days past there were even humans who specialized in playing animals on stage. Among the best was actor George Ali, who starred in the comic fantasy *White Wings* (1926) as a horse named Joseph, who is killed at the end of the play. The play takes its name from the sanitation workers, white wings, who clean up after horses in city streets. Another such entertainer was English pantomimist Fred Conquest (1871–1941), famous in his day for his portrayal of a goose, and his brother Arthur (1875–1945), who played the chimp in the music hall act "Daphne, the Chimpanzee."

Of Mouse and Man: The Authorized Biography of the Real Mickey Mouse (Via Firm Agreements with His Heirs)

Mirabile dictu! He'll be seventy-five this year (1999), a star who surely ranks with Chaplin in stature and influence and is among the greatest entertainers of this or any other century. Yet no biography has ever been written of the most popular performer in all history, doubtless the most famous of all animals endowed with human characteristics. Certainly "Mouse, Mickey," as one scholarly index lists him, deserves space somewhere, so following is a biography of a mouse—there have surely been biographies (recent ones, too) penned of far less appealing creatures.

To begin with, all scholars should know that Mickey's progenitor was a *real* mouse. For the sake of convenience we will call our mouse "him," though the original may just as well have been a Ms. as a Mr.

Mortimer Mouse (b. 1924), as Disney christened him, came into this world somewhere within the musty, malodorous cobwebbed walls of the garage that served as Walt Disney's Laugh-O-Gram studio in Kansas City, Missouri. The ur-material is scarce, but he appears to have come from a family of ten, though no accurate biography of his immediate ancestors is available. Yet to those cynics who question his reality, we submit abundant testimony that our hero did indeed exist. Disney's daughter confirms this: "Several stories have been told about Father's having had a mouse who lived on his desk during his early days in Kansas City," she testifies. "The thought back of this tale is that the mouse had given Father a special fondness for mice. 'Unlike most of the stories that have been printed,' Father told me, 'that one is true. . . . Mice gathered in my wastebasket when I worked late at night. I lifted them out and kept them in little cages on my desk. One of them was my particular friend. Then before I left Kansas City I carefully carried him out into a field and let him go.'"

Another Disney biographer informs us that he let his mouse go in an empty lot, through exactly where in Kansas City still remains something of a mystery: "Nine mice skittered off into the weeds, but the tenth stayed put. It was Mortimer, watching him with bright eyes. Walt stamped his feet and shouted. The mouse took fright and ran. 'I walked away,' Walt would later recall, 'feeling such a cur.' "

Other sources go as far as to say that Mortimer even "trespassed on his master's drawing board, cleaning his whiskers with unconcern or hitching up his imaginary trousers," that he plagued the other cartoonists to the extent of gnawing their pencils and erasers, that Walt often brought two lunches to the office, one for himself and the other for his pet—at a time when the artist more than once actually had to scrounge stale bread for his own supper. There is even a tale that Disney forbade his employers to set traps for *any* marauding mice, keeping his favorite Mortimer in an inverted wire basket during the day and letting him romp free with his friends at night. Here we have the familiar story of the neglected artist in his garret, the variation being that this artist starved with a pet mouse who was to become the inspiration for his greatest creation. "Other people would leave lunch scraps in the wastebaskets," Disney later recalled in referring to his mouse. "What I didn't eat the mice came around to eat. One (Mortimer) was bolder than the rest. There was a shelf above my drawing board and he wouldn't move off it."

Those are the hard-core facts on our mouse's real life before Disney left Kansas City for Hollywood with just forty bucks in his pocket. But we can speculate that Mortimer was about six months of age when Walt let him go free in that empty lot, and judging by the one and a half year lifespan of mousekind, lived until August 1925—unless famine, feline, or other bad fortune befell him. As for his vital statistics, Mortimer probably measured a little smaller than the average *Mus musculus* at two and a half to three inches in length. His heart, however, though weighing only about the usual 1.15 grams, was infinitely larger in the way of soul, having inspired Disney to the greatness he achieved.

No one had ever created a mouse anything like Disney's. The idea came almost five years after he let Mortimer go—to be exact, as biographers must be in monumental works, on the evening of March 16, 1928, aboard a train carrying the cartoonist from New York to Hollywood, when Disney dreamed of his all but forgotten pet. Call it what you like—fate, serendipity, Tyche, Lady Luck—but while he dozed that night another world was born. Walt didn't know it, but he was gestating a mouse realer than real. Mortimer was actually put on paper for the first time the next day, somewhere between Toluca, Illinois, and La Junta, Colorado. Disney at first drew him with ruffled hair like Charles Lindbergh's—for his first cartoon, *Plane Crazy*, being about a mouse who built a plane in his own backyard, was to parody that great Viking flier who had just flown across the Atlantic. But the familiar red velvet pants with red buttons, the black dots for eyes, the pear-shaped body, pencil limbs, big yellow clodhoppers, and three-fingered hands in white gloves were already all present. So was a tail, which the rarest of rodents lost to the eraser in the future. Walt doodled and drew all day. Suddenly, in the midst of his sketching that evening, he shouted to his wife, Lillian, "I've got him—Mortimer Mouse!"

"Mortimer is a *horrible* name for a mouse," Lilly said with the certainty only artists' wives and film critics can affect.

"How about Mickey then?" Walt replied. "Mickey Mouse has a good friendly sound."

Lilly agreed, suggesting "Minnie Mouse" as a helpmate for Mickey in the process. It was both a second life, a reincarnation for Mortimer probably long in his grave, and a new birth for Disney, who even became the Mouse's squeaky voice when he made sound films about Mickey. "I fathered him when he was called Mortimer Mouse," the artist once told reporters, "and he was my first born and the means by which I ultimately achieved all the other things I ever did—from Snow White to Disneyland."

Disney produced both *Plane Crazy* and *Galloping Gaucho* before, having solved many technical problems, he was able to sell Mickey Mouse in the black-and-white talkie *Steamboat Willie*, the world's first animated sound cartoon. First booked on Broadway at the Colony Theatre, *Steamboat Willie* ran for a solid two weeks amid roars of appreciative laughter. Mickey, with his squeaky voice and jerky walk, played the captain of a Mississippi River steamboat who danced and tooted his boat whistle with gay abandon. "Mickey growls, whines, squeaks and makes various sounds that add to the mirthful quality," the *New York Times* film critic wrote, applauding the cartoon. Other critics all over the world joined in praising Mickey. With *Steamboat Willie*'s appearance in 1928 the mouse became an overnight sensation.

That year Mickey began to win fame enough to satisfy the most ambitious human. His popularity knew no national boundaries; sojourners everywhere found home in his cartoons. In France he became known as Michael Souris; in Italy as Topolino; in Japan, Miki Kuchi; in Spain, Miguel Ratoncito; in Latin America, El Raton Miguelto; in Sweden, Muse Pigg; in Germany, Michael Maus; and in Russia, Mikki Maus. At its peak, Mickey's fan mail approached ten thousand letters a day.

Mickey inspired Disney to invent a host of fantabulous anthropomorphic cartoons and characters. Father Goose, as Disney was dubbed, invented characters millions will never forget and untold millions will learn never to forget. You could count on the knuckles of your fingers folk heroes as appealing as Mickey and Disney's other creations: Pluto, that most amiable of clumsy dogs; Donald Duck; Goofy; Scrooge McDuck; Horace Horsecollar; José Carioca; Clarabelle Cow; even a relative of Mickey's named Mortimer. This is not to mention immortal screen versions of characters like Pinocchio, Dumbo, Bambi (Henry Ford's favorite), Peter Pan, the Three Little Pigs, Ferdinand the Bull, Herbie the Love Bug, Maleficent the evil witch, Winnie the Pooh, Cinderella, Sleeping Beauty, Br'er Rabbit, Snow White—and, of course, the Seven Dwarfs (Dopey, Grumpy, Bashful, Sneezy, Happy, Sleepy, and Doc). Then there were the songs from Walt's many films, such as "Whistle While You Work," "Hi-Ho, Hi-Ho, It's Off to Work We Go," "Someday My Prince Will Come," "Who's Afraid of the Big Bad Wolf?," "When You Wish upon a Star," and many others. Disney was probably the only artist to be praised by both the American Legion and the Soviet Union. His film with Donald Duck singing "We heil, we heil, right in the Führer's face" proved to be among the most effective propaganda weapons of World War II when it was translated into a dozen languages and dropped behind enemy lines to be used by resistance groups. Because of Mickey and his friends, Disney won thirty-two Oscars (more than anyone else in movie history), four Emmys, honorary degrees from Harvard and Yale, the French Legion of Honor, and the Presidential Medal of Freedom—more than nine hundred awards in all, not including the nomination by a leading French magazine in 1964 for the Nobel Prize. Pretty good for a modest country boy who once told reporters, "I'm selling corn, and I like corn!"

Disney, the natural genius, the simple man totally alien to intellectual analysis, perhaps best explained the phenomenon of his and his mouse's popularity. "Sometimes I've tried to figure out why Mickey appealed to the whole world," he once told a reporter. "So far as I know, nobody really has. He's a pretty nice fellow who never does anybody any harm, who gets into scrapes through no fault of his own, but always manages to come up grinning. Why Mickey's even been faithful to one girl, Minnie, all his life. Mickey is so simple and uncomplicated, so easy to understand that you can't help liking him."

There is no doubt that Mickey Mouse embodied everything that Walt Disney liked, whereas Mickey's near equal in popularity, Donald Duck—said to be based loosely on the Old Curmudgeon of Franklin Roosevelt's administration, Harold Ickes—was a combination of all the qualities he disliked in people. In any event, the esteemed British cartoonist David Low called

Mickey's creator "the most significant figure in graphic arts since Leonardo da Vinci." And in a tribute to Disney after his death in 1965, age sixty-five, a *New York Times* editorial observed that what Disney "gave to us and the world . . . is all summed up in a friendly, engaging mouse named Mickey. It is not a small bequest . . . he was simply the father of Mickey Mouse."

Mickey's Credits

Today Mickey Mouse's name is a part of the language, adorning thousands of things, having appeared by now on some five thousand commercial products alone—from those ubiquitous Mickey Mouse watches (now collector's items) to sweatshirts, sheets, and a diamond-studded Mickey Mouse locket selling for more than a thousand dollars. Altogether the rodent has starred in more than 125 cartoons, winning two Oscars, one in 1932 and the other in 1941 while he was busy selling war bonds. *Mickey Mousing* is now the name of a cartoon soundtrack–synchronizing process invented for the mouse's films—each of the more than one hundred ten-minute cartoons required 14,440 pictures; sixteen drawings were needed to show a single step. *Mickey Mouse* was the password chosen by intelligence officers in planning the greatest invasion in the history of warfare—Normandy, 1944. *Mickey Mouse diagrams* were maps made for plotting positions of convoys and bombarding forces at Normandy. The special insulated boots issued to combat troops in Korea were called *Mickey Mouse boots*, and *Mickey Mouse discipline* was used and is still applied to childish rear-echelon inspections. . . . All this and much more in honor of a *real* mouse who lived and died one year half a century ago, a real mouse reborn to revitalize fantasy and take his unassailable place among the great folk heroes of all time.

Disney's Credo

Walt Disney's basically optimistic view of the world is apparent in his description of his favorite relative, his mentally retarded uncle Ed, whom the Disney clan always looked after. "Uncle Ed may have been touched in the head," Disney once told a reporter, "but he was happy. He spent hours wandering through the woods. He knew all the birds and their calls and he knew the names of all the plants. It was a privilege to wander with him. . . . There wasn't anybody happier or friendlier and I loved him so. To me he represented fun in its simplest and purest form.... I could never figure out who was crazy, Uncle Ed or everybody else."

A Bambi Quiz

Try these questions about the only movie masterpiece made for three-year-olds.

1. When did Walt Disney make the classic animated feature *Bambi* (which has been called "the world's first environmental film")?
2. Name Bambi's rabbit friend.
3. What was Bambi's skunk friend called?
4. Give the name of Bambi's "wife."
5. Describe the difference between the tails of Bambi's skunk pal and the skunk's wife.

Answers

1. 1942
2. Thumper
3. Flower
4. Falene
5. Flower's tail was black edged with white and his nameless wife's white edged with black.

King of the Beasts

Disney's animated film *The Lion King* (1994) became the world's bestselling video of all time when its sales reached 55 million copies in mid-1997. In the year of its theatrical release it grossed $300 million. It has been released recently on laser disc, along with an extensive, fascinating commentary on how the movie was made.

Late Recognition

Pinocchio (1940) is often acclaimed as the best feature-length cartoon ever made. *New York Times* critic Vincent Canby called it Disney's "pinnacle of creativity and technical mastery." Yet the film was not even nominated for an Academy Award for best picture or best cartoon in 1940. Neither was it nominated for best art direction. *Pinocchio* did win an Oscar that year for best original score and for best song—"When You Wish upon a Star," music by Leigh Harline and lyrics by Ned Washington. Time, however, often improves tastes, and the classic movie is now on the list of the National Film Registry. (*See* Chapter 8.)

Most Famous Cartoon Characters

For the top three of these comic geniuses many would pick, in order of preference:

1. Mickey Mouse
2. Donald Duck
3. Bugs Bunny

Our apologies to the supporters of, among many others:

Felix the Cat	Heckle and Jeckle
Krazy Kat	Woody Woodpecker
Betty Boop	Elmer Fudd
Porky Pig	Mighty Mouse
Mr. Magoo	Oswald Rabbit
Goofy	Bullwinkle
Tweety Bird	Rocky
Sylvester	Road Runner
Pluto	Big Bird
Scrooge McDuck	Yogi Bear
Daffy Duck	Quick Draw McGraw
Huey, Louie, and Dewey	The Simpsons

Censoring Betty Boop

Betty Boop, the short-skirted cartoon character of the 1920s, had to behave more decorously in the 1930s at the Hays Office's request. Betty is said to have been suggested by the voice, appearance, and personality of musical comedy star Helen Kane, who hailed from the Bronx.

One of a Kind

The only animated film ever nominated for the Oscar for best picture was Disney's *Beauty and the Beast* (1991), produced by Don Hahn (Buena Vista). It lost the Oscar to the suspense-horror film *The Silence of the Lambs* but did win Oscars for best song ("Belle") and best original score.

Best Cartoon Oscars

Of the Academy Award Oscars given for best cartoon since the category was instituted in 1931–32, Walt Disney Productions has won thirteen times, including the first eight awards. Disney cartoons have additionally been nominated twenty-seven times for Oscars. Disney's nearest competition is the Tom and Jerry series produced by Frederick Quimby, which has won seven Oscars. Bugs Bunny, Mr. Magoo, and Tweety Bird have also been well represented. The cartoon award was changed to "Animated Short Subject" in 1971. Here are the winners:

- Walt Disney—*Flowers and Trees* (1931–32)
- Disney—*The Three Little Pigs* (1932–33)
- Disney—*The Tortoise and the Hare* (1934)
- Disney—*Three Orphan Kittens* (1935)
- Disney—*The Country Cousin* (1936)
- Disney—*The Old Mill* (1937)
- Disney—*Ferdinand the Bull* (1938)
- Disney—*The Ugly Duckling* (1939)
- Rudolf Ising—*The Milky Way* (1940)
- Disney—*Lend a Paw* (1941)
- Disney—*Der Führer's Face* (1942)
- Tom & Jerry Series—*Yankee Doodle Dandy* (1943)
- Tom & Jerry Series—*Mouse Trouble* (1944)
- Tom & Jerry Series—*Quiet Please!* (1945)
- Tom & Jerry Series—*The Cat Concerto* (1946)
- Merrie Melodies Series—*Tweetie Pie* (1947)
- Tom & Jerry Series—*The Little Orphan* (1948)
- Merrie Melodies Series—*For Scent-Imental Reasons* (1949)

- Jolly Frolics Series—*Gerald McBoing-Boing* (1950)
- Tom & Jerry Series—*Two Mouseketeers* (1951)
- Tom & Jerry Series—*Johann Mouse* (1952)
- Disney—*Toot, Whistle, Plunk and Boom* (1953)
- Mr. Magoo Series—*When Magoo Flew* (1954)
- Merrie Melodies Series—*Speedy Gonzales* (1955)
- Mr. Magoo Series—*Mister Magoo's Puddle Jumper* (1956)
- Tweety and Sylvester Series—*Birds Anonymous* (1957)
- Bugs Bunny Series—*Knighty Knight, Bugs* (1958)
- Storyboard, Inc.—*Moonbird* (1959)
- Noveltoon Series—*Munro* (1960)
- Zabeb Films—*Ersatz (The Substitute)* (1961)
- Storyboard, Inc.—*The Hole* (1962)
- Pintoff-Crossbow Productions—*The Critic* (1963)
- Pink Panther Series—*The Pink Phink* (1964)
- Chuck Jones and Les Goldman, producers—*The Dot and the Line* (1965)
- I Feel Special Series—*Herb Alpert and the Tijuana Brass Double Feature* (1966)
- Murakami-Wolf Films—*The Box* (1967)
- Disney—*Winnie the Pooh and the Blustery Day* (1968)
- Disney—*It's Tough to Be a Bird* (1969)
- Stephen Bosustow Productions—*Is It Always Right to Be Right?* (1970)
- Maxwell-Petok-Petrovich Productions—*The Crunch Bird* (1971)
- Richard Williams Productions—*A Christmas Carol* (1972)
- Frank Morris, producer—*Frank Film* (1973)
- Will Vinton and Bob Gardiner, producers—*Closed Mondays* (1974)
- Grandstern Ltd.—*Great* (1975)
- Susan Baker, producer; Film Australia—*Leisure* (1976)
- Canadian National Film Board—*The Sand Castle* (1977)
- Canadian National Film Board—*Special Delivery* (1978)

- Paul Fierlinger, producer—*It's So Nice to Have a Wolf Around the House* (1979)
- Ferenc Rofusz, producer—*The Fly* (1980)
- Frédéric Back, producer; Société Radio Canada—*Crac* (1981)
- Film Polski Productions—*Tango* (1982)
- Jimmy Picker, producer—*Sundae in New York* (1983)
- Joe Minnis, producer—*Charade* (1984)
- Netherlands, producer—*Anna & Bella* (1985)
- Linda Van Tulden and William Thijssen, producers—*A Greek Tragedy* (1986)
- Frédéric Back, producer—*The Man Who Planted Trees* (1987)
- John Lasseter and William Reeves, producers—*Tin Toy* (1988)
- Christoph and Wolfgang Lauenstein, producers—*Balance* (1989)
- Nick Park, producer—*Creature Comforts* (1990)
- Daniel Greaves, producer—*Manipulation* (1991)
- Joan C. Gratz, producer—*Mona Lisa Descending a Staircase* (1992)
- Nick Park, producer—*The Wrong Trousers* (1993)
- Alison Snowden and David Fine, producers—*Bob's Birthday* (1994)
- Nick Park, producer—*A Close Shave* (1995)
- Tyron Montgomery and Thomas Stellmach, producers—*Quest* (1996)
- Jan PinRava, producer—*Geri's Game* (1997)
- Chris Wedge, producer—*Bunny* (1998)

That's All, Folks!

Mel Blanc (1908–89), as Bugs Bunny, first uttered the immortal words "Er, what's up, Doc?" to Elmer Fudd when the first Merrie Melodies cartoons were launched in 1937, though the words may be an old Western expression suggested by Tex Avery, one of the cartoons' animators. It is said that when Blanc emerged from a coma in 1983, he looked up at his physician and asked, "Er, what's up, Doc?"

Mel Blanc was the voice of many Merrie Melodies cartoon characters and chose the phrase "That's all, folks!" for his epitaph. These were the concluding words of all Merrie Melodies cartoons, spoken by Porky Pig, and have been chosen by a number of cartoon fans over the years for *their* epitaphs.

I Am Dracula . . . I Bid You Welcome: Count Dracula, the Immortal Vampire

As the recent film *Bram Stroker's Dracula* reminds us, the Irish-born English author Bram Stoker, who managed Sir Henry Irving's acting company, first called a vampire "Dracula" in his novel of that title published in 1897. Stoker's novel, written after a nightmare caused by too much rich food (as the legend goes) became the most famous of all vampire tales. Not that vampires hadn't been treated before—Goethe and Lord Byron, among others, had written novels about vampirism, and history tells of many real human monsters, male and female, who drank the blood of hundreds of their murder victims. But Stoker's vampire—tall and thin with pointed ears, beaklike nose, cruel and sensuous features, and "peculiarly sharp white teeth protruding over his lips"—became the inspiration for every movie made about vampires since the novel appeared.

The first film about Count Dracula to reach the screen was German director F. W. Murnau's silent *Nosferatu* (1922). Because of copyright problems with Stoker's widow, Murnau had to change Dracula's name to Graf Orlak and even then a court action against the director resulted in all but a few clandestine copies of the movie being destroyed. There is nothing sinisterly seductive about the vampire played by Max Schreck in this picture. He is a completely repulsive monster with a head resembling a skull, hands like claws, and ratlike teeth. His coffin is infested with squirming rats.

Lon Chaney Sr., the "Man of a Thousand Faces" (*see* Chapter 2), played a truly terrifying vampire in Tod Browning's *London After Midnight* (1927), but Browning's talkie *Dracula* (1930) was a better picture because Browning did not try to explain away the vampire legend as he did in the first film. This was the first movie starring the inimitable Bela Lugosi as Dracula, though the talented Hungarian actor had previously played the lead in a New York stage production of the story. Here is the Count with flowing opera cloak and evening dress and the Transylvanian accent imitated by others ever since, but he sports no fangs and no blood is spilled in the film. At the end of the movie the character Van Helsing addresses the audience off camera: "Please. One moment. Just a word before you go. We hope the memories of Dracula won't give you bad dreams—so just a word of reassurance. When you get home tonight and lights have been turned out and you're afraid to look behind the curtains—and you dread to see a face appear at the window—why, just pull yourself together and remember . . . that . . . after all . . . *there are such things!*"

Lugosi's *Dracula* became the biggest movie of 1931, opening a gold mine in which Hollywood producers quickly filed claims. The character Dracula appeared in 262 films after Browning's effort—the record for any monster.

As for Bela Lugosi, he became a star thanks to Count Dracula, but after twenty years or so he found it hard to get parts in even grade B films. He had predicted his fate to a reporter while he was basking in glory: "I can blame it all on Dracula. When I made my stage debut in New York, after leaving Hungary, I played a sympathetic role. Then came Dracula and I've been Dracula ever since. Since then Hollywood has scribbled a little card of classification for me and it looks as though I'll never be able to prove my mettle in any other kind of role."

Bela Lugosi, addicted to narcotics in his last years, was committed to a hospital in 1955 to be cured. He died at home the following year, buried in his Dracula cape as was his last wish.

Even more ironically, film critics today rank British actor Christopher Lee as filmdom's greatest Dracula, for his performance in *The Curse of Dracula* (1956), made in living (often bloodred) color. Yet Lee's performance might not have been possible if it wasn't for Lugosi, who gave not only his talent but his life for it.

Other Noted Dracula Movies

Dracula and Frankenstein, 1932

Dracula's Daughter, 1936

Son of Dracula, 1943

House of Dracula, 1945

Blood of Dracula, 1957

Return of Dracula, 1958

Dracula, 1958

Brides of Dracula, 1960

Billy the Kid vs. Dracula, 1965

Dracula—Prince of Darkness, 1965

Dracula Has Risen from the Grave, 1968

Blood of Dracula's Castle, 1969

Count Dracula, 1970

Scars of Dracula, 1970

Taste the Blood of Dracula, 1970

Countess Dracula, 1971

Blacula, 1972

Dracula A.D., 1972, 1972

Blood for Dracula, 1973

The Satanic Rites of Dracula, 1973

Bram Stoker's Dracula, 1992

The Golem

The legendary golem, a huge supernatural creature made of clay who fights against the persecution of Jews, is far older than Mary Shelley's Frankenstein monster, but the first movie made about it (set in modern times) came four years after the first Frankenstein film, in 1914. That was the year German actor-director Paul Wegener filmed *The Golem*. The clay man in his picture is found in the ruins of an ancient synagogue and brought to life by an antiquarian who finds the secret formula to revive him in an old book of magic. But the keeper loses control of his creation, and the monster becomes a force of evil before it is destroyed. Wegener, however, brought the creature back in two more movies that in costume and cinematography greatly influenced the major Frankenstein films to come.

My Dear Old Monster: Dr. Frankenstein's Boy

Contrary to popular notion, Dr. Frankenstein's monster does have a name. The good doctor, played by Boris Karloff, named him Adam in the 1931 film *Frankenstein*. Because many other movies about the monster give him no name, the name Adam has been all but forgotten. Dr. Frankenstein's first name, incidentally, was Victor.

Frankenstein's monster has been portrayed in 117 movies around the world, making him the second most portrayed horror movie character in film history—Count Dracula is in first place by a large margin.

Frankenstein was written 183 years ago by English novelist Mary Wollstonecraft Shelley, after the idea came to her in a dream, and has never been out of print since. Some critics consider it the first sci-fi novel. It was initially staged as a play in London in 1823 and became a great hit. The first Frankenstein movie (lost until it surfaced in a Milwaukee suburb in 1990) was a twelve-minute film starring Charles Ogle made by Thomas Edison at his Edison Film Company in 1910. Since then the monster's films have given him a bride (1935), two sons (in 1939 and 1957), and a daughter (1958).

The greatest and most successful Frankenstein film is director James Whale's chilling but not gruesome *Frankenstein* (1931), which starred Boris Karloff as the monster that ran amok. One critic has pointed out that "Dr. Frankenstein's creature, when newly born, ecstatically raises his hands and face to the warmth of the sun—it is only after meeting his fellow-beings' implacable hostility and incomprehension that he becomes a monster."

Frankenstein's monster did not speak in Whale's movie, uttering only fierce snarls and moans. The most memorable words in the film—and probably in all monster films—are Dr. Frankenstein's "It's alive! It's alive! It's alive!" when his creature first moves, followed by the equally chilling observation, "Now I know what it feels like to be God!"

Boris Karloff played in only three Frankenstein films, but the part transformed him from a bit player to a star. Unlike Bela Lugosi he had no regrets about playing a monster. "My dear old monster, I owe everything to him; he's my best friend!" he once said of the Frankenstein creature. Modestly, he gave all the credit to his success to legendary makeup artist Jack Pierce. "When you get right down to it," he told a reporter, "it was Jack Pierce who really created the Frankenstein monster. I was merely the animation in the costume." Everything from the monster's matted hair and ghostly pallor to the bolts in the sides of his neck and the clothing was Pierce's invention. The bolts, of course, were there to take the electrical charges that brought the monster to life. "There are six ways a surgeon can cut the skull," Pierce told a reporter later, "and I figured Dr. Frankenstein, who was not a practicing surgeon, would take the easiest. That is, he would cut the top of the skull straight across like a pot lid, hinge it, pop the brain in, and clamp it tight. That's the reason I decided to make the monster's head square and flat like a box and dig that big scar across his forehead and have two metal clamps hold it together. . . . The lizard eyes were made of rubber, as was his false head. I made his arms look longer by shortening the sleeves of his coat. His legs were stiffened by steel struts and two pairs of pants. . . . His fingernails were blackened with shoe polish. . . . His face was coated with blue-green greasepaint."

Pierce labored five hours every day to put on Karloff's makeup, but the makeup was only applied down to the actor's eyelids, so that he could express the gamut of emotions with his face. When the shooting stopped Karloff had lost twenty pounds in making what many consider the greatest monster picture of all. (*See also* Chapter 2.)

Famous Frankenstein Films and Their Stars

Frankenstein, Boris Karloff (1931)

The Bride of Frankenstein, Boris Karloff and Elsa Lancaster (1935)

Son of Frankenstein, Boris Karloff (1939)

Ghost of Frankenstein, Lon Chaney Jr. (1942)

Frankenstein Meets the Wolf Man, Bela Lugosi (1943)

Abbott and Costello Meet Frankenstein, Glenn Strange (1948)

The Curse of Frankenstein, Christopher Lee (1956)

I Was a Teenage Frankenstein, Gary Conway (1957)

Revenge of Frankenstein, Michael Gwynn (1958)

Frankenstein's Daughter, Sandra Knight (1958)

Frankenstein Created Woman, Susan Denberg (1959)

Frankenstein Must Be Destroyed, Freddie Jones (1969)

The Horror of Frankenstein, David Prowse (1970)

Frankenstein and the Monster from Hell, David Prowse (1973)

Young Frankenstein, Peter Boyle (1974)

The Bride, Jennifer Beals (1985)

Mary Shelley's Frankenstein, Robert De Niro (1994)

My Baby, the Wolf Man

Werewolves have been the subject of legend throughout the world for centuries, but the most memorable portrayal of one on the stage or screen was by Lon Chaney Jr. in *The Wolf Man* (1941). Chaney played a lycanthrope who turned into the beast after being bitten by a real wolf (played by Bela Lugosi), and could be killed only by a silver bullet. He thought it was the best performance of his career, calling it "My Baby." But makeup man Jack Pierce, so instrumental in Boris Karloff's Frankenstein film, deserves as much credit for this great monster film. Pierce worked on Chaney's makeup for up to eight hours every day while the movie was being made, fashioning the monster's hideous claws and gluing single threads of yak hair on his face and hands. Scores of werewolf films have been made since, including *Wolf* (1994), which starred Jack Nicholson as the wolf man, but Chaney's beast remains the best. Pierce never won a best makeup Oscar for this or any of his efforts (such awards not given at the time), but Rick Baker did win one for *An American Werewolf in London* (1981).

Monster Robots

Robotlike creatures can be traced at least as far back as the ancient Greeks and their legend of Talos, a huge bronze monster who guarded the island of Rhodes. Talos is depicted in the movie *Jason and the Argonauts* (1963), but the term *robot* was first used in a stage play, which was performed by actors who wore no special costumes or makeup. In Karel Capek's play *R.U.R.*, first produced in 1921, mechanical men manufactured by the Rossum Universal Robot Corporation revolt and threaten to take over the world. This play marked the first time mechanical men were called *robots*, a word which has since been extended to include people devoid of human feelings who act like mechanical men and to any mechanism guided by automatic controls. Capek coined *robot* from the Czech word *robota*, "work," to mean "a slave." The world is saved in the play when the robots miraculously become human.

The Only Monster Oscar

The only Academy Award given for acting in a horror film was won by Fredric March for *Dr. Jekyll and Mr. Hyde* in 1932. March's excellent performance was all the more remarkable because he had been regarded mainly as a comedic actor. This film remains the best movie ever made from Robert Louis Stevenson's famous novel, though it was not the first—a film version had been made as early as 1912. March went on to win another Oscar for *The Best Years of Our Lives* (1946) and was nominated for three more.

In Stevenson's book, written in 1886, Dr. Jekyll, a physician, discovers a drug that creates in him a personality that absorbs all his evil instincts. This personality, which he calls Mr. Hyde, is repulsive in appearance and gradually gains control of him until he finally commits a horrible murder. Jekyll can rid himself of Hyde only by committing suicide. Stevenson, who wrote the novel in three days locked in his study after he had a dream about the story, based the main character on an Edinburgh cabinetmaker and deacon named William Brodie (1741–88), who was a "double being," by day a respected businessman and by night the leader of a gang of burglars. Brodie was finally hanged for his crimes, but Stevenson, who was raised in Edinburgh, knew his story well and in fact wrote a play entitled *Deacon Brodie, or The Double Life* when he was only fifteen. This was the germ of the idea for his dream and his later work. Stevenson's wife wrote about the dream: "In the small hours one morning I was awakened by cries of horror from Louis. Thinking he had a nightmare I awakened him. He said angrily: 'Why did you awaken me? I was dreaming a fine bogey tale.'" The "bogey tale" turned out to be *Dr. Jekyll and Mr. Hyde*.

More Memorable Monster and Sci-Fi Masterpieces

It would be impossible to list the thousands of memorable horror and sci-fi films made since the early days of cinema, but here are some interesting selections. A number of these films have become great hits—especially the later sci-fi movies—escaping their genre classification. In fact, three sci-fi films—*E.T.*, *Jurassic Park*, and *Star Wars*—are among the top five movie box-office hits of all time, grossing well over $2 billion collectively. Add *Jaws* and *The Return of the Jedi* and that figure becomes five out of the top ten. The films here were chosen for their excellence, historic importance, or special interest:

- *Robbing Cleopatra's Tomb* (1899). French moviemaker Georges Méliès's film featured a mummy that the hero tried to chop up and burn—only to see it rise phoenixlike from the fire as Cleopatra.
- *Voyage to the Moon* (1902). Lobster claws for hands, hideous bodies, and hawklike faces—these are the moon creatures who attacked humans in director Georges Méliès's science fiction film, based on H. G. Wells's novel.
- *The Doctor's Experiment, or Reversing Darwin's Theory* (1908). Here was the first movie monster, made when a scientist's secret formula turned a man into an ape.
- *The Cabinet of Dr. Caligari* (1919). Probably the most influential of early horror films, this German movie, directed by Robert Wiene,

tells the story of the mad Dr. Caligari, who uses Cesare, an inmate of the mental hospital he runs, in a hypnotism act he performs at a local fair. Caligari keeps Cesare in a cabinet, but at night, after the fair crowds have all departed, he sends his hypnotized subject out to murder and maim his enemies. Conrad Veidt played the murderous zombie slinking through the night streets and Werner Krauss played Dr. Caligari. Altogether the acting, direction, and designs set a horror film standard and style for years to come, and many critics still consider it the best horror film ever made.

- *The Hunchback of Notre Dame* (1932). (*See* Chapter 3, "The Man of a Thousand Faces.")

- *The Phantom of the Opera* (1925). (*See* Chapter 3, "The Man of a Thousand Faces.")

- *The Mummy* (1932). Boris Karloff stars in the title role, as the mummy of Egyptian king Im-Ho-Tep, who comes back to life after three thousand years. Karloff's acting is as excellent as Jack Pierce's makeup work.

- *King Kong* (1933). (*See* Chapter 3.)

- *The Invisible Man* (1933). Claude Rains plays a mad doctor who takes a drug to make himself invisible so that he can rule the world. He is finally shot after leaving footprints in the snow. As he lays dying his body reappears piece by piece.

- *The Man They Could Not Hang* (1939). Here Boris Karloff, as Dr. Savaard, invents a mechanical heart that can bring the dead back to life, probably the first heart transplant in movie history and possibly an inspiration to future real-life surgeons!

- *Cat People* (1942). A horror film without a hideous monster. Brilliant camera work, lighting, sound effects, and editing made this subtle film a classic. Simone Simon stars as a beautiful young woman who turns into a panther, silently, eerily tracking down rivals for the affection of the man she loves.

- *I Walked with a Zombie* (1943). A suspenseful, terrifying movie set in the West Indies.

- *The Thing* (1951). One of the first "flying saucers" appeared in this sci-fi film, but the Thing from outer space itself, a vegetable that feeds on human blood, though it looks like a giant hairless human, stole the show. James Arness, who played the creature, went on to greater glory as TV's Marshal Dillon on *Gunsmoke*. "What do you do with a vegetable?" the film's heroine asks rhetorically. "You cook it!" Which is just what is done with the monster.

- *The Day the Earth Stood Still* (1951). The giant flying saucer in this one lands near the White House, complete with a ten-foot robot named Gort. If Earth doesn't stop nuclear testing, we are warned, the extraterrestrials will reduce Earth to "a burned-out cinder." We soon get the message.

- *The Beast from 20,000 Fathoms* (1953). Based on a Ray Bradbury story, this low-budget film features a dinosaur freed from the ice by a nuclear-test explosion, which slinks toward Brooklyn destroying and eating everything in its path, including people, until it is finally killed at Coney Island—but not before it destroys the famed amusement park roller coaster.

- *Them* (1954). *They* are menacing, gigantic ants, their mutation caused by atomic radiation.

- *Tarantula* (1955). A giant spider turns on its scientist creator, played by the formidable Leo G. Carroll.

- *The Incredible Shrinking Man* (1957). A sci-fi movie masterpiece rated by some as the best ever. A man caught in a cloud of insecticide begins slowly shrinking until he becomes smaller than a mouse, losing everything but his life in the process. The film certainly should have at least won an Academy Award for special effects, but it wasn't even nominated.

- *The Fly* (1957). A fly with a human head and one human arm is crushed to pulp in CinemaScope. The 1986 remake of this film starred Jeff Goldblum.

- *The Blob* (1958). A gooey amoeba-like creature eats and grows, devouring everything that gets in its way, including a diner, until it meets up with the hero, played by Steve McQueen. The film was so popular it inspired a sequel—*Son of the Blob*.

- *I Married a Monster from Outer Space* (1958). About a monster who can assume human shape; the title became a U.S. catchphrase between husbands and wives.

- *One Million Years B.C.* (1966). Fabulous prehistoric creatures created by special effects genius Ray Harryhausen—and Raquel Welch besides.

- *The Dance of the Vampires* (1967). Director Roman Polanski actually played a vampire in this satirical film, as did his wife, Sharon Tate. Their lives were of course later to be violated by all too real monsters, Charles Manson and his disciples. (*See* Chapter 7.)
- *Planet of the Apes* (1968). Features the apelike inhabitants of Earth's future (the result of a nuclear war). Brilliant makeup by John Chambers and excellent acting by Roddy McDowell, Kim Hunter, and Maurice Evans, who play the simians.
- *2001: A Space Odyssey* (1968). Fantastic special effects and its memorable computer "monster" HAL make this one of the best and most profitable of all science fiction films.
- *Westworld* (1969). Here Yul Brynner plays an android gunslinger in the Old West.
- *Night of the Living Dead* (1969). Probably the bloodiest, most repulsive horror film ever made—which obviously makes it one of the best.
- *The Andromeda Strain* (1970). The best of "the plague from outer space" films, directed by the brilliant, versatile Robert Wise, who got his start in low-budget horror films in the 1940s but also won an Academy Award for directing *The Sound of Music* (1965).
- *The Thing with Two Heads* (1971). Football star Rosey Grier and Ray Milland in a kind of horror film *Defiant Ones*. Here a black-hating racist and a black convict share the same body.
- *Blacula* (1972). The first of the African American Draculas comes to the screen to fight against the slave trade.
- *Tales from the Crypt* (1972). Among the best of anthology-type horror films featuring several stories; all are superbly acted.
- *Psychomania* (1972). Features a horrific biker gang, the "Living Dead," who actually have come back from the dead after making a deal with the devil. Motorcycle gangs often get stoned, but this one is literally turned to stone at the end of the movie.
- *Sssnake* (1973). Another great title for the genre. The monster is a human-reptile created by still another mad scientist.
- *Jaws* (1975). The monster mechanical shark, dubbed "Bruce," didn't win an Academy Award for special effects, as would be expected.

Neither did *Jaws* win best picture, though it was nominated. Director Steven Spielberg's flick did win Oscars for sound, film editing, and, of course, for its all too memorable (for ocean swimmers) score by composer John Williams.

- *Star Wars* (1977). One of the all-time box-office hits, with a domestic gross of more than $340 million—so well known, along with its sequels, that no description is necessary. It received an Academy Award nomination for best picture and won Oscars for art direction, sound, original score, film editing, costume design, and visual effects. All in all it had ten Oscar nominations, two more than its sci-fi competitor *Close Encounters of the Third Kind*.

- *Close Encounters of the Third Kind* (1977). Steven Spielberg, who at least once professed a belief in UFOs, directed this best of the flying saucer films, which has grossed about $175 million domestically to date. It won an Academy Award for cinematography and earned Spielberg a nomination for best director.

- *Time After Time* (1979). H. G. Wells, who didn't write the story the film is based upon, invents a time machine and chases Jack the Ripper into the future—modern-day San Francisco.

- *Alien* (1979). An innovative film in that a woman finally gets to kill the ugly monster from outer space.

- *E.T. the Extra-Terrestrial* (1982). A critically acclaimed film that has been compared to *The Wizard of Oz*, this is one of the biggest movie hits in history, grossing about $415 million domestically to date. Nominated for an Academy Award for best picture, it lost to *Gandhi* but won Oscars for visual effects, sound, sound editing, and original score. Steven Spielberg was nominated for best director.

- *Jurassic Park* (1993). Steven Spielberg's *Schindler's List* won the Academy Award for best picture in 1993, and Spielberg won an Oscar for best director, not to mention the five other Oscars the film won. That didn't leave much for Spielberg's big box-office hit *Jurassic Park*, but it managed to win Academy Awards for visual effects, sound, and sound effects editing.

Psycho, *The Birds*, and *The Silence of the Lambs* could also be regarded as great horror films, but they were made to appeal to a general audience, not as genre films.

The Ten Worst Sci-Fi Films

Most of these are so bad that they're great fun. Can you think of any you'd add to the list?

- *Robot Monster* (1953). Its reviews were supposedly so bad that its young director attempted suicide.
- *It Came from Beneath the Sea* (1955). A giant sleeping octopus, awakened by nuclear testing, attacks the Bay Area, pulling down the Golden Gate Bridge, among other landmarks, before its brain is obliterated by a torpedo and it leaves its heart in San Francisco.
- *The Attack of the Killer Tomatoes* (1957). Brobdingnagian tomatoes (yes!) go on a rampage. It was so bad that it inspired a sequel—*Return of the Killer Tomatoes.*
- *Womaneater* (1957). A carniverous Amazon plant as hairy as a barber shop has a favorite entrée—beautiful young women.
- *The 30 Foot Bride of Candy Rock* (1959). Even Lou Costello, the bridegroom, couldn't save this one.
- *Dr. Terror's House of Horror* (1964). Love that title, but nothing else.
- *Santa Claus Conquers the Martians* (1964). The title says it all. Never try to kidnap St. Nick from the North Pole.
- *The Horror of Party Beach* (1964). At once among the worst of horrible horror, sci-fi, and beach party flicks.
- *The Blood Beast Terror* (1967). A giant moth mates with a blood-drinking woman.

Humphrey Bogart the Vampire: Unlikely Stars Who Acted in Horror Films

- Early in his career Humphrey Bogart played a child murderer in *The Return of Dr. X* (1937)—a vampire who needed the blood of children to stay alive. "This was one of the pictures," he later recalled, "that made me march in to Jack Warner [of Warner Bros. Studio] and ask for more money. You can't believe what this one was like. I had a part like Bela Lugosi or Boris Karloff should have played. I was this doctor, brought back to life, and the only thing that nourished this poor bastard was blood. If it had been Jack Warner's blood, or Harry Warner's or Pops' I wouldn't have minded as much!" Bogart never made another horror film.

- The late Michael Landon, the wholesome hero of television series like *Bonanza* and *Little House on the Prairie*, played a werewolf in *I Was a Teenage Werewolf* (1957). Like Bogart, he never appeared in the genre again.
- James Arness, well known for portraying Matt Dillon in the television series *Gunsmoke* and respected as an excellent actor, played a horrible vegetable creature from outer space in the classic horror movie *The Thing* (1951). It was his first film—and his last horror film.
- Charles Bronson, well known for his hard-boiled hero roles today, played the brutish shuffling assistant to the mad museum owner (Vincent Price) in *House of Wax* (1953). Acting under his real name, Charles Buchinsky, he saw fit to take the stage name Charles Bronson after this performance.
- Spencer Tracy starred in *Dr. Jekyll and Mr. Hyde* (1941), which was both a critical and box-office failure. Fredric March had won an Oscar playing the part in a 1932 film of the Stevenson classic. Another star who played the role was the Great Profile, John Barrymore, who in a 1920 film of the story used no makeup for his brilliant transformation from Jekyll to Hyde. Still another was Kirk Douglas, who starred in a 1973 TV musical based on the tale. Inevitably, there was also a film called *Abbott and Costello Meet Dr. Jekyll and Mr. Hyde* (1953).
- Jack Nicholson, considered one of Hollywood's finest actors, played a good guy in the horror film *The Raven* (1963). Later in his career he starred in Stephen King's *The Shining* (1980) and played a werewolf in still another film, *Wolf* (1994).

The Worm Eaters

In a 1977 horror movie appropriately called *The Worm Eaters*, the cast ate about $200 worth of worms supplied free by the Minnesota Worm & Fly Corporation—and this was in just the first five weeks of production. Filmmaker Ted Nickels—whose credits include *The Undertaker and His Pals*, *The Corpse Grinders*, and *Children Shouldn't Play with Dead Things*—promised free admission at the premiere to anyone who would swallow a worm. It is reported that there were a number of takers.

The Weirdest Oscar

In the cult horror film *The Creature from the Black Lagoon* (1954) the hideous "Gill Man" from the Amazon River was the creation of director Jack Arnold. Arnold had been staring at an Academy Award in his office when the idea came to him—use the Oscar body as the monster's body and attach gills and fins to it.

VI

OF BARNS AND PALACES: FAMOUS THEATERS AND MOVIE HOUSES

The First Theaters

The word *theater* itself comes from a Greek word meaning "a place for seeing." No theater existed in this sense of the word before the planned theaters of the ancient Greeks; all previous plays were performed in such places as temple courts and terraces.

The very first theater, so far as is known, was the theater of Dionysus at Athens, the ruins of which can be seen today. It was patterned on "natural theaters" at the foot of hillsides on which spectators stood or sat. "From this natural form the first theaters took their main outlines," a nineteenth-century historian wrote. "There was a circle or orchestra for the chorus and actor or actors, and rising tiers of wooden seats, built against a hillside for the spectators. These seats extended usually around two-thirds or more of the orchestra, since at this time dancing or movement was more important than acting, and there was no stage for the spectators to face."

Super Theaters and Stages

- Rome's Colosseum, built in A.D. 180, remains the world's largest amphitheater, measured by seating capacity, with a capacity of 87,000 seats.
- Australia's Perth Entertainment Centre, built in 1976, is the world's largest indoor theater, with 8,003 seats.

- The Gershwin Theater, boasting 1,933 seats, is the biggest in use on Broadway.
- The Hilton Theater of Reno, Nevada, has the world's largest theater stage, which measures 175 by 241 feet.
- Hollywood, as would be expected, boasts the largest complex of movie studios: the Universal City Complex, which has 31 sound stages and 479 buildings on a site of more than 420 acres.
- The largest single studio stage is at Pinewood Studios in England. This "007" stage built for the James Bond film *The Spy Who Loved Me* (1976) measures 336 by 139 by 41 feet.
- The largest movie set was built in Madrid, Spain, for *The Fall of the Roman Empire* (1964). It was a replica of the Roman Forum measuring 1,312 by 754 feet.

Naming the Colosseum

Contrary to popular belief, its size had nothing to do with the naming of the Roman arena called the Colosseum, which gave its name to all future colosseums. The original Colosseum took its name from a "colossal" statue of Nero that stood near it, the statue placed there after the dissolute emperor's palace had burned to the ground in the great fire that destroyed most of Rome.

No Obscenity (Violence) on Stage

According to one theory, *obscene* originally meant "off the stage" in ancient Greek drama, deriving from the Greek *ob*, "against," and *scaena*, "stage." What was kept off the stage in Greek drama was violence (always reported by a messenger), not sex, of which there was plenty in comedies and satyr plays complete with actors fitted with huge artificial phalluses. *Obscenity* wasn't associated with sex until the word made its appearance in England toward the end of the seventeenth century. Shakespeare was the first to use *obscene* in the sense of offensive to the senses, that is, disgusting, filthy, foul, etc., in *Richard II*: ". . . so heinous, black, obscene a deed." The Bard probably based the word on the French *obscene*, meaning the same, which came from the Latin *obscenus*. Within five years or so, *obscene* was being used to mean "indecent and lewd" as well.

Young Folk of the Pear Garden

In about A.D. 720 Chinese emperor Ming Huang visited the moon, according to Chinese legend, and was royally entertained there by plays and players. This inspired the good emperor to establish a lavish theater and the world's first school of acting in the Pear Garden of the Imperial Park. Perhaps Ming Huang visited the moon in his dreams—no astronaut has reported resident actors there—but in any case, he did build his theater and dramatic academy. His actors were called "Disciples (or Young Folk, or Students) of the Pear Garden" and, indeed, all Chinese actors were so called up until the mid-twentieth century. Although the Pear Garden no longer exists, the empress dowager's theater can still be seen in Peking's Summer Palace. According to one British reporter it has "three storeys with special devices which allowed evil spirits to appear on the stage from below and celestial beings from the second story above."

Deus ex Machina

Some unlikely event that extricates one from a difficult situation, usually in a play or other work of fiction, is called a *deus ex machina*, which literally means "a god (let down upon the stage) from a machine." In ancient Greek drama a god was often lowered onto the stage by a pulley system to help the hero out of trouble; this practice gave rise to the expression. Euripides used the device widely, while Sophocles and Aeschylus avoided it—as almost all writers avoid it today. Much later Bertolt Brecht parodied the practice at the end of *The Threepenny Opera* when Mack the Knife is saved from hanging by Queen Victoria's proclamation.

France's First Theater—and Theatrical Real Estate Firm

The Brotherhood of Passion, France's first theatrical organization, opened the first French theater in 1548. The Hotel de Bourgogne, built on the ruins of the duke of Burgundy's palace in Paris, was more elegant than any English Elizabethan playhouse, boasting two tiers of boxes and chandeliers to light the wide, long hall. But the brotherhood, a band of trade-guild members and artisans who held the monopoly on acting in Paris, soon gave up producing plays, realizing they could not compete with professional acting troupes. Instead, they became the first theatrical real estate firm in history, leasing their theater to other groups. The most famous of these was the King's Players, who performed many of the seventeenth century's finest plays at the Hotel de Bourgogne until they left the theater in 1673 and joined other actors in Paris to form the Comédie-Française.

The Comédie-Française

The French national theater, famous for its extensive repertoire of classical French drama, is also called the Théâtre-Français and La Maison de Molière, but it is best known as the Comédie-Française. Celebrated as "the glory of the French theater" by more than one critic, it was founded in 1680 and before the end of the decade moved into a playhouse built for it in an indoor tennis court, whose layout, with its boxes for spectators, was easily converted to a theater. Since 1770, it has remained at the site of what was the Palais Royal Theater, which is now called the Comédie-Française. The acting company is a cooperative society, each actor holding from one-quarter to one full share (depending on the actor's experience or importance) once he or she is admitted to the company. Admission comes after the actor successfully performs a role of his or her choosing and serves a salaried probationary period of up to several years. At that point the actor becomes a full member, sharing in the company's profits, and is entitled to a pension after twenty years' service. The head of the company, called the *doyen*, is its oldest member.

Segregated Theaters

In Renaissance Spanish theaters, unlike their French and English counterparts, all women were required to sit in a special section in the rear that was popularly called the "stew pan" (*cazuela*). This special gallery was on the first floor, facing the stage, and no men were permitted to enter it.

London's First Theater

James Burbage, considered by some to be the most famous actor of his day and the father of Shakespeare's friend and fellow actor Richard Burbage, designed and built London's first theater in 1576 in partnership with his father-in-law. The playhouse, erected at a cost of about seven hundred pounds, was a circular, roofless building with some boxes and galleries that cost two pennies for admission. For one penny, patrons could buy standing room on the grounds.

Burbage had trouble with the Corporation of the City of London, which disapproved of playacting, but he managed to keep his playhouse operating for more than twenty years by putting on sword fighting competitions and other athletic contests as well as the plays that his acting company produced. Then his landlord terminated the lease and the theater had to be pulled down. Luckily, a clause in the lease stipulated that Burbage owned the building itself. This enabled his sons to dismantle the structure and use the lumber to build the illustrious Globe Theatre on the other side of the Thames. (*See* "The 'Wooden O' and Its Burning.")

The Golden Age of Attendance

In Shakespeare's time theater attendance reached its peak. There was an average weekly audience of more than 20,000 people from a London population of 160,000, about one out of eight people attending. In the history of entertainment this has been matched only by the movie audiences in the modern era. Theaters flew flags all morning if there was to be a performance that afternoon and a trumpeter on the theater roof signaled that the playing time of two o'clock was approaching.

The "Wooden O" and Its Burning

Shakespeare described London's famous Globe Theatre as a "wooden O,[218]" and his playhouse did have a doughnut shape. The Globe was built from timbers used in the construction of London's first theater, which was constructed in 1576 on the north side of the Thames by actor James Burbage and torn down when Burbage's sons decided to build the Globe on Bankside in Southwark in 1599. Shakespeare had a share in the Globe and performed there.

The auditorium of the Globe was an old innyard. Shilling patrons sat on stage near the actors, threepenny patrons rated stools in the balcony, while one-penny customers stood in the yard. As the large stage jutted into the yard the actors found themselves with an audience pressing on three sides of them. The balconies and stage were roofed but the center innyard was open to the sky.

The Globe had a capacity, at most, of two thousand people and was only used in the daytime. This most important of English theaters burned to the ground in 1613 after an ordinance shot discharged at the entrance of the king in *Henry VIII* (a play attributed in part to Shakespeare) set fire to the thatched roof over the stage and balconies. It was rebuilt the following year and finally demolished thirty years later. Other contemporary theaters similar to it included the Swan, the Curtain, the Rose, and the Fortune. A replica of the famous Globe was built on the banks of the Thames in 1997. There are also replicas in Stratford, Ontario, and Stratford, Connecticut.

Diplomat Sir Henry Wotton, who later penned the famous words "An Ambassador is an honest man sent abroad to lie for his country," jokingly described the burning of the Globe Theatre in a 1613 letter. His eyewitness account follows:

> *Now King Henry making a masque at the Cardinal Wolsey's house, and certain chambers [cannons] being shot off at his entry, some of the paper, or other stuff, wherewith one of them was stopped, did light on the thatch [roof], where being thought at first but an idle smoke, and their eyes more attentive to the show, it kindled inwardly, and ran round like a train [fuse], consuming within less than an hour the whole house, to the very grounds. This was the fatal period of that virtuous fabric, wherein yet nothing did perish but wood and straw, and a few forsaken cloaks; only one man had his breeches set on fire, that would perhaps have broiled him, if he had not by the benefit of a provident wit put it out with a bottle of ale.*

"Behind the Scenes"

Though the origins of this phrase are theatrical, as would be expected, it goes back to the English theater in the time of Charles I, when elaborate paintings were commonly used for the first time to create atmosphere on the stage. Since these paintings were often landscapes, they were called *scenes*. Behind them much of the important action of a play went on—birth, murders, intrigues, and the like—action that wasn't represented on the stage. As early as 1658 we find the playwright John Dryden writing about "Things happening in the Action of the Play, and suppos'd to be done behind the Scenes." It wasn't long before the phrase began to be used figuratively to describe any important action hidden from the ordinary spectator, especially in places of power.

The display involved in *making a scene*, "making a disturbance, usually in public," suggests that this expression, too, is theatrical in origin. Strong emotions often portrayed in short scenes of stage plays probably are responsible for the phrase. In fact, the first literary use of the idea is in Samuel Foote's farce *The Liar* (1762), where one of the characters says, "We parted this moment. Such a scene!"

The Drury Lane

The long-famous street and theater in London called Drury Lane get their names from the Drury House, which once stood just south of the present site. The house was built by statesman-soldier Sir William Drury during the reign of Henry VIII. There have been four Drury Lane theaters, including the present one; the first was originally a cockpit that was converted into a theater under James I. All the great English actors, from Garrick and Booth on, have performed at one or another Drury Lane.

British theater manager Augustus Harris took over the Drury Lane in 1881 when its owners went bankrupt, and he made a great success of it, putting on popular big shows in a theater where "Shakespeare spelled ruin and Byron bankruptcy." Few, if any, producers have become so intimately connected with a theater as the ambitious Harris, who managed to assume ownership of Drury Lane when he had only five pounds in his pocket. He was so closely identified with the theater that he soon was called "Augustus Druriolanus."

The Greenroom

The lounge in the theater where performers rest when they aren't on stage, or where people who are to appear on television wait before they go on, probably takes its name from such a room in London's Drury Lane Theatre, which just happened to be painted green sometime in the late seventeenth century. Most authorities reject the old story that the room was painted green to soothe the actors' eyes. Another theory holds that the greenroom was also called the scene room because stage scenery was stored there. According to this theory, *greenroom* is simply a corruption of *scene room*.

Getting the Audience off the Stage

As early as Shakespearean times rich patrons were allowed to buy seats on the stage in English theaters, usually to the dismay of the actors, who objected to these gentlemen fops proudly displaying their new clothes and chattering endlessly, paying no attention to the play. In France, Voltaire by 1759 banned spectators from the stage, blaming them for the failure of several of his plays, and three years later David Garrick tried with some success to ban them at London's Drury Lane. By the mid-nineteenth century the practice was all but obsolete. One old story has Molière himself sitting on the stage watching a play satirizing his own work and his company. The actor who was satirizing him, however, was so nervous about being physically close to the great playwright that he gave a terrible performance, providing Molière with an evening of laughter.

Boxes

Opera houses were the first theaters to feature the enclosed rooms that came to be called boxes. While opera houses still have boxes encircling the auditorium, most other theaters have abandoned them because of their poor view of the stage. Once, however, they were the only possible choice for those who came to the theater to be seen as much as to see. Some held as many as twenty people, and they were often equipped with blinds in the front that could be pulled down to give their occupants complete privacy when for one reason or another they didn't care to watch the play.

Box Office

The term *box office* may derive from the theater office that sold box seats to playgoers. However, an old story insists that the expression goes back to Shakespeare's day, when theater admission was collected by passing a box attached to a long stick among the audience.

Really Bringing Down the House

A player who brings down the house is so good that the theater seems to vibrate from all the applause he or she receives, as if the building will collapse. The common expression, first recorded in 1754, is from the British theater but is widely used everywhere today.

During an early performance of Christopher Marlowe's *The Tragicall History of Dr. Faustus*, the story of a man who sold his soul to the devil, timbers in The Theater Playhouse suddenly began to crack. Many in the audience thought the building was on the verge of collapse—some attributing this to supernatural causes—and alarmed patrons hurried from the premises. It turned out to be a false alarm, but no one ever established the cause of the cracking timbers.

Playing to the Gallery

Like *playing to the grandstand*, this saying means "showing off." It is an older phrase, however, having its origins in the eighteenth-century English theater, when many actors overacted their roles and raised their voices in order to be appreciated by the larger audience up in the gallery beyond the orchestra.

After the Show: Taverns Where Shakespeare and Co. Drank

The Devil Tavern in London was long a favorite haunt of players in Shakespeare's time, and Ben Jonson often watered there. It isn't the origin of the expression "go to the devil," but its habitués often made a play on the words—old even then.

The White Hart Inn in Southwark must be counted as another famous thespian tavern. Shakespeare mentioned it in *2 Henry VI* as the headquarters of Jack Cade, the Irish adventurer who marched on London leading a mob.

Most famous of all thespian taverns was The Mermaid on Broad Street in London, which Shakespeare, Richard Burbage, Ben Jonson, Beaumont and Fletcher, and many other great playwrights and players frequented. This was the noted watering place that John Keats wrote about in his poem "Lines on the Mermaid Tavern":

Souls of Poets dead and gone,
What Elysium have ye known,
Happy field or mossy cavern,
Choicer than the Mermaid Tavern?
Have ye tippled drink more fine
Than mine host's Canary wine?
Or are fruits of Paradise
Sweeter than those dainty pies
Of venison? O generous food!
Dressed as though bold Robin Hood
Would, with his Maid Marian,
Sup and bowse from horn and can.

I have heard that on a day
Mine host's sign-board flew away
Nobody knew whither, till
An astrologer's old quill
To a sheepskin gave the story,
Said he saw you in your glory,
Underneath a new old sign
Sipping beverage divine,

*And pleading with contented smack
The Mermaid in the Zodiac.*

*Souls of poets dead and gone,
What Elysium have ye known,
Happy field or mossy cavern,
Choicer than the Mermaid Tavern?*

New York City's First Theater

"On the 6th instant, the *New Theater* in the building of the Hon. Rip Van Dam, Esq. was opened with the comedy of *The Recruiting Officer*," read a newspaper article dated December 11, 1732. *The Recruiting Officer* was a play by English dramatist George Farquhar that has been revived many times since, and the New Theater was located in what is now the New York City financial district. The Honorable Rip Van Dam (1660–1749) had served as governor of the Province of New York before opening the city's first playhouse, which remained in use until about the time of his death. On that first opening night in New York a circle of candles on nails projecting from a barrel hoop illuminated the stage, and a stove in the foyer provided the only heat for the bare bench-lined room. A large notice on the wall urged the audience not to spit. From these inconspicuous premises the great New York stage tradition began.

Penny Theaters

Small makeshift theaters that charged only a penny for admission were common in England and France during the early nineteenth century. These theaters held only about a hundred people and put on several shows nightly. The plays presented were usually crude, lurid melodramas catering to what were called "the lower classes." One such play, entitled *The Red-Nosed Monster or The Tyrant of the Mountains* (c. 1850) was a kind of early Western in which the lone hero rescued the heroine from the Indians. The cast included the Red-Nosed Monster (the Indian), the Assassin, the Ruffian of the Hur, the Villain of the Valley, the Wife of the Red-Nosed Monster, the Daughter of the Assassin, and of course the Hero and the Heroine. The theaters themselves might be said to be the ancestors of the little theaters (the equivalent of Off-Off-Broadway playhouses) of today.

When the Bowery Was in Bloom

After the erection in 1826 of the famous Bowery Theatre, the first playhouse on the Bowery, the area soon became lined with playhouses, concert halls, saloons, and dives. As late as 1898 there were ninety-nine houses of entertainment, only fourteen of which were approved by the police. These theaters were a thrilling attraction for visitors to the city. Many of them were three-story buildings with dime museums upstairs and a theater below. Upstairs the patrons paid their dimes to see attractions like Madame Rosa, the bearded lady; Big Hannah, the fat woman; Bosco, the Smoke Eater; and Jo-Jo, the Dog-Faced Man. Then the lecturer would launch into a lyrical spiel coaxing them downstairs to the theater:

> *Now that you've seen our wonder wares,*
> *Next is the big show given downstairs,*
> *You'll see a drama most intense,*
> *The seats they'll cost you but five cents.*
> *Our star has long been known to fame;*
> *Fanny Herring is her name!*
> *Yes, Fanny Herring gives below*
> *A drama laid in O-hi-O.*
> *As the heroine she'll thrawt her foes,*
> *Shoot the villain and goodness knows*
> *She'll prove her lover guiltless of crime—*
> *Remember,* seat costs but half a dime!

"For many years some Bowery theaters presented first-class plays," Herbert Asbury tells us in *The Gangs of New York* (1927),

> but as the character of the street changed and the dives and gangsters made it a byword from coast to coast, they offered blood and thunder thrillers of so distinct a type that they became known as Bowery plays, and could be seen nowhere else. Among them were The Boy Detective, Marked for Life, and Neck and Neck. From these productions developed the "ten, twent,' thirt' " melodrama which was so popular throughout the United States, until its place was taken by the moving pictures. . . . The pit and topmost galleries fairly swarmed with ragamuffins of all degrees and both sexes who stamped and whistled and shouted "h'ist dat rag!" when the curtain failed to rise promptly. . . . "These places were jammed to suffocation on Sunday nights," wrote an author who visited the Bowery theaters about the time of the Civil War. "Actresses too corrupt or dissolute to play elsewhere appear

on the boards at the Bowery. Broad farces, indecent comedies, plays of highwaymen and murderers, are received with shouts by the reeking crowds which fill the low theaters. Newsboys, street sweepers, rag-pickers, begging girls, collectors of cinders, all who can beg or steal a six pence, fill the galleries of these corrupt places of amusement. There is not a dancehall, a concert saloon, or a vile drinking place that presents such a view of the depravity and degradation of New York as the gallery of a Bowery theater.

At the Old Bowery Theatre

The pseudonymous "Q. K. Philander Doesticks," surely one of the most curiously named of New York critics, wrote that the average Bowery theater audience expected "maximum violence from stage battles and deaths, often forcing the too subtle actor to repeat an unsuccessful death (on stage) with the right number of jerks, spasms and groans. For them, a tragedy hero is a milksop, unless he rescues some forlorn maiden from an impregnable castle, carries her down a forty-foot ladder in his arms, holds her with one hand, while with the other he annihilates a score or so of pursuers." According to Edward K. Sparn, in his *The New Metropolis* (1981), "In the 1840s and early 1850s, the legendary hero of the Bowery stage was Mose Humphrey . . . an eight-foot tall urban Paul Bunyan, a giant who uprooted lampposts as weapons in his triumphs over his evil enemies and who carried street cars for blocks in one hand."

Getting the Hook at Miner's Bowery

"At Miner's Bowery Theatre in New York were presented the first amateur nights in burlesque. Here the aspirants for footlight fame were given the opportunity to show their goods. The audience was at liberty to give full expression to their approval or dislike to the offerings of the contestants for the prizes. One Friday night, in October 1903, at Miner's Bowery, a particularly bad amateur was inflicting upon a patient audience an impossible tenor solo. Despite howls, groans and cat-calls, the artist persisted in staying on, when Tom Miner, who was running the show, chanced to see a large old-fashioned, crook-handled cane which had been used by one of the Negro impersonators. Quickly, he had Charles Guthinger, the stage manager, lash it to a long pole. With this, he stepped to the wings without getting into sight of the audience, deftly slipped the hook around the neck of the singer and yanked him off the stage before

Of Barns and Palaces: Famous Theaters and Movie Houses

he knew what happened. The next amateur was giving an imitation of Booth when a small boy yelled, "Get the hook!" The audience roared and the actor fled in dismay. Many later stars including Fanny Brice, Joe Cook, and George White endured the ordeal of the hook."
—The Actor's Fair Bulletin, *1931*

Huber's Barker

Huber's Dime Museum on East 14th Street in New York was almost as famous in its heyday as Barnum's Museum. It was especially noted for its remarkable barker attired at all times in evening dress, who looked like "a bankrupt count of the grand old school of pancake and wax." His spiel in verse went like this:

> *Ladies and gents*
> *for only ten cents*
> *you can see all the sights.*
> *And there on your right*
> *is the great fat lady;*
> *she's a healthy baby*
> *weighing three hundred pounds;*
> *she's six foot around.*
> *Her husband is the living*
> *skeleton—see him shivering.*
> *The dog-faced boy*
> *will give you all joy,*
> *and the tattooed man*
> *does the best he can.*
> *The human horse*
> *is wonderful, of course,*
> *and I'll show to you*
> *the boxing kangaroo.*
> *The lady lion tamer*
> *will please every stranger.* . . .

The Original Broadway Production

By the mid-nineteenth century most New York playhouses were located on Broadway or nearby, but the name "Broadway" wasn't used to attract customers until 1866, when *The Black Crook*, a strange hybrid of ballet and melodrama, was produced. This extravaganza ran over a year on Broadway and toured for more than twenty years, advertising itself as "the original Broadway production." After that the name of Broadway was commonly used both in describing a successful touring company and in attracting visitors to New York as well. *The Black Crook* also did much to further burlesque, employing a long chorus line of girls in flesh-colored tights that proved sensational at the time.

Great White Way Theaters

The nickname the Great White Way for Broadway or the Manhattan theatrical or entertainment district—a reference to all the lights there—was coined by Albert Bigelow Paine, best known today as Mark Twain's first biographer, who used it as the title of his novel *The Great White Way* (1901), which, oddly enough, is about the Antarctic, not Broadway. An early map of New York City shows a "Playhouse on Broadway" operating as early as 1735. Today ten million visitors yearly visit Broadway theaters; they are New York's "biggest single tourist draw," according to Mayor Rudy Giuliani. Some of these often beautifully restored theaters are listed below. Those with stars are named after prominent theatrical figures. Many are rich in theatrical history, such as the Palace, where every vaudevillian once dreamed of playing.

Ambassador Theater
219 West 49th Street

Belasco Theatre★
111 West 44th Street

Booth Theater★
222 West 45th Street

Broadhurst Theatre★
235 West 44th Street

Broadway Theater
1681 Broadway

Brooks Atkinson Theater★
256 West 47th Street

Cort Theatre★
138 West 48th Street

Ethel Barrymore Theatre★
243 West 47th Street

Eugene O'Neill Theatre★
230 West 49th Street

Gershwin Theater★
222 West 51st Street

Helen Hayes Theatre★
240 West 44th Street

Imperial Theater
249 West 45th Street

John Golden Theatre★
252 West 45th Street

Longacre Theatre
220 West 48th Street

Lunt-Fontanne Theatre★
205 West 46th Street

Lyceum Theatre
149 West 45th Street

Majestic Theatre
247 West 44th Street

Marquis Theatre
1535 Broadway

Martin Beck Theatre★
302 West 45th Street

Minskoff Theatre★
200 West 45th Street

Music Box
239 West 45th Street

Nederlander Theater★
208 West 41st Street

Neil Simon Theatre★
250 West 52nd Street

Palace Theatre
1564 Broadway

Plymouth Theatre
236 West 45th Street

Richard Rodgers★
226 West 45th Street

Roundabout Theatre
1530 Broadway

Royale Theatre
242 West 45th Street

Shubert Theater★
225 West 44th Street

St. James Theatre
246 West 44th Street

Virginia Theatre
245 West 52nd Street

Walter Kerr Theatre★
219 West 48th Street

Winter Garden Theater
1634 Broadway

Off-Broadway

At first *Off-Broadway* meant a play produced in the big playhouses within the New York City area two blocks right or left of Broadway south of 59th Street and north of 38th Street. But it came to mean any economically produced and "idealistically intended" play put on anywhere in the city. Though the term had been used many years before, it came into common use during the 1934 theater season when critic Burns Mantle began an Off-Broadway section in his annual *Best Plays of the Year* volumes. Some famous Off-Broadway groups over the years have included the Washington Square Players, the Provincetown Players (who moved from Provincetown, Massachusetts, to New York City in 1916), the Civic Repertory Theater, Orson Welles's Mercury Theater, and the Circle-in-the-Square Theater. Many important plays have first been presented in such little theater groups. The Provincetown Players, for example, first performed seven of Eugene O'Neill's plays, including *Bound East for Cardiff* (1916), *The Emperor Jones* (1918), *The Hairy Ape* (1921), and *Desire Under the Elms* (1924). Dylan Thomas's poetic *Under Milk Wood* (1953) was first played in the auditorium of the Young Men's Hebrew Association.

The Tree of Hope

Outside New York's Lafayette Theatre, often called "The House Beautiful," stood an elm tree called the "Tree of Hope" that black actors always touched before a performance for good luck. The tree is gone now, as is the theater, which burned to the ground in 1968.

Tin Pan Alley

Tin Pan Alley is located between 48th and 52nd Streets on Seventh Avenue in New York City, an area where many music publishers, recording studios, composers, and arrangers have offices. The place was probably named for the tinny sound of the cheap, much-abused pianos in the offices of music publishers there, or for the constant noise emanating from the area, which sounded like the banging of tin pans to some. The term *Tin Pan Alley*, first recorded in 1914, today means any place where popular music is published and can even stand for popular music itself.

But another version of how the place got its name is told in Isaac Goldberg's *Tin Pan Alley* (1930):

> *It was [music publisher] Harry Von Tilzer's custom when playing the piano in his office, to achieve a queer effect by weaving strips of newspaper through the strings of his upright piano. It is not a musical effect; it is wispy, sometimes mandolin-like, and blurs the music just enough to accentuate the rhythms. Monroe H. Rosenfeld was a frequent visitor, not only as a composer and jingle-man, but as a newspaper writer in quest of material. He had just finished an article upon the music business . . . and was casting about for a title. Harry happened to sit down and strum a tune, when Rosenfeld, catching the thin, "panny" effect, bounced up with the exclamation "I have it!" It was another "Eureka!"*
>
> *"There's my name!" exclaimed Rosenfeld. "Your Kindler and Collins [piano] sounds exactly like a Tin Pan. I'll call the article 'Tin Pan Alley'!"*

The 1940 film *Tin Pan Alley* won an Oscar for Alfred Newman's musical score.

Stage Door Canteen

Probably the only "theater" celebrated in a song—Irving Berlin's "I Left My Heart at the Stage Door Canteen"—is the Stage Door Canteen that the United Service Organization (USO) and American Theater Wing ran during World War II in the basement of Broadway's 44th Street Theater. This was the first USO canteen in the country. Admission was free to all armed forces personnel and Broadway players performed there gratis, danced with the GIs, and even waited on tables. The New York Stage Door Canteen was featured in several movies, as was its counterpart in Hollywood.

Lay Them in the Aisles

Theatrical slang for "to have a sensational success," *to lay* (or *knock*) *them in the aisles* may derive partly from the expression to *knock 'em cold*, which has its origins in boxing. Both expressions date only from about the 1920s. British listeners would have trouble making sense of the phrase, because until fairly recently they have used *aisle* for a section of a theater, not a passageway. Since the word is from the Latin *ala*, "a wing"—corrupted to *aisle* over the years—their use of the word is more true to its original meaning.

The Little Church Around the Corner

Several New York City churches refused to hold funeral services for eminent comedian George Holland (1791–1870) on the grounds that he was an actor. "Holland was the merriest man I ever knew," fellow comedian Joseph Jefferson wrote in his *Autobiography* (1889).

> *Practical joking was a passion with him and though his pranks were numerous, by some good fortune they always ended innocently and with harmless mirth. I remember that on one occasion, when some goldfish had been placed in the ornamental fountain in Union Square, Holland dressed himself in a full sporting suit, and with a fish basket strapped upon his shoulder, a broad-brimmed hat upon his head, and a rod in his hand, he unfolded a campstool, and quietly seating himself in front of the fountain, began to fish, with such a patient and earnest look in his face, that no one could have supposed that it was intended as a practical joke. This strange spectacle soon attracted a curious crowd about the sportsman, who, with a vacant and idiotic smile, sat there quietly awaiting a nibble. A policeman soon forced his way through the crowd and arrested Holland, who explained with a bewildered look that he was fishing in his own private grounds. The policeman naturally concluded that the intruder was some harmless lunatic, and, patting him kindly on the shoulder, bade him go home to his friends. Holland burst into a flood of tears, and while affectionately embracing the*

guardian of the law contrived to fasten the fish-hook into the collar of the policeman's coat, who walked slowly and sympathetically away, unconsciously dragging the line and rod after him. The crowd, seeing the joke, roared with laughter as Holland quickly made his way to the nearest omnibus, which he reached before the infuriated policeman could catch him.

Holland was also noted for his unique acting style. "He was unlike any actor I have ever seen," one theatrical manager recalled. "His appreciation of a part . . . [came from] the amount of practical fun he could extract from it. An opportunity of tumbling over a chair, upsetting a table, or burning his nose with a candle, was worth to him more than all the finest sentences of wit and sentiment. In the overstrained, unnatural, and exaggerated style of farce . . . George Holland was in many respects unequalled."

Remembering all the fun he had had with him, Jefferson was deeply saddened when Holland's son told him that no church would allow his old friend funeral services. Jefferson accompanied the son to still another church. There pompous Episcopal minister Lorenzo Sabine again refused Holland burial services, but told Jefferson that "there is a little church around the corner where they do that sort of thing." The funeral was finally held there, at 1 East 29th Street in the Protestant Episcopal Church of the Transfiguration, which soon became known as the Little Church Around the Corner and is still the scene of many theatrical funerals and weddings.

Playing the Barns

Cows, pigs, horses, and chickens were among the audiences that theatrical troupes have performed before in barns throughout America since as early as the eighteenth century. *Barnstorming* has been used to describe such performances since at least 1815, when an itinerant New York City theatrical troupe gave such performances in upstate New York barns. The word also came to mean acting characterized by ranting, shouting, and broad or violent gestures. Later it was applied to tours of rural areas by political candidates.

Corny, for something old-fashioned, unsophisticated, mawkishly sentimental and unsubtle—what is often called "tacky" in today's slang—has its origin in America's Corn Belt barns. Comedians playing to unsophisticated "corn-fed" audiences in Midwest barns gave them the corn-fed humor they wanted, so much so that corn came to be known as "what farmers feed pigs and comedians feed farmers." Soon *corn-fed humor* became simply *corny jokes*, the phrase possibly helped along by the Italian word *carne*, "cheap meat," being applied to the "cheap jokes" the comedians told.

Unholy Hollywood

There is no proof for the tale that Hollywood was first called *Holywood* by its pious founders, and that the word was corrupted to Hollywood as the town corrupted. The film capital of the world, laid out in 1887, is probably named for the California holly or toyon (*Heteromeles arbutifolia*), a large shrub that isn't a tree holly but whose scarlet berries, borne from Christmas to Easter, suggest the holly and are much used for Christmas ornaments. Hollywood may, however, be the transferred name of another place named Hollywood for a true holly, someplace where hollies are a native tree.

Imprints for Posterity: Grauman's Chinese Theater

Since 1927 scores of movie stars have left imprints of their feet and hands in cement outside Grauman's Chinese Theater in Los Angeles, the first of them Hollywood actress Norma Talmadge. A good number of stars, however, have left more imaginative imprints for posterity. Jimmy "The Schnoz" Durante, for example, impressed his impressive nose in the forecourt sidewalk, and comedian Joe E. Brown left a likeness of his huge mouth, while Betty Grable laid down one of her "million dollar legs" and Mickey Mouse left his paw prints. The hoofprints of cowboy star Gene Autry's faithful horse, Champ, and Roy Rogers's Trigger are also enshrined outside Grauman's, as is Al Jolson's right knee, which he knelt on singing "Mammy." So are matinee idol John Barrymore's profile and actor Monty Woolley's beard. The theater, now owned by the Mann Theaters Corporation, has no plans to discontinue this tradition begun in the first year it was built.

Dish Houses

During the Great Depression in the 1930s, theaters sponsored many promotions to lure patrons to the movies. Among the most popular were "dish nights," when anyone buying a ticket received a piece of china. The china was part of a matching set so that those who attended regularly could acquire all fifty-two or so pieces. Such theaters soon came to be called *dish houses*.

Holden Caulfield

The famous fictional character created by J. D. Salinger in *Catcher in the Rye* (1951) was named in an unusual way. The author happened to be passing a movie theater and looked up at the marquee to see the names William

Holden and Joan Caulfield starring in *Dear Ruth*. He focused on the last names, which were featured in large letters, and the two names seemed a natural to him for the name of the teenager in the book he was writing.

Movie Palaces Today

The largest movie theater in the world today is New York's Radio City Music Hall, which opened in 1932 and now has 5,910 seats. America's largest *screen*, however, is the three-dimensional screen measuring 96 feet by 70½ feet at the Six Flags Great America Pictorium in Gurnee, Illinois.

Chicago has more movie screens than any other American city, according to the National Association of Theater Owners—with 453 as of 1996. But San Francisco has the most movie screens per 100,000 people—20.3 at last count.

There are few great movie palaces or multiplexes in mainland China, but the Chinese go to the movies more than people in any other country—a record-breaking 21.8 billion of them in 1988. The Chinese, however, don't have to pay the often outrageous prices American cinemophiles dish out to see a flick. A ticket costs as much as $9.50 in New York first-run theaters today, $1.50 more if you call to reserve a seat—a far cry from the nickelodeons of seventy years ago.

VII

Fanatics, Fires, and Murders Most Foul

The Bloodiest Performer of All

Cruel, vindictive, dissolute, spindle-shanked, pot-bellied, profligate, treacherous, tyrannical, murderous—it would take a far longer string of derogatory adjectives to describe Nero, the last of the Caesars. But this bloody-minded Roman emperor, who killed his own mother and kicked to death one of his wives, thought he was a great actor. That Nero fiddled while Rome burned is essentially true, though he probably sang and played the harp, not the fiddle, while regarding the fiery spectacle with cynical detachment. For Nero considered himself a peerless singer with "a divine voice." Though he performed as a dancer in pantomime—he had the pantomime artist Paris put the death because Paris got more applause than he, Nero, did—his favorite stage performances were in tragic roles such as the matricide Orestes, the mad Hercules, and the blind Oedipus. Here he thought he excelled "singing" the parts. One time Nero toured Greece in such roles and won 1,808 triumphal crowns. But it should be remembered that he brought five thousand trained applauders with him and was never really disguised behind the masks he wore. Everyone knew he was Nero—and voted prudently—because the masks he wore were modeled either on his own features or on the features of his mistress of the moment.

If one includes as theaters the Roman circuses, where chariot races and other bloodier entertainments took place, Nero may have been responsible for the greatest theater fire of all time. The fire he may have set to burn down Rome began in the stalls of the Circus Maximus, spreading swiftly to destroy three-fourths of the city. It is said that Nero set Rome afire in A.D. 64 because he wanted to see what Troy looked like when it burned, although there is no proof of the story.

In any event, the madman (he could charitably be called this) rebuilt Rome, including a grandiose "Golden House" for himself, blamed the blaze on Christians, and persecuted them with such fury that they regarded him as the fantastic beast called 666 in Revelation 13:11–18. Fortunately he died young—in A.D. 68 at only thirty-one—before he could do any more damage to people or property. His last words were "What an artist dies in me!"

Reprehensible Scum, the Dirty Rotten Scoundrel

Nobody would expect anything from someone nicknamed "Scum," and leading British actor Cardonnell "Scum" Goodman (1649–99) provided nothing. Nicknamed Scum since his schooldays, when he was kicked out of Cambridge, Cardonnell, the son of a clergyman, probably had the most reprehensible manners of any actor who ever trod the boards. Once he fatally stabbed a fellow actor in an argument over a shirt the two men shared—Goodman wanted to wear it out of turn. On another occasion he was fined for trying to poison the two older sons of his mistress, the duchess of Cleveland, by whom he had a son of his own—apparently to get the two boys out of the way so that his own son could inherit her fortune. Later he turned highwayman but was soon caught. James II pardoned him, and Scum returned the royal favor by becoming involved in a plot to kill William II. Scum Goodman finally fled to Paris; a British syndicate paid the dirty rotten scoundrel an annual pension to remain there for the rest of his life.

A Poison Plot

Jean Racine (1639–99), one of France's greatest dramatists, was accused by the actress Catherine Voisen of poisoning her to make room in one of his plays for the actress Mlle Champmeslé. There is no proof of this, but Mlle Champmeslé did later become Racine's mistress and starred in his renowned play *Phèdre*.

Murder over a Wig

The long-lived English actor Charles Macklin, famous for his portrayal of Shylock in *The Merchant of Venice*, killed fellow player Adam Hallam, one of a large family of English actors, in the greenroom at the Drury Lane Theatre in 1735. Macklin, an extremely jealous and quarrelsome man, wanted to wear a wig Hallam had chosen for a play both men were appearing in. The Wild Irishman, as he was called, got away with the murder and went his tempestuous way, celebrated as a great lover, boxer, card player, distance walker, and drinker, expending more energy off the stage than on it. Macklin constantly quarreled with one person or another and frequently wound up in court, though, paradoxically, he was known as a man of great charm, generosity, and critical acuity. His most bitter quarrel was with an audience. In 1772 he was appearing as Macbeth in Covent Garden, when the audience demanded to see the great crowd pleaser William Smith in the part. "Gentleman Smith"—who boasted that he had never blackened his face for a part, never played in a farce, never ascended through a trap door, and never, ever acted during the hunting season—was a handsome, elegant Cambridge graduate but hardly rivaled Macklin as an actor. Macklin refused to give him the stage and a few nights later, in retaliation, the audience refused to hear the Wild Irishman in his famous Shylock role. The theater company fired him in order to avoid a riot. Macklin sued and the courts ruled in his favor, awarding him six hundred pounds and costs, though Macklin chose instead to have the defendants buy one hundred pounds' worth of tickets at three benefits—one for himself, one for his daughter, and one for the management. Macklin, who was among England's greatest actors, only retired from the theater at age ninety-three, when he could no longer remember his lines. He lived until one hundred—or one hundred seven, according to some accounts—outliving all of his children before he died in 1797. It is said that his favorite entertainment in his old age was to attend the theater and heckle the actors.

Most Deaths on Stage

Only the bloodiest Hollywood movies can match the violence of the classic Japanese play *The Forty-Seven Ronins*. In this sixteenth-century Kabuki drama—a version of which was written by Chikamatsu Monzaemon, the Japanese Shakespeare—forty-seven *ronins*, or servants, set out to murder an official who has forced their master to commit suicide. After much mayhem they accomplish their goal and in the last act—called the bloodiest in theater history—all forty-seven of them commit hara-kiri, too.

Attacking the Audience

George Washington Lafayette Fox, an American pantomime artist, started his career in Boston when six or so with his family troupe. Fox went out on his own after he came of age, joining the National Theater Company and playing many roles, including a burlesque of *Hamlet*. It is said that Fox's quick movements, darting eyes, and sharp features actually resembled those of a fox. Playing under the name Lafayette Fox he was for a while the highest paid American performer, making over $20,000 a year during the 1870s. His greatest success was in his own musical pantomime *Humpty Dumpty* (1868), which was the longest-running show of its time, marking the high point of American pantomime. (A former mayor of New York City, A. Oakey Hall, collaborated with Fox on the play.) Fox played in numerous versions of *Humpty Dumpty* in his last years, but his behavior became extremely erratic, and his career all but ended one night when he leaped off the stage and assaulted members of the audience without provocation. He died a short time later, in 1877, when only fifty-two, apparently either of paresis, a late manifestation of syphilis characterized by progressive dementia and paralysis, or from lead poisoning caused by the white clown makeup he used.

Dictator D'Annunzio

Gabriele D'Annunzio's prose style was admired by James Joyce, and his play *Le Martyre de Saint Sebastien* was set to music by Claude Debussy, but the Italian poet, playwright, and novelist, who died in 1938, age seventy-five, is better remembered today for his sexual and military adventures than for his lyric writings. D'Annunzio's whole life was onstage. His spectacular exploits by sea and air were widely reported in the press when he fought for the Allies during World War I. He is the only playwright (if not director) ever to become an actual dictator—for two years beginning in 1919, when he and his small volunteer force occupied the city of Fiume. His sexual adventures were legion, making Casanova look like an amateur. Stating that "a good soldier is prepared for anything," D'Annunzio would carry condoms into battle in Napoléon's snuffbox, which he had won as a prize of war. There are legends that he rode to the hounds in the raw with a naked lady at the front of his saddle, nonchalantly strode nude into the dining room of an illustrious hotel, slept on a pillow filled with locks of hair from his conquests, served wine from a carafe made from the skull of a virgin who had committed suicide because of him, and used strychnine as an aphrodisiac. Once he boasted that he had eaten a roasted baby. D'Annunzio, whose most famous affair was with the great actress Eleonora Duse (about whom he wrote a callous tell-all biography), publicly boasted that he was "hated by a thousand husbands." It is said that but for his often "swinish behavior," he would have won the Nobel Prize in 1926.

The Bromo Seltzer Murder

Playwright Roland Molineaux (1866–1917) was convicted of killing the cousin of the manager of New York's Knickerbocker Athletic Club after an altercation with the manager. Molineaux, so the charge went, had mailed a bottle of poisoned Bromo Seltzer to the manager and the man's cousin had inadvertently drunk it for an upset stomach. Molineaux spent three years in prison before a new trial resulted in his acquittal. The playwright wrote several plays after his release, but apparently all his troubles drove him insane. After the failure of his play *The Man Inside* (1913) he was committed to an insane asylum, where he remained for the rest of his life.

More Murders Most Foul

- Young Christopher Marlowe (1564–93), at age twenty-nine second only to Shakespeare among Elizabethan dramatists, was having supper in a private room at a tavern with Ingram Frizer, his host; Robert Poley; and Nicholas Skeres when a brawl broke out among them. According to one version, the heated dispute arose over the dinner bill, with Marlowe wrestling Frizer for his dagger, which accidentally penetrated two inches into Marlowe's eye and killed him instantly. But all four men were active in espionage circles at the time, and Marlowe's death was possibly a planned assassination due to his secret service activities. Some even say that Marlowe wasn't killed, that his assassination was faked, he was hidden, and he later returned to write his last plays under Shakespeare's name. In any case, Frizer was tried but acquitted of the killing on grounds of self-defense.

- Renowned English playwright Ben Jonson was an arrogant and quarrelsome man, but brave and fearless. While serving as an English soldier in Flanders he fought and killed an enemy champion in single combat. Later, in a duel he fought at London's Hogsden Fields in 1598, Jonson killed actor Gabriel Spenser, probably in self-defense, and was in danger of the gallows. However, a Roman Catholic priest visited him in prison and he converted to Catholicism. Pleading guilty to manslaughter, he served a short term in jail and was finally released by benefit of clergy, forfeiting all his possessions and being branded with an *M* for "murderer" on his left thumb. The playwright remained a heavy drinker. One story, probably apocryphal, claims that he and the poet Michael Drayton visited Shakespeare in Stratford and drank so hard with him as to bring on the fatal fever that killed the Swan of Avon.

- When John Dryden, the outstanding English playwright of the Restoration period, dedicated a play to the earl of Rochester's enemy Lord Mulgrave in 1657, Rochester hired a band of thugs who almost beat Dryden to death in Covent Garden. Rather than feeling any guilt for the attack, Rochester later quipped in a poem: "Who'd be a wit in Dryden's cudgelled skin?"

    Rochester's tongue, sharp and cruel as an assassin's knife, went to work again when playwright Samuel Pordage left a copy of his rhymed tragedy *Herod and Mariamme* at his house, hoping that Rochester, whom he didn't know, would back it. A week later Pordage went to collect the play and found that Rochester had written on the cover:

    Poet, who'er thou art, God damn thee,
    Go hang thyself, and burn thy Mariamme.

    Luckily, Pordage did neither.

- The German dramatist August von Kotzebue (1761–1819) proved luckier with his plays, some of them famous in their time, than he did with his politics. In Russia, where he served as a minor official, he fell from grace and spent a few months in Siberia as a convict. Soon afterward he was restored to favor, only to see his patron, Czar Paul I, assassinated. After wandering between Russia and his own country, Kotzebue finally returned to Germany in 1817 as a secret political informant for Czar Alexander I. Liberal Germans suspected his activities, and he was stabbed to death by zealous nationalist Karl Sand, who became a martyr after being executed for the assassination.

- Actor John Wilkes Booth assassinated President Abraham Lincoln on April 14, 1865, at 10:15 in the evening in Ford's Theatre, Washington, D.C., a murder that has become part of world folklore. (See "A Tragedy in the Audience" for a fuller account.)

- Popular British actor William Terris (1847–97), "Breezy Bill" to his many admirers, was assassinated by a madman after he left London's Adelphi Theatre one evening.

- Virginia Rappe, a pretty, struggling young film actress, died of massive internal injuries a few days after attending a wild party thrown by popular slapstick comedian Roscoe "Fatty" Arbuckle in a San Francisco hotel suite on September 5, 1921. The three-hundred-pound Arbuckle was charged with raping the young woman and causing her death, allegedly by penetrating her with a long, jagged chunk of ice or with a champagne bottle—there were a number of stories about the instrument used. Several witnesses gave graphic testimony against him, but Arbuckle's first two trials for the crime ended with hung juries and a third jury acquitted him. Nevertheless, outraged movie fans throughout the country judged the comedian guilty, the watchdog Hayes Office banned his films, and Arbuckle's career was ruined. Until his death in 1933, age forty-six, the former millionaire actor barely scraped by as a vaudeville performer and as a director working under the pseudonym William Goodrich.

- Former child star Carl Switzer (1926–59), who played Alfalfa in the classic Our Gang comedy series, couldn't make it as an actor after his early success. He became an alcoholic, living on the fringes of Hollywood society. Switzer was stabbed to death by another drunken panhandler in an argument over money. His last words were "I want that fifty bucks you owe me and I want it now!"

- Lana Turner's teenage daughter, Cheryl Crane, stabbed to death Turner's boyfriend, mobster Johnny Stompanato, on April 4, 1958, after he had brutally beaten the movie star.

- Self-proclaimed messiah Charles Manson, the abused, deranged son of a prostitute, sent three of his brainwashed "Manson girls" and his disciple Charles Watson into actress Sharon Tate's Hollywood home on August 9, 1969, to brutally murder Tate and four guests. They stabbed and bludgeoned them all seventy or eighty times and stabbed Sharon Tate, eight months pregnant, repeatedly in the womb. The next night the same four zombies executed Mr. and Mrs. Leno La Bianca in their Los Angeles home. For these seven murders, among the most vicious in all history, let alone theater history, Manson and his followers were all tried and sentenced to death, but their sentences were later commuted to life imprisonment.

The President Threatens a Critic

"Miss Truman is a unique American phenomenon with a pleasant voice of little size and fair quality," music critic Paul Hume wrote in 1950 of a singing recital by Margaret Truman. "Yet Miss Truman cannot sing very well. She is flat a good deal of the time. . . . She communicates almost nothing of the music she presents. . . . There are few moments during her recital when one can relax and feel confident that she will make her goal, which is the end of the song."

When Margaret's father, President "Give 'em Hell" Harry Truman, read the review in the *Washington Post* the next morning, he slashed off the following reply to Hume: "I have just read your lousy review buried in the back pages. You sound like a frustrated old man who never made a success, an eight-ulcer man on a four-ulcer job, and all four ulcers working. I have never met you, but if I do you'll need a new nose and plenty of beefsteak and perhaps a supporter below."

Hissing Away a Career

English actor William Smith (d. 1696) was arguing with a nobleman behind the scenes of George Etherege's play *The Man of Mode*, in which he was appearing as Sir Fopling Flutter, "The Prince of Fops." The nobleman grew so angry about Smith's characterization (which was said to suggest the peer) that he severely beat the actor. When word got back to Charles II, who admired the handsome Smith's work, the king severely reprimanded the nobleman. But justice wasn't really served. A large party of the nobleman's gentleman friends formed a club whose sole purpose was to drive Smith from the stage. They followed Smith from theater to theater, their hisses and catcalls ruining his every performance. Smith soon retired, his only consolation the small fortune he had accumulated over the years.

The Actor Who Saved an Audience: History's First Theater Assassination

History records several assassinations and assassination attempts of heads of state in theaters long before John Wilkes Booth killed Abraham Lincoln at Ford's Theatre. In 1807, for example, an unknown man tried to assassinate England's mad King George III during a performance of *She Would and She Wouldn't* at the Drury Lane Theatre in London. But the most famous of such acts was the killing of the tyrannical Roman emperor Caligula.

The insane Caligula met his end in a Roman theater after watching the famed Greek actor Mnester play the role of an assassinated tyrant. Mnester was repeatedly stabbed to death in the play, blood from a bladder concealed under his robe drenching his costume. When the play ended, Caligula tried to leave the theater but was set upon by assassins in a corridor and stabbed to death in exactly the same way. Caligula's feared mercenary bodyguards were ready to massacre all the audience in retaliation when Mnester took the stage again in the confusion and made a long, eloquent speech convincing the guards that Caligula had miraculously been saved and was even now making a speech to his subjects in the forum. While the dreaded mercenaries rushed out to check his story, the audience of hundreds escaped unharmed from the theater.

A Tragedy in the Audience: Actors View Lincoln's Assassination

The real drama, a play for the ages, wasn't onstage but out in the audience, where several actors in the cast of Tom Taylor's *Our American Cousin* saw John Wilkes Booth assassinate President Abraham Lincoln on April 14, 1865, at 10:15 in the evening in Ford's Theatre. Actress Kathryne M. Evans, playing the part of a servant, wasn't onstage when it happened. "My husband and I were sitting in the greenroom waiting for our 'call,' when we heard a shot that we knew was not a part of the play," she recalled twenty years later in her memoirs.

> *Everybody rushed frantically to the stage, and as we arrived there we saw the President's head fall forward on his breast. The members of the company were terribly excited and refused to believe that the assassin was an actor, much less that it was Booth, as he was loved by everyone who knew him. A great gloom fell over all theatrical people that the deed had been committed by one of their number, and many did not go back to Washington for years. My husband and everybody that had been seen in the company during the day was put under arrest on suspicion of being an accessory to the great crime.*

Harry Hawk, another actor in the play, saw much more than Mrs. Evans. It began that Friday afternoon, he told a *Billboard* correspondent many years later on July 20, 1907:

> *I was at the theater early at the rehearsal of a song composed by William Withers, the leader of the orchestra, in honor of President Lincoln, and about 2 o'clock I went out to get some lunch. On the steps of the theatre sat J. Wilkes Booth, reading a letter. I spoke to him, and he started, folded the letter with a muttered "Damn that woman," and came with me, and we had a light lunch together.*
>
> *I can see him yet, tall, handsome, and gifted. He was dressed all in black and wore a black hat, the same clothing he wore that night at the theatre. He was morose, as he always was, for John Booth, as we called him, was disappointed, and burning with the shame and wrongs of the*

South, as he bitterly called them. He thought the whole South would rise up with open arms to greet him when he committed that awful crime, and in his poor, diseased imagination, he pictured himself as the idol of the Confederacy.

Well, after we had finished our lunch I returned to the theatre and saw no more of Booth until after the shot had been fired. When the assassination occurred I was alone on the stage, but my back was turned toward the President, and therefore I did not see the actual shooting.

Mrs. Muzzy, who played the part of Mrs. Mount Chessington in the play, had just discovered that I, as The American Cousin, had destroyed a will which gave me a large fortune, and in anger she cried, "Sir, it is plain to be seen that you are not accustomed to the manners of good society," and with this parting shot she flounced out.

"Not accustomed to the manners of good society?" I replied. "Well, I know enough to turn you inside out, woman. You darned old sockdolliger of a man trap." Those were the last words the President heard, for just as I finished them I heard a shot. It was not loud, and I supposed some one had fired a pistol by mistake in the property room. As I turned to go on with my part, not realizing what had taken place, the house was as silent as the grave for an instant, and then through the quietness came the now famous "Sic Semper Tyrannis," followed by a scene of wild confusion.

Booth was advancing over the stage with a big dagger in his hand, and I took a step toward him, then, as he waved his weapon, I went off the stage, to return a moment later, when I was grasped by Colonel Stewart, who had gained the stage, and who shouted, "Where is that man?"

"By God I don't know," I shouted in return and then went into the green room. Even then the members of the company did not know who had fired the shot, and were rushing about in wild disorder.

After this I was arrested and was taken before Mayor Wallach, who held me under $1,000 bail as a witness. This was furnished by Dr. Brown, an undertaker, who afterwards embalmed the body of the President. Dr. Brown took me with him to his home, and at about three in the morning I was taken under escort of six soldiers to the Peterson House, where the members of the Cabinet and other officials were gathered. Here also was the wounded President lying, and it was not until seven in the morning that he died. I gave my testimony before Judge Carter, and was allowed to return to my friend's home.

A spurious account has John Wilkes Booth's brother Edwin Booth in the audience at Ford's Theatre when Lincoln was assassinated, but Edwin was not even in Washington at the time. However, less than five months previous to this, America's greatest actor of the day and a founder of the Players Club performed in New York's Winter Garden Theatre in *Julius Caesar* with his two brothers. Edwin played Brutus, his brother Junius played Cassius, and John Wilkes played Mark Antony.

The Jinx Theater

Ford's Theatre in Washington, D.C., was a Baptist Church before theatrical manager John Thompson Ford converted it to a playhouse in 1861. Only a year later it burned to the ground in a mysterious fire. Ford rebuilt it in brick the following year, only to see it become the most famous—or infamous—American theater on April 14, 1865, when Abraham Lincoln was assassinated there. The theater was then purchased by the U.S. government and converted into an office building. But the jinx continued in 1890, when part of the building collapsed, killing twenty-two government workers. Since it reopened as the restored Ford's Theatre in 1965 there have been no further incidents.

Edison's Electrocuted Elephant

One of the worst fates to befall a performing animal was visited upon Topsy, the famous performing elephant at Coney Island's Luna Park early in the century. An enraged Topsy killed three visitors after one of them fed her a lighted cigar or cigarette. Her keepers were ordered to feed her poisoned carrots, but she survived this first execution attempt. There was talk of hanging Topsy, but that method was ruled out by public protest. Finally, Thomas Edison, the founder of motion pictures, offered to execute the elephant and prove the power of his alternating current invention at the same time. The ever practical Edison charged admission to the demonstration-execution. Attaching electrodes to the huge elephant, he threw the switch and Topsy, smoking like a house on fire, fell down dead in a few seconds. Luckily Edison didn't film the execution.

Off with Their Heads!

At the time of the French Revolution audiences were probably more unruly than any other playgoers in history. Patrons often physically stopped plays and demanded that another drama from the company's repertoire be performed.

Zealots rioted and halted one play to ceremonially unfurl the national flag onstage. On numerous occasions spectators interrupted performances to demand that aristocratic forms of address such as *duc*, *marquis*, and *comte* be changed to the all-encompassing, revolutionary *citoyen*. First the Revolution closed all the theaters; then they were opened to everyone at low prices. Finally, melodramas like those of Guilbert de Pixerécourt, who boasted that he wrote for those who could not read, became the most popular in Paris. It is said that a performing monkey on one of the boulevards drew greater audiences than the Comédie-Française.

During the Revolution, revolutionary actors acted in a troupe called the Théâtre de la République, while those who didn't share their beliefs organized themselves into the Théâtre de la Nation. The public, of course, favored the first group, considering all others *aristos* (aristocrats) and rioting against them several times. During a performance of *Pamela*, based on Richardson's novel, a riot ensued that resulted in the arrest of all the actors, who were imprisoned for nearly a year.

England's O.P. Riots

After the Covent Garden Theatre burned down in 1808—twenty-three firemen losing their lives trying to put out the fire—a new theater that cost more than £150,000 to build was erected on the site. Its owner, John Philip Kemble, found it necessary to raise the prices for seats, much to the dismay of theatergoers, who rioted at the first performance on September 18, 1809. The audience wanted the old prices back and shouted their disapproval throughout the play, yelling, hooting, and stamping their feet. The riots didn't end that night, either, continuing for more than two months. "O.P.," a shortening of *old prices*, became the rallying cry of the rioters, who attended the theater waving banners that they hung from the boxes reading JOHN BULL AGAINST JOHN KEMBLE, BRING BACK O.P., and NO ITALIANS (the last referred to Italian actress Madame Catalini, a favorite of the management who was unpopular with the patrons). O.P. medals, hats, waistcoats, and handkerchiefs were among the items hawked in the streets outside theaters. Catcalls (trumpetlike instruments) and rattles interrupted the actors' speeches, and members of the audience danced a special O.P. dance on the pit benches. It grew worse every one of the sixty-seven nights and Kemble had to return to the old prices, dismiss Madame Catalini, and formally apologize to the rioters before the most prolonged interruption by any audience in theater history came to an end.

The Rioters Who (Possibly) Gave the Cops Their Name

In 1826 the Bowery Theatre was erected in New York, on the site of the old Bull's Head Tavern, where George Washington had a last drink before evacuating New York during the Revolutionary War. "The new playhouse," Herbert Asbury writes in *The Gangs of New York*,

> *opened with a comedy,* The Road to Ruin, *but its first important production was in November 1826, when Edwin Forrest played the title role in* Othello. *For many years it was one of the foremost theaters on the continent; its boards creaked beneath the tread of some of the greatest players of the time. It was then the largest playhouse in the city, with a seating capacity of 3,000, and was the first to be equipped with gas [lighting]. The structure was burned three times between 1826 and 1838, and again caught fire some fifteen years before the Civil War, when the police, recently uniformed by order of Mayor Harper, appeared on the scene in all the glory of their new suits and glistening brass buttons. They ordered the spectators to make way for the firemen, but the Bowery gangsters jeered and laughed at them as liveried lackeys, and refused to do their bidding. The thugs attacked with great ferocity when someone howled that the policemen were trying to imitate the English bobbies, and many were injured before they were subdued. So much ill-feeling arose because of this and similar incidents that the uniforms were called in, and for several years the police appeared on the street with no other insignia than a star-shaped copper shield, whence came the name* coppers *and* cop.

Note: Other authorities say that the word *cop* has nothing to do with copper buttons, tracing it back to the verb *cop*, which was first recorded in the sense of "to catch or capture" in early eighteenth-century England.

The Ireland Hoax

While working as a clerk in a lawyer's office, William Henry Ireland (1777–1835) discovered blank Elizabethan parchments and used them and a faded brown ink he concocted to forge a number of documents purporting to be in the handwriting of William Shakespeare. Ireland, only seventeen at the time, claimed that he received the documents from an old "gentleman of fortune" who "had many old papers which had descended to him from his ancestors" but wanted to remain anonymous. When Ireland's father, an engraver and bookseller, pronounced the first documents authentic and notified scholars of the find, his forger-son proceeded to turn out scores of

Shakespeare documents, including letters to the Earl of Southampton, a "Profession of Protestant Faith," and even a love letter to Anne Hathaway enclosing a lock of hair. The young man published his findings in book form and exhibited them, charging admission and gulling people like Pitt, Burke, Boswell, and the Prince of Wales. Ireland's masterworks, however, were two new "Shakespearean" plays: *Vortigern and Rowena* and *Henry II.* Playwright Richard Sheridan actually purchased *Vortigern* for three hundred pounds and half of any royalties, producing it at Drury Lane on April 2, 1796. By this time many people had sensed that Ireland's "discoveries" were forgeries, and the play proved it. A complete fiasco, it was treated as a joke by the actors and practically hooted off the stage by the rioting audience, never to be played again. Its failure and an exposé by Shakespearean scholar Edmund Malone at the end of the year prompted Ireland to confess his forgeries in print. The only punishment he received was the condemnation of literary critics, and he went on to write several forgettable novels.

America's Astor Place Riots

Edwin Forrest, the first star of the American stage, America's first great tragedian, was a vain, jealous, "utterly selfish" man, while William Charles Macready, who ranked behind only Garrick and Kean on the English stage, was arrogant, terrible-tempered, and openly contemptuous of American actors. Both considered themselves rivals from the time they made their New York debuts in 1826.

Time far from improved matters. When Forrest played London nineteen years later he blamed Macready for the cold reception he received, believing without any real proof that the English actor had demeaned his acting ability. He retaliated by taking a box seat and childishly hissing at Macready when he performed in Edinburgh.

Forrest didn't stop there, for it is almost certain that he was an instigator of New York's Astor Place Theatre riots when Macready performed *Macbeth* there on May 7, 1849. Forrest announced that he, too, would play the role of Macbeth that evening at the Bowery Theatre. A perfectly peaceful acting contest might have resulted, but Forrest's supporters, who considered the contest to be a struggle of democracy's rank and file versus elite Americans supporting the British, attended Macready's performance and almost forced the English actor from the theater. Chairs were thrown upon the stage, and rotten food and asafetida (a foul-smelling resinous plant material) were hurled from the gallery at Macready.

Fanatics, Fires, and Murders Most Foul 241

Macready was by now ready to sail home, but a group of his American admirers, including Washington Irving, petitioned him to repeat his performance three days later. This time Forrest's loyalists were led by E. Z. C. Judson—a disreputable character who wrote dime novels under the pen name Ned Buntline and had helped found the reactionary Know Nothing political party. They not only marched on the Astor Place Theatre but planned to wreck the homes of all the "Anglophiles" who had petitioned Macready to perform again. However, when they reached the theater, the rioters found it surrounded by New York police and militia. Still they charged, armed with stones and clubs, and in the ensuing shambles, which almost wrecked the theater, twenty-two people were killed and thirty-six wounded, many of them seriously.

Macready barely escaped with his life before America's worst theater riot ended that night; he never performed in America again. Later the shady Judson was sentenced to a year in the penitentiary for his part in the affair. As for Forrest, whom many considered the real instigator behind the scenes, his popularity began to wane, his reputation tarnished, though he still had a large following upon his death twenty years later.

More Stupid Theater Riots

1670. A riot broke out in the theater when a younger actress replaced popular French actress Catherine Leclerc du Rozet (1630-1706) in her customary role as Agnes in Molière's *L'École des Femmes*. In order to calm the clamoring Parisian audience Catherine was sent for after the play began, in such haste that she had to play the costume part in her street clothes.

1737. The custom of allowing footmen waiting for their employers at the theater to see the play for free was abolished, causing a number of riots in London playhouses.

1749. The Quart Bottle Playhouse Riot. The British duke of Portland bet that if "a man advertised the most impossible thing in the world, he will find fools enough to fill a playhouse and pay handsomely for the privilege of being there." His friends took him up on the wager and they advertised in the newspapers that on the next Monday, January 16, on the stage of Mr. John Potter's London playhouse, a man would "jump into a quart bottle placed on a table . . . in the sight of all spectators." On the appointed night the playhouse was "crowded to suffocation" with people who had paid up to seven shillings and sixpence a seat. When the man failed to appear and jump into the bottle, the mob went wild and totally destroyed the theater, burning it to the ground after vandalizing or stealing everything in it. Yet some people believed the duke and his friends when they advertised again that the man would have appeared if someone watching him rehearse hadn't corked him up in his bottle and carried him off to parts unknown!

1794. When the first command performance was given at London's Haymarket Theatre, an enormous crowd attended hoping to see the king and queen. Fifteen people were trampled to death and a larger number were badly injured.

1796. The Tailors' Riot took place at the Haymarket Theatre after a throng of London's tailors, taking offense at Samuel Foote's satirical play *The Tailors*, attended a performance, throwing shears at him and driving the actors from the stage.

1831. When the French Inspector General of Theaters censored passages in Victor Hugo's *Hernani* that were disrespectful of the monarchy, a literary war ensued in which romanticists supporting Hugo took sides against the classicists. There were pitched battles for weeks inside and out of the theater. Professional claques were hired by the classicists, and Théophile Gautier led romanticist volunteers, urging them to take their stand "upon the rugged mount of Romanticism, and to valiantly defend its passes against the assault of the Classics." It was a costly victory for the romanticists; many were injured and at least one young man died in a duel. The novelist Balzac, who was hit in the head with a cabbage, remarked that "if the play had had six acts, we should all have collapsed asphyxiated."

1834. The Farren Riots broke out on July 9 at the Bowery Theatre at a benefit for English comedian George F. Farren in which American actor Edwin Forrest was scheduled to perform. The riots were a cause of the bloody anti-British Astor Place Riots (*see* "America's Astor Place Riots") that occurred fifteen years earlier. New York City diarist Philip Hone (1780–1851) described how the riots began:

> *Our city last evening was the scene of disgraceful riots. The first was at the Bowery Theatre. An actor by the name of Farren, whose benefit it was, had made himself obnoxious by some ill-natural reflections upon the country, which called down the vengeance of the mob, who seemed determined to deserve the bad name which he had given them. An hour after the performance commenced, the mob broke open the doors, took possession of every part of the house, committed every species of outrage, hissed and pelted poor*

> *Hamblin [the theater manager], not regarding the talisman which he relied upon, the American flag, which he waved over his head. This they disregarded, because the hand that held it was that of an Englishman, and they would listen to nobody but "American Forrest."*

1907. John M. Synge's great play *The Playboy of the Western World* aroused great anger when first performed at Dublin's Abbey Theatre. The audience was outraged at the idea that Irish peasants would condone a murder, as they did in the play, and at Synge's language, frank for the time—Christy Mahon, the play's main character, at one point speaks of "all the girls in Mayo . . . standing before me in their shifts." A riot broke out during the first-night performance on January 26, 1907, and the police had to be called in to restore order. When *Playboy* visited the United States for the first time in 1911, performed by the Abbey Players, there were riots among "Irish patriots" in several cities and the entire company was actually arrested in Philadelphia, where they were hauled before a magistrate and charged with "performing an immoral play." More trouble broke out during U.S. tours in 1913 and 1914. It wasn't until another decade or so had passed that Synge's play was widely acknowledged for the masterpiece it is. (See "1926.")

1907. The Night of the Long Kiss. On January 3 the marquise de Morny's pantomime play *Rêve d'Egypte* premiered at the Moulon Rouge music hall in Paris with the famous French author and actress Colette starring as a woman reunited with her lover. Colette, scantily clad—almost unclad—played opposite her lesbian lover, the marquise de Morny, who played the male role. It was a realistic performance, especially the long uninhibited kiss between the two women toward the end of the play. Unfortunately, the marquise de Morny's husband and a group of his friends had front-row seats. Their outrage spread to most of the audience and a riot broke out in the theater, with people throwing bottles and glasses at the actors and fighting with each other in the aisles.

1913. At the premiere performance of Igor Stravinsky's *Rites of Spring* on May 29 at the Théâtre des Champs Élysées in Paris, traditional ballet lovers were shocked by Nijinsky's sensual dancing and the composer's revolutionary score, which many regard today as "the cornerstone of modern music." They rose to their feet whistling, booing, and shouting, punching and wrestling to the ground anyone who tried to silence them. Finally, the police had to be called in, but as soon as silence was restored, disturbances broke out again in another part of the theater. Pandemonium reigned long after the performance ended.

1914. The Pugilist Musicians. A performance of Luigi Russolo's *Fourth Network of Noise* in Paris on April 14 was far ahead of its time for most of the audience. Russolo was a Futurist composer, whose music largely consisted of a cacophony of noises made by combining sounds of streetcars, engines, automobiles, busy crowds, hisses, laughs, and even farts. He and his fellow avant-garde musicians had not been received kindly anywhere before and this time took the precaution of learning how to box before the performance took place. Their plan was to split into two groups if the audience assaulted them again—one group to continue playing and the boxers to protect them. All went according to plan when the enraged audience rose and attacked not long after the concert began. The boxers successfully defended the stage without injury to any of the other musicians or themselves, while eleven of the rioters wound up in the hospital with concussions and broken bones.

1919. Violinist Fritz Kreisler, who had been badly wounded in World War I as a German soldier, made a concert tour of the United States, many of the concerts canceled because of anti-German feelings. Prior to his Cornell University concert in Ithaca in December, New York City's mayor and numerous others urged people not to attend. Kreisler was forced to play in the dark for forty-five minutes when angry American Legionnaires cut the electric wires, and before the performance was over the police had to be called in to put down rioters.

1920. The outraged audience pelted the performers with eggs, tomatoes, and even slabs of beef during a performance of dadaists at the Salle Gaveau in Paris on May 26. The Dada anti-art movement, founded in 1916, flouted conventional values, advocating works marked by nonsense and incongruity. The French child's word *dada*, a "plaything" or hobbyhorse, admirably suited the group's purpose and was chosen, according to the old story, by one member opening a dictionary and pointing randomly to the word. This nihilistic group was composed of painters, poets, playwrights, and other writers. At the Salle Gaveau performance, Paul Eluard dressed as a ballerina, André Breton read from his works with a revolver tied to each side of his head, and other costumes were just as outrageous. Though their negative comments were hardly heard by the rioting audience, the dadaists were quite pleased with their performance. After all, the group's chief aim was a denial of sense and order.

1923. Avant-garde composer George Antheil performed at the Philharmonic in Budapest early in the year. He learned something from his first concert, which had been ruined by rioting traditionalists. On the second night he had the doors of the theater locked, placed a revolver on top of the piano, and proceeded to play uninterrupted until he finished.

1926. Sean O'Casey's play *The Plough and the Stars*, about the 1916 Easter Rebellion against the British, caused a riot when performed at Dublin's Abbey Theatre on February 11. When, during the second act, the Irish flag was brought into a tavern setting on stage, many took this as a national insult. Boos and catcalls drowned the actor's words, audience members fought in the aisles, and others climbed up on stage to fight with the actors. Poet William Butler Yeats, a director of the playhouse, lectured to the audience from the stage, but few listened and the police had to be called in. During all future performances that year the police were present. Though there were no more riots, several stink bombs were thrown and there was a threat to blow up the Abbey. (*See also* "1907.")

1930. At one of the first showings of Luis Buñuel and Salvador Dalí's *L'Age d'Or* in Paris, the audience, objecting to the violent, erotic, antifamily, and antireligion images of the surrealistic film, attacked in force and began to destroy the movie theater, *even assaulting the actors on the screen*. Egged on by reactionary newspapers, the rioters and hundreds more continued their attack for six days, inflicting over 120,000 francs' worth of damage on the theater. The film had to be withdrawn and wasn't shown again in a French theater until 1965.

1954. In September some three thousand roughneck Teddy Boys, stirred up by a showing of *Rock Around the Clock* starring Bill Haley and his Comets, left the theater and started one of the biggest riots in London's history.

1977. The Hanafi Muslim sect demanded that the film *Mohammed, Messenger of God* be withdrawn from the Washington, D.C., theater where it was being shown on the grounds that it blasphemously depicted the image of the Prophet. On March 10 bands of Hanafi gunmen took over three D.C. buildings, including the city hall, killing one person and holding one hundred hostages for two days. After the sect members surrendered it was found that all their charges were false, that the Prophet was never seen in the film.

1977. An Iranian Muslim extremist group violently opposed to the Shah set fire to the Cinema Rex Theater in Abadan on August 20, protesting the showing of a film called *The Deer*. Some 420 people were killed in the fire.

Rat Riots

When the antiwar film *All Quiet on the Western Front*, based on Erich Maria Remarque's famous novel, opened in Berlin in 1929, Nazi protestors caused riots in theaters throughout the city by releasing rats and snakes in the aisles. Several people were injured in the stampedes from the theaters. Other films that the Nazis protested, banned, or confiscated included pacifist Jean Renoir's *Grand Illusion* (1938) and Charlie Chaplin's *The Great Dictator* (1940). In the last case, Chaplin's amazing resemblance to Hitler astonished even his fellow actors.

One Hundred Thousand Dead: Terrible Theater Fires

Tens of thousands of deaths have been caused by theater fires over the past four centuries alone. Just a single such fire in a Chinese playhouse in 1845 led to the loss of 1,670 people, according to one authority. Theater fires were indeed so common in the United States in the nineteenth century that the average life of a playhouse was generally estimated to be only fifteen years. A list of famous theater fires follows. At least 6,569 people died or were severely injured in just these twenty blazes, but more than two hundred theater fires occurred in the United States and Britain alone in the nineteenth century. Keeping these figures in mind it isn't rash to estimate that more than *one hundred thousand* people have been killed or injured in theater fires throughout the world from Shakespeare's day until the present.

1613. The famous Globe or "wooden O" burned. (*See* Chapter 6.)

1672. Drury Lane, London's most famous theater, was almost destroyed by fire on June 25. The only casualty was actor Richard Bell, who was killed in an explosion set off to prevent the fire from spreading. The theater was rebuilt.

1798. The first recorded theater fire in American history completely destroyed the thousand-seat Federal (or Boston) Theatre designed by famed architect Charles Bulfinch. There have been more than one hundred serious theater fires in America up to the present day.

1808. When Covent Garden Theatre in London burned to the ground, twenty-three firemen lost their lives. It was rebuilt, only to burn down again in 1856 and to be rebuilt a second time. A theater still stands on the site.

1809. The Drury Lane Theatre in London—owned since 1777 by playwright Richard Sheridan—burned to the ground for the second time (*see*

"1672") and was rebuilt once again at a cost of about £400,000, a huge sum at the time. Some fifteen years before the 1809 fire, patrons had been assured that the new iron safety curtain over the Drury Lane stage made any fire impossible. Drury Lane still stands as a theater today.

1811. Virginia's governor and sixty-nine other patrons died in a Richmond playhouse on December 26 during a performance of *The Bleeding Nun*, when burning candles in a chandelier set fire to the play's scenery.

1828. London's Royal Brunswick Theatre had burned to the ground in 1826. It was so badly reconstructed that when it reopened two years later it collapsed during a rehearsal and at least fifteen actors were killed.

1836. A fire in the Lehman Theatre, St. Petersburg, Russia, caused some eight thousand casualties.

1846. A Quebec, Canada, theater fire resulted in one hundred casualties.

1847. More than six hundred casualties were reported in a Karlsruhe, Germany, theater fire.

1857. A Leghorn, Italy, theater fire caused one hundred casualties.

1865. P. T. Barnum's American Museum and its theater seating three thousand were totally destroyed by fire in July. The building, on Chambers Street in New York, was rebuilt only to burn to the ground again three years later. In that three-year period four other New York theaters burned to the ground: "444" Broadway; the Academy of Music; the New Bowery; and the old Winter Garden.

1876. A fire in the Brooklyn Theatre in Brooklyn, New York, broke out during the last act of a melodrama entitled *The Two Orphans* and resulted in three hundred deaths, including two actors.

1887. A fire at the Opera Comique in London claimed two hundred lives.

1887. Fire killed 186 people in the Theatre Royal, Exeter, England. Just two years earlier the theater had been destroyed by fire and rebuilt.

1891. A fire at the famous Ring Theatre in Vienna, Austria, left six hundred people dead.

1903. On December 30, 589 lives were lost in a fire at Chicago's Iroquois Theatre. (*See* "America's Worst Theater Fire.")

1942. Some 490 people were killed in a fire at Boston's Coconut Grove nightclub on November 28. Firemen called the club a firetrap.

1944. On July 6 Ringling Brothers, Barnum & Bailey Circus was performing before an audience of more than seven thousand in Hartford, Connecticut. A fire of unknown origin suddenly broke out and 168 people, mostly children, perished in the flames, and at least 487 people were badly injured. To this day the identity of a little girl of about six years old who died in the fire has not been established, though her picture was widely circulated for months afterward throughout the United States.

1977. *See* "More Stupid Theater Riots."

By the Fireside

In 1776 Richard Brinsley Sheridan acquired a share in the famous Drury Lane Theatre, and he produced his plays there afterward. He rebuilt the deteriorating theater eighteen years later at a huge cost. When in 1809 this new Drury Lane Theatre was destroyed by fire, Sheridan sat in a nearby coffeehouse watching the raging flames burn it to the ground. "How can you bear your misfortune so calmly?" a friend inquired. Replied Sheridan, "Ah, a man may surely be allowed to take a glass of wine by his own fireside."

America's Worst Theater Fire

Puckish comedian Eddie Foy, later head of the famous Seven Little Foys vaudeville act, became one of America's greatest thespian heroes during Chicago's terrible Iroquois Theatre fire, but even his bravery couldn't prevent the deaths of 589 people.

Foy was starring in a bargain matinee performance of *Mr. Bluebeard*, playing the role of Sister Anne. The low admission price attracted a large number of mothers and children and the house was overcrowded with 2,400 people, too many of them standing. The Iroquois had been widely advertised as "fireproof" by the syndicate that owned it, and few people gave a thought to the possibility of fire. But the syndicate—a clique of producers who tried to corner the market in American theater entertainment—had little but contempt for safety regulations, as the coming tragedy would prove.

During the musical number "In the Pale Moonlight," not far into the play's second act, a high-temperature carbon arc lamp used to create the illusion of moonlight brushed against a flammable painted canvas wing and the canvas caught fire. The blaze quickly spread to the flammable props and drops made of gauze and muslin. Soon ropes, catwalks, and second curtains were on fire. It all took only seconds, and it seemed as if only Foy had the presence of mind to do anything about it.

Foy rushed out to center stage and ordered the asbestos fire curtain lowered so that the flames could be contained backstage. He pleaded with the audience to remain calm and had the orchestra play a loud overture. But sight of the flames and smoke panicked the packed house. While Foy improvised an act onstage, dancing acrobatically and singing loudly, many people began fighting their way toward the theater's thirty unlighted exits. Women and children fell in the aisles and were trampled by the stampeding crowd. The panic increased when it was found that all the exit doors were locked and opened inward so that they were blocked by the pressure of the crowds of people around them. Those who seized fire extinguishers found them defective; there were no water hoses in working order.

It took only about eight minutes for 589 people to die. None of them succumbed to the flames—Foy had seen to this by containing the fire. All were trampled to death before the doors could be opened and order restored. Later, the Chicago fire commissioner said that Foy's quick thinking and heroic actions in calming some of the crowd had saved another six hundred lives.

The loss of life in the Iroquois disaster created a national scandal that inspired stringent theater safety regulations throughout America, including the requirement of the common "panic doors" in today's theaters that open outward from pressure on a bar. As a result, fires in theaters have become comparatively rare, almost always occurring only when safety regulations are evaded.

Early Film Fires and Other Hazards

Film historians believe that cinema fires in the first few years of the twentieth century numbered in the thousands due to the notoriously flammable nitrate film used in the booming nickelodeons and the use of old buildings not adapted to their new function. It is indeed amazing that there weren't bigger and more fatal fires considering how many small ones broke out in theater projection boxes. Lethal fumes, carbon, and asbestos dust were other hazards both projectionists and audiences shared before much-needed local regulation of the nickelodeons came into play.

The Towering Inferno

Soon after the movie ended at the El Ray Theatre in Manteca, California, in 1975, a fire of unknown origin raged completely out of control and burned the theater to its four walls. The movie playing was *The Towering Inferno*.

The Twilight Zone Crash

It was two o'clock in the morning of July 23, 1982; director John Landis and his crew were working late to finish a scene of *Twilight Zone: The Motion Picture* on the set of a Vietnamese village built beside a river outside Los Angeles, California. Actor Vic Morrow was to save two children from a Viet Cong attack by carrying them across the river while a helicopter hovered above, shooting at them.

Morrow carried the child actors into the water, and special-effects explosions detonated all around them, six cameras recording the action. The pilot descended, circling, but a special-effects explosion shook the copter, which went out of control. The pilot struggled in vain to keep it aloft.

The helicopter went down in the river, its huge blade spinning wildly, landing directly on top of Morrow and the children in his arms. It all happened so quickly that there was nothing anyone could do about it, though Landis and several crew members rushed into the water. Vic Morrow, seven-year-old Myca Dinh Le, and six-year-old Renee Shinn Chen were killed instantly.

Making the Best of It

When Coney Island's Steeplechase Park burned down in 1907, its owners wasted no tears and didn't hesitate to make the best of it. The very next day they posted a sign announcing: ADMISSION TO THE BURNING RUINS—10 CENTS. Business was brisk.

A Theatergoer Who Died Laughing

John Gay's *The Beggar's Opera* (1728) is supposed to have made Gay rich and Rich (the producer) gay (though not in today's sexual meaning of the word). Gay's *Opera*, produced by John Rich, is one of the few plays at which someone literally died laughing. Fifty years after Gay's death, at an April 1782 performance, a certain Mrs. Fitzherbert broke into laughter at the sight of a male actor, dressed up as a girl, playing the part of Polly. She laughed so loudly all the way through the second act that she had to be ejected from the Drury Lane Theatre. Mrs. Fitzherbert's laughter never ended, however. Her hysterical laughter lasted all that Wednesday and all of Thursday until she died of laughter early on Friday morning.

The Great Lover's Funeral

After Rudolph Valentino died of a perforated ulcer in 1926, more than one hundred thousand people, mostly women, lined up for a full ten blocks waiting to view him laid out at the Campbell Funeral Home in New York City—including the Great Lover's professed lover, actress Pola Negri, who wore a $3,000 gown for the occasion. Some one hundred mourners were injured in the weeping, pressing crowd, one wag contending that a few drowned in all the tears. Meanwhile, back in Hollywood all the major studios halted production for two minutes on the day of Valentino's funeral—no great sacrifice considering the millions that were to be made on the rerelease of all his films. Perhaps the worst of all this star worship was the trick photo the *New York Evening Graphic* ran on its front page—it showed Valentino's head attached to another man's body lying in a casket.

The Naughty Play That Ruined Rector's

"Paul Potter's play *The Girl from Rector's* really ruined the million-dollar hotel which George Rector and his father had made one of the great hostelries of the world. Potter, an English-born dramatist, had completed the translation of a French farce for producer Al Woods and the title was undecided. One day Woods arrived at the hotel for a conference with Potter on the forthcoming production. It was raining, and as Woods stepped from his cab a beautiful young girl leaped out of a hansom cab and ran for the door of the restaurant. In those days skirts were worn to the heel, but this shapely and exquisite lady took no chances with the muddy pavements. Skirts high, rippling laughter, the most gorgeous legs and hosiery imaginable made an immediate and dazzling impression on the producer. In later years [Woods] could never recall whether he paid the cabman, but when he arrived at Potter's rooms he announced the title of the new play: *The Girl from Rector's.* It was one of the first of the naughty French type of plays and though it aided Rector's to the pinnacle of success briefly, the association of the name with the play gradually gave the hinterlands the impression that Rector's was the most daring and emotionally dangerous place in New York. The transient trade—bossed by wives from a distance—stopped coming there."

—*Edward Dean Sullivan,* The Fabulous Wilson Mizner, *1935*

Haunted Playhouses

During an early rebuilding of the Drury Lane Theatre, workers found a skeleton bricked up in the walls, a dagger stuck in its ribs. Whether this skeleton has any connection with the ghost of Drury Lane is unknown, but many people have claimed that they've seen a ghost in the theater. He has only been spotted at matinee performances when the house is full, walking in from one wall of the upper circle and walking out the other. The ghost has been described as "an eighteenth-century gentleman in a long gray riding cloak, riding boots, sword, three-cornered hat, and powdered hair." Some say he's the ghost of the murdered man; others claim he is the murderer.

London's venerable Haymarket Theatre is another famous playhouse said to be haunted—by the ghost of popular comedic actor John Baldwin Buckstone (1802–79). Buckstone loved the theater, acted there many times, and toward the end of his life managed the Haymarket.

VIII

Oscars, Tonys, Pulitzers, and Other Prestigious Prizes

The Oscar

Hollywood's gold-plated Oscar remained nameless four years after the Academy of Motion Picture Arts and Sciences first presented the celebrated awards in 1927. Called simply the Statuette, the trophy was designed by Cedric Gibbons; each weigh about seven pounds and originally cost about one hundred dollars. It is thirteen and one-half inches high, depicting a naked man with a sword standing on a reel of film and made mainly of Britannia metal coated with copper, then nickel, silver, and finally 24-carat gold. The Statuette quickly became a symbol of film fame, but it wasn't until 1931 that it got a name. At that time Mrs. Margaret Herrick reported to work as librarian of the Academy and when shown one of the trophies, observed, "He reminds me of my uncle Oscar." As fate would have it Sidney Skolsky, a newspaper columnist, happened to be in the room when she made her remark, and he soon reported to his readers that "Employees of the Academy have affectionately dubbed their famous statuette 'Oscar.'" The name stuck and Mrs. Herrick's uncle won immortality. Uncle Oscar was in reality Oscar Pierce, a wealthy Texan from a pioneer family who had made his fortune in wheat and fruit and migrated to California, where he could now bask in glory as well as the sun. The Oscars that bear his name are given annually in twenty-six categories, the seven most widely known being best motion picture, best leading actor and actress, best supporting actor and actress, best direction, and best screenplay. Cedric Gibbons, the Oscar's designer, received six Oscars for best art director. Here are a few fascinating facts about Oscars past and present:

- The only silent film to win an Oscar was *Wings*, made in 1927, the first year the Oscar was awarded. Gary Cooper had a bit part in the movie.
- The first talkie to win the Oscar for best picture was *The Broadway Melody* (1929).
- In 1941 Joan Fontaine won the best actress Oscar for her performance in *Suspicion*, beating out her sister Olivia de Havilland, who had been nominated for her performance in *Hold Back the Dawn*. This sparked a feud between the sisters that lasted for years.
- The Oscars were made of plaster in 1942 due to World War II wartime austerity.
- A black-and-white film hasn't won the Oscar for best picture since *The Apartment* (1960).
- *Midnight Cowboy* (1969) is the only X-rated film ever to win an Oscar.
- Hattie McDaniel became the first African American to win an Oscar, for best supporting actress in *Gone with the Wind* (1939).
- Sidney Poitier was the first African American actor to win the best actor award, for *Lilies of the Field* (1963).
- Greer Garson's acceptance speech for best actress in *Mrs. Miniver* was the longest in Oscar history, five and a half minutes.
- The briefest role ever to win an Oscar was that of Paul Gauguin in *Lust for Life* (1956), played by Anthony Quinn, who won best supporting actor for his approximately eight-minute portrayal.
- Three films have won Oscars for best picture, director, actor, actress, *and* screenplay: *It Happened One Night* (1934); *One Flew over the Cuckoo's Nest* (1975); and *The Silence of the Lambs* (1991).
- *Beauty and the Beast* (1991) is the only animated movie ever nominated for best picture.
- Over the years the Oscar lost its sharply defined chin. But in 1998 a change in its casting by the Chicago firm that makes the statuette today brought it back to its original glory.

And the Winner Is: A Century of Academy Awards

1927–28

BEST PICTURE: *Wings*

BEST ACTOR: Emil Jannings, *The Last Command* and *The Way of All Flesh*

BEST ACTRESS: Janet Gaynor, *Seventh Heaven* and *Sunrise*

BEST DIRECTOR: Frank Borzage, *Seventh Heaven*

BEST WRITER (adaptation): Benjamin Glazer, *Seventh Heaven*

BEST WRITER (original screenplay): Ben Hecht, *Underworld*

1928–29

BEST PICTURE: *The Broadway Melody*

BEST ACTOR: Warner Baxter, *In Old Arizona*

BEST ACTRESS: Mary Pickford, *Coquette*

BEST DIRECTOR: Frank Lloyd, *The Divine Lady*

BEST WRITER (adaptation): Hanns Kräly, *The Patriot*

1929–30

BEST PICTURE: *All Quiet on the Western Front*

BEST ACTOR: George Arliss, *Disraeli*

BEST ACTRESS: Norma Shearer, *The Divorcee*

BEST DIRECTOR: Lewis Milestone, *All Quiet on the Western Front*

BEST WRITER: Frances Marion, *The Big House*

1930–31

BEST PICTURE: *Cimarron*

BEST ACTOR: Lionel Barrymore, *A Free Soul*

BEST ACTRESS: Marie Dressler, *Min and Bill*

BEST DIRECTOR: Norman Taurog, *Skippy*

BEST WRITER (adaptation): Howard Estabrook, *Cimarron*

BEST WRITER (original screenplay): John Monk Saunders, *The Dawn Patrol*

1931–32

    BEST PICTURE: *Grand Hotel*

    BEST ACTOR: Wallace Beery, *The Champ* and Fredric March, *Dr. Jekyll and Mr. Hyde*

    BEST ACTRESS: Helen Hayes, *The Sin of Madelon Claudet*

    BEST DIRECTOR: Frank Borzage, *Bad Girl*

    BEST WRITER (adaptation): Edwin J. Burke, *Bad Girl*

    BEST WRITER (original screenplay): Frances Marion, *The Champ*

1932–33

    BEST PICTURE: *Cavalcade*

    BEST ACTOR: Charles Laughton, *The Private Life of Henry VIII*

    BEST ACTRESS: Katharine Hepburn, *Morning Glory*

    BEST DIRECTOR: Frank Lloyd, *Cavalcade*

    BEST WRITER (adaptation): Victor Heerman and Sarah Y. Mason, *Little Women*

    BEST WRITER (original screenplay): Robert Lord, *One Way Passage*

1934

    BEST PICTURE: *It Happened One Night*

    BEST ACTOR: Clark Gable, *It Happened One Night*

    BEST ACTRESS: Claudette Colbert, *It Happened One Night*

    BEST DIRECTOR: Frank Capra, *It Happened One Night*

    BEST WRITER (adaptation): Robert Riskin, *It Happened One Night*

    BEST WRITER (original screenplay): Arthur Caesar, *Manhattan Melodrama*

1935

    BEST PICTURE: *Mutiny on the Bounty*

    BEST ACTOR: Victor McLaglen, *The Informer*

    BEST ACTRESS: Bette Davis, *Dangerous*

    BEST DIRECTOR: John Ford, *The Informer*

    BEST WRITER (adaptation): Dudley Nichols, *The Informer*

    BEST WRITER (original screenplay): Ben Hecht and Charles MacArthur, *The Scoundrel*

1936

BEST PICTURE: *The Great Ziegfeld*

BEST ACTOR: Paul Muni, *The Story of Louis Pasteur*

BEST ACTRESS: Luise Rainer, *The Great Ziegfeld*

BEST SUPPORTING ACTOR: Walter Brennan, *Come and Get It*

BEST SUPPORTING ACTRESS: Gale Sondergaard, *Anthony Adverse*

BEST DIRECTOR: Frank Capra, *Mr. Deeds Goes to Town*

BEST WRITER (original story): Pierre Collings and Sheridan Gibney, *The Story of Louis Pasteur*

BEST WRITER (screenplay): Pierre Collings and Sheridan Gibney, *The Story of Louis Pasteur*

1937

BEST PICTURE: *The Life of Émile Zola*

BEST ACTOR: Spencer Tracy, *Captains Courageous*

BEST ACTRESS: Luise Rainer, *The Good Earth*

BEST SUPPORTING ACTOR: Joseph Schildkraut, *The Life of Émile Zola*

BEST SUPPORTING ACTRESS: Alice Brady, *In Old Chicago*

BEST DIRECTOR: Leo McCarey, *The Awful Truth*

BEST WRITER (original story): William A. Wellman and Robert Carson, *A Star Is Born*

BEST WRITER (screenplay): Heinz Herald, Geza Herczeg, and Norman Reilly Raine, *The Life of Émile Zola*

1938

BEST PICTURE: *You Can't Take It with You*

BEST ACTOR: Spencer Tracy, *Boys Town*

BEST ACTRESS: Bette Davis, *Jezebel*

BEST SUPPORTING ACTOR: Walter Brennan, *Kentucky*

BEST SUPPORTING ACTRESS: Fay Bainter, *Jezebel*

BEST DIRECTOR: Frank Capra, *You Can't Take It with You*

BEST WRITER (original story): Eleanore Griffin and Dore Schary, *Boys Town*

BEST WRITER (screenplay): George Bernard Shaw, writer; Ian Dalrymple, Cecil Lewis, and W. P. Lipscomb, adaptation, *Pygmalion*

1939

BEST PICTURE: *Gone with the Wind*

BEST ACTOR: Robert Donat, *Goodbye, Mr. Chips*

BEST ACTRESS: Vivien Leigh, *Gone with the Wind*

BEST SUPPORTING ACTOR: Thomas Mitchell, *Stagecoach*

BEST SUPPORTING ACTRESS: Hattie McDaniel, *Gone with the Wind*

BEST DIRECTOR: Victor Fleming, *Gone with the Wind*

BEST WRITER (original story): Lewis R. Foster, *Mr. Smith Goes to Washington*

BEST WRITER (screenplay): Sidney Howard, *Gone with the Wind*

1940

BEST PICTURE: *Rebecca*

BEST ACTOR: Jimmy Stewart, *The Philadelphia Story*

BEST ACTRESS: Ginger Rogers, *Kitty Foyle*

BEST SUPPORTING ACTOR: Walter Brennan, *The Westerner*

BEST SUPPORTING ACTRESS: Jane Darwell, *The Grapes of Wrath*

BEST DIRECTOR: John Ford, *The Grapes of Wrath*

BEST WRITER (original story): Benjamin Glazer and John S. Toldy, *Arise My Love*

BEST WRITER (original screenplay): Preston Sturges, *The Great McGinty*

1941

BEST PICTURE: *How Green Was My Valley*

BEST ACTOR: Gary Cooper, *Sergeant York*

BEST ACTRESS: Joan Fontaine, *Suspicion*

BEST SUPPORTING ACTOR: Donald Crisp, *How Green Was My Valley*

BEST SUPPORTING ACTRESS: Mary Astor, *The Great Lie*

BEST DIRECTOR: John Ford, *How Green Was My Valley*

BEST WRITER (original story): Harry Segall, *Here Comes Mr. Jordan*

BEST WRITER (original screenplay): Herman J. Mankiewicz and Orson Welles, *Citizen Kane*

1942

BEST PICTURE: *Mrs. Miniver*

BEST ACTOR: James Cagney, *Yankee Doodle Dandy*

BEST ACTRESS: Greer Garson, *Mrs. Miniver*

BEST SUPPORTING ACTOR: Van Heflin, *Johnny Eager*

BEST SUPPORTING ACTRESS: Teresa Wright, *Mrs. Miniver*

BEST DIRECTOR: William Wyler, *Mrs. Miniver*

BEST WRITER (original story): Emeric Pressburger, *The Invaders*

BEST WRITER (original screenplay): Michael Kanin and Ring Lardner Jr., *Woman of the Year*

1943

BEST PICTURE: *Casablanca*

BEST ACTOR: Paul Lukas, *Watch on the Rhine*

BEST ACTRESS: Jennifer Jones, *The Song of Bernadette*

BEST SUPPORTING ACTOR: Charles Coburn, *The More the Merrier*

BEST SUPPORTING ACTRESS: Katina Paxinou, *For Whom the Bell Tolls*

BEST DIRECTOR: Michael Curtiz, *Casablanca*

BEST WRITER (original story): William Saroyan, *The Human Comedy*

BEST WRITER (original screenplay): Norman Krasna, *Princess O'Rourke*

1944

BEST PICTURE: *Going My Way*

BEST ACTOR: Bing Crosby, *Going My Way*

BEST ACTRESS: Ingrid Bergman, *Gaslight*

BEST SUPPORTING ACTOR: Barry Fitzgerald, *Going My Way*

BEST SUPPORTING ACTRESS: Ethel Barrymore, *None but the Lonely Heart*

BEST DIRECTOR: Leo McCarey, *Going My Way*

BEST WRITER (original story): Leo McCarey, *Going My Way*

BEST WRITER (original screenplay): Lamar Trotti, *Wilson*

1945

BEST PICTURE: *The Lost Weekend*

BEST ACTOR: Ray Milland, *The Lost Weekend*

BEST ACTRESS: Joan Crawford, *Mildred Pierce*

BEST SUPPORTING ACTOR: James Dunn, *A Tree Grows in Brooklyn*

BEST SUPPORTING ACTRESS: Anne Revere, *National Velvet*

BEST DIRECTOR: Billy Wilder, *The Lost Weekend*

BEST WRITER (original story): Charles G. Booth, *The House on 92nd Street*

BEST WRITER (original screenplay): Richard Schweizer, *Marie-Louise*

1946

BEST PICTURE: *The Best Years of Our Lives*

BEST ACTOR: Fredric March, *The Best Years of Our Lives*

BEST ACTRESS: Olivia de Havilland, *To Each His Own*

BEST SUPPORTING ACTOR: Harold Russell, *The Best Years of Our Lives*

BEST SUPPORTING ACTRESS: Anne Baxter, *The Razor's Edge*

BEST DIRECTOR: William Wyler, *The Best Years of Our Lives*

BEST WRITER (original story): Clemence Dane, *Vacation from Marriage*

BEST WRITER (original screenplay): Muriel Box and Sydney Box, *The Seventh Veil*

1947

BEST PICTURE: *Gentleman's Agreement*

BEST ACTOR: Ronald Colman, *A Double Life*

BEST ACTRESS: Loretta Young, *The Farmer's Daughter*

BEST SUPPORTING ACTOR: Edmund Gwenn, *Miracle on 34th Street*

BEST SUPPORTING ACTRESS: Celeste Holm, *Gentleman's Agreement*

BEST DIRECTOR: Elia Kazan, *Gentleman's Agreement*

BEST WRITER (original story): Valentine Davies, *Miracle on 34th Street*

BEST WRITER (original screenplay): Sidney Sheldon, *The Bachelor and the Bobby-Soxer*

1948

BEST PICTURE: *Hamlet*

BEST ACTOR: Laurence Olivier, *Hamlet*

BEST ACTRESS: Jane Wyman, *Johnny Belinda*

BEST SUPPORTING ACTOR: Walter Huston, *The Treasure of the Sierra Madre*

BEST SUPPORTING ACTRESS: Claire Trevor, *Key Largo*

BEST DIRECTOR: John Huston, *The Treasure of the Sierra Madre*

BEST WRITER (original story): Richard Schweizer and David Wechsler, *The Search*

BEST WRITER (original screenplay): John Huston, *The Treasure of the Sierra Madre*

1949

BEST PICTURE: *All the King's Men*

BEST ACTOR: Broderick Crawford, *All the King's Men*

BEST ACTRESS: Olivia de Havilland, *The Heiress*

BEST SUPPORTING ACTOR: Dean Jagger, *Twelve O'Clock High*

BEST SUPPORTING ACTRESS: Mercedes McCambridge, *All the King's Men*

BEST DIRECTOR: Joseph L. Mankiewicz, *A Letter to Three Wives*

BEST WRITER (original story): Douglas Morrow, *The Stratton Story*

BEST WRITER (original screenplay): Joseph L. Mankiewicz, *A Letter to Three Wives*

1950

BEST PICTURE: *All About Eve*

BEST ACTOR: José Ferrer, *Cyrano de Bergerac*

BEST ACTRESS: Judy Holliday, *Born Yesterday*

BEST SUPPORTING ACTOR: George Sanders, *All About Eve*

BEST SUPPORTING ACTRESS: Josephine Hull, *Harvey*

BEST DIRECTOR: Joseph L. Mankiewicz, *All About Eve*

BEST WRITER (original story): Edna Anhalt and Edward Anhalt, *Panic in the Streets*

BEST WRITER (screenplay): Joseph L. Mankiewicz, *All About Eve*

BEST WRITER (story and screenplay): Charles Brackett, Billy Wilder, and D. M. Marshman Jr., *Sunset Boulevard*

1951

BEST PICTURE: *An American in Paris*

BEST ACTOR: Humphrey Bogart, *The African Queen*

BEST ACTRESS: Vivien Leigh, *A Streetcar Named Desire*

BEST SUPPORTING ACTOR: Karl Malden, *A Streetcar Named Desire*

BEST SUPPORTING ACTRESS: Kim Hunter, *A Streetcar Named Desire*

BEST DIRECTOR: George Stevens, *A Place in the Sun*

BEST WRITER (original story): Paul Dehn and James Bernard, *Seven Days to Noon*

BEST WRITER (original screenplay): Michael Wilson and Harry Brown, *A Place in the Sun*

1952

BEST PICTURE: *The Greatest Show on Earth*

BEST ACTOR: Gary Cooper, *High Noon*

BEST ACTRESS: Shirley Booth, *Come Back, Little Sheba*

BEST SUPPORTING ACTOR: Anthony Quinn, *Viva Zapata!*

BEST SUPPORTING ACTRESS: Gloria Grahame, *The Bad and the Beautiful*

BEST DIRECTOR: John Ford, *The Quiet Man*

BEST WRITER (original story): Fredric M. Frank, Theodore St. John, and Frank Cavett, *The Greatest Show on Earth*

BEST WRITER (original screenplay): Charles Schnee, *The Bad and the Beautiful*

1953

- BEST PICTURE: *From Here to Eternity*
- BEST ACTOR: William Holden, *Stalag 17*
- BEST ACTRESS: Audrey Hepburn, *Roman Holiday*
- BEST SUPPORTING ACTOR: Frank Sinatra, *From Here to Eternity*
- BEST SUPPORTING ACTRESS: Donna Reed, *From Here to Eternity*
- BEST DIRECTOR: Fred Zinnemann, *From Here to Eternity*
- BEST WRITER (original story): Ian McLellan Hunter and Dalton Trumbo, *Roman Holiday*
- BEST WRITER (original screenplay): Daniel Taradash, *From Here to Eternity*

1954

- BEST PICTURE: *On the Waterfront*
- BEST ACTOR: Marlon Brando, *On the Waterfront*
- BEST ACTRESS: Grace Kelly, *The Country Girl*
- BEST SUPPORTING ACTOR: Edmond O'Brien, *The Barefoot Contessa*
- BEST SUPPORTING ACTRESS: Eva Marie Saint, *On the Waterfront*
- BEST DIRECTOR: Elia Kazan, *On the Waterfront*
- BEST WRITER (motion picture story): Philip Yordan, *Broken Lance*
- BEST WRITER (original story and screenplay): Budd Schulberg, *On the Waterfront*
- BEST WRITER (screenplay): George Seaton, *The Country Girl*

1955

- BEST PICTURE: *Marty*
- BEST ACTOR: Ernest Borgnine, *Marty*
- BEST ACTRESS: Anna Magnani, *The Rose Tattoo*
- BEST SUPPORTING ACTOR: Jack Lemmon, *Mister Roberts*
- BEST SUPPORTING ACTRESS: Jo Van Fleet, *East of Eden*
- BEST DIRECTOR: Delbert Mann, *Marty*
- BEST WRITER (original story): Daniel Fuchs, *Love Me or Leave Me*
- BEST WRITER (original screenplay): Paddy Chayefsky, *Marty*

1956

    BEST PICTURE: *Around the World in 80 Days*

    BEST ACTOR: Yul Brynner, *The King and I*

    BEST ACTRESS: Ingrid Bergman, *Anastasia*

    BEST SUPPORTING ACTOR: Anthony Quinn, *Lust for Life*

    BEST SUPPORTING ACTRESS: Dorothy Malone, *Written on the Wind*

    BEST DIRECTOR: George Stevens, *Giant*

    BEST WRITER (motion picture story): Dalton Trumbo, *The Brave One*

    BEST WRITER (adapted screenplay): James Poe, John Farrow, and S. J. Perelman, *Around the World in 80 Days*

    BEST WRITER (original screenplay): Albert Lamorisse, *The Red Balloon*

1957

    BEST PICTURE: *The Bridge on the River Kwai*

    BEST ACTOR: Alec Guinness, *The Bridge on the River Kwai*

    BEST ACTRESS: Joanne Woodward, *The Three Faces of Eve*

    BEST SUPPORTING ACTOR: Red Buttons, *Sayonara*

    BEST SUPPORTING ACTRESS: Miyoshi Umeki, *Sayonara*

    BEST DIRECTOR: David Lean, *The Bridge on the River Kwai*

    BEST WRITER (screenplay based on material from another medium): Pierre Boulle, Michael Wilson, and Carl Foreman, *The Bridge on the River Kwai*

    BEST WRITER (story and screenplay written for the screen): George Wells, *Designing Woman*

1958

    BEST PICTURE: *Gigi*

    BEST ACTOR: David Niven, *Separate Tables*

    BEST ACTRESS: Susan Hayward, *I Want to Live!*

    BEST SUPPORTING ACTOR: Burl Ives, *The Big Country*

    BEST SUPPORTING ACTRESS: Wendy Heller, *Separate Tables*

    BEST DIRECTOR: Vincente Minnelli, *Gigi*

    BEST WRITER (screenplay based on material from another medium): Alan Jay Lerner, *Gigi*

BEST WRITER (story and screenplay written for the screen): Nedrick Young and Harold Jacob Smith, *The Defiant Ones*

1959

BEST PICTURE: *Ben-Hur*

BEST ACTOR: Charlton Heston, *Ben-Hur*

BEST ACTRESS: Simone Signoret, *Room at the Top*

BEST SUPPORTING ACTOR: Hugh Griffith, *Ben-Hur*

BEST SUPPORTING ACTRESS: Shelley Winters, *The Diary of Anne Frank*

BEST DIRECTOR: William Wyler, *Ben-Hur*

BEST WRITER (screenplay based on material from another medium): Neil Paterson, *Room at the Top*

BEST WRITER: (story and screenplay written for the screen): Russell Rouse and Clarence Greene, story; Stanley Shapiro and Maurice Richlin, screenplay, *Pillow Talk*

1960

BEST PICTURE: *The Apartment*

BEST ACTOR: Burt Lancaster, *Elmer Gantry*

BEST ACTRESS: Elizabeth Taylor, *Butterfield 8*

BEST SUPPORTING ACTOR: Peter Ustinov, *Spartacus*

BEST SUPPORTING ACTRESS: Shirley Jones, *Elmer Gantry*

BEST DIRECTOR: Billy Wilder, *The Apartment*

BEST WRITER (screenplay based on material from another medium): Richard Brooks, *Elmer Gantry*

BEST WRITER (story and screenplay written for the screen): Billy Wilder and I. A. L. Diamond, *The Apartment*

1961

BEST PICTURE: *West Side Story*

BEST ACTOR: Maximilian Schell, *Judgment at Nuremberg*

BEST ACTRESS: Sophia Loren, *Two Women*

BEST SUPPORTING ACTOR: George Chakiris, *West Side Story*

BEST SUPPORTING ACTRESS: Rita Moreno, *West Side Story*

BEST DIRECTOR: Robert Wise and Jerome Robbins, *West Side Story*

BEST WRITER (screenplay based on material from another medium): Abby Mann, *Judgment at Nuremberg*

BEST WRITER (story and screenplay written for the screen): William Inge, *Splendor in the Grass*

1962

BEST PICTURE: *Lawrence of Arabia*

BEST ACTOR: Gregory Peck, *To Kill a Mockingbird*

BEST ACTRESS: Anne Bancroft, *The Miracle Worker*

BEST SUPPORTING ACTOR: Ed Begley, *Sweet Bird of Youth*

BEST SUPPORTING ACTRESS: Patty Duke, *The Miracle Worker*

BEST DIRECTOR: David Lean, *Lawrence of Arabia*

BEST WRITER (screenplay based on material from another medium): Horton Foote, *To Kill a Mockingbird*

BEST WRITER (story and screenplay written for the screen): Ennio De Concini, Alfredo Giannetti, and Pietro Germi, *Divorce—Italian Style*

1963

BEST PICTURE: *Tom Jones*

BEST ACTOR: Sidney Poitier, *Lilies of the Field*

BEST ACTRESS: Patricia Neal, *Hud*

BEST SUPPORTING ACTOR: Melvyn Douglas, *Hud*

BEST SUPPORTING ACTRESS: Margaret Rutherford, *The V.I.P.s*

BEST DIRECTOR: Tony Richardson, *Tom Jones*

BEST WRITER (screenplay based on material from another medium): John Osborne, *Tom Jones*

BEST WRITER (story and screenplay written for the screen): Pasquale Festa Campanile, Massimo Franciosa, Vasco Pratolini, and Nanni Loy, story; Pasquale Festa Campanile, Massimo Franciosa, Nanni Loy, and James R. Webb, screenplay, *How the West Was Won*

1964

BEST PICTURE: *My Fair Lady*

BEST ACTOR: Rex Harrison, *My Fair Lady*

BEST ACTRESS: Julie Andrews, *Mary Poppins*

BEST SUPPORTING ACTOR: Peter Ustinov, *Topkapi*

BEST SUPPORTING ACTRESS: Lila Kedrova, *Zorba the Greek*

BEST DIRECTOR: George Cukor, *My Fair Lady*

BEST WRITER (screenplay based on material from another medium): Edward Anhalt, *Becket*

BEST WRITER (screenplay and story written directly for the screen): S. H. Barnett, story; Peter Stone and Frank Tarloff, screenplay, *Father Goose*

1965

BEST PICTURE: *The Sound of Music*

BEST ACTOR: Lee Marvin, *Cat Ballou*

BEST ACTRESS: Julie Christie, *Darling*

BEST SUPPORTING ACTOR: Martin Balsam, *A Thousand Clowns*

BEST SUPPORTING ACTRESS: Shelley Winters, *A Patch of Blue*

BEST DIRECTOR: Robert Wise, *The Sound of Music*

BEST WRITER (screenplay based on material from another medium): Robert Bolt, *Doctor Zhivago*

BEST WRITER (story and screenplay written for the screen): Frederic Raphael, *Darling*

1966

BEST PICTURE: *A Man for All Seasons*

BEST ACTOR: Paul Scofield, *A Man for All Seasons*

BEST ACTRESS: Elizabeth Taylor, *Who's Afraid of Virginia Woolf?*

BEST SUPPORTING ACTOR: Walter Matthau, *The Fortune Cookie*

BEST SUPPORTING ACTRESS: Sandy Dennis, *Who's Afraid of Virginia Woolf?*

BEST DIRECTOR: Fred Zinnemann, *A Man for All Seasons*

BEST WRITER (screenplay based on material from another medium): Robert Bolt, *A Man for All Seasons*

BEST WRITER (story and screenplay written for the screen): Claude Lelouch, story; Pierre Uytterhoeven and Claude Lelouch, screenplay, *A Man and a Woman*

1967

Best Picture: *In the Heat of the Night*

Best Actor: Rod Steiger, *In the Heat of the Night*

Best Actress: Katharine Hepburn, *Guess Who's Coming to Dinner?*

Best Supporting Actor: George Kennedy, *Cool Hand Luke*

Best Supporting Actress: Estelle Parsons, *Bonnie and Clyde*

Best Director: Mike Nichols, *The Graduate*

Best Writer (screenplay based on material from another medium): Stirling Silliphant, *In the Heat of the Night*

Best Writer (story and screenplay written for the screen): William Rose, *Guess Who's Coming to Dinner?*

1968

Best Picture: *Oliver!*

Best Actor: Cliff Robertson, *Charley*

Best Actress: Katharine Hepburn, *The Lion in Winter* and Barbra Streisand, *Funny Girl*

Best Supporting Actor: Jack Albertson, *The Subject Was Roses*

Best Supporting Actress: Ruth Gordon, *Rosemary's Baby*

Best Director: Carol Reed, *Oliver!*

Best Writer (screenplay based on material from another medium): James Goldman, *The Lion in Winter*

Best Writer (story and screenplay written for the screen): Mel Brooks, *The Producers*

1969

Best Picture: *Midnight Cowboy*

Best Actor: John Wayne, *True Grit*

Best Actress: Maggie Smith, *The Prime of Miss Jean Brodie*

Best Supporting Actor: Gig Young, *They Shoot Horses, Don't They?*

Best Supporting Actress: Goldie Hawn, *Cactus Flower*

Best Director: John Schlesinger, *Midnight Cowboy*

Best Writer (screenplay based on material from another medium): Waldo Salt, *Midnight Cowboy*

BEST WRITER (story and screenplay written for the screen):
William Goldman, *Butch Cassidy and the Sundance Kid*

1970

BEST PICTURE: *Patton*

BEST ACTOR: George C. Scott, *Patton* (refused the award)

BEST ACTRESS: Glenda Jackson, *Women in Love*

BEST SUPPORTING ACTOR: John Mills, *Ryan's Daughter*

BEST SUPPORTING ACTRESS: Helen Hayes, *Airport*

BEST DIRECTOR: Franklin J. Schaffner, *Patton*

BEST WRITER (screenplay based on material from another medium):
Ring Lardner Jr., *M*A*S*H*

BEST WRITER (original screenplay): Francis Ford Coppola and
Edmund H. North, *Patton*

1971

BEST PICTURE: *The French Connection*

BEST ACTOR: Gene Hackman, *The French Connection*

BEST ACTRESS: Jane Fonda, *Klute*

BEST SUPPORTING ACTOR: Ben Johnson, *The Last Picture Show*

BEST SUPPORTING ACTRESS: Cloris Leachman, *The Last Picture Show*

BEST DIRECTOR: William Friedkin, *The French Connection*

BEST WRITER (screenplay based on material from another medium):
Ernest Tidyman, *The French Connection*

BEST WRITER (original screenplay): Paddy Chayefsky, *The Hospital*

1972

BEST PICTURE: *The Godfather*

BEST ACTOR: Marlon Brando, *The Godfather* (refused the award)

BEST ACTRESS: Liza Minnelli, *Cabaret*

BEST SUPPORTING ACTOR: Joel Gray, *Cabaret*

BEST SUPPORTING ACTRESS: Eileen Heckart, *Butterflies Are Free*

BEST DIRECTOR: Bob Fosse, *Cabaret*

Best Writer (screenplay based on material from another medium): Mario Puzo and Francis Ford Coppola, *The Godfather*

Best Writer (original screenplay): Jeremy Larner, *The Candidate*

1973

Best Picture: *The Sting*

Best Actor: Jack Lemmon, *Save the Tiger*

Best Actress: Glenda Jackson, *A Touch of Class*

Best Supporting Actor: John Housman, *The Paper Chase*

Best Supporting Actress: Tatum O'Neal, *Paper Moon*

Best Director: George Roy Hill, *The Sting*

Best Writer (screenplay based on material from another medium): William Peter Blatty, *The Exorcist*

Best Writer (original screenplay): David S. Ward, *The Sting*

1974

Best Picture: *The Godfather: Part II*

Best Actor: Art Carney, *Harry and Tonto*

Best Actress: Ellen Burstyn, *Alice Doesn't Live Here Anymore*

Best Supporting Actor: Robert De Niro, *The Godfather: Part II*

Best Supporting Actress: Ingrid Bergman, *Murder on the Orient Express*

Best Director: Francis Ford Coppola, *The Godfather: Part II*

Best Writer (screenplay adapted from other material): Francis Ford Coppola and Mario Puzo, *The Godfather: Part II*

Best Writer (original screenplay): Robert Towne, *Chinatown*

1975

Best Picture: *One Flew over the Cuckoo's Nest*

Best Actor: Jack Nicholson, *One Flew over the Cuckoo's Nest*

Best Actress: Louise Fletcher, *One Flew over the Cuckoo's Nest*

Best Supporting Actor: George Burns, *The Sunshine Boys*

Best Supporting Actress: Lee Grant, *Shampoo*

BEST DIRECTOR: Milos Forman, *One Flew over the Cuckoo's Nest*

BEST WRITER (screenplay adapted from other material): Lawrence Hauben and Bo Goldman, *One Flew over the Cuckoo's Nest*

BEST WRITER (original screenplay): Frank Pierson, *Dog Day Afternoon*

1976

BEST PICTURE: *Rocky*

BEST ACTOR: Peter Finch, *Network*

BEST ACTRESS: Faye Dunaway, *Network*

BEST SUPPORTING ACTOR: Jason Robards, *All the President's Men*

BEST SUPPORTING ACTRESS: Beatrice Straight, *Network*

BEST DIRECTOR: John G. Avildsen, *Rocky*

BEST WRITER (screenplay based on material from another medium): William Goldman, *All the President's Men*

BEST WRITER (screenplay written directly for the screen): Paddy Chayefsky, *Network*

1977

BEST PICTURE: *Annie Hall*

BEST ACTOR: Richard Dreyfuss, *The Goodbye Girl*

BEST ACTRESS: Diane Keaton, *Annie Hall*

BEST SUPPORTING ACTOR: Jason Robards, *Julia*

BEST SUPPORTING ACTRESS: Vanessa Redgrave, *Julia*

BEST DIRECTOR: Woody Allen, *Annie Hall*

BEST WRITER (screenplay based on material from another medium): Alvin Sargent, *Julia*

BEST WRITER (screenplay written directly for the screen): Woody Allen and Marshall Brickman, *Annie Hall*

1978

BEST PICTURE: *The Deer Hunter*

BEST ACTOR: Jon Voight, *Coming Home*

BEST ACTRESS: Jane Fonda, *Coming Home*

BEST SUPPORTING ACTOR: Christopher Walken, *The Deer Hunter*

BEST SUPPORTING ACTRESS: Maggie Smith, *California Suite*

BEST DIRECTOR: Michael Cimino, *The Deer Hunter*

BEST WRITER (screenplay based on material from another medium):
Oliver Stone, *Midnight Express*

BEST WRITER (screenplay written directly for the screen):
Nancy Dowd, Waldo Salt, and Robert C. Jones, *Coming Home*

1979

BEST PICTURE: *Kramer vs. Kramer*

BEST ACTOR: Dustin Hoffman, *Kramer vs. Kramer*

BEST ACTRESS: Sally Field: *Norma Rae*

BEST SUPPORTING ACTOR: Melvyn Douglas, *Being There*

BEST SUPPORTING ACTRESS: Meryl Streep, *Kramer vs. Kramer*

BEST DIRECTOR: Robert Benton, *Kramer vs. Kramer*

BEST WRITER (screenplay based on material from another medium):
Robert Benton, *Kramer vs. Kramer*

BEST WRITER (screenplay written directly for the screen):
Steve Tesich, *Breaking Away*

1980

BEST PICTURE: *Ordinary People*

BEST ACTOR: Robert De Niro, *Raging Bull*

BEST ACTRESS: Sissy Spacek, *Coal Miner's Daughter*

BEST SUPPORTING ACTOR: Timothy Hutton, *Ordinary People*

BEST SUPPORTING ACTRESS: Mary Steenburgen,
Melvin and Howard

BEST DIRECTOR: Robert Redford, *Ordinary People*

BEST WRITER (screenplay based on material from another medium):
Alvin Sargent, *Ordinary People*

BEST WRITER (screenplay written directly for the screen):
Bo Goldman, *Melvin and Howard*

1981

Best Picture: *Chariots of Fire*

Best Actor: Henry Fonda, *On Golden Pond*

Best Actress: Katharine Hepburn, *On Golden Pond*

Best Supporting Actor: John Gielgud, *Arthur*

Best Supporting Actress: Maureen Stapleton, *Reds*

Best Director: Warren Beatty, *Reds*

Best Writer (screenplay based on material from another medium): Ernest Thompson, *On Golden Pond*

Best Writer (screenplay written directly for the screen): Colin Welland, *Chariots of Fire*

1982

Best Picture: *Gandhi*

Best Actor: Ben Kingsley, *Gandhi*

Best Actress: Meryl Streep, *Sophie's Choice*

Best Supporting Actor: Louis Gossett Jr., *An Officer and a Gentleman*

Best Supporting Actress: Jessica Lange, *Tootsie*

Best Director: Richard Attenborough, *Gandhi*

Best Writer (screenplay based on material from another medium): Costa-Gavras and Donald Stewart, *Missing*

Best Writer (screenplay written directly for the screen): John Briley, *Gandhi*

1983

Best Picture: *Terms of Endearment*

Best Actor: Robert Duvall, *Tender Mercies*

Best Actress: Shirley MacLaine, *Terms of Endearment*

Best Supporting Actor: Jack Nicholson, *Terms of Endearment*

Best Supporting Actress: Linda Hunt, *The Year of Living Dangerously*

Best Director: James L. Brooks, *Terms of Endearment*

Best Writer (screenplay based on material from another medium): James L. Brooks, *Terms of Endearment*

BEST WRITER (screenplay written directly for the screen): Horton Foote, *Tender Mercies*

1984

BEST PICTURE: *Amadeus*

BEST ACTOR: F. Murray Abraham, *Amadeus*

BEST ACTRESS: Sally Field, *Places in the Heart*

BEST SUPPORTING ACTOR: Haing S. Ngor, *The Killing Fields*

BEST SUPPORTING ACTRESS: Peggy Ashcroft, *A Passage to India*

BEST DIRECTOR: Milos Forman, *Amadeus*

BEST WRITER (screenplay based on material from another medium): Peter Shaffer, *Amadeus*

BEST WRITER (screenplay written directly for the screen): Robert Benton, *Places in the Heart*

1985

BEST PICTURE: *Out of Africa*

BEST ACTOR: William Hurt, *Kiss of the Spider Woman*

BEST ACTRESS: Geraldine Page, *The Trip to Bountiful*

BEST SUPPORTING ACTOR: Don Ameche, *Cocoon*

BEST SUPPORTING ACTRESS: Angelica Huston, *Prizzi's Honor*

BEST DIRECTOR: Sydney Pollack, *Out of Africa*

BEST WRITER (screenplay based on material from another medium): Kurt Luedtke, *Out of Africa*

BEST WRITER (screenplay written directly for the screen): Earl W. Wallace and William Kelley, screenplay; William Kelley, Pamela Wallace, and Earl W. Wallace, story, *Witness*

1986

BEST PICTURE: *Platoon*

BEST ACTOR: Paul Newman, *The Color of Money*

BEST ACTRESS: Marlee Matlin, *Children of a Lesser God*

BEST SUPPORTING ACTOR: Michael Caine, *Hannah and Her Sisters*

BEST SUPPORTING ACTRESS: Dianne Wiest, *Hannah and Her Sisters*

BEST DIRECTOR: Oliver Stone, *Platoon*

BEST WRITER (screenplay based on material from another medium): Ruth Prawer Jhabvala, *A Room with a View*

BEST WRITER (screenplay written directly for the screen): Woody Allen, *Hannah and Her Sisters*

1987

BEST PICTURE: *The Last Emperor*

BEST ACTOR: Michael Douglas, *Wall Street*

BEST ACTRESS: Cher, *Moonstruck*

BEST SUPPORTING ACTOR: Sean Connery, *The Untouchables*

BEST SUPPORTING ACTRESS: Olympia Dukakis, *Moonstruck*

BEST DIRECTOR: Bernardo Bertolucci, *The Last Emperor*

BEST WRITER (screenplay based on material from another medium): Mark Peploe and Bernardo Bertolucci, *The Last Emperor*

BEST WRITER (screenplay written directly for the screen): John Patrick Shanley, *Moonstruck*

1988

BEST PICTURE: *Rain Man*

BEST ACTOR: Dustin Hoffman, *Rain Man*

BEST ACTRESS: Jodie Foster, *The Accused*

BEST SUPPORTING ACTOR: Kevin Kline, *A Fish Called Wanda*

BEST SUPPORTING ACTRESS: Geena Davis, *The Accidental Tourist*

BEST DIRECTOR: Barry Levinson, *Rain Man*

BEST WRITER (screenplay based on material from another medium): Christopher Hampton, *Dangerous Liaisons*

BEST WRITER (original screenplay): Ronald Bass and Barry Morrow, screenplay; Barry Morrow, story, *Rain Man*

1989

BEST PICTURE: *Driving Miss Daisy*

BEST ACTOR: Daniel Day-Lewis, *My Left Foot*

BEST ACTRESS: Jessica Tandy, *Driving Miss Daisy*

BEST SUPPORTING ACTOR: Denzel Washington, *Glory*

BEST SUPPORTING ACTRESS: Brenda Fricker, *My Left Foot*

BEST DIRECTOR: Oliver Stone, *Born on the Fourth of July*

BEST WRITER (screenplay based on material from another medium): Alfred Uhry, *Driving Miss Daisy*

BEST WRITER (screenplay written directly for the screen): Tom Schulman, *Dead Poets Society*

1990

BEST PICTURE: *Dances with Wolves*

BEST ACTOR: Jeremy Irons, *Reversal of Fortune*

BEST ACTRESS: Kathy Bates, *Misery*

BEST SUPPORTING ACTOR: Joe Pesci, *GoodFellas*

BEST SUPPORTING ACTRESS: Whoopi Goldberg, *Ghost*

BEST DIRECTOR: Kevin Costner, *Dances with Wolves*

BEST WRITER (screenplay based on material from another medium): Michael Blake, *Dances with Wolves*

BEST WRITER (screenplay written directly for the screen): Bruce Joel Rubin, *Ghost*

1991

BEST PICTURE: *The Silence of the Lambs*

BEST ACTOR: Anthony Hopkins, *The Silence of the Lambs*

BEST ACTRESS: Jodie Foster, *The Silence of the Lambs*

BEST SUPPORTING ACTOR: Jack Palance, *City Slickers*

BEST SUPPORTING ACTRESS: Mercedes Ruehl, *The Fisher King*

BEST DIRECTOR: Jonathan Demme, *The Silence of the Lambs*

BEST WRITER (screenplay based on material from another medium): Ted Tally, *The Silence of the Lambs*

BEST WRITER (screenplay written directly for the screen): Callie Khouri, *Thelma and Louise*

1992

BEST PICTURE: *Unforgiven*

BEST ACTOR: Al Pacino, *Scent of a Woman*

BEST ACTRESS: Emma Thompson, *Howards End*

Oscars, Tonys, Pulitzers, and Other Prestigious Prizes

BEST SUPPORTING ACTOR: Gene Hackman, *Unforgiven*

BEST SUPPORTING ACTRESS: Marisa Tomei, *My Cousin Vinny*

BEST DIRECTOR: Clint Eastwood, *Unforgiven*

BEST WRITER (screenplay based on material from another medium): Ruth Prawer Jhabvala, *Howards End*

BEST WRITER (screenplay written directly for the screen): Neil Jordan, *The Crying Game*

1993

BEST PICTURE: *Schindler's List*

BEST ACTOR: Tom Hanks, *Philadelphia*

BEST ACTRESS: Holly Hunter, *The Piano*

BEST SUPPORTING ACTOR: Tommy Lee Jones, *The Fugitive*

BEST SUPPORTING ACTRESS: Anna Paquin, *The Piano*

BEST DIRECTOR: Steven Spielberg, *Schindler's List*

BEST WRITER (screenplay based on material from another medium): Steven Zaillian, *Schindler's List*

BEST WRITER (screenplay written directly for the screen): Jane Campion, *The Piano*

1994

BEST PICTURE: *Forrest Gump*

BEST ACTOR: Tom Hanks, *Forrest Gump*

BEST ACTRESS: Jessica Lange, *Blue Sky*

BEST SUPPORTING ACTOR: Martin Landau, *Ed Wood*

BEST SUPPORTING ACTRESS: Dianne Wiest, *Bullets over Broadway*

BEST DIRECTOR: Robert Zemeckis, *Forrest Gump*

BEST WRITER (screenplay based on material from another medium): Eric Roth, *Forrest Gump*

BEST WRITER (screenplay written directly for the screen): Quentin Tarantino and Roger Avary, *Pulp Fiction*

1995

BEST PICTURE: *Braveheart*

BEST ACTOR: Nicolas Cage, *Leaving Las Vegas*

BEST ACTRESS: Susan Sarandon, *Dead Man Walking*

BEST SUPPORTING ACTOR: Kevin Spacey, *The Usual Suspects*

BEST SUPPORTING ACTRESS: Mira Sorvino, *Mighty Aphrodite*

BEST DIRECTOR: Mel Gibson, *Braveheart*

BEST WRITER (screenplay based on material from another medium): Emma Thompson, *Sense and Sensibility*

BEST WRITER (screenplay written directly for the screen): Christopher McQuarrie, *The Usual Suspects*

1996

BEST PICTURE: *The English Patient*

BEST ACTOR: Geoffrey Rush, *Shine*

BEST ACTRESS: Frances McDormand, *Fargo*

BEST SUPPORTING ACTOR: Cuba Gooding Jr., *Jerry McGuire*

BEST SUPPORTING ACTRESS: Juliette Binoche, *The English Patient*

BEST DIRECTOR: Anthony Minghella, *The English Patient*

BEST WRITER (screenplay based on material from another medium): Billy Bob Thornton, *Sling Blade*

BEST WRITER (screenplay written directly for the screen): Ethan and Joel Coen, *Fargo*

1997

BEST PICTURE: *Titanic*

BEST ACTOR: Jack Nicholson, *As Good as It Gets*

BEST ACTRESS: Helen Hunt, *As Good as It Gets*

BEST SUPPORTING ACTOR: Robin Williams, *Good Will Hunting*

BEST SUPPORTING ACTRESS: Kim Basinger, *L.A. Confidential*

BEST DIRECTOR: James Cameron, *Titanic*

BEST WRITER (screenplay based on material from another medium): Brian Helgeland and Curtis Hanson, *L.A. Confidential*

BEST WRITER (screenplay written directly for the screen): Ben Affleck and Matt Damon, *Good Will Hunting*

1998

BEST PICTURE: *Shakespeare in Love*

BEST ACTOR: Roberto Benigni, *Life Is Beautiful*

BEST ACTRESS: Gwyneth Paltrow, *Shakespeare in Love*

BEST SUPPORTING ACTOR: James Coburn, *Affliction*

BEST SUPPORTING ACTRESS: Judi Dench, *Shakespeare in Love*

BEST DIRECTOR: Steven Spielberg, *Saving Private Ryan*

BEST WRITER (screenplay based on material from another medium): Marc Norman and Tom Stoppard, *Shakespeare in Love*

BEST WRITER (screenplay written directly for the screen): Bill Condon, *Gods and Monsters*

And the Biggest Winners Are

Walt Disney won the most Oscars, thirty-two of them in various categories, and designer Edith Head won the most Oscars in any one category—eight for best costume design. Here are some other big winners in the Oscar sweepstakes:

- Most Academy Awards for a movie: *All About Eve* (1950) and *Titanic* (1997)—14 Oscars each.
- Most Academy Awards for best actress: Katharine Hepburn—4 Oscars.
- Most Academy Awards for best actor: Jack Nicholson, Fredric March, Spencer Tracy, Gary Cooper, Marlon Brando, Dustin Hoffman, Tom Hanks—2 Oscars each.
- Most Academy Awards for supporting actor: Walter Brennan—3 Oscars.
- Most Academy Awards for supporting actress: Shelley Winters and Dianne Wiest—2 Oscars each.
- Most Academy Awards for director: John Ford—4 Oscars.
- Most Academy Awards for writer of an original screenplay: Billy Wilder—3 Oscars. (Wilder also won 3 Oscars for best director.)
- Most Academy Awards for musical score: Alfred Newman—9 Oscars.

Oldest and Youngest Oscar Winners

- The oldest player to win a best actress Oscar was Jessica Tandy (at 80 years, 293 days), for *Driving Miss Daisy* (1989), which makes her also the oldest actor ever to win an Academy Award. Charlie Chaplin, however, won a special honorary award in 1971, when 83 years old.
- The oldest player to win a best actor Oscar was Henry Fonda (76 years, 317 days) for *On Golden Pond* (1981).
- The oldest player to win an Oscar for best supporting actor was George Burns (80 years, 69 days) for *The Sunshine Boys* (1975).
- The youngest player ever to win an Oscar was Tatum O'Neal (10 years, 148 days) for best supporting actress in *Paper Moon* (1973). Shirley Temple won a special honorary miniature Oscar in 1934 when 5 years and 10 months old. Anna Paquin was 11 when she won an Oscar for best supporting actress in *The Piano* (1993).
- The youngest player ever to win an Oscar for best actor was Richard Dreyfuss (29 years, 156 days) for *The Goodbye Girl* (1977).
- George Cukor (65) was the oldest director to win an Oscar, for *My Fair Lady* (1964).
- Norman Taurog (31) was the youngest director to win an Oscar, for *Skippy* (1930).
- George Bernard Shaw (82) was the oldest writer to win a best screenplay Oscar, for the scenario of his *Pygmalion* (1938).

The Completely Naked Oscar Nominee

Sally Kirkland is said to have been the first modern actress to appear completely naked on the stage, in an otherwise forgotten play called *Sweet Eros.* This may not be provable, but she is surely the only actress to appear naked on the stage who later won an Academy Award nomination for best actress. Sally Kirkland was nominated in 1987 for her excellent performance in *Anna.* Her competitors were Glenn Close (*Fatal Attraction*), Holly Hunter (*Broadcast News*), Meryl Streep (*Ironweed*), and Cher, who won for her work in *Moonstruck.* Kirkland's nomination was secured in some part by Hollywood publicist Dale Olson's high-powered publicity campaign.

The only other naked story about the Oscars features Hollywood advertising man Robert Opal, who managed to sneak past security guards and streak naked across the stage during the nationally televised 1973 Academy

Awards ceremony. British actor David Niven, who was speaking at that instant, got off the best ad-lib in Academy history: "The only way he could get a laugh was by showing his shortcomings."

Oscar Oscars

Oscar Lagerstrom, Oskar Homolka, Oscar Brodney, and Oskar Werner were all nominated for Oscars. However, the only Oscar ever to win an Oscar was Oscar Hammerstein II. In fact, Oscar Hammerstein won two Oscars for best song. In 1941 he and composer Jerome Kern won for "The Last Time I Saw Paris" from *Lady Be Good*. In 1945 he and composer Richard Rodgers won an Oscar for "It Might as Well Be Spring," from *State Fair*.

Long Shot

The biggest long shot in the history of the Oscars came when Loretta Young won for her performance in *The Farmer's Daughter* (1947). She beat Joan Crawford (*Possessed*), Rosalind Russell (*Mourning Becomes Electra*), Susan Hayward (*Smash-Up*), and Dorothy McGuire (*Gentleman's Agreement*). Rosalind Russell, the favorite, actually stood up while the winner's envelope was being opened, and then her beads broke, scattering all over. She remembered how she had turned down the part Miss Young won with. All the polls had proved wrong; as had the *Los Angeles Times* early edition headline ROZ RUSSELL WINS OSCAR. Harry Truman would win a similar upset a year later.

Oddest-Shaped Oscars

When ventriloquist Edgar Bergen received an honorary Academy Award in 1937 for his creation of Charlie McCarthy (Mortimer Snerd was not mentioned), he was given a wooden Oscar.

Walt Disney's *Snow White and the Seven Dwarfs* received an honorary award in 1938 that consisted of an Oscar and seven miniature Oscars.

Shirley Temple got a miniature statuette for her honorary award in 1934, beginning a tradition that awarded the same size statuette to Deanna Durbin and Mickey Rooney (both in 1938), Judy Garland (1939), Margaret O'Brien (1944), Peggy Ann Garner (1945), Claude Jarman Jr. (1946), Ivan Jandl (1948), Bobby Driscoll (1949), Jon Whiteley and Vincent Winter (both 1954), and Hayley Mills (1960).

Who Did It?: A Quick Oscar Quiz

1. Who was the only actor to win an Oscar posthumously?
2. Who gave the longest Oscar acceptance speech?
3. Who was the only actor to direct himself in an Oscar-winning performance?
4. Who directed the only sequel to win an Oscar for best picture?
5. Who was the only woman ever nominated as best director?

A. Lina Wertmüller
B. Laurence Olivier
C. Francis Ford Coppola
D. Peter Finch
E. Greer Garson

Answers

1. D (for best actor in *Network*, 1976)
2. E (for best actress in *Mrs. Miniver*, 1942, five and a half minutes)
3. B (in *Hamlet*, 1948)
4. C (*The Godfather: Part II*, 1974; *The Godfather* had won in 1972)
5. A (for *Seven Beauties*, 1976)

Never the Bridegroom, Always the Usher

Richard Burton and Peter O'Toole hold the record for the most nominations for best actor—seven—without a single win.

Insulting Oscar

George Bernard Shaw is the only Oscar winner who also won the much more prestigious Nobel Prize. Shaw won in 1938 for his screenplay for *Pygmalion*, thirteen years after his Nobel. "Not the least regard will be paid to American ideas, except to avoid them as much as possible," the British author had said after accepting his screenwriting commission from producer Gabriel Pascal, who had acquired the film rights to Shaw's plays after far richer men had failed. Pascal had made a successful film in London and then migrated to Hollywood, where he could get no work. Arriving back in London, he impulsively called on Shaw, whom he had never met, without an invitation, and told him he wanted to film his plays. "How much capital do you have?" Shaw asked him. "Fifteen shillings and sixpence—but I owe a pound," Pascal replied. Delighted with Pascal's admiration, effrontery, and wit, Shaw gave him a pound to pay his debts and signed a contract.

Despite all his bluster about American ideas, Shaw did conform to them in part—he even changed the ending, letting the professor get the girl Hollywood-style. Yet, predictably, he didn't attend the ceremonies and had something acid to say: "It's an insult for them to offer me any honor, as if they had never heard of me before—and it's likely they never have."

Players Who Refused the Oscar

George C. Scott, who felt that it was "degrading for actors to compete against one another" said he didn't want the Oscar and tried to withdraw his name from contention, but he nevertheless won the award for *Patton* in 1970. Scott didn't attend the ceremony, and his producer returned the statuette to the Academy.

Two years later Marlon Brando became the second actor to reject poor Oscar. Brando, who had won the Oscar for best actor in *The Godfather*, apparently turned the award down as a protest against "treatment of American Indians today by the film industry." He sent "Sacheen Littlefeather," self-described "president of the National American Affirmative Image Committee" to refuse the Oscar for him. But it turned out that she was actress María Cruz posing as an American Indian. She was not permitted to read the long speech Brando had written for her, giving a short extempore version, but later read Brando's words in full to the press.

Still another person to turn down an Oscar was director Walter Wanger. Wanger, furious that his film *Joan of Arc* hadn't even been nominated in 1948, was offered the consolation prize of a special Oscar for the movie, but refused it.

Miracle Year

The year 1939, when *Gone with the Wind* won the Academy Award for best picture, brought forth the greatest number of memorable pictures of any single year in movie history. These included *The Wizard of Oz*; *Stagecoach*; *Wuthering Heights*; *Goodbye, Mr. Chips*; *Mr. Smith Goes to Washington*; *Of Mice and Men*; *Ninotchka*; *Dark Victory*; *Union Pacific*; *Drums Along the Mohawk*; *Intermezzo*; *Beau Geste*; *Gunga Din*; and several others. There was even a Disney contribution—his Oscar-winning cartoon *The Ugly Duckling*.

Top Money Earners

As of March 1998 *Titanic* (1997) became the biggest moneymaker in movie history, with a worldwide box-office gross of more than $1.1 billion dollars (which is sure to go much higher). When adjustments are made for inflation, however, the three most profitable films of all time thus far are:

1. *Gone with the Wind* (1939)
2. *Star Wars* (1977)
3. *Snow White* (1937)

Snow White, a perennial favorite, and *Gone with the Wind* were recently digitally restored at a cost of several million dollars each.

More Megabuck Movies

- The *Star Wars* trilogy has grossed over $1.7 billion as of 1997.
- *Jurassic Park* (1993) passed the billion-dollar mark in worldwide earnings in 1999.
- *Il Postino* (*The Postman*, 1996), an Italian production, has earned over $22 million to become the highest-grossing foreign film in the United States as of 1997.
- *Mad Max* (1983), an Australian film made on a $350,000 budget, has thus far grossed over $100 million worldwide.
- As of 1997 actor Tom Cruise had acted in five consecutive movies that each grossed over $100 million.
- Director Steven Spielberg's films have grossed over $5 billion, earning him the title of Hollywood's most bankable director.
- *Cutthroat Island* (1995) may be filmdom's biggest flop, critically and financially; it cost over $100 million to make and earned back only $11 million as of 1997.

The Raspberry Awards

The Raspberry Awards, modeled on the Oscars, were devised to give the *worst* films of the year their due. The most recent Raspberry for worst picture went to Kevin Costner's *The Postman* (1998), which also won Raspberries in the director, actor, and screenplay categories.

The Ten Worst Movies Ever Made

According to critics Harry Medved and Randy Dreyfus, authors of *The Fifty Worst Films of All Time*, these would be, in chronological order:

1. *The Terror of Tiny Town* (1938), a Western with a cast of midgets.
2. *That Hagen Girl* (1947), which Ronald Reagen wished he'd never starred in.
3. *Robot Monster* (1953), whose director attempted suicide upon its completion.
4. *The Conqueror* (1956), starring John Wayne as Genghis Khan.
5. *Solomon and Sheba* (1959), with Yul Brynner as King Solomon.
6. *Santa Claus Conquers the Martians* (1964), for which no comment is needed.
7. *The Horror of Party Beach* (1964), a science fiction beach-party flick.
8. *Che!* (1969), with Jack Palance as Fidel Castro.
9. *Myra Breckinridge* (1970), a sex-change movie as bad as any movie ever made.
10. *Lost Horizon* (1973), a remake of the classic original film.

The World's Longest Film—More than a Day Long

Everyone can see the world's longest film, for director Edgar Reitz's *Die Zweite Heimat* (1992), a classic chronicle of life in a small German town from 1919 to 1982, is available on home video now. Be prepared to spend a long weekend with it, for the acclaimed movie runs twenty-five hours and thirty-two minutes.

The late artist Andy Warhol's *Sleep* (1963) shows a naked man sleeping for eight hours in an eight-hour film. His *Empire* is a seven-and-a-half-hour view of the Empire State Building, but it was cut from more than twenty-five hours.

Movie Sequel Quiz

Name five sequel films that have a II or III or IV in their titles.

Answer

Choose from:

Rocky	*Beverly Hills Cop*
Jaws	*Home Alone*
The Godfather	*Lethal Weapon*
Rambo	*Die Hard*
Psycho	*Karate Kid*
The French Connection	*Back to the Future*
Terminator	*Ghostbusters*

among other movies less well known and/or profitable.

Winners of the Cannes Film Festival

In the world of cinema and cineasts only the Cannes International Film Festival awards are as well known as the Academy Awards. Held on the French Riviera every May since 1946 except when funds were not available, the Cannes Festival at first gave Grand Prix awards to the best films, then switched in 1955 to the now famous Palme d'Or, only to add the Grand Prix again in 1990. Awards are given in a varying number of categories, but just the prize-winning films, actors, actresses, and directors are recorded here.

1946

GRAND PRIX: This first year grand prizes were given to films from eleven different countries:

The Red Earth (Denmark)

The Lost Weekend (United States)

La Symphonie Pastorale (France)

Brief Encounter (United Kingdom)

Neecha Nagar (India)

Rome—Open City (Italy)

María Candelaria (Mexico)

The Prize (Sweden)

The Last Chance (Switzerland)

Men Without Wings (Czechoslovakia)

The Great Turning Point (U.S.S.R.)

BEST ACTOR: Ray Milland, *The Lost Weekend* (United States)

BEST ACTRESS: Michèle Morgan, *La Symphonie Pastorale* (France)

DIRECTION: René Clément, *Battle of the Rails* (France)

1947

GRAND PRIX: Not given; instead awards went to *Antoine et Antoinette* (France) for "Psychological and Love Films" and to *The Damned* (France) for "Adventure and Thriller Films." No awards were given for best actor, actress, or direction.

1948

No festival held

1949

GRAND PRIX: *The Third Man* (United Kingdom)

BEST ACTOR: Edward G. Robinson, *House of Strangers* (United States)

BEST ACTRESS: Isa Miranda, *The Walls of Malapaga* (France/Italy)

DIRECTION: René Clément, *The Walls of Malapaga* (France/Italy)

1950

No festival held

1951

GRAND PRIX: *Miracle in Milan* (Italy) and *Miss Julie* (Sweden)

BEST ACTOR: Michael Redgrave, *The Browning Version* (United Kingdom)

BEST ACTRESS: Bette Davis, *All About Eve* (United States)

DIRECTION: Luis Buñuel, *Los Olvidados* (Mexico)

1952

GRAND PRIX: *Two Pennyworth of Hope* (Italy) and *Othello* (Morocco)

BEST ACTOR: Marlon Brando, *Viva Zapata!* (United States)

BEST ACTRESS: Lee Grant, *Detective Story* (United States)

DIRECTION: Christian-Jaque, *Fanfan la Tulipe* (France)

1953

GRAND PRIX: *The Wages of Fear* (France/Italy)

BEST ACTOR: Charles Vanel, *The Wages of Fear* (France/Italy)

BEST ACTRESS: Shirley Booth, *Come Back, Little Sheba* (United States)

DIRECTION: No award given

1954

GRAND PRIX: *Gate of Hell* (Japan)

BEST ACTOR: No award given

BEST ACTRESS: No award given

DIRECTION: No award given

1955

PALM D'OR: *Marty* (United States)

DIRECTION: Sergei Vassiliev, *The Heroes of Ship Ra* (Bulgaria); and Jules Dassin, *Rififi* (France)

1956

PALM D'OR: *The Silent World* (France)

BEST ACTOR: No award given

BEST ACTRESS: Susan Hayward, *I'll Cry Tomorrow* (United States)

DIRECTION: Sergei Yutkevich, *Othello* (U.S.S.R.)

1957

PALM D'OR: *Friendly Persuasion* (United States)

BEST ACTOR: John Kitzmiller, *Valley of Peace* (Yugoslavia)

BEST ACTRESS: Giulietta Masina, *Nights of Cabiria* (Italy)

DIRECTION: Robert Bresson, *A Man Escaped* (France)

1958

PALM D'OR: *The Cranes Are Flying* (U.S.S.R.)

BEST ACTOR: Paul Newman, *The Long Hot Summer* (United States)

BEST ACTRESS: Bibi Anderson, Eva Dahlbecj, Ingrid Thulin, and Barbro Hiort-Af-Ornas for their performances in *Brink of Life* (Sweden)

DIRECTION: Ingmar Bergman, *Brink of Life*

1959

PALM D'OR: *Black Orpheus* (France)

BEST ACTOR: Dean Stockwell, Bradford Dillman, and Orson Welles for their performances in *Compulsion* (United States)

BEST ACTRESS: Simone Signoret, *Room at the Top* (United Kingdom)

DIRECTION: François Truffaut, *The 400 Blows* (France)

1960

PALM D'OR: *La Dolce Vita* (Italy)

BEST ACTOR: No award given

BEST ACTRESS: Melina Mercouri, *Never on Sunday*

DIRECTION: No award given

1961

PALM D'OR: *Viridiana* (Spain) and *A Long Absence* (France/Italy)

BEST ACTOR: Anthony Perkins, *Goodbye Again* (France/United States)

BEST ACTRESS: Sophia Loren, *Two Women* (France/Italy)

DIRECTION: Yultna Solntzava, *History of the Flaming Years* (U.S.S.R.)

1962

PALM D'OR: *The Given Word* (Brazil)

BEST PERFORMANCES: Katharine Hepburn, Ralph Richardson, Jason Robards Jr., and Dean Stockwell in *Long Day's Journey into Night* (United States); and Sidney Lumet, Rita Tushingham, and Murray Melvin in *A Taste of Honey* (United Kingdom)

DIRECTION: No award given

1963

PALM D'OR: *The Leopard* (France/Italy)

BEST ACTOR: Richard Harris, *This Sporting Life* (United Kingdom)

BEST ACTRESS: Marina Vlady, *The Conjugal Bed* (Italy)

DIRECTION: No award given

1964

PALM D'OR: *The Umbrellas of Cherbourg* (France/Germany)

BEST ACTOR: Antal Páger, *Pacsirta* (Hungary) and Saro Urzì, *Seduced and Abandoned* (Italy)

BEST ACTRESS: Anne Bancroft, *The Pumpkin Eater* (United States) and Barbara Barrie, *One Potato, Two Potato* (United States)

DIRECTION: No award given

1965

PALM D'OR: *The Knack . . . and How to Get It* (United Kingdom)

BEST ACTOR: Terence Stamp, *The Collector* (United States)

BEST ACTRESS: Samantha Eggar, *The Collector* (United States)

DIRECTION: Liviu Ciulei, *The Lost Forest* (Romania)

1966

PALM D'OR: *A Man and a Woman* (France) and *The Birds, the Bees, and the Italians* (France/Italy)

BEST ACTOR: Per Oscarsson, *Hunger* (Denmark)

BEST ACTRESS: Vanessa Redgrave, *Morgan!* (United Kingdom)

DIRECTION: Sergei Yutkevich, *Portrait of Lenin* (U.S.S.R.)

1967

PALM D'OR: *Blow Up* (United Kingdom/Italy)

BEST ACTOR: Oded Kotler, *Three Days and a Child* (Israel)

BEST ACTRESS: Pia Degermark, *Elvira Madigan* (Denmark)

DIRECTION: Ferenc Kósa, *Ten Thousand Suns* (Hungary)

1968

No festival held

1969

PALM D'OR: *If* (United Kingdom)

BEST ACTOR: Jean-Louis Trintignant, *Z* (France)

BEST ACTRESS: Vanessa Redgrave, *Isadora* (United Kingdom)

DIRECTION: Glauber Rocha, *Antonio das Mortes* (Brazil) and Vojtech Jasny, *All My Countrymen* (Czechoslovakia)

1970

PALM D'OR: *M*A*S*H* (United States)

BEST ACTOR: Marcello Mastroianni, *Drama of Jealousy* (Italy)

BEST ACTRESS: Ottavia Piccolo, *Metello* (Italy)

DIRECTION: John Boorman, *Leo the Last* (United Kingdom)

1971

PALM D'OR: *The Go-Between* (United Kingdom)

BEST ACTOR: Riccardo Cucciolla, *Sacco and Vanzetti* (Italy)

BEST ACTRESS: Kitty Winn, *Panic in Needle Park* (United States)

DIRECTION: No award given

1972

PALM D'OR: *The Mattei Affair* (Italy) and *The Working Class Go to Heaven* (Italy)

BEST ACTOR: Jean Yanne, *We Will Not Grow Old Together* (France)

BEST ACTRESS: Susannah York, *Images* (Ireland)

DIRECTION: Miklós Jancsó, *Red Psalm* (Hungary)

1973

PALM D'OR: *Scarecrow* (United States) and *The Hireling* (United Kingdom)

BEST ACTOR: Giancarlo Giannini, *Love and Anarchy* (Italy)

BEST ACTRESS: Joanne Woodward, *The Effect of Gamma Rays on Man-in-the-Moon Marigolds* (United States)

DIRECTION: No award given

1974

PALM D'OR: *The Conversation* (United States)

BEST ACTOR: Jack Nicholson, *The Last Detail* (United States)

BEST ACTRESS: Marie-José Nat, *Les Violons du Bal* (France)

DIRECTION: No award given

1975

PALM D'OR: *Chronicle of the Burning Years* (Algeria)

BEST ACTOR: Vittorio Gassman, *Scent of a Woman* (Italy)

BEST ACTRESS: Valerie Perrine, *Lenny* (United States)

DIRECTION: Costa-Gavras, *Special Section* (France) and Michel Brault, *The Orders* (Canada)

1976

PALM D'OR: *Taxi Driver* (United States)

BEST ACTOR: José Luis Gómez, *Pascual Duarte* (Spain)

BEST ACTRESS: Dominique Sanda, *The Inheritance* (Italy) and Mari Torocsikc, *Mrs. Dery, Where Are You?* (Hungary)

DIRECTION: Ettore Scola, *Down and Dirty* (Italy)

1977

PALM D'OR: *Padre Padrone* (Italy)

BEST ACTOR: Fernando Rey, *Elisa My Love* (Spain)

BEST ACTRESS: Shelley Duvall, *Three Women* (United States) and Monique Mercure, *J. A. Martin, Photographer* (Canada)

DIRECTION: No award given

1978

PALM D'OR: *The Tree of Wooden Clogs* (Italy)

BEST ACTOR: Jon Voight, *Coming Home* (United States)

BEST ACTRESS: Jill Clayburgh, *An Unmarried Woman* (United States) and Isabelle Huppert, *Violette* (France)

DIRECTION: Nagisa Oshima, *Empire of Passion* (Japan)

1979

PALM D'OR: *The Tin Drum* (Germany) and *Apocalypse Now* (United States)

BEST ACTOR: Jack Lemmon, *The China Syndrome* (United States)

BEST ACTRESS: Sally Field, *Norma Rae* (United States)

DIRECTION: Terrence Malick, *Days of Heaven* (United States)

1980

PALM D'OR: *Kagemusha* (Japan) and *All That Jazz* (United States)

BEST ACTOR: Michel Piccoli, *Leap into the Void* (Italy)

BEST ACTRESS: Anouk Aimée, *Leap into the Void* (Italy)

DIRECTION: Krzysztof Zanussi, *The Constant Factor* (Poland)

1981

PALM D'OR: *Man of Iron* (Poland)

BEST ACTOR: Ugo Tognazzi, *The Tragedy of a Ridiculous Man* (Italy)

BEST ACTRESS: Isabelle Adjani, *Quartet* (United Kingdom/France) and *Possession* (France/Germany)

DIRECTION: No award given

1982

PALM D'OR: *Missing* (United States)

BEST ACTOR: Jack Lemmon, *Missing* (United States)

BEST ACTRESS: Jadwiga Jankowska-Cieslak, *Another Way* (Hungary)

DIRECTION: Werner Herzog, *Fitzcarraldo* (Germany)

1983

PALM D'OR: *The Ballad of Narayama* (Japan)

BEST ACTOR: Gian Maria Volonte, *The Death of Mario Ricci* (Switzerland)

BEST ACTRESS: Hanna Schygulla, *The Story of Piera* (Italy)

DIRECTION: No award given

1984

PALM D'OR: *Paris, Texas* (Germany)

BEST ACTOR: Alfredo Landa and Francisco Rabal, *The Holy Innocents* (Spain)

BEST ACTRESS: Helen Mirren, *Cal* (Ireland)

DIRECTION: Bertrand Tavernier, *A Sunday in the Country* (France)

1985

    PALM D'OR: *When Father Was Away on Business* (Yugoslavia)

    BEST ACTOR: William Hurt, *Kiss of the Spider Woman* (United States)

    BEST ACTRESS: Norma Aleandro, *The Official Story* (Argentina) and Cher, *Mask* (United States)

    DIRECTION: André Téchiné, *Rendez-Vous* (France)

1986

    PALM D'OR: *The Mission* (United Kingdom)

    BEST ACTOR: Michel Blanc, *Tenue de Soirée* (France) and Bob Hoskins, *Mona Lisa* (United Kingdom)

    BEST ACTRESS: Barbara Sukowa, *Rosa Luxemburg* (Germany) and Fernanda Torres, *Speak to Me of Love* (Brazil)

    DIRECTION: Martin Scorsese, *After Hours* (United States)

1987

    PALM D'OR: *Under Satan's Sun* (France)

    BEST ACTOR: Marcello Mastroianni, *Dark Eyes* (Italy)

    BEST ACTRESS: Barbara Hershey, *Shy People* (United States)

    DIRECTION: Wim Wenders, *Wings of Desire* (Germany/France)

1988

    PALM D'OR: *Pelle the Conqueror* (Denmark/Sweden)

    BEST ACTOR: Forest Whitaker, *Bird* (United States)

    BEST ACTRESS: Barbara Hershey, Jodhi May, and Linda Mvusi, *A World Apart* (United States)

    DIRECTION: Fernando E. Solanas, *The South* (Argentina)

1989

    PALM D'OR: *sex, lies and videotape* (United States)

    BEST ACTOR: James Spader, *sex, lies and videotape* (United States)

    BEST ACTRESS: Meryl Streep, *A Cry in the Dark* (United States/Australia)

    DIRECTION: Emir Kusturica, *Time of the Gypsies* (Yugoslavia)

1990

PALM D'OR: *Wild at Heart* (United States)

GRAND PRIX: *Shi No Toge* (Japan) and *Tilai* (France)

BEST ACTOR: Gérard Depardieu, *Cyrano de Bergerac* (France)

BEST ACTRESS: Krystyna Janda, *Interrogation* (Poland)

DIRECTION: Pavel Lunguine, *Taxi Blues* (U.S.S.R./France)

1991

PALM D'OR: *Barton Fink* (United States)

GRAND PRIX: *La Belle Noiseuse* (France)

BEST ACTOR: John Turturro, *Barton Fink* (United States)

BEST ACTRESS: Irène Jacob, *The Double Life of Veronique* (Poland/France)

DIRECTION: Joel Coen, *Barton Fink* (United States)

1992

PALM D'OR: *The Best Intentions* (Sweden)

GRAND PRIX: *Stolen Children* (Italy/France)

BEST ACTOR: Tim Robbins, *The Player* (United States)

BEST ACTRESS: Pernilla August, *The Best Intentions* (Sweden)

DIRECTION: Robert Altman, *The Player* (United States)

1993

PALM D'OR: *The Piano* (Australia/France) and *Farewell, My Concubine* (Hong Kong)

GRAND PRIX: *Faraway, So Close!* (Germany)

BEST ACTOR: David Thewlis, *Naked* (United Kingdom)

BEST ACTRESS: Holly Hunter, *The Piano* (Australia/France)

DIRECTION: Mike Leigh, *Naked* (United Kingdom)

1994

PALM D'OR: *Pulp Fiction* (United States)

GRAND PRIX: *Burnt by the Sun* (Russia/France) and *To Live* (China)

BEST ACTOR: Ge You, *To Live* (China)

BEST ACTRESS: Virna Lisi, *Queen Margot* (France)

DIRECTION: Nanni Moretti, *Caro Diaro* (Italy)

1995

PALM D'OR: *Underground* (France/Germany/Hungary)

GRAND PRIX: *Ulysses' Gaze* (Greece/France/Italy)

BEST ACTOR: Jonathan Pryce, *Carrington* (United Kingdom)

BEST ACTRESS: Helen Mirren, *The Madness of King George* (United Kingdom/United States)

DIRECTION: Matthieu Kassovitz, *Hate* (France)

1996

PALM D'OR: *Secrets and Lies* (United Kingdom)

GRAND PRIX: *Breaking the Waves* (Denmark)

BEST ACTOR: Pascal Duquenne and Daniel Auteuil, *Eighth Day* (France)

BEST ACTRESS: Brenda Blethyn, *Secrets and Lies* (United Kingdom)

DIRECTION: Joel Coen, *Fargo* (United States)

1997

PALM D'OR: *The Taste of Cherry* (Iran) and *Unagi* (Japan)

GRAND PRIX: *The Sweet Hereafter* (Canada)

BEST ACTOR: Sean Penn, *She's So Lovely* (United States)

BEST ACTRESS: Kathy Burke, *Nil by Mouth* (United Kingdom)

DIRECTION: Wong Kar-Wai, *Happy Together* (Hong Kong)

1998

PALM D'OR: *Eternity and a Day* (Greece)

GRAND PRIX: *Life Is Beautiful* (Italy)

BEST ACTOR: Peter Mullan, *My Name Is Joe* (United Kingdom)

BEST ACTRESS: Elodie Bouchez and Natacha Régnier, *The Dreamlife of Angels* (France)

DIRECTION: John Boorman, *The General* (United Kingdom)

1999

PALM D'OR: *Rosetta* (Belgium)

GRAND PRIX: *L'humanité* (France)

BEST ACTOR: Emmanuel Schotté, *L'humanité* (France)

BEST ACTRESS: Séverine Caneele, *L'humanité* (France) and Emelie Dequenne, *Rosetta* (Belgium)

DIRECTION: Pedro Almodóvar, *All About My Mother* (Spain)

The National Film Registry: 150 *Great Movies*

The National Film Registry is administered by the Librarian of Congress, who since 1989 has selected twenty-five films a year to be preserved in the National Library. Films are chosen for "their historical, cultural and aesthetic significance" and must be at least ten years old to be eligible. The list totals 150 films to date. There are a great number of others that weren't chosen, to be sure, including foreign films like *Pather Panchali, 8½, La Strada, L'Atalante, Rashomon, The Rules of the Game, Battleship Potemkin, Jules and Jim, L'Avventura, The Passion of Joan of Arc, Wild Strawberries, The Bicycle Thief, Ivan the Terrible,* and *Brief Encounter.*

Adam's Rib (1949)

The African Queen (1951)

All About Eve (1950)

All Quiet on the Western Front (1930)

An American in Paris (1951)

Annie Hall (1977)

The Apartment (1960)

Badlands (1973)

The Bank Dick (1940)

The Battle of San Pietro (1945)

The Best Years of Our Lives (1946)

Big Business (1929)

The Big Parade (1925)

The Birth of a Nation (1915)

The Black Pirate (1926)
Blade Runner (1982)
The Blood of Jesus (1941)
Bonnie and Clyde (1967)
Bringing Up Baby (1938)
Carmen Jones (1954)
Casablanca (1942)
Castro Street (1966)
Cat People (1942)
The Cheat (1915)
Chinatown (1974)
Chulas Fronteras (1976)
Citizen Kane (1941)
City Lights (1931)
The Cool World (1963)
A Corner in Wheat (1909)
The Crowd (1928)
David Holtzman's Diary (1968)
Detour (1946)
Dodsworth (1936)
Dog Star Man (1964)
Double Indemnity (1944)
Dr. Strangelove or: How I Learned to Stop Worrying and Love the Bomb (1964)
Duck Soup (1933)
Eaux d'Artifice (1953)
E.T. the Extra-Terrestrial (1982)
The Exploits of Elaine (1914)
Fantasia (1940)
Footlight Parade (1933)
Force of Evil (1948)

Frankenstein (1931)
Freaks (1932)
The Freshman (1925)
The General (1927)
Gerti the Dinosaur (1914)
Gigi (1958)
The Godfather (1972)
The Godfather: Part II (1974)
The Gold Rush (1925)
Gone with the Wind (1939)
The Grapes of Wrath (1940)
The Great Train Robbery (1903)
Greed (1924)
Harlan County, U.S.A. (1976)
Hell's Hinges (1916)
High Noon (1952)
High School (1968)
His Girl Friday (1940)
Hospital (1970)
How Green Was My Valley (1941)
I Am a Fugitive from a Chain Gang (1932)
Intolerance (1916)
Invasion of the Body Snatchers (1956)
It Happened One Night (1934)
The Italian (1915)
It's a Wonderful Life (1946)
Killer of Sheep (1977)
King Kong (1933)
The Lady Eve (1941)
Lassie Come Home (1943)
Lawrence of Arabia (1962)

The Learning Tree (1969)
Letter From an Unknown Woman (1948)
Louisiana Story (1948)
Love Me Tonight (1932)
Magical Maestro (1952)
The Magnificent Ambersons (1942)
The Maltese Falcon (1942)
The Manchurian Candidate (1962)
March of Time: Inside Nazi Germany (1938)
Marty (1955)
Meet Me in St. Louis (1944)
Meshes of the Afternoon (1943)
Midnight Cowboy (1969)
Modern Times (1936)
Morocco (1930)
A Movie (1958)
Mr. Smith Goes to Washington (1939)
My Darling Clementine (1946)
Nanook of the North (1922)
Nashville (1975)
A Night at the Opera (1935)
The Night of the Hunter (1955)
Ninotchka (1939)
Nothing but a Man (1964)
On the Waterfront (1954)
One Flew over the Cuckoo's Nest (1975)
Out of the Past (1947)
Paths of Glory (1957)
Pinocchio (1940)
A Place in the Sun (1951)
Point of Order (1964)

The Poor Little Rich Girl (1917)
Primary (1960)
The Prisoner of Zenda (1937)
Psycho (1960)
Raging Bull (1960)
Rebel Without a Cause (1955)
Red River (1948)
Ride the High Country (1962)
The River (1937)
Safety Last (1923)
Salesman (1969)
Salt of the Earth (1954)
Scarface (1932)
The Searchers (1956)
Shadow of a Doubt (1943)
Shadows (1959)
Shane (1953)
Sherlock, Jr. (1924)
Singin' in the Rain (1952)
Snow White (1933)
Snow White and the Seven Dwarfs (1937)
Some Like It Hot (1959)
Star Wars (1977)
Sullivan's Travels (1941)
Sunrise (1927)
Sunset Boulevard (1950)
Sweet Smell of Success (1957)
Tabu (1931)
Taxi Driver (1976)
Tevye (1939)
Top Hat (1935)

Touch of Evil (1958)

The Treasure of the Sierra Madre (1948)

Trouble in Paradise (1932)

2001: A Space Odyssey (1968)

Vertigo (1958)

What's Opera, Doc? (1957)

Where Are My Children? (1916)

The Wind (1928)

Within Our Gates (1920)

The Wizard of Oz (1939)

A Woman Under the Influence (1974)

Yankee Doodle Dandy (1942)

Zapruder film of John F. Kennedy's assassination (1963)

More Great Movies

Here is a short list of movies that many critics believe should be added to the preceding National Film Registry list. Add your own favorites to it.

Apocalypse Now (1979)

Bambi (1942)

Being There (1979)

Blow-Up (1966)

Cabaret (1972)

The Conversation (1974)

The Elephant Man (1980)

A Face in the Crowd (1957)

Five Easy Pieces (1970)

Gallipoli (1981)

A Hard Day's Night (1964)

The Informer (1935)

The Innocents (1961)

The Last Picture Show (1971)
The Lost Weekend (1945)
My Man Godfrey (1936)
North by Northwest (1959)
Notorious (1946)
The Ox-Bow Incident (1943)
The Philadelphia Story (1940)
Queen Christina (1933)
Rear Window (1954)
Rebecca (1940)
The Third Man (1949)
The 39 Steps (1935)
To Kill a Mockingbird (1962)
West Side Story (1961)

The Sundance Film Festival Awards

Founded by actor Robert Redford and a group of friends and associates in Sundance, Utah, the Sundance awards are dedicated to the support of new, independent films unaffiliated with any major studio. Of the many awards issued annually, only the Grand Jury Prizes for dramatic films are listed in this sampling.

1990—*Chameleon Street*, director Wendell B. Harris, Jr.

1991—*Poison*, director Todd Haynes

1992—*In the Soup*, director Alexandre Rockwell

1993—*Ruby in Paradise*, director Victor Nunez

1994—*What Happened Was*, director Tom Noonan

1995—*The Brothers McMullen*, director Edward Burns

1996—*Welcome to the Dollhouse*, director Todd Solondz

1997—*Sunday*, director Jonathan Nositer

1998—*Slam*, director Marc Levin

An Amateur Affair: The World's Longest-Running Play

The world's longest-running play, an entirely amateur production, has been playing for more than three centuries, longer than any modern-day professional play. The record-holder is the Oberammergau Passion Play, portraying Christ's last days, his suffering and death, in Jerusalem. In 1633, the villagers of Oberammergau, in Germany's Bavarian Alps, vowed that if God would spare them from the terrible plague raging through Europe, they would enact Christ's last days on earth every ten years "until the end of time." Since then the Oberammergau Passion Play, performed for thirty-eight years out of its 354-year history, has become synonymous with passion play itself.

The amateur players at Oberammergau are paid very little for their one hundred or so six-and-a-half-hour performances during the year of the play, at most about $2,000 for a year of work rehearsing and presenting the drama. Some 1,700 villagers are involved in each production. No one makes any great personal monetary gain; the profits are mainly divided between the Catholic Church and the fund for the next play.

More than half a million people visit Oberammergau every year the passion play is presented, watching from hard seats in a 5,200-seat theater whose stage is out in the open against an Alpine backdrop. Twice as many usually have to be turned away.

Other Long-Running Plays

- Agatha Christie's play *The Mousetrap*, which opened in London on November 25, 1952, has been performed 18,503 times as of May 9, 1997, grossing more than $36 million and making a rich man of the author's nephew, to whom she had bequeathed all royalties.
- *The Fantasticks*, which opened Off-Broadway on May 3, 1960, was the longest-running musical of all time with 15,429 performances up until 1998.
- The musical *Cats*, which opened on June 19, 1982, took the title of Broadway's longest-running show on June 19, 1997, with its 6,138th performance. It has grossed more than $2.2 billion.
- Danish comedian Victor Borge had the longest-running one-man show in theater history, performing his *Comedy in Music* on Broadway 849 consecutive times from October 2, 1953, through January 21, 1956.

America's Oldest Play

America's first play was of course produced centuries after Greek classical dramas or even the medieval mystery plays in England and other European countries. In fact, only two plays by American playwrights were produced for the American stage before the Revolutionary War. Neither showed promise as native drama. George Cocking's *The Conquest of Canada, or The Siege of Quebec* is a weak attempt at historical drama, and *The Prince of Parthia* (1759) is a blank verse romantic tragedy by Philadelphia poet Thomas Godfrey the Younger (who died in 1763 when he was only twenty-seven), about Arsaces, son of King Artabanus of Parthia. Godfrey's effort is said to be a patchwork of passages imitated from at least seven English writers, including Shakespeare and Marlowe. It was, however, the first American play to be produced professionally. Royall Tyler's comedy *The Contrast* was the second, in 1787, and was the first native work to introduce the character now known as the stage Yankee, as well as America's first play to be a box-office success.

Much earlier than any of the above plays is *Androboros*, which has never been produced but was the first American play to be printed, in 1714. Its two prominent authors were New York governor Robert Hunter and New York's chief justice, Lewis Morris. This political satire bears the imprint Moronapolis ("Fool's Town") on the title page and is a thinly veiled attack on New York colonial administrator Francis Nicholson, who is called Androboros ("Maneater") in the play. When Androboros proposes an attack on the French, the Moronapolis senate passes a resolution that he has behaved gallantly in the attack, which he hasn't made yet. Asked why the resolution has been passed before the attack, the senators reply that there will be less reason to do so after it is made.

Pulitzer Prize–Winning Plays

Established and endowed by newspaper publisher Joseph Pulitzer, the Pulitzer Prizes are the most prestigious of all American literary prizes. The awards in drama have been given since 1918. Eugene O'Neill won four Pulitzers, while Robert E. Sherwood and Edward Albee are tied for second place with three each. Here are the winning plays and playwrights to date. It should be noted that William Saroyan turned down the Pulitzer Prize he was awarded in 1940 for *The Time of Your Life*. He is the only playwright ever to have done so, though Sinclair Lewis had earlier turned down the Pulitzer for his novel *Arrowsmith* (1926).

1918—*Why Marry?*, Jesse Lynch Williams
1919—No award given
1920—*Beyond the Horizon*, Eugene O'Neill
1921—*Miss Lulu Bett*, Zona Gale
1922—*Anna Christie*, Eugene O'Neill
1923—*Icebound*, Owen Davis
1924—*Hell-Bent fer Heaven*, Hatcher Hughes
1925—*They Knew What They Wanted*, Sidney Howard
1926—*Craig's Wife*, George Kelly
1927—*In Abraham's Bosom*, Paul Green
1928—*Strange Interlude*, Eugene O'Neill
1929—*Street Scene*, Elmer L. Rice
1930—*The Green Pastures*, Marc Connelly
1931—*Alison's House*, Susan Glaspell
1932—*Of Thee I Sing*, George S. Kaufman, Morrie Ryskind, and Ira Gershwin
1933—*Both Your Houses*, Maxwell Anderson
1934—*Men in White*, Sidney Kingsley
1935—*The Old Maid*, Zoe Akins
1936—*Idiots Delight*, Robert E. Sherwood
1937—*You Can't Take It with You*, Moss Hart and George S. Kaufman
1938—*Our Town*, Thornton Wilder
1939—*Abe Lincoln in Illinois*, Robert E. Sherwood
1940—*The Time of Your Life*, William Saroyan
1941—*There Shall Be No Night*, Robert E. Sherwood
1942—No award given
1943—*The Skin of Our Teeth*, Thornton Wilder
1944—No award given
1945—*Harvey*, Mary Chase

1946—*State of the Union*, Russel Crouse and Howard Lindsay

1947—No award given

1948—*A Streetcar Named Desire*, Tennessee Williams

1949—*Death of a Salesman*, Arthur Miller

1950—*South Pacific*, Richard Rodgers, Oscar Hammerstein II, and Joshua Logan

1951—No award given

1952—*The Shrike*, Joseph Kramm

1953—*Picnic*, William Inge

1954—*The Teahouse of the August Moon*, John Patrick

1955—*Cat on a Hot Tin Roof*, Tennessee Williams

1956—*The Diary of Anne Frank*, Frances Goodrich and Albert Hackett

1957—*Long Day's Journey into Night*, Eugene O'Neill

1958—*Look Homeward, Angel*, Ketti Frings

1959—*J.B.*, Archibald MacLeish

1960—*Fiorello!*, George Abbott, Jerome Weidman, Jerry Bock, and Sheldon Harnick

1961—*All the Way Home*, Tad Mosel

1962—*How to Succeed in Business Without Really Trying*, Frank Loesser and Abe Burrows

1963—No award given

1964—No award given

1965—*The Subject Was Roses*, Frank D. Gilroy

1966—No award given

1967—*A Delicate Balance*, Edward Albee

1968—No award given

1969—*The Great White Hope*, Howard Sackler

1970—*No Place to Be Somebody*, Charles Gordone

1971—*The Effect of Gamma Rays on Man-in-the-Moon Marigolds*, Paul Zindel

1972—No award given

1973—*That Championship Season*, Jason Miller

1974—No award given

1975—*Seascape*, Edward Albee

1976—*A Chorus Line*, Michael Bennett, James Kirkwood, Nicholas Dante, Marvin Hamlisch, and Edward Kleban

1977—*The Shadow Box*, Michael Cristofer

1978—*The Gin Game*, Donald L. Coburn

1979—*Buried Child*, Sam Shepard

1980—*Talley's Folly*, Lanford Wilson

1981—*Crimes of the Heart*, Beth Henley

1982—*A Soldier's Play*, Charles Fuller

1983—*'Night, Mother*, Marsha Norman

1984—*Glengarry Glen Ross*, David Mamet

1985—*Sunday in the Park with George*, Stephen Sondheim and James Lapine

1986—No award given

1987—*Fences*, August Wilson

1988—*Driving Miss Daisy*, Alfred Uhry

1989—*The Heidi Chronicles*, Wendy Wasserstein

1990—*The Piano Lesson*, August Wilson

1991—*Lost in Yonkers*, Neil Simon

1992—*The Kentucky Cycle*, Robert Schenkkan

1993—*Angels in America: Millennium Approaches*, Tony Kushner

1994—*Three Tall Women*, Edward Albee

1995—*The Young Man from Atlanta*, Horton Foote

1996—*Rent*, Jonathan Larson

1997—No award given

1998—*How I Learned to Drive*, Paula Vogel

The Movies' Only Pulitzer

Composer Virgil Thomson won the movies' only Pulitzer Prize for his original score to the film *Louisiana Story* (1948). He was not even nominated for an Oscar, which went that year to Brian Easdale for *The Red Shoes* and to Johnny Green and Roger Edens for *Easter Parade*.

The Tony Awards

Officially called the Antoinette Perry Awards, after the distinguished actor and director who died in 1946, the Tonys are given annually by the American Theatre Wing, Inc., and the League of American Theatres and Producers to honor "distinguished achievement in the theater." All categories aren't covered here.

1947

ACTORS—PLAY: José Ferrer, *Cyrano de Bergerac* and Fredric March, *Years Ago*

ACTRESSES—PLAY: Ingrid Bergman, *Joan of Lorraine* and Helen Hayes, *Happy Birthday*

DIRECTOR: Elia Kazan, *All My Sons*

1948

PLAY: *Mister Roberts*

ACTORS: Henry Fonda, *Mister Roberts*; Paul Kelly, *Command Decision*; Basil Rathbone, *The Heiress*

ACTRESSES: Judith Anderson, *Medea*; Katharine Cornell, *Antony and Cleopatra*; Jessica Tandy, *A Streetcar Named Desire*

DIRECTOR: No award given

1949

PLAY: *Death of a Salesman*

MUSICAL: *Kiss Me Kate*

ACTOR: Rex Harrison, *Anne of a Thousand Days*

ACTRESS: Marita Hunt, *The Madwoman of Chaillot*

ACTOR—MUSICAL: Ray Bolger, *Where's Charley?*

ACTRESS—MUSICAL: Nanette Fabray, *Love Life*

AUTHOR—PLAY: Arthur Miller, *Death of a Salesman*

AUTHOR—MUSICAL: Bella and Samuel Spewack, *Kiss Me Kate*

DIRECTOR: Elia Kazan, *Death of a Salesman*

1950

    PLAY: *The Cocktail Party*

    MUSICAL: *South Pacific*

    ACTOR—PLAY: Sidney Blackmer, *Come Back, Little Sheba*

    ACTRESS—PLAY: Shirley Booth, *Come Back, Little Sheba*

    ACTOR—MUSICAL: Ezio Pinza, *South Pacific*

    ACTRESS—MUSICAL: Mary Martin, *South Pacific*

    AUTHOR—PLAY: T. S. Eliot, *The Cocktail Party*

    AUTHOR—MUSICAL: Oscar Hammerstein II and Joshua Logan, *South Pacific*

    DIRECTOR: Joshua Logan, *South Pacific*

1951

    PLAY: *The Rose Tattoo*

    MUSICAL: *Guys and Dolls*

    ACTOR—PLAY: Claude Rains, *Darkness at Noon*

    ACTRESS—PLAY: Uta Hagen, *The Country Girl*

    ACTOR—MUSICAL: Robert Alda, *Guys and Dolls*

    ACTRESS—MUSICAL: Ethel Merman, *Call Me Madam*

    AUTHOR—PLAY: Tennessee Williams, *The Rose Tattoo*

    AUTHOR—MUSICAL: Jo Swerling and Abe Burrows, *Guys and Dolls*

    DIRECTOR: George S. Kaufman, *Guys and Dolls*

1952

    PLAY: *The Fourposter*

    MUSICAL: *The King and I*

    ACTOR—PLAY: José Ferrer, *The Shrike*

    ACTRESS—PLAY: Julie Harris, *I Am a Camera*

    ACTOR—MUSICAL: Phil Silvers, *Top Banana*

    ACTRESS—MUSICAL: Gertrude Lawrence, *The King and I*

    AUTHOR—PLAY: No award given

AUTHOR—MUSICAL: No award given

DIRECTOR: José Ferrer, *The Shrike*, *The Fourposter*, and *Stalag 17*

1953

PLAY: *The Crucible*

MUSICAL: *Wonderful Town*

ACTOR—PLAY: Tom Ewell, *The Seven Year Itch*

ACTRESS—PLAY: Shirley Booth, *Time of the Cuckoo*

ACTOR—MUSICAL: Thomas Mitchell, *Hazel Flagg*

ACTRESS—MUSICAL: Rosalind Russell, *Wonderful Town*

AUTHOR—PLAY: Arthur Miller, *The Crucible*

AUTHOR—MUSICAL: Joseph Fields and Jerome Chodorov, *Wonderful Town*

DIRECTOR: Joshua Logan, *Picnic*

1954

PLAY: *The Teahouse of the August Moon*

MUSICAL: *Kismet*

ACTOR—PLAY: David Wayne, *The Teahouse of the August Moon*

ACTRESS—PLAY: Audrey Hepburn, *Ondine*

ACTOR—MUSICAL: Afred Drake, *Kismet*

ACTRESS—MUSICAL: Dolores Gray, *Carnival in Flanders*

AUTHOR—PLAY: John Patrick, *The Teahouse of the August Moon*

AUTHOR—MUSICAL: Charles Lederer and Luther Davis, *Kismet*

DIRECTOR: Alfred Lunt, *Ondine*

1955

PLAY: *The Desperate Hours*

MUSICAL: *The Pajama Game*

ACTOR—PLAY: Alfred Lunt, *Quadrille*

ACTRESS—PLAY: Nancy Kelly, *The Bad Seed*

ACTOR—MUSICAL: Walter Slezak, *Fanny*

ACTRESS—MUSICAL: Mary Martin, *Peter Pan*
AUTHOR—PLAY: Joseph Hayes, *The Desperate Hours*
AUTHOR—MUSICAL: George Abbott and Richard Bissell, *The Pajama Game*
DIRECTOR: Robert Montgomery, *The Desperate Hours*

1956

PLAY: *The Diary of Anne Frank*
MUSICAL: *Damn Yankees*
ACTOR—PLAY: Paul Muni, *Inherit the Wind*
ACTRESS—PLAY: Julie Harris, *The Lark*
ACTOR—MUSICAL: Ray Walston, *Damn Yankees*
ACTRESS—MUSICAL: Gwen Verdon, *Damn Yankees*
AUTHOR—PLAY: Frances Goodrich and Albert Hackett, *The Diary of Anne Frank*
AUTHOR—MUSICAL: George Abbott and Douglass Wallop, *Damn Yankees*
DIRECTOR: Tyrone Guthrie, *The Matchmaker*

1957

PLAY: *Long Day's Journey into Night*
MUSICAL: *My Fair Lady*
ACTOR—PLAY: Fredric March, *Long Day's Journey into Night*
ACTRESS—PLAY: Margaret Leighton, *Separate Tables*
ACTOR—MUSICAL: Rex Harrison, *My Fair Lady*
ACTRESS—MUSICAL: Judy Holliday, *Bells Are Ringing*
AUTHOR—PLAY: Eugene O'Neill, *Long Day's Journey into Night*
AUTHOR—MUSICAL: Alan Jay Lerner, *My Fair Lady*
DIRECTOR: Moss Hart, *My Fair Lady*

1958

PLAY: *Sunrise at Campobello*
MUSICAL: *The Music Man*
ACTOR—PLAY: Ralph Bellamy, *Sunrise at Campobello*

ACTRESS—PLAY: Helen Hayes, *Time Remembered*

ACTOR—MUSICAL: Robert Preston, *The Music Man*

ACTRESS—MUSICAL: Thelma Ritter, *New Girl in Town* and Gwen Verdon, *New Girl in Town*

AUTHOR—PLAY: Dore Schary, *Sunrise at Campobello*

AUTHOR—MUSICAL: Meredith Willson and Franklin Lacey, *The Music Man*

DIRECTOR: Vincent J. Donehue, *Sunrise at Campobello*

1959

PLAY: *J.B.*

MUSICAL: *Redhead*

ACTOR—PLAY: Jason Robards Jr., *The Disenchanted*

ACTRESS—PLAY: Gertrude Berg, *A Majority of One*

ACTOR—MUSICAL: Richard Kiley, *Redhead*

ACTRESS—MUSICAL: Gwen Verdon, *Redhead*

AUTHOR—PLAY: Archibald MacLeish, *J.B.*

AUTHOR—MUSICAL: Herbert and Dorothy Fields, Sidney Sheldon, and David Shaw, *Redhead*

DIRECTOR: Elia Kazan, *J.B.*

1960

PLAY: *The Miracle Worker*

MUSICAL: *Fiorello!* and *The Sound of Music*

ACTOR—PLAY: Melvyn Douglas, *The Best Man*

ACTRESS—PLAY: Anne Bancroft, *The Miracle Worker*

ACTOR—MUSICAL: Jackie Gleason, *Take Me Along*

ACTRESS—MUSICAL: Mary Martin, *The Sound of Music*

AUTHOR—PLAY: William Gibson, *The Miracle Worker*

AUTHOR—MUSICAL: Jerome Weidman and George Abbott, *Fiorello!* and Howard Lindsay and Russel Crouse, *The Sound of Music*

DIRECTOR—PLAY: Arthur Penn, *The Miracle Worker*

DIRECTOR—MUSICAL: George Abbott, *Fiorello!*

1961

    PLAY: *Becket*
    MUSICAL: *Bye, Bye Birdie*
    ACTOR—PLAY: Zero Mostel, *Rhinoceros*
    ACTRESS—PLAY: Joan Plowright, *A Taste of Honey*
    ACTOR—MUSICAL: Richard Burton, *Camelot*
    ACTRESS—MUSICAL: Elizabeth Seal, *Irma la Douce*
    AUTHOR—PLAY: Jean Anouilh, *Becket*
    AUTHOR—MUSICAL: Michael Stewart, *Bye, Bye Birdie*
    DIRECTOR—PLAY: Sir John Gielgud, *Big Fish, Little Fish*
    DIRECTOR—MUSICAL: Gower Champion, *Bye, Bye Birdie*

1962

    PLAY: *A Man for All Seasons*
    MUSICAL: *How to Succeed in Business Without Really Trying*
    ACTOR—PLAY: Paul Scofield, *A Man for All Seasons*
    ACTRESS—PLAY: Margaret Leighton, *Night of the Iguana*
    ACTOR—MUSICAL: Robert Morse, *How to Succeed in Business Without Really Trying*
    ACTRESS—MUSICAL: Anna Maria Alberghetti, *Carnival* and Diahann Carroll, *No Strings*
    AUTHOR—PLAY: Robert Bolt, *A Man for All Seasons*
    AUTHOR—MUSICAL: Abe Burrows, Jack Weinstock, and Willie Gilbert, *How to Succeed in Business Without Really Trying*
    DIRECTOR—PLAY: Noel Willman, *A Man for All Seasons*
    DIRECTOR—MUSICAL: Abe Burrows, *How to Succeed in Business Without Really Trying*

1963

    PLAY: *Who's Afraid of Virginia Woolf?*
    MUSICAL: *A Funny Thing Happened on the Way to the Forum*
    ACTOR—PLAY: Arthur Hill, *Who's Afraid of Virginia Woolf?*

ACTRESS—PLAY: Uta Hagen, *Who's Afraid of Virginia Woolf?*

ACTOR—MUSICAL: Zero Mostel, *A Funny Thing Happened on the Way to the Forum*

ACTRESS—MUSICAL: Vivien Leigh, *Tovarich*

AUTHOR—PLAY: No award given

AUTHOR—MUSICAL: Burt Shevelove and Larry Gelbart, *A Funny Thing Happened on the Way to the Forum*

DIRECTOR—PLAY: Alan Schneider, *Who's Afraid of Virginia Woolf?*

DIRECTOR—MUSICAL: George Abbott, *A Funny Thing Happened on the Way to the Forum*

1964

PLAY: *Luther*

MUSICAL: *Hello, Dolly!*

ACTOR—PLAY: Alec Guinness, *Dylan*

ACTRESS—PLAY: Sandy Dennis, *Any Wednesday*

ACTOR—MUSICAL: Bert Lahr, *Foxy*

ACTRESS—MUSICAL: Carol Channing, *Hello, Dolly!*

AUTHOR—PLAY: John Osborne, *Luther*

AUTHOR—MUSICAL: Michael Stewart, *Hello, Dolly!*

DIRECTOR—PLAY: Mike Nichols, *Barefoot in the Park*

DIRECTOR—MUSICAL: Gower Champion, *Hello, Dolly!*

1965

PLAY: *The Subject Was Roses*

MUSICAL: *Fiddler on the Roof*

ACTOR—PLAY: Walter Matthau, *The Odd Couple*

ACTRESS—PLAY: Irene Worth, *Tiny Alice*

ACTOR—MUSICAL: Zero Mostel, *Fiddler on the Roof*

ACTRESS—MUSICAL: Liza Minnelli, *Flora, the Red Menace*

AUTHOR—PLAY: Neil Simon, *The Odd Couple*

AUTHOR—MUSICAL: Joseph Stein, *Fiddler on the Roof*

DIRECTOR—PLAY: Mike Nichols, *Luv* and *The Odd Couple*
DIRECTOR—MUSICAL: Jerome Robbins, *Fiddler on the Roof*

1966

PLAY: *Marat/Sade*
MUSICAL: *Man of La Mancha*
ACTOR—PLAY: Hal Holbrook, *Mark Twain Tonight!*
ACTRESS—PLAY: Rosemary Harris, *The Lion in Winter*
ACTOR—MUSICAL: Richard Kiley, *Man of La Mancha*
ACTRESS—MUSICAL: Angela Lansbury, *Mame*
DIRECTOR—PLAY: Peter Brook, *Marat/Sade*
DIRECTOR—MUSICAL: Albert Marre, *Man of La Mancha*

1967

PLAY: *The Homecoming*
MUSICAL: *Cabaret*
ACTOR—PLAY: Paul Rogers, *The Homecoming*
ACTRESS—PLAY: Beryl Reid, *The Killing of Sister George*
ACTOR—MUSICAL: Robert Preston, *I Do! I Do!*
ACTRESS—MUSICAL: Barbara Harris, *The Apple Tree*
DIRECTOR—PLAY: Peter Hall, *The Homecoming*
DIRECTOR—MUSICAL: Harold S. Prince, *Cabaret*

1968

PLAY: *Rosencrantz and Guildenstern Are Dead*
MUSICAL: *Hallelujah, Baby!*
ACTOR—PLAY: Martin Balsam, *You Know I Can't Hear You When the Water's Running*
ACTRESS—PLAY: Zoe Caldwell, *The Prime of Miss Jean Brodie*
ACTOR—MUSICAL: Robert Goulet, *The Happy Time*
ACTRESS—MUSICAL: Patricia Routledge, *Darling of the Day* and Leslie Uggams, *Hallelujah, Baby!*

DIRECTOR—PLAY: Mike Nichols, *Plaza Suite*

DIRECTOR—MUSICAL: Gower Champion, *The Happy Time*

1969

PLAY: *The Great White Hope*

MUSICAL: *1776*

ACTOR—PLAY: James Earl Jones, *The Great White Hope*

ACTRESS—PLAY: Julie Harris, *Forty Carats*

ACTOR—MUSICAL: Jerry Orbach, *Promises, Promises*

ACTRESS—MUSICAL: Angela Lansbury, *Dear World*

DIRECTOR—PLAY: Peter Dews, *Hadrian VII*

DIRECTOR—MUSICAL: Peter Hunt, *1776*

1970

PLAY: *Borstal Boy*

MUSICAL: *Applause*

ACTOR—PLAY: Fritz Weaver, *Child's Play*

ACTRESS—PLAY: Tammy Grimes, *Private Lives* (revival)

ACTOR—MUSICAL: Cleavon Little, *Purlie*

ACTRESS—MUSICAL: Lauren Bacall, *Applause*

DIRECTOR—PLAY: Joseph Hardy, *Child's Play*

DIRECTOR—MUSICAL: Ron Field, *Applause*

1971

PLAY: *Sleuth*

MUSICAL: *Company*

ACTOR—PLAY: Brian Bedford, *The School for Wives*

ACTRESS—PLAY: Maureen Stapleton, *Gingerbread Lady*

ACTOR—MUSICAL: Hal Linden, *The Rothschilds*

ACTRESS—MUSICAL: Helen Gallagher, *No, No, Nanette*

DIRECTOR—PLAY: Peter Brook, *A Midsummer Night's Dream*

DIRECTOR—MUSICAL: Harold Prince, *Company*

1972

    PLAY: *Sticks and Bones*

    MUSICAL: *Two Gentlemen of Verona*

    ACTOR—PLAY: Cliff Gorman, *Lenny*

    ACTRESS—PLAY: Sada Thompson, *Twigs*

    ACTOR—MUSICAL: Phil Silvers, *A Funny Thing Happened on the Way to the Forum* (revival)

    ACTRESS—MUSICAL: Alexis Smith, *Follies*

    DIRECTOR—PLAY: Mike Nichols, *The Prisoner of Second Avenue*

    DIRECTOR—MUSICAL: Harold Prince and Michael Bennett, *Follies*

1973

    PLAY: *That Championship Season*

    MUSICAL: *A Little Night Music*

    ACTOR—PLAY: Alan Bates, *Butley*

    ACTRESS—PLAY: Julie Harris, *The Last of Mrs. Lincoln*

    ACTOR—MUSICAL: Ben Vereen, *Pippin*

    ACTRESS—MUSICAL: Glynis Johns, *A Little Night Music*

    DIRECTOR—PLAY: A. J. Antoon, *That Championship Season*

    DIRECTOR—MUSICAL: Bob Fosse, *Pippin*

1974

    PLAY: *The River Niger*

    MUSICAL: *Raisin*

    ACTOR—PLAY: Michael Moriarty, *Find Your Way Home*

    ACTRESS—PLAY: Colleen Dewhurst, *A Moon for the Misbegotten*

    ACTOR—MUSICAL: Christopher Plummer, *Cyrano*

    ACTRESS—MUSICAL: Virginia Capers, *Raisin*

    DIRECTOR—PLAY: José Quintero, *A Moon for the Misbegotten*

    DIRECTOR—MUSICAL: Harold Prince, *Candide*

1975

    PLAY: *Equus*

    MUSICAL: *The Wiz*

ACTOR—PLAY: John Kani and Winston Ntshona, *Sizwe Banzi Is Dead* and *The Island*

ACTRESS—PLAY: Ellen Burstyn, *Same Time, Next Year*

ACTOR—MUSICAL: John Cullum, *Shenandoah*

ACTRESS—MUSICAL: Angela Lansbury, *Gypsy*

DIRECTOR—PLAY: John Dexter, *Equus*

DIRECTOR—MUSICAL: Geoffrey Holder, *The Wiz*

1976

PLAY: *Travesties*

MUSICAL: *A Chorus Line*

ACTOR—PLAY: John Wood, *Travesties*

ACTRESS—PLAY: Irene Worth, *Sweet Bird of Youth*

ACTOR—MUSICAL: George Rose, *My Fair Lady* (revival)

ACTRESS—MUSICAL: Donna McKechnie, *A Chorus Line*

DIRECTOR—PLAY: Ellis Rabb, *The Royal Family*

DIRECTOR—MUSICAL: Michael Bennett, *A Chorus Line*

1977

PLAY: *The Shadow Box*

MUSICAL: *Annie*

ACTOR—PLAY: Al Pacino, *The Basic Training of Pavlo Hummel*

ACTRESS—PLAY: Julie Harris, *The Belle of Amherst*

ACTOR—MUSICAL: Barry Bostwick, *The Robber Bridegroom*

ACTRESS—MUSICAL: Dorothy Loudon, *Annie*

DIRECTOR—PLAY: Gordon Davidson, *The Shadow Box*

DIRECTOR—MUSICAL: Gene Saks, *I Love My Wife*

1978

PLAY: *Da*

MUSICAL: *Ain't Misbehavin'*

ACTOR—PLAY: Barnard Hughes, *Da*

ACTRESS—PLAY: Jessica Tandy, *The Gin Game*

ACTOR—MUSICAL: John Cullum, *On the Twentieth Century*

ACTRESS—MUSICAL: Liza Minnelli, *The Act*
DIRECTOR—PLAY: Melvin Bernhardt, *Da*
DIRECTOR—MUSICAL: Richard Maltby Jr., *Ain't Misbehavin'*

1979

PLAY: *The Elephant Man*
MUSICAL: *Sweeney Todd*
ACTOR—PLAY: Tom Conti, *Whose Life Is It Anyway?*
ACTRESS—PLAY: Constance Cummings, *Wings* and Carole Shelley, *The Elephant Man*
ACTOR—MUSICAL: Len Cariou, *Sweeney Todd*
ACTRESS—MUSICAL: Angela Lansbury, *Sweeney Todd*
DIRECTOR—PLAY: Jack Hofsiss, *The Elephant Man*
DIRECTOR—MUSICAL: Harold Prince, *Sweeney Todd*

1980

PLAY: *Children of a Lesser God*
MUSICAL: *Evita*
ACTOR—PLAY: John Rubinstein, *Children of a Lesser God*
ACTRESS—PLAY: Phyllis Frelich, *Children of a Lesser God*
ACTOR—MUSICAL: Jim Dale, *Barnum*
ACTRESS—MUSICAL: Patti LuPone, *Evita*
DIRECTOR—PLAY: Vivian Matalon, *Morning's at Seven*
DIRECTOR—MUSICAL: Harold Prince, *Evita*

1981

PLAY: *Amadeus*
MUSICAL: *42nd Street*
ACTOR—PLAY: Ian McKellen, *Amadeus*
ACTRESS—PLAY: Jane Lapotaire, *Piaf*
ACTOR—MUSICAL: Kevin Kline, *The Pirates of Penzance*
ACTRESS—MUSICAL: Lauren Bacall, *Woman of the Year*

DIRECTOR—PLAY: Peter Hall, *Amadeus*

DIRECTOR—MUSICAL: Wilford Leach, *The Pirates of Penzance*

1982

PLAY: *The Life and Adventures of Nicholas Nickleby*

MUSICAL: *Nine*

ACTOR—PLAY: Roger Rees, *The Life and Adventures of Nicholas Nickleby*

ACTRESS—PLAY: Zoe Caldwell, *Medea*

ACTOR—MUSICAL: Ben Harney, *Dreamgirls*

ACTRESS—MUSICAL: Jennifer Holliday, *Dreamgirls*

DIRECTOR—PLAY: Trevor Nunn and John Caird, *The Life and Adventures of Nicholas Nickleby*

DIRECTOR—MUSICAL: Tommy Tune, *Nine*

1983

PLAY: *Torch Song Trilogy*

MUSICAL: *Cats*

ACTOR—PLAY: Harvey Fierstein, *Torch Song Trilogy*

ACTRESS—PLAY: Jessica Tandy, *Foxfire*

ACTOR—MUSICAL: Tommy Tune, *My One and Only*

ACTRESS—MUSICAL: Natalia Makarova, *On Your Toes*

DIRECTOR—PLAY: Gene Saks, *Brighton Beach Memoirs*

DIRECTOR—MUSICAL: Trevor Nunn, *Cats*

1984

PLAY: *The Real Thing*

MUSICAL: *La Cage aux Folles*

ACTOR—PLAY: Jeremy Irons, *The Real Thing*

ACTRESS—PLAY: Glenn Close, *The Real Thing*

ACTOR—MUSICAL: George Hearn, *La Cage aux Folles*

ACTRESS—MUSICAL: Chita Rivera, *The Rink*

DIRECTOR—PLAY: Mike Nichols, *The Real Thing*
DIRECTOR—MUSICAL: Arthur Laurents, *La Cage aux Folles*

1985

PLAY: *Biloxi Blues*
MUSICAL: *Big River*
ACTOR—PLAY: Derek Jacobi, *Much Ado About Nothing*
ACTRESS—PLAY: Stockard Channing, *Joe Egg*
DIRECTOR—PLAY: Gene Saks, *Biloxi Blues*
DIRECTOR—MUSICAL: Des McAnuff, *Big River*

1986

PLAY: *I'm Not Rappaport*
MUSICAL: *The Mystery of Edwin Drood*
ACTOR—PLAY: Judd Hirsch, *I'm Not Rappaport*
ACTRESS—PLAY: Lily Tomlin, *The Search for Signs of Intelligent Life in the Universe*
ACTOR—MUSICAL: George Rose, *The Mystery of Edwin Drood*
ACTRESS—MUSICAL: Bernadette Peters, *Song & Dance*
DIRECTOR—PLAY: Jerry Zaks, *The House of Blue Leaves*
DIRECTOR—MUSICAL: Wilford Leach, *The Mystery of Edwin Drood*

1987

PLAY: *Fences*
MUSICAL: *Les Misérables*
ACTOR—PLAY: James Earl Jones, *Fences*
ACTRESS—PLAY: Linda Lavin, *Broadway Bound*
ACTOR—MUSICAL: Robert Lindsay, *Me and My Girl*
ACTRESS—MUSICAL: Maryann Plunkett, *Me and My Girl*
DIRECTOR—PLAY: Lloyd Richards, *Fences*
DIRECTOR—MUSICAL: Trevor Nunn and John Caird, *Les Misérables*

1988

PLAY: *M. Butterfly*
MUSICAL: *The Phantom of the Opera*
ACTOR—PLAY: Ron Silver, *Speed-the-Plow*
ACTRESS—PLAY: Joan Allen, *Burn This*
ACTOR—MUSICAL: Michael Crawford, *The Phantom of the Opera*
ACTRESS—MUSICAL: Joanna Gleason, *Into the Woods*
DIRECTOR—PLAY: John Dexter, *M. Butterfly*
DIRECTOR—MUSICAL: Harold Prince, *The Phantom of the Opera*

1989

PLAY: *The Heidi Chronicles*
MUSICAL: *Jerome Robbins' Broadway*
ACTOR—PLAY: Philip Bosco, *Lend Me a Tenor*
ACTRESS—PLAY: Pauline Collins, *Shirley Valentine*
ACTOR—MUSICAL: Jason Alexander, *Jerome Robbins' Broadway*
ACTRESS—MUSICAL: Ruth Brown, *Black and Blue*
DIRECTOR—PLAY: Jerry Zaks, *Lend Me a Tenor*
DIRECTOR—MUSICAL: Jerome Robbins, *Jerome Robbins' Broadway*

1990

PLAY: *The Grapes of Wrath*
MUSICAL: *City of Angels*
ACTOR—PLAY: Robert Morse, *Tru*
ACTRESS—PLAY: Maggie Smith, *Lettuce and Lovage*
ACTOR—MUSICAL: James Naughton, *City of Angels*
ACTRESS—MUSICAL: Tyne Daly, *Gypsy* (revival)
DIRECTOR—PLAY: Frank Galati, *The Grapes of Wrath*
DIRECTOR—MUSICAL: Tommy Tune, *Grand Hotel, The Musical*

1991

PLAY: *Lost in Yonkers*

MUSICAL: *The Will Rogers Follies*

ACTOR—PLAY: Nigel Hawthorne, *Shadowlands*

ACTRESS—PLAY: Mercedes Ruehl, *Lost in Yonkers*

ACTOR—MUSICAL: Jonathan Pryce, *Miss Saigon*

ACTRESS—MUSICAL: Lea Salonga, *Miss Saigon*

DIRECTOR—PLAY: Jerry Zaks, *Six Degrees of Separation*

DIRECTOR—MUSICAL: Tommy Tune, *The Will Rogers Follies*

1992

PLAY: *Dancing at Lughnasa* (revival)

MUSICAL: *Crazy for You*

ACTOR—PLAY: Judd Hirsch, *Conversations with My Father*

ACTRESS—PLAY: Glenn Close, *Death and the Maiden*

ACTOR—MUSICAL: Gregory Hines, *Jelly's Last Jam*

ACTRESS—MUSICAL: Faith Prince, *Guys and Dolls* (revival)

DIRECTOR—PLAY: Patrick Mason, *Dancing at Lughnasa* (revival)

DIRECTOR—MUSICAL: Jerry Zaks, *Guys and Dolls*

1993

PLAY: *Angels in America: Millennium Approaches*

MUSICAL: *Kiss of the Spider Woman—The Musical*

ACTOR—PLAY: Ron Leibman, *Angels in America: Millennium Approaches*

ACTRESS—PLAY: Madeline Kahn, *The Sisters Rosensweig*

ACTOR—MUSICAL: Brent Carver, *Kiss of the Spider Woman—The Musical*

ACTRESS—MUSICAL: Chita Rivera, *Kiss of the Spider Woman—The Musical*

DIRECTOR—PLAY: George C. Wolfe, *Angels in America: Millennium Approaches*

DIRECTOR—MUSICAL: Des McAnuff, *The Who's Tommy* (revival)

1994

    PLAY: *Angels in America: Perestroika*

    MUSICAL: *Passion*

    ACTOR—PLAY: Stephen Spinella, *Angels in America: Perestroika*

    ACTRESS—PLAY: Diana Rigg, *Medea*

    ACTOR—MUSICAL: Boyd Gaines, *She Loves Me*

    ACTRESS—MUSICAL: Donna Murphy, *Passion*

    DIRECTOR—PLAY: Stephen Daldry, *An Inspector Calls*

    DIRECTOR—MUSICAL: Nicholas Hytner, *Carousel* (revival)

1995

    PLAY: *Love! Valour! Compassion!*

    MUSICAL: *Sunset Boulevard*

    ACTOR—PLAY: Ralph Fiennes, *Hamlet*

    ACTRESS—PLAY: Cherry Jones, *The Heiress*

    ACTOR—MUSICAL: Matthew Broderick, *How to Succeed in Business Without Really Trying*

    ACTRESS—MUSICAL: Glenn Close, *Sunset Boulevard*

    DIRECTOR—PLAY: Gerald Gutierrez, *The Heiress*

    DIRECTOR—MUSICAL: Harold Prince, *Show Boat*

1996

    PLAY: *Master Class*

    MUSICAL: *Rent*

    ACTOR—PLAY: George Grizzard, *A Delicate Balance*

    ACTRESS—PLAY: Zoe Caldwell, *Master Class*

    ACTOR—MUSICAL: Nathan Lane, *A Funny Thing Happened on the Way to the Forum* (revival)

    ACTRESS—MUSICAL: Ann Duquesnay, *Bring in 'Da Noise, Bring in 'Da Funk*

    DIRECTOR—PLAY: Gerald Gutierrez, *A Delicate Balance*

    DIRECTOR—MUSICAL: George C. Wolfe, *Bring in 'Da Noise, Bring in 'Da Funk*

1997

PLAY: *The Last Night of Ballyhoo*
MUSICAL: *Titanic*
ACTOR—PLAY: Christopher Plummer, *Barrymore*
ACTRESS—PLAY: Janet McTeer, *A Doll's House*
ACTOR—MUSICAL: James Naughton, *Chicago*
ACTRESS—MUSICAL: Bebe Neuwirth, *Chicago*
DIRECTOR—PLAY: Anthony Page, *A Doll's House*
DIRECTOR—MUSICAL: Walter Bobbie, *Chicago*

1998

PLAY: *Side Man*
MUSICAL: *Fosse*
ACTOR—PLAY: Brian Dennehy, *Death of a Salesman*
ACTRESS—PLAY: Judi Dench, *Amy's View*
ACTOR—MUSICAL: Martin Short, *Little Me*
ACTRESS—MUSICAL: Bernadette Peters, *Annie Get Your Gun*
DIRECTOR—PLAY: Robert Falls, *Death of a Salesman*
DIRECTOR—MUSICAL: Matthew Bourne, *Swan Lake*

Tony Superlatives

- Most Tonys won by an individual: Harold Prince—17 (9 as a producer and 8 as a director).
- Most Tonys won by a play: *A Man for All Seasons* (1962), *Who's Afraid of Virginia Woolf?* (1963), *Amadeus* (1977)—5 each.
- Most Tonys won by a leading actor: John Cullum, Richard Kiley, Robert Preston, George Rose, Phil Silvers—2 each.
- Most Tonys won by a leading actress: Julie Harris—5.
- Most Tonys won by a director (comedy or drama): Mike Nichols—5.
- Most Tonys won by a director (musical): Harold Prince—8.
- Most Tonys won by an author (book for a musical): George Abbott, James Lapine, Hugh Wheeler—3 each.

- Most Tonys won for best score: Stephen Sondheim—6.
- Most Tonys won by a producer: Harold Prince—9.

Broadway's Biggest Flop

The musical *Carrie* (1988) cost more than $7 million to produce and closed after only five performances.

New York Drama Critics Circle Awards

These prestigious awards were first given in 1935 by the New York Drama Critics Circle, an association of local critics, in large part because of dissatisfaction with the Pulitzer Prize drama selections. At first, only dramatic American plays were selected, but in later years other awards were given, including those for best foreign plays and musicals. Only the drama winners selected over the years are noted here. Tennessee Williams, Tom Stoppard, and August Wilson are tied for the most wins, with four each.

1935–1936: *Winterset*, Maxwell Anderson

1936–1937: *High Tor*, Maxwell Anderson

1937–1938: *Of Mice and Men*, John Steinbeck

1938–1939: No award given

1939–1940: *The Time of Your Life*, William Saroyan

1940–1941: *Watch on the Rhine*, Lillian Hellman

1941–1942: No award given

1942–1943: *The Patriots*, Sidney Kingsley

1943–1944: No award given

1944–1945: *The Glass Menagerie*, Tennessee Williams

1945–1946: No award given

1946–1947: *All My Sons*, Arthur Miller

1947–1948: *A Streetcar Named Desire*, Tennessee Williams

1948–1949: *Death of a Salesman*, Arthur Miller

1949–1950: *The Member of the Wedding*, Carson McCullers

1950–1951: *Darkness at Noon*, Sidney Kingsley

1951–1952: *I Am a Camera*, John Van Druten

1952–1953: *Picnic*, William Inge

1953–1954: *The Teahouse of the August Moon*, John Patrick

1954–1955: *Cat on a Hot Tin Roof*, Tennessee Williams

1955–1956: *The Diary of Anne Frank*, Frances Goodrich and Albert Hackett

1956–1957: *Long Day's Journey into Night*, Eugene O'Neill

1957–1958: *Look Homeward, Angel*, Ketti Frings

1958–1959: *A Raisin in the Sun*, Lorraine Hansberry

1959–1960: *Toys in the Attic*, Lillian Hellman

1960–1961: *All the Way Home*, Tad Mosel

1961–1962: *The Night of the Iguana*, Tennessee Williams

1962–1963: *Who's Afraid of Virginia Woolf?*, Edward Albee

1963–1964: *Luther*, John Osborne

1964–1965: *The Subject Was Roses*, Frank D. Gilroy

1965–1966: *The Persecution and Assassination of Marat as Performed by the Inmates of the Asylum of Charenton Under the Direction of the Marquis de Sade*, Peter Weiss and *The Man of La Mancha*, Dale Wasserman, Mitch Leigh, and Joe Darion

1966–1967: *The Homecoming*, Harold Pinter

1967–1968: *Rosencrantz and Guildenstern Are Dead*, Tom Stoppard

1968–1969: *The Great White Hope*, Howard Sackler

1969–1970: *Borstal Boy*, Frank McMahon

1970–1971: *Home*, David Storey

1971–1972: *That Championship Season*, Jason Miller

1972–1973: *The Changing Room*, David Storey

1973–1974: *The Contractors*, David Storey

1974–1975: *Equus*, Peter Shaffer

1975–1976: *Travesties*, Tom Stoppard

1976–1977: *Otherwise Engaged*, Simon Gray

1977–1978: *Da*, Hugh Leonard

1978–1979: *The Elephant Man*, Bernard Pomerance

1979–1980: *Talley's Folly*, Landford Wilson and *Evita*, Andrew Lloyd Webber and Tim Rice

1980–1981: *A Lesson from Aloes*, Athol Fugard

1981–1982: *The Life and Adventures of Nicholas Nickleby*, adapted by David Edgar

1982–1983: *Brighton Beach Memoirs*, Neil Simon

1983–1984: *The Real Thing*, Tom Stoppard

1984–1985: *Ma Rainey's Black Bottom*, August Wilson

1985–1986: *Lie of the Mind*, Sam Shepard

1986–1987: *Fences*, August Wilson

1987–1988: *Joe Turner's Come and Gone*, August Wilson

1988–1989: *The Heidi Chronicles*, Wendy Wasserstein

1989–1990: *The Piano Lesson*, August Wilson

1990–1991: *Six Degrees of Separation*, John Guare

1991–1992: *Dancing at Lughnasa*, Brian Friel

1992–1993: *Angels in America: Millennium Approaches*, Tony Kushner

1993–1994: *Three Tall Women*, Edward Albee

1994–1995: *Arcadia*, Tom Stoppard

1995–1996: *Seven Guitars*, August Wilson

1996–1997: *How I Learned to Drive*, Paula Vogel

1997–1998: *Wit,* Margaret Edson

The Obies

Since 1955 the New York newspaper *The Village Voice* has presented *The Village Voice* Off-Broadway Awards, popularly called the Obies, honoring the best Off-Broadway productions. A different panel of judges each year is picked to select the best play, playwright, actor, director, composer, designer, etc. Another annual award for outstanding Off-Broadway achievement is the Lucille Lortel Awards.

Nielsen Ratings

Nielsen ratings are a survey conducted by the A. C. Nielsen Company since about 1960 to measure television viewership of various programs. The ratings are based on meters placed in TV sets and viewer diaries of a preselected sample of viewers. A. C. Nielsen has been measuring *radio* audiences since

1922. The ratings, especially the Sweeps, taken in the months of February, May, July, and November, determine what the networks charge sponsors.

The Q rating is a poll that tries to measure the familiarity of actors, products, etc., to the television viewing audience. It is named for its devisor, the TVQ/Marketing Evaluations Co.

The Emmys

The Emmys are any of several statuettes awarded annually for excellence in television programming, productions, or performance. No one is sure of the origin of the name, which may be an alteration (influenced by the name "Emmy") of *immy*, which, in turn, could be an alteration of *image orthicon*. An image orthicon is a sensitive television camera pickup tube. On the other hand, it could just have been named for some now unknown Emmy.

The Emmy Awards were instituted in 1948 by the Academy of Television Arts and Sciences, but today this body administers the prime-time awards in a full ceremony, while the National Academy of Television Arts and Sciences presents the daytime awards every spring. All and all there are some forty categories in which Emmys are given.

The first television program to win an Emmy (for most popular television program) was "Pantomime Quiz Time" in 1948. Most outstanding television personality was Shirley Dinsdale, with her puppet Judy Splinter, neither exactly a household name today. The next year, however, storied comedians Ed Wynn and Milton Berle won Emmys. Here are some Emmy record holders.

- Most Emmy Awards won by an individual: Producer Dwight Hemion—17 (out of 47 nominations).
- Most Emmy Awards won by an actress: Dinah Shore—8.
- Most Emmy Awards won by an actor: Ed Asner—7.
- Most Emmy Awards won by a series: "Sesame Street"—64.
- Most Emmy Awards won by an adult series: "The Mary Tyler Moore Show"—29.
- Most Emmy Awards won by a miniseries: "Roots"—9.
- Most Emmy Awards won by a crime drama series: "Hill Street Blues"—26.

Longest-Running TV Talk Show

"Meet the Press," which John F. Kennedy called "the fifty-first state" (so important is it politically), has been televised since 1947, having aired 2,600 shows as of June 4, 1997. But "The Joe Franklin Show," running from 1951 to 1993, has broadcast nearly twelve times as many shows—31,015, to be exact. None of the hosts or panelists on these two talk shows come anywhere near earning as much as talk show host Oprah Winfrey, who reportedly makes about $150 million a year.

Radio Days: The Longest-Lived Radio Shows

Radio is but a shadow of what it was in those "thrilling days of yesteryear" when the Lone Ranger and the Shadow (voice by Orson Welles) ruled the airwaves, when the medium offered listeners scores of comedies and mysteries and dramas and soap operas ranging from "Stella Dallas" to "The Goldbergs." Today America's 12,177 stations (the most in the world) broadcast mainly music, weather, news and talk shows of conservative political stripe. But two shows from the very earliest days of radio are still with us: the early morning "Rambling with Gambling" (since March 1925) and the weekly "Grand Old Opry" (since November 1925). The record-holding "Rambling with Gambling" has been hosted by three John Gamblings over the years—John B., the show's founder; his son John A.; and, presently, his grandson, John R. It is on the air all year, six days a week, and has been broadcast 22,948 times as of July 29, 1998.

Most Awards

Bob Hope (b. 1903) has won more awards of various kinds than any performer in history, or any person, for that matter—2,001 at this writing. Hope, considered the most popular American comedian of all time (excepting, possibly, Charlie Chaplin), has won four honorary Oscars.

IX

SCURRILOUS CRITICS AND INSIDIOUS CENSORS

Brickbats for the Bard

Critics. How can any player or playwright avoid them if even Shakespeare couldn't? Here are some brickbats hurled at the Bard over the years. Most are from critics who should have known better.

- "Shakespeare never had six lines without a fault," the Great Cham, Dr. Samuel Johnson remarked. "Perhaps you may find seven, but this does not refute my general assertion."
- *A Midsummer Night's Dream*, according to Samuel Pepys, was "the most insipid, ridiculous play that I ever saw in my life." The famous English diarist hated many of Shakespeare's plays.
- English poet Alexander Pope wrote sneeringly about the Bard: "Shakespeare whom you and every play-house bill / Style the divine, the matchless, what you will . . ."
- French playwright Victorien Sardou called Hamlet an "empty windbag hero" and wrote there is "nothing good in the play . . . except the scene with the actors."
- Lord Byron scoffed at "One Shakespeare and his plays so doting, / Which many pass for wits by quoting."
- "I hear a great deal, too, of Shakespeare, but I cannot read him," England's George II said of the Bard, "he is such a *bombast* fellow."

- Philosopher David Hume called Shakespeare "a disproportioned and misshapen giant."
- Joseph Addison failed to include Shakespeare in his *Account of the Greatest English Poets.*
- Critic John Dennis thought the Bard "devoid of celestial fire."
- Said poet John Dryden: "[Shakespeare] writes in many places below the dullest of our or any precedent age. Never did any author precipitate himself from such heights of thought to so low expression. . . . He is the very Janus of poets; he wears almost everywhere two faces; and you have scarce begun to admire the one ere you despise the other."
- Playwright Robert Greene on Shakespeare: "There is an upstart Crow, beautified with our feathers, that with his *Tygers hart wrapt in a Players hyde*, supposes he is well able to bombast out a blanke verse as the best of you: and beeing an absolute *Johannes fac totum* is in his owne conceit the onely Shakescene in a countrey." (The jealous Greene parodied here a line from *3 Henry VI*: "Oh Tiger's heart wrapt in a woman's hide.")
- "Shakespeare undoubtably wanted taste," said English novelist Hugh Walpole.
- Said Ben Jonson on hearing Shakespeare's boast that he had never blotted out a single line: "Would that he had blotted out a thousand."
- Dostoyevsky had strange reservations about Shakespeare. In a letter to his brother (May 31, 1858) he perhaps echoed Ben Jonson when he wrote: "A thing that has been written all at once cannot be ripe. They say there was not a blot on Shakespeare's manuscripts. That is why there are so many enormities and so much bad taste in him; he would have done better if he had worked harder."
- Wrote George Bernard Shaw: "With the single exception of Homer, there is no eminent writer, not even Sir Walter Scott, whom I can despise so entirely as I despise Shakespeare, when I measure my mind against his. . . . It would positively be a relief to me to dig him up and throw stones at him."

Nothing Changes

"The applause I have met with has often flattered me a great deal," said the great French playwright Jean Racine to his son. "But the smallest critical censure always caused me more vexation than all the pleasure given me by praise."

Extreme Criticism

- Legend holds that the great Greek dramatist Euripides was ripped apart by a mob of women who objected to one of his plays, though another tradition claims he was accidentally torn to pieces by a pack of hunting dogs. (*See* Chapter 3.)
- According to still another legend, the Greek poet Terpander was happily singing one of his songs on stage when a critic threw a fig at him that entered his mouth and lodged in his windpipe, "choking him to death in the very ecstasy of song."
- The famous Athenian orator Aeschines was a great tragic actor before he turned political speaker. Though a highly regarded thespian, he very nearly didn't live out his career, performing before audiences who expressed their displeasure by throwing olives, figs, or stones at actors. One time he appeared in a play that the audience regarded as highly offensive and was almost stoned to death. It was at this point that he turned to oratory.
- Dramatist-philosopher Giordano Bruno, "The Nuisance," was convicted of heresy by the Inquisition for one of his plays. He was stripped naked, bound to a stake over a pyre, his tongue tied so that he could make no speeches, and burned alive before a huge crowd.
- Prosper Jolyot de Crébillon, known as Crébillon Le Tragique, loved the high life and was notorious in his time, serving as the French censor of literature. But his dramatist father called him "the worst of my productions."
- Few critics have been as insistent as Jacques Vaché, the dadaist who climbed up on the stage of a Paris theater, pulled out a revolver, and threatened to shoot anyone who applauded a play he disliked. No one applauded.
- Danish critic Georg Morris Brandes (George Morris Cohen) made so many enemies with his slashing pen that he carried a pistol at all times to protect himself from their retaliation.

"Courage, Molière!"

Molière's *Tartuffe*, which has been performed more often than any other French play, is an exposé of the hypocritically pious. This theme obviously included a great number of real-life clergymen of his day, considering their reaction to the play. The archbishop of Paris, for example, threatened to excommunicate anyone who read, heard, or performed it, and another clergyman cried that "[Molière] should be burned at the stake as a foretaste of the fires of hell." Sometimes, however, Molière had help from his admirers. When he invented the French comedy of manners with *Les Précieuses Ridicules* in 1659, for example, he was uncertain about how successful he had been. His fears were laid to rest on opening night when a woman rose in the audience and cried, "Courage! Courage! Molière, this is good comedy!"

Word of Mouth

Honoré de Balzac spread the rumor that the premiere of his play *Les Resources* was sold out, hoping to spur demand by exaggerating the play's popularity. His plan backfired, however, when hordes of would-be attendees returned home, disappointed, before reaching the theater.

Puffery

In his play *The Critic* (1779) English dramatist Richard Brinsley Sheridan created a cast of characters including the bogus, verbose critic and author Mr. Puff. Sheridan named Mr. Puff after the English word *puff*, meaning inflated praise, which is suggestive of the sound made by puffing wind from the mouth and was commonly applied to exaggerated newspaper ads at the time. But Mr. Puff added a new dimension to the word in Sheridan's satire of the malignant literary criticism of the day. Puff talks with the spiteful critics Dangle and Sneer about the absurd, bombastic "tragedy" he has written called *The Spanish Armada*, pushing his play all the while, for he has refined the art of puffery to a science. At one time he even catalogs the puff: "Yes, the puff preliminary, the puff collateral, the puff collusive, and the puff oblique, or puff by implication. These all assume, as circumstances require, the various forms of letter to the editor, occasional anecdote, impartial critique, observation from correspondent, or advertisement from the party." So absurdly does Mr. Puff overpraise or blow up his work that *puffery* became the word for the kind of criticism produced by literary cliques, the mutual back-scratching or logrolling that is usually subtler but still as common today among the Sneers and Dangles of literature as it was in Sheridan's time.

The Man Without a Skin

Richard Cumberland, a British writer of popular sentimental comedies and turgid tragedies, was dubbed the "Man Without a Skin" by actor David Garrick because "he was so extremely sensitive that he could not bear to be touched by the finger of criticism." At a performance of Richard Brinsley Sheridan's acclaimed *The School for Scandal*, the jealous Cumberland tried to keep his children from laughing at Sheridan's successful comedy, often pinching them as he asked, "What are you laughing at, my dear little folks? You should not laugh, my angels, there is nothing to laugh at. . . . Keep still, you little dunces!" The story eventually got back to Sheridan, who pretended to be deeply hurt. "That was very ungrateful of Cumberland to have been displeased with his poor children for laughing at my comedy," he said gravely, "for I went the other night to see his tragedy, and laughed at it from beginning to end." Sheridan took further revenge on Cumberland by caricaturing him in *The Critic* as the savage, inept theater critic Sir Fretful Plagiary.

Rigoletto Reviled

Giuseppe Verdi's great opera *Rigoletto*, containing the famous melody "*La donna e mobile*," was abused by many critics as "uninspired" and "puerile and queer" for over ten years before being generally recognized as a masterpiece, though the public loved it from the first time it was performed in 1851 at the Venice Theater in Venice, Italy. One newspaper critic went so far as to say that to even discuss it "would be a loss of time and space."

Criticizing Beginners

- French dramatist Alexis Piron, called a "*machine à sailles*" (a machine that makes jokes) by a critic of the day, was cornered by a young would-be author who began reading him an entire five-act play. Piron listened politely but soon found a way to escape from a work so blatantly lifted from other authors. He began to bow to each line he recognized as another author's effort and soon the would-be playwright asked him why he was bowing so much. Said Piron, "Why, that is the way I am accustomed to greeting old friends when I run into them."

- A young playwright sent French actor Lucien Guitry a play he had written, with a covering note saying, *I bet you a louis that you don't read this script*. The busy Guitry returned the manuscript unopened along with an envelope containing a louis and a note reading, *You win.*

- Actor Sir Herbert Beerbohm Tree, half brother of critic and caricaturist Max Beerbohm, wrote this brief letter to a young aspiring dramatist who had sent him a play:

> *My dear Sir:*
>
> *I have read your play. Oh, my dear Sir!*
>
> *Yours faithfully.*

Free to Flee

A friend took the Hungarian dramatist Ferenc Molnár to the theater on complimentary tickets, but the playwright had enough of the play after one act and started to leave. "You can't walk out," his friend whispered, "we're guests of the management." Molnár thought for a moment and then got up again. "Where are you going now?" his friend demanded. "To the box office," explained Molnár, "to buy two tickets so we can leave."

Sardoodledum

French playwright Victorien Sardou was born to great wealth, but when his family lost its fortune he descended into poverty he could not have imagined. Sardou was found near death of typhoid fever in a garret, covered only by a pile of rejected play manuscripts. The woman who found him nursed him back to health and he later married her. He became among the most successful playwrights of his day, writing many vehicles for Sarah Bernhardt, but his well-made, often contrived, shallow plays led George Bernard Shaw to coin the word *Sardoodledum* for such dramas.

Abusing Ibsen

Here are some essential excerpts from reviews of the first plays by the Norwegian playwright Henrik Ibsen, the founder of modern drama.

- "A bad escape of moral sewer gas."
- "An open drain; a loathsome sore unbandaged."
- "Foul and filthy."
- "Morbid and unwholesome."

- "Garbage and offal."
- "Photographic studies of vice and morbidity."
- "Three acts of gibberish."
- "Repulsive and degrading."
- "Unnatural, immoral."
- "Simply blasphemous."

The plays so criticized were the masterpieces *A Doll's House*, *Ghosts*, *Hedda Gabler*, and *The Master Builder*.

Chekhov on Critics

"Critics are like horseflies which prevent the horse from ploughing," Anton Chekhov wrote to a friend. "For over twenty years I have read criticism of my work and I do not remember a single remark of any value or one word of valuable advice. Only once Skabichevsky wrote something which made an impression on me. He said I would die in a ditch drunk."

Married to a Critic

His own wife, Lady Rosina Bulwer-Lytton, was the worst critic of prolific British playwright and novelist Edward George Bulwer-Lytton. She not only vilified everything he wrote, but herself wrote a novel in which her husband was the villain. Finally, when Baron Lytton ran for political office, the lady followed him around England viciously heckling his speeches. She was certified insane in 1858 and was briefly in the care of a physician, but she outlived the baron by almost a decade.

A Shavian Shaft

George Bernard Shaw submitted the following review when he was drama critic for the *London Saturday Review* in the late nineteenth century:

> *I am in the somewhat foolish position concerning a play at the Opera Comique, whither I was bidden this day week. For some reason I was not supplied with a program; so that I never learned the name of the play. At the end of the second act the play had advanced about as far as an ordinary dramatist would have brought it five minutes after the first rising of the curtain; or say, as far as Ibsen would have brought it ten years before*

that event. Taking advantage of the second interval [intermission] to stroll out into the Strand for a little exercise, I unfortunately forgot all about my business, and actually reached home before it occurred to me that I had not seen the end of the play. Under these circumstances, it would ill become me to dogmatize the merits of the work or its performance and I can only offer the management my apologies.

Famous Counterattacks

- Among the most successful playwrights of his time, British author Douglas Jerrold seems in retrospect wittier than any of the characters he left to posterity. On the first night of his first play, *Fifteen Years of a Drunken Life* (1828), Jerrold was kidded about his nervousness by a seasoned, successful playwright. "I," he intoned, "never feel nervous on the first night of my pieces."

  "Ah, my boy," replied Jerrold, "you are always certain of success. Your pieces have all been tried before."

- German dramatist Hermann Sudermann was persuaded to make up with his enemy, playwright Richard Voss. "Herr Sudermann," Voss said as they shook hands, "I wish for your next play the same success as you wish me." Sudermann threw up his hands in desperation: "Did you hear that? There he goes again!"

- One evening Alexandre Dumas *père* sat with rival French playwright Alexander Soumet at the final performance of Soumet's latest play. Dumas pointed Soumet's attention to a sleeping spectator, saying, "You see, my dear Soumet, why your play must close." The next evening, however, a Dumas drama was playing in the same theater and Soumet thought he had revenged himself when he drew Dumas's attention to a spectator sound asleep through the whole performance. "It seems, my dear Dumas," he said archly, "that one can be put asleep by your plays, too." Dumas never blinked. "Why, that's the same man who was asleep last night," he said. "He hasn't been able to wake up yet."

- "How did your play go tonight?" asked someone of Oscar Wilde, knowing full well that it had flopped. "Ah," Wilde replied loftily, "the play was a great success but I'm afraid the audience was a failure."

- "Who am I to tamper with a masterpiece?" Wilde said when asked to make minor changes in one of his plays.

- Another time one of Wilde's critics presented him with a rotten cabbage instead of the usual flowers on the opening night of one of his plays.

"Thanks, dear fellow," Wilde told him. "Every time I smell it I shall be reminded of you."

- One opening night George Bernard Shaw stepped forward on stage to accept the plaudits of the audience. Amid all the applause, however, a lone dissenter shouted out, "Shaw, your play stinks!" G.B.S. hardly missed a beat after the brief silence that followed. "My friend," he said almost immediately, "I agree with you completely, but what are we two"—he gestured toward the audience—"against the great majority?"

- "Did you see my last play, *Private Lives*?" Noël Coward asked the actress Lady Diana Manners.

    "Yes," Manners replied. "Not at all amusing. Speaking of plays, did you see me play the role of the Virgin in *The Miracle*?"

    "Yes," said Coward. "*Very* amusing."

- Immediately after arguing with Sarah Bernhardt about her interpretation of a role in one of his plays, Oscar Wilde took out a cigarette. "Do you mind if I smoke, madam?" he asked. "I don't care if you burn," said the Divine Sarah.

The Divine vs. the Incomparable

The "Incomparable Max" Beerbohm, British critic, essayist, and caricaturist, reviewed Sarah Bernhardt when she portrayed Hamlet in 1899, when she was sixty-five. Wrote Beerbohm of the Divine Sarah's performance:

> *Her friends ought to have restrained her. The native critics ought not to have encouraged her. The customhouse officials at Charing Cross ought to have confiscated her sable doublet and horse. . . . The only compliment one can conscientiously pay her is that her Hamlet was, from first to last,* très grande dame.

An Unholy Alliance

Eugene O'Neill once explained in a letter his contempt for drama critics: "Me that was born on Times Square . . . and have heard dramatic critics called sons of bitches . . . ever since I was old enough to recognize the Count of Monte Cristo's voice [played on the stage for many years by his father]." When asked by the New York Drama Critics Circle to provide a welcoming statement on its founding in 1939, he wrote: "It is a terrible, harrowing experience for a playwright to be forced by his conscience to praise critics for anything. . . . There is something morbid and abnormal about it, something destructive to the noble traditions of what is correct for dramatists."

Years later, at the fiftieth anniversary dinner party of the New York Drama Critics Circle in 1985, attendance was poor for no apparent reason; only two writers of all the play award winners accepted their invitations. A critic later mentioned the poor attendance to one of the absent playwrights, who replied: "Why should anyone want to have dinner with critics?"

The Jukes Family of Journalism

After New York critics panned Maxwell Anderson's play *Truckline Café*, the Pulitzer Prize–winning playwright took out an ad in the *New York Times* calling critics "The Jukes family of journalism, who bring to the theater nothing but their own hopelessness, recklessness, and despair."

Bob's Best Barbs

Author and drama critic Robert Benchley was one of the few critics who could be ranked among the world's greatest wits. Benchley is also the only writer ever to win an Academy Award for a film he starred in (*see* Chapter 4). Here are some of his critical barbs.

- Benchley attended the Broadway premiere of *The Squall*, a turkey about gypsies who spoke in broken English. He bore the pain as long as he could, until a young gypsy girl character came on stage and delivered the immortal lines, "Me Nubi. Nubi good girl. Nubi stay."
  Benchley immediately rose.
  "Me Bobby," he said. "Bobby bad boy. Bobby go." And he left the theater.
- "It was one of the plays in which all the actors enunciated very clearly," he wrote of a Broadway flop.
- "Some laughter was heard in the back rows," the critic reported after attending the opening of a decidedly unfunny stage comedy. "Someone must have been telling jokes back there."
- Usually a man of impeccable judgment, Benchley made a bad mistake as theater adviser to millionaire John Hay Whitney. "I could smell it when the postman came whistling down the lane," he told the millionaire about a play he had received that was based on several popular *New Yorker* magazine stories. "Don't put a dime in it."

Luckily, Whitney decided to back *Life with Father* anyway, and it ran for seven and a half years.

- At the end of his career, when he was no longer reviewing plays, Benchley went to a Broadway opening with a friend. He fell asleep during the first act, but when a telephone rang onstage he awoke with a start, shouting, "Will someone please answer that—I think it's for me!" The next day one review read, "Show terrible but Benchley superb in small part."

Putting Criticism Behind One

German composer Max Reger received a terrible review from newspaper critic Rudolf Lewis. He immediately replied: "I am sitting in the smallest room in my house. I have your review before me. Soon it will be behind me."

The Peerless Percy

One of the sharp, witty Broadway drama critics of the 1920s, Percy Hammond worked for several Midwestern newspapers before becoming drama critic of the *New York Tribune* in 1921, remaining there until his death fifteen years later. The peerless Percy, much admired by his fellow critics, was responsible for several legendary quips that he often isn't given credit for, including his famous brief review of a tired vaudeville act: "They've played it so often that they can play it in their sleep, which yesterday they did."

One time impresario Florenz Ziegfeld telegraphed Hammond protesting his review of a Ziegfeld show and demanding that he print the long telegram as a rebuttal. Hammond not only printed the telegram—he printed all the far worse notices other New York critics had given the show.

He didn't spare his fellow critics, either. In reviewing rotund critic Alexander Woollcott's acting debut, he wrote of Smart Alec: "Observation of his billowy amplitudes suggests that the world might be a safer globe on which to live were the abdomens of its inhabitants more convex and less concave."

A Kaufman Collection

From his earliest days, American playwright George S. Kaufman had a precocious wit and vocabulary. When he was only four, his mother told him that his aunt would be visiting soon. "It wouldn't hurt to be nice to her, would it?" she asked. "That depends," Kaufman replied, "on your threshold of pain." And he got better as he got older; he is as much remembered today for his incisive wit as for his enduring plays.

- One afternoon at the famed Algonquin Round Table, Kaufman was asked to supply a definition of satire. "Satire," he replied, "is what closes on Saturday night."
- "There's no scenery at all," an actress told him, describing a new play she was rehearsing. "In the first scene, I'm on the left side of the stage and the audience has to imagine I'm eating dinner in a restaurant. Then in scene two, I move over to the right side of the stage and the audience has to imagine I'm in my drawing room."
  "And the second night," Kaufman said, "*you* have to imagine there's an audience out front."
- When Kaufman was scriptwriter for the Marx Brothers' *The Cocoanuts*, Groucho tried to slip one of his jokes into a scene. Kaufman thought it was terrible. "They laughed at Fulton and his steamboat, too," Groucho groused. "Not at matinees," Kaufman said.
- Kaufman worried about the lyrics of Irving Berlin's "Always." "'Always' seems like such a long time," he told the composer. "Why don't you make it, 'I'll be loving you on Thursday'?"
- "How do I get our leading lady's name in the *Times*?" the press agent for a musical asked Kaufman when he was drama critic at the newspaper. "Shoot her," Kaufman advised.
- "After all, it's only a small, insignificant theater," a summer stock producer who had used a Kaufman play without paying royalties explained. "Then you'll go to a small, insignificant jail," Kaufman replied.
- After Clifford Odets had written a rather anemic play, Kaufman asked him, "Odets, where is thy sting?"
- The author of a panned Broadway show had the misfortune to run into Kaufman shortly afterward. "I understand," Kaufman said, "that your play is full of single entendre."
- Charlie Chaplin was said to be richer than he was famous. One day he remarked to Kaufman that his blood pressure was down to 108. "Common or preferred?" Kaufman inquired.
- After the flop of his adaptation of the French farce *Someone in the House*, Kaufman suggested the following advertising slogan to the producer: "Avoid Crowds, See *Someone in the House* at the Knickerbocker Theatre."

Ouch!

Critic Wolcott Gibbs is credited with the shortest dramatic criticism in theatrical history. Reviewing the Broadway farce *Wham!* he wrote only "Ouch!"

More Broadway Barbs

- Reviewing a production of *Antony and Cleopatra*, John Mason Brown wrote: "Tallulah Bankhead barged down the Nile last night as Cleopatra—and sank."
- "Kate's wonderful, isn't she?" a friend said of Katharine Hepburn's Broadway performance in *The Lake*, between acts at the Martin Beck Theatre. "Oh, yes," Dorothy Parker agreed. "She runs the gamut of emotions all the way from A to B." These words became as celebrated as any of her ripostes, but years later she told Garson Kanin that she didn't think there was a finer actress anywhere than Katharine Hepburn; she had made the remark for the same reason she said many things—because it was funny. Miss Hepburn, however, agreed with her assessment of *The Lake*.
- George Jean Nathan reviewed the great American actor John Barrymore in one of his worst performances: "I always said that I'd like Barrymore's acting till the cows came home. Well, ladies and gentlemen, last night the cows came home."
- Wrote *New York Post* drama critic Richard Watts of Clare Booth Luce's first play: "One almost forgave *Abide with Me* its faults when its lovely playwright, who must have been crouched in the wings for a sprinter's start as the final curtain mercifully descended, heard a cry of 'Author,' which was not audible in my vicinity, and arrived to accept the audience's applause just as the actors, who had a head start on her, were properly lined up and smoothed out to receive their customary adulation."
- "*Hook and Ladder* is the sort of play that gives failures a bad name," Walter Kerr said of another turkey.
- *Oh! Calcutta!* said critic Clive Barnes, "is the sort of play that gives pornography a bad name."
- "The scenery was beautiful, but the actors got in front of it," wrote Alexander Woollcott of a lavish musical.
- Describing the performance of actor Creston Clarke in *King Lion*, Eugene Field wrote: "He played the King as though under the momentary apprehension that someone else was about to play the ace."

- George Jean Nathan on a contemporary playwright: "He writes his plays for the ages—the ages between five and twelve."
- Critic Percy Hammond summed up his review of a new musical comedy: "I have knocked everything but the knees of the chorus girls, and Nature has anticipated me there."
- After viewing a terrible performance of *Hamlet*, drama critic Robert Hendrickson wrote: "There has long been a controversy over who wrote Shakespeare's plays—Shakespeare or Bacon. I propose to settle it today by opening their graves. Whoever turned over last night wrote *Hamlet*."
- "Oh for an hour of Herod!" wrote Anthony Hope after sitting through the opening of *Peter Pan*.
- Critic Louis Kronenberger reviewed Tallulah Bankhead in *The Europeans*: "Only Mae West as Snow White could have seemed more unsuited to a part."

Outwitting the Critics

When controversial producer David Merrick (b. 1912) saw that reviews of one of his plays were terrible, he hired a group of men with the same names as the leading Broadway critics, made them write favorable reviews of the play, and published the glowing reviews in an ad he took out in all the New York papers.

Critics as Eunuchs

Irish playwright Brendan Behan had little use for drama critics. "Critics are like eunuchs in a harem," he remarked after reading an especially savage review of one of his plays. "They're there every night, they see how it should be done every night, but they can't do it themselves."

First Movie Review

A *New York Times* critique of D. W. Griffith's film *Pippa Passes* in 1909 is sometimes called the first movie review, but there are many descriptions of films before this and several among them might be considered film criticism as well, at least in part. The *Times* itself had this to say of the performances in several of Edison's Vitascope shorts on April 24, 1896: "People whose minds are not oversensitive find Miss [Florrie] West intensely amusing. But everybody likes [Albert] Chevalier, though it is doubtful if the perfect naturalness and delicate finish of his impersonations are generally appreciated. He is not 'sensational.'"

Some negative film criticism is expressed in a generally good discussion of *The Great Train Robbery* in the *Philadelphia Inquirer* of June 26, 1904: "In the pursuit by the sheriff one [rider] is shot in the back as he dashes madly downhill, and the way in which he tumbles from his horse and strikes the ground leaves the spectators wondering if he is not a dummy, for it does not seem possible that a man could take such a fall and live."

Stix Nix Hix Pix

This is among the most famous of the colorful headlines that have appeared in the show business newspaper *Variety*. It referred to a survey indicating that residents of small towns don't like movies about small town life.

One Critic's Credo

"In front of the screen, I'm still a kid. Movie love is abiding throughout life. The movies have a fascination that our ordinary lives don't have. The people are more beautiful, the vistas more splendid. When the theater lights go down, we want to be charmed and entertained. We're lovers who are let down all the time, and go on loving."
—*Pauline Kael, from a 1998* New York Times *interview*

Boos and Hisses

- Anton Chekhov was booed from the theater after the first performance of *The Sea Gull*. He angrily vowed never to write another play, but fortunately changed his mind two years later after Konstantin Stanislavsky restaged the drama and made it a resounding success.
- Henry James counted January 5, 1895, the worst night of his life. That was the opening night of his play *Guy Domville*, which he described as "a little white Christian virgin thrown to the tigers and lions." Not only was the play booed and hissed, but when he was led onstage, James, too, was booed. Despite good reviews from H. G. Wells and George Bernard Shaw, among others, he plunged into a deep depression.
- Though one of the greatest modern playwrights, Tennessee Williams saw his second play, *Battle of Angels* (revised in 1957 as *Orpheus Descending*),

hissed off the stage in 1940. His producers then took the unprecedented step of going onstage and apologizing to the audience for the production.

- French critic Francisque Sarcey attended a play in which a mechanical asp raised its head from a box and hissed. Later, when asked his opinion of the play, he replied, "I agree with the asp."
- A loud hiss came forth from somewhere in the audience while British poet-playwright Charles Lamb was delivering a lecture. After a brief silence, Lamb, showing no emotion, simply said: "There are only three things that hiss—a goose, a snake, and a fool. Come forth and be identified." On another occasion Lamb was present when his first play was hissed off the stage and actually joined in the hissing so that he couldn't be recognized as the author by the violent audience. Lamb, however, had the last word about the hissing, writing:

  Mercy on us, that God should give his favorite children, men, mouths to speak with, discourse rationally, to promise smoothly, to flatter agreeably, to encourage warmly, to counsel wisely; to sing with, to drink with, and to kiss with; and that they should turn them into mouths of adders, bears, wolves, hyennas, and whistle like tempests, and emit breath through them like distillations of aspic poison, to asperse and vilify the innocent labour of their fellow creatures who are desirous to please them. God be pleased to make the breath stink and the teeth rot out of them all therefore!

- One of French playwright Georges Feydeau's early farces was almost booed off the stage on opening night, and a friend spotted the playwright himself standing in the aisle, joining in the hissing and catcalls. "Have you gone crazy?" his friend asked him. "No, this way I can't hear them, and it doesn't hurt so much," Feydeau replied.

Silencing the Audience

Annoyed with a row of people coughing in the audience, John Barrymore sent out for a fish during intermission and threw it at them when he came back onstage. "Busy yourself with that, you damned walruses," the actor cried, "and let the rest of us proceed with the play!"

Banning the Bard

Shakespeare never made the Roman Catholic Church's *Index Librorum Prohibitorum*, but several of his plays were censored or banned in other places. Queen Elizabeth I disliked the scene where the king is deposed in *Richard II* and had it deleted from all copies of the play. From 1788 to 1820 *King Lear* was forbidden on the English stage, due to George III's insanity. Thomas Bowdler expurgated Shakespeare, as Coleridge had suggested before him, and in recent times *The Merchant of Venice* has been banned on the grounds that Shylock is a vicious characterization of a Jew. Moreover, Shakespeare has often been revised to the point of bowdlerization over the centuries. Conspicuous among examples are Nahum Tate's rewrite giving *King Lear* a happy ending; the Honorable James Howard, Dryden's brother-in-law, rewriting *Romeo and Juliet* so that the young lovers are happily married; and poet laureate Sir William D'Avenant's jolly production of *Macbeth*, complete with singing and dancing.

Bowdler the Bloodletter

Dr. Thomas Bowdler was not the first of the Bowdler clan to expurgate Shakespeare—his sister, Harriet, worked over the body of the Bard's work first. But Dr. Bowdler did more than enough gouging on his own to deserve to be known as the man behind the word *bowdlerize*. His inability to stand the sight of human blood and suffering had forced Dr. Thomas Bowdler to abandon his medical practice in London, but this weakness apparently did not apply where vendors of words were concerned. Bowdler so thoroughly purged Shakespeare that the Bard would have screamed in pain from the bloodletting had he been alive.

Bowdler, the most renowned of self-appointed literary censors, was born at Ashley, near Bath, England, on July 11, 1754. After he retired from medical practice, a considerable inheritance enabled him to travel about Europe, writing accounts of the grand tour that seem to have neither offended nor pleased anyone. Though he came from a religious family, Bowdler never earned the Reverend Doctor title often applied to him and his early years are conspicuous for the lack of any real accomplishments, unless one counts membership in organizations such as the Society for the Suppression of Vice. Only when he was middle-aged did he retire to the Isle of Wight and begin to sharpen his rusty scalpel on the Bard of Avon's bones.

In 1807 Bowdler's sister had published an expurgated edition of Shakespeare's work called *The Family Shakespeare* without signing her name to it as editor—probably because people would have wondered how a spinster knew what to look for to expurgate. Dr. Bowdler, however, had no such fears about signing his name. He was proud of the revised and enlarged *Family Shakespeare* that he published in 1818. In justifying this ten-volume edition, Bowdler explained on the title page that "nothing is added to the text; but those expressions are omitted which cannot with propriety be read aloud in a family," adding later that he had also expunged "whatever is unfit to be read by a gentleman in a company of ladies." What this really meant was that Bowdler (and his sister before him) had completely altered the characters of Hamlet, Macbeth, Falstaff, and others, and totally eliminated "objectionable" characters like Doll Tearsheet. Strangely enough, the poet Swinburne, who saw his own works bowdlerized by others, applauded the doctor many years later, writing that "no man ever did better service to Shakespeare than the man who made it possible to put him into the hands of intelligent and imaginative children."

Few playwrights then or now would agree with Swinburne, though *The Family Shakespeare* was a bestseller and won some critical acclaim. Bowdler firmly believed that Shakespeare would have "desired nothing more ardently" than his literary vandalism and he would probably have turned his scalpel to other great authors if death had not excised him in 1825. About ten years later Bowdler's name was first used as a verb, the official definition then "to expurgate by omitting or modifying words or passages considered indelicate or offensive." Today the word more often implies "prudish, arbitrary, ridiculous censorship." Bowdler himself has been described by a British critic as "the quivering moralist who is certain in his soul that others will be contaminated by what he himself reads with impunity."

A Banned Critic

Critic Alexander Woollcott had to take the management of the Shubert Theaters to court in 1915 in order to review plays in their houses. They had banned him from all Shubert productions for the "rancor and malice and venom" in his reviews.

Banning, Branding, and Beheading

In 1633 English author William Prynne was branded and had his ears cut off for writing a criticism of plays and playgoing which the queen enjoyed. Archbishop William Laud prosecuted him and had his book burned publicly. But Prynne got his revenge. Nine years later he was Laud's prosecutor when the archbishop was tried for high treason and beheaded.

Evading the Censors

Finding that his more prominent victims had his satiric impersonations of them suppressed under the licensing laws of the British theater, playwright Samuel Foote, known to his contemporaries as the "English Aristophanes," would invite the audience to join him for tea the next day, promising some diverting comedy. While the tea was being made he would present his uproarious mimicry of prominent people.

Disregarding the Censors

Mrs. Pat Campbell got the starring role in Shaw's *Pygmalion* because all the reigning London actresses refused to say the then taboo word *bloody* that the playwright put in the mouth of Eliza.

Getting Even

Comedian Stuart Robson (1836–1903) was constantly criticized by clergymen, as were many actors of his day. Robson retaliated by keeping a scrapbook of newspaper articles about sinning ministers and releasing appropriate portions of it to the press whenever attacked by a clergyman critic.

Shafting Shaw

Censorship caused George Bernard Shaw's play *Mrs. Warren's Profession* (1905), about the evils of prostitution, to be performed first in America, where it got even worse reviews than could have been expected in England.

"Offensive . . . Contemptible . . . Abominable," the *New York Post* reported.

"A dramatized stench," offered the *New York Sun*.

"A superabundance of foulness . . . Wholly immoral and degenerate," the *New York Herald* cried.

"Decaying and reeking," said the *New York Times*.

Nevertheless Shaw became the most famous living playwright in the world by the 1920s. "Obscenity," he once said in defending authors from censorship, "can be found in every book except the telephone directory."

The Coining of Comstockery

About 160 tons of books, photographs, magazines, film, and paintings were destroyed by Anthony Comstock (1844–1915), founder of the New York Society for the Suppression of Vice, in his long career as a self-appointed crusader against immorality in literature. Comstock, who inspired Boston's Watch and Ward Society, headed a YMCA campaign against obscene literature in 1873, the same year in which he came to national prominence by founding his society and securing federal passage of the so-called Comstock Laws to exclude objectionable matter from the mails. Appointed special agent of the Post Office Department and chief special agent for the society, Comstock had the power of an inquisitor, and *Comstockery* became a synonym for "narrow-minded, bigoted, and self-righteous moral censorship." The crusader particularly objected to George Bernard Shaw's play *Mrs. Warren's Profession*, and Shaw coined the word, making good clean fun of the censor's name.

The Case of the Moving Navel

One of the most ridiculous acts of censorship in stage history was the arrest of Mae West and the closing of her popular play *Sex* (1926), in which the Ooo-La-La Lady of the Stage played a tantalizing prostitute. West was charged with "corrupting the morals of youth" by swinging her hips and licking her lips. Furthermore, said an undercover cop "she moved her navel up and down and from left to right" while performing a belly dance. Rather than put herself in the hands of the courts, Mae West fled to Hollywood.

Banned in Boston

During the Roaring Twenties the familiar words *banned in Boston* made a number of plays and movies big hits throughout the rest of America. Plays and films were frequently banned in Boston for foolish reasons at the time because the ultraconservative Watch and Ward Society wielded great power over the city censor, often an ignorant and unreasonable man. The Boston censor who banned Eugene O'Neill's plays, for example, was the mayor's cousin, appointed because he had lost an arm in an accident and was fired from his job as drummer in a burlesque show band.

Czar of the Movies

Censorship of the Hollywood movie studios dates back to the early twentieth century, when one of the film's critics tried to censor D. W. Griffith's classic *The Birth of a Nation*, a movie notorious for its prejudice against blacks. But fully organized censorship didn't come until the 1920s, when scandals like those involving comedian Fatty Arbuckle (*see* Chapter 6), "the Ideal of American Manhood," made Hollywood look like a modern Gomorrah. At that time the studios founded the Motion Picture Producers and Distributors of America headed by Will Harrison Hays (1879–1954). Will Hays became known as the czar of filmdom when he formulated the so-called Hays Code in 1934, helped by representatives of the Catholic Church. Hays, a former chairman of the Republican National Committee who had been Postmaster General under President Harding, zealously administered the code until he retired in 1945. During his reign the studios only distributed movies that had the Production Code Administration's Seal of Approval.

The Hays Office regulated "indecent or under exposure," "inference of sexual perversion," "excessive and lustful kissing," "licentious or suggestive nudity," "ridicule of clergy," and "miscegenation." Violence fared better than sex in the code, which decreed that "actual hangings or electrocutions . . . brutality and possibly gruesomeness [may be shown] within the careful limits of good taste."

Since 1968, after the constitutionality of the provisions of the Hays Code was questioned, the precensorship of the code has been replaced by a classification system designed to advise moviegoers of the content of any film. This Motion Picture Association of America self-regulating system rates films ranging from G, "general, all ages permitted," to X, "restricted, no one under 17 admitted." The X rating referred to explicit sex and violence in a movie and became so common that the expression *X-rated* became a term for anything pornographic or sexy, from a film to a book or even a person.

Midnight Cowboy (1969), starring Jon Voight and Dustin Hoffman, is the only X-rated film ever to win an Oscar for best picture. It also won Oscars for best director (John Schlesinger), best screenplay (Waldo Salt), and its stars Voight and Hoffman were nominated for best actor.

Sex Sells

Under the Hays Code movies could not expose the nipple on a woman's breast or show the inside of her thigh. In 1960 cameraman Russ Myer made a low-budget ($25,000) film which exposed the human breast. The film could not be shown in legitimate theaters but it nevertheless grossed more than $1 million.

The Banning of Mickey Mouse

One would think Walt Disney's Mickey Mouse among the most innocuous, least objectionable characters in literature, but in truth Disney's creation was banned over a dozen times. In 1933, for example, Mickey Mouse was banned in Nazi Germany, and three years later he was banned in the Soviet Union. In 1937, Mickey was banned in Yugoslavia because a cartoon he starred in depicted a revolution against a monarchy; in 1938 Fascist Italy banned the mouse; and in 1954 East Germany banned Mickey as an anti-Red rebel. In the United States one Mickey Mouse syndicated comic strip was suppressed in 1932 because it depicted a cow in a pasture reading Elinor Glyn's then controversial *Three Weeks*.

Bugging the Censors

The Welsh poet Dylan Thomas went to great lengths to play practical jokes. When he wrote his radio play *Under Milk Wood*, everyone who read the script assumed that the name of fictional village Llareggub therein was authentically Welsh—until someone spelled it backward, after the play had already aired, and realized the poet's bawdy joke. For *bugger* in British English never means a child, as it does in American expressions like "he's just a little bugger." A bugger in England is a sodomite and *to bugger* is "to sodomize"—in fact, use of the word in print was actionable in England for many years. *Bugger* in this sense, which is American slang as well, derives, down a tortuous path, from the medieval Latin *Bulgarus*, meaning both a Bulgarian and a sodomite. The word first referred to a Bulgarian and then to the Bulgarian Albigenes or Bulgarian Heretics, an eleventh-century religious sect whose monks and nuns were believed, rightly or wrongly, to practice sodomy.

Was Hiawatha a Red?

The cold war Red Scare of the 1950s went to ridiculous extremes that seem almost unbelievable today, as can be seen in the following *New York Times* report from Hollywood in June 1950:

> *Fear that a motion picture dealing with the life and exploits of Hiawatha might be regarded as Communist propaganda has caused Monogram Studio to shelve such a project. It was Hiawatha's efforts as a peacemaker among the warring Indian tribes of his day, which brought about the federation of 5 nations, that gave Monogram particular concern, according to a studio spokesman. These, it was decided, might cause the picture to be regarded as a message for peace and therefore helpful to present Communist designs.*

X

Entertaining Words and Memorable Lines

Memorable Movie Lines

- "Why don't you come up some time and see me?" —Mae West to Cary Grant in *She Done Him Wrong*

- "Well, come see a fat old man sometime!" —John Wayne as parting words in *True Grit*

- "If you need me, just whistle." —Lauren Bacall to Humphrey Bogart in *To Have and Have Not*

- "Catherine had three hundred lovers. I did the best I could in a couple of hours." —Mae West's curtain speech during her run as Russian empress Catherine the Great in *Catherine Was Great*

- "Made it, Ma! Top of the world!" —Jimmy Cagney, as he goes to his death in *White Heat*

- "Physically, I'm in pretty good shape." —Marilyn Monroe in *There's No Business Like Show Business*

- "Beulah, peel me a grape." —Mae West to her maid in *She Done Him Wrong*

- "Frankly, my dear, I don't give a damn." —Clark Gable as Rhett Butler to Scarlett O'Hara in *Gone with the Wind*

- "My mother thanks you. My father thanks you. My sister thanks you. And I thank you." —James Cagney in *Yankee Doodle Dandy*

- "Me Tarzan, you Jane." —Johnny Weissmuller in *Tarzan*

- "We could have made beautiful music together." —Gary Cooper to Madeleine Carroll in *The General Died at Dawn*
- "The natives are restless tonight." —Charles Laughton in *The Island of Lost Souls*
- "Do you mind if I slip into something comfortable?" —Jean Harlow in *Hell's Angels*
- "I'd like to stay longer, but I'm having an old friend for dinner." —Anthony Hopkins as "Hannibal the Cannibal" Lecter in *The Silence of the Lambs*
- "Bond. James Bond." —Sean Connery as words of introduction in the James Bond films series
- "The problems of the world are not my department. I'm a saloon keeper." —Humphrey Bogart in *Casablanca*
- "Here's lookin' at you, kid." —Humphrey Bogart in *Casablanca*
- "The Germans have outlawed miracles." —Sydney Greenstreet in *Casablanca*
- "Louis, I think this is the beginning of a beautiful friendship." —Humphrey Bogart in *Casablanca*
- "The problems of three little people don't amount to a hill of beans in this crazy world." —Humphrey Bogart in *Casablanca*
- "Round up the usual suspects." —Claude Rains in *Casablanca*
- "I'm only a poor corrupt official." —Claude Rains in *Casablanca*
- "Of all the gin joints in all the towns in all the world, she walks into mine." —Humphrey Bogart in *Casablanca*
- "Play it again, Sam, play 'As Time Goes By.'" —Ingrid Bergman in *Casablanca* to the piano player, played by Dooley Wilson
- "I always say a kiss on the hand might feel good, but a diamond tiara lasts forever." —Marilyn Monroe in *Gentlemen Prefer Blondes*
- "Real diamonds! They must be worth their weight in gold." —Marilyn Monroe in *Gentlemen Prefer Blondes*
- "She really needs someone like I to educate her." —Marilyn Monroe in *Gentlemen Prefer Blondes*
- "With all the unrest in the world, I don't think anybody should have a yacht that sleeps more than twelve." —Tony Curtis in *Some Like It Hot*
- "If I'd been a ranch, they would have named me the Bar Nothing." —Rita Hayworth in *Gilda*

- "I *am* big. It's the pictures that got small." —Gloria Swanson in *Sunset Boulevard*
- "If you know what's good for you, you won't be messing around with Fred C. Dobbs." —Humphrey Bogart in *The Treasure of the Sierra Madre*
- "Gimme a whiskey, ginger ale on the side. And don't be stingy, baby." —Greta Garbo in *Anna Christie*, the first words of her first talking film (for "I vant to be alone" *see* Chapter 1)
- "I'd love to kiss you, but I just washed my hair." —Bette Davis in *Cabin in the Cotton*
- "I was an orphan until I was twenty, and then a rich and beautiful woman adopted me." —Humphrey Bogart in *Beat the Devil*
- "The limb is mightier than the thumb." —Claudette Colbert, while extending her leg to hitch a ride in *It Happened One Night*
- "There comes a time in every woman's life when the only thing that helps is a glass of champagne." —Ethel Merman in *Call Me Madam*
- "I'm gonna make him an offer he can't refuse." —Marlon Brando as the Godfather in *The Godfather* (variations on the line were used twice more in the film and once more in *The Godfather: Part II*)
- "I'm a businessman. Blood is a big expense." —Al Lettieri as the character Sollozzo in *The Godfather*
- "The higher I go, the crookeder it becomes." —Al Pacino as the Godfather in *The Godfather: Part III*
- "You're right, Rico. You shouldn't have been deported; you should have been exterminated." —Lionel Barrymore to Edward G. Robinson in *Key Largo*
- "Go ahead. Make my day." —Clint Eastwood as Dirty Harry in *Sudden Impact*
- "If you want to call me that, smile." —Gary Cooper in *The Virginian* (this was a variation on novelist Owen Wister's "When you call me that, smile!")
- "She wore diamonds and honeysuckle perfume. I was drunk with it. I never knew murder could smell like honeysuckle." —Fred MacMurray in *Double Indemnity*
- "Mother of Mercy!—is this the end of Rico?" —Edward G. Robinson, as the last line of *Little Caesar*
- "Don't apologize. It's a sign of weakness." —John Wayne in *She Wore a Yellow Ribbon*

- "Consider that a divorce." —Arnold Schwarzenegger to his wife, Sharon Stone, in *Total Recall* as he kills her
- "Ah!" —Jack Nicholson, the last word in *As Good as It Gets*, as he looks at some warm bakery rolls
- "We rob banks." —Warren Beatty in *Bonnie and Clyde*
- "Is that a pistol in your pocket, big boy, or have I inspired you?" —Mae West in *She Done Him Wrong*
- "He was some kind of man. What does it matter what you say about someone?" —Marlene Dietrich about the Orson Welles character in *Touch of Evil*
- "What a dump!" —Bette Davis in *Beyond the Forest*
- "Was you ever bit by a dead bee?" —Walter Brennan; a nonsensical joke repeated several times in *To Have and Have Not*
- "Ah, yes, of course I've heard of her husband. I saw him do *Hamlet*. And let me say, what he did to Shakespeare, we are now doing to Poland." —A German officer about Carole Lombard, playing the wife of the world's biggest ham, played by Jack Benny, in *To Be or Not to Be*
- "I'm mad as hell and I'm not gonna take this anymore." —Peter Finch in *Network*
- "My mama always said life was like a box of chocolates; never know what you're gonna get." —Tom Hanks in *Forrest Gump*
- "Stupid is as stupid does." —Tom Hanks in *Forrest Gump*
- "That's all I have to say about that." —Tom Hanks in *Forrest Gump*
- "You blasted idiot! You stupid fathead!" —Peter Lorre to Sydney Greenstreet in *The Maltese Falcon*
- "The only causes worth fighting for are lost causes." —Claude Rains, as Senator Paine, in *Mr. Smith Goes to Washington*
- "Goodnight, Gracie." —George Burns to his wife and costar Gracie Allen at the end of each of their radio programs
- "Can't nobody wipe us out. Can't nobody lick us. We'll go on forever, Pa. We're the people." —Jane Darwell as Ma Joad in *The Grapes of Wrath*
- "Tara. I'll go home to Tara. And I'll think of some way to get him back. After all, tomorrow is another day." —Vivien Leigh, in *Gone with the Wind*

Some words that don't qualify have often been cited as memorable movie lines. The famous "Come with me to the Casbah," for example, was never said by Charles Boyer in *Algiers* (1938) or any other film, and Jimmy Cagney never exclaimed "You dirty rat!" in any film. Neither did Humphrey Bogart ever say "Tennis, anyone?" on the screen or stage (no one else did, either, as far as can be ascertained). Some of these lines may have been invented by press agents. Mae West's "I do most of my best work in bed" was uttered not in a film but to a newspaper reporter interviewing the Screen's Bad Girl. Finally, "There but for the grace of God goes God," wasn't said of Orson Welles on or off the screen. It was a description of Winston Churchill by a fellow Briton. Other famous lines are discussed elsewhere in these pages.

What a Line!

English playwright Richard Sheridan once asked a beautiful young actress: "Won't you come into my garden? I would like my roses to see you."

Don Juans on the Stage

Of the names most frequently applied to great lovers—Don Juan, Casanova, Cyrano, Valentino, Romeo, and Lothario—all are connected with the theater and only the last is completely fictional. Don Juan, the most famous of them, is immortalized in *El Burlador de Sevilla* (1630) by Gabriel Téllez, Molière's *Le Desrin de Pierre*, and Mozart's *Don Giovanni*. He is based on the fourteenth-century Spanish nobleman Don Juan Tenorio. That this original Don Juan had 2,594 mistresses, according to the valet's figures in Mozart's opera, is doubtful if not impossible, but the aristocratic lover's conquests were legion. His last was the daughter of Seville's commandant. While attempting to ravish young Donna Anna, the legendary lover was surprised by her father, whom he dispatched in a duel. But local Franciscan monks decided that this was one debauchery too many and lured Don Juan to their monastery, where he was killed with his boots on. The monks, to conceal their crime, claimed that he had been carried off to hell by a statue of the commandant on the grounds, and thus the legend of Don Juan had its basis in fact.

Not to leave out "Donna Juanitas," it should be noted that the Russian empress Catherine the Great, an accomplished playwright, surely topped Don Juan's total conquests, and that actress Sarah Bernhardt claimed she had one thousand lovers. Another French actress, a certain Mademoiselle Dubois, put Don Juan and all others to shame with her 16,527 "affairs" over a twenty-year period—the lady's own figures, although unconfirmed.

Hamlet, U.S.A.

Someone who can't make up his mind is often called *Hamletlike*, after Shakespeare's tragic character. This certainly didn't apply to comedian Jimmy Durante, who got his start, along with Eddie Cantor, as a singing waiter in Coney Island. "You should play Hamlet," John Barrymore once said jokingly to the great comic.

"To hell with them small towns," said the Schnozzola confidently. "I'll take Broadway anytime."

Theatrical "Act of God" Clause

Producer Jed Harris (1900–79), for a time called the "Wonder Boy" of Broadway, was noted for his eccentricities. One time Harris sued actress Helen Hayes when she left his production of *Coquette* because she was pregnant. An actress should not become pregnant while playing a part, he contended, but Hayes successfully countered that having a baby was an "act of God." As a result of this lawsuit all actresses have "act of God" clauses in their contracts today.

On another occasion playwright George S. Kaufman met with Harris at the producer's Waldorf Astoria suite, and for some reason known only to himself Harris squatted naked on the floor for the whole meeting. If he meant to shock Kaufman it didn't work, for the great wit didn't say a word about Harris's nakedness until he was leaving. Then, with hand on the doorknob, Kaufman stared at Harris and advised, "Jed, your fly is open."

The Thespian Dictionary: Show Biz Words and Phrases

All of these more than one hundred words, phrases, technical terms, and superstitions—which include expressions deriving from the names of famous actors or characters in plays and movies—have some connection with the world of show business. Other interesting word and phrase stories are treated in preceding chapters.

Acrobat

Acrobat comes from the Greek *akros*, "aloft," plus *batos*, "climbing or walking," referring of course to the stunts early acrobats performed in the air, which included ropewalking. The greatest of the ancient Greek acrobats were called *neurobats*, from the Greek *neuron*, "sinew." These men performed on sinewy rope that was only as thick as the catgut or plastic used for fishing line today, appearing from the ground as if they were walking on air.

Ameche

Don Ameche's performance in *The Story of Alexander Graham Bell* was ignored by the critics, as was the film itself in 1939, that golden year that brought us such film classics as *Gone with the Wind*, *Wuthering Heights*, *The Wizard of Oz*, and many others. Ameche may not have been worthy of a best actor Oscar like Robert Donat, the winner, or nominees Laurence Olivier and Clark Gable, but he did achieve an immortality none of them ever matched. Though hardly used anymore, *Ameche* has been American slang for "telephone" ever since he played the lead role portraying the inventor of the telephone. Ameche did win an Oscar for his supporting role in *Cocoon* (1985).

Anchor

The strongest member of a track team, the runner who runs the last leg in a relay race, has been called the *anchorman* since the late nineteenth century. Possibly the term has its roots in the anchor man at the end of a tug of war, but there is no proof that this usage came first. In any case, anchorman came to be applied to the last swimmer in a relay race, too, and by the 1930s was being used for the strongest member of a radio broadcasting team. With the rise of women in sports and television news broadcasting, the term is increasingly heard as *anchor*, not *anchorman*.

Annie Oakley

Annie Oakley was the stage name of Ohio-born Phoebe Oakley Mozee (1860–1926), star rifle shot with Buffalo Bill's Wild West Show. Annie joined Buffalo Bill at age twenty-five and amazed audiences for more than forty years with her expert marksmanship and trick shooting. Annie once broke 942 glass balls thrown into the air with only 1,000 shots. Her most famous trick was to toss a playing card, usually a five of hearts, into the air and shoot holes through all its pips. The riddled card reminded circus performers of their punched meal tickets, which they began to call Annie Oakleys, and the name was soon transferred to free railroad and press passes, both of which were customarily punched with a hole in the center. Today *Annie Oakley* refers to all complimentary passes, punched or not.

Anvil Chorus

When the opposition, especially in politics, joins collectively in condemning an action or proposal, the criticism is called an *anvil chorus.* The reference is to the famous "Anvil Chorus" based on the "Gypsy Song" in Giuseppe Verdi's opera *Il Trovatore*, complete with the sound of many loud anvils and cymbals.

Auteur

A movie director who displays a strong unique personal style in his films is often called an auteur, from the French for "originator" or "author," though the word has something of an affected air. (*See* CINEAST.)

"Beam Me Up, Scotty"

This has become a very popular humorous expression, often used on bumper stickers as well as in conversation, for "get me out of here, free me from this mess," etc. It originally requested transportation back to the ship, a frequent order Captain Kirk gave to chief engineer Montgomery "Scotty" Scott on the immensely popular television series "Star Trek," which premiered in 1966. It meant that Scotty should transform Kirk's body into energy. Trekkies and interplanetary polyglots will be interested to know that a 1996 video game, Star Trek Klingon, teaches players the Klingon language. "Beam me up!" in Klingon is *Hljol! Klingon* itself has become a synonym for any brutal, barbaric, warlike person, the Klingons in the series being debased warlike beings from the planet Klingon.

Bel Canto

Bel canto is virtuoso singing, a vocal technique emphasizing the quality of sound rather than emotion, a style found in some Italian operas. The words are Italian for "beautiful singing." Bel canto writing might be writing with more style than substance, though some would say the only substance is style.

Best Boy

This term, often puzzling to moviegoers when seen in film credits, simply means the main gaffer, the electrician's chief assistant, on a movie set.

Big Daddy

An affectionate term for one's grandfather or the paternalistic head of a family, made famous by Tennessee Williams as the nickname of the wealthy cotton planter in his play *Cat on a Hot Tin Roof* (1955).

Blackout

A *blackout* is the extinguishing of all stage lights to show the end of a scene in a play, to indicate the passing of time, or to mark the end of a vaudeville skit.

Blue Movies

A series of off-color nineteenth-century French books called La Bibliotheque Bleu contributed to the coining of the word *blue* for "obscene," as in pornographic blue movies. The term *blue laws*, which might repress *blue movies*, has an entirely different derivation. It usually refers to Never-on-Sunday morals laws and may take its name from a nonexistent Connecticut "blue book" rumored to contain fanatical laws. The vengeful rumor was spread by the Reverend Samuel Peters, an American Tory who returned to England after the Revolution. Peters claimed that the fictitious blue-bound book contained laws prohibiting such activities as kissing one's wife on Sunday.

Boards

Refers to the stage of a theater; frequently used in the expression *on the boards* in the theatrical profession, as in, "The Booths were on the boards for three generations."

Break a Leg!

Break a leg! means "good luck" in theatrical circles, probably *not* because the great Sarah Bernhardt "had but one leg and it would be good luck to be like her." No one is sure, but one theory has the expression meaning "may you get a big break," that is, good luck leading to success. Or actors simply may wish someone bad luck, like breaking a leg, because they are a superstitious lot and have long believed that wishing good luck guarantees something terrible will happen.

Buying Back the Nut

Troupes of actors often traveled by wagon to theaters where they performed. Innkeepers would rent them rooms on credit if they would leave or deposit the nut holding one of the wheels to the wagons. When the troupe was paid for its performance, they would pay the bill and receive the essential wheel nut in return. This came to be called *buying back the nut*, a term purely of historical interest today.

Cancan

University scholars in Paris often prefaced their erudite arguments about anything and everything with the Latin word *quamquam*, "although." This ridiculous habit grew so common that the word soon meant "a piece of nonsense," with *quamquam* coming to be pronounced *concon*. Carousing French students of the 1830s, punning bawdily on the sound of *concon*, then made it the name of the high-kicking, skirt-lifting dance of Parisian cafes.

Caviar to the General

"I heard thee speak me a speech once," Hamlet says to the players at Elsinore, "but it was never acted . . . ; for the play, I remember, pleased not the million, 'twas caviar to the general." When Shakespeare says "general" here, he means the general public, the generality, the masses as they were later called, not the general of an army. The play he refers to (which was actually pretty bad, judging by the fragments presented) is, like caviar, for the tastes of only the most discriminating people; others would find it repugnant because they haven't acquired fine taste. The rather snobbish remark is still commonplace in describing something for which one has to acquire a taste.

Chairman of the Board

(*See* RAT PACK.)

Chew Up the Scenery

A term meaning "to overact or ham it up." Originally only a theatrical expression, these words can be traced to their inventor, Dorothy Parker, who used them first in a 1930 theater review: "More glutton than artist . . . he commences to chew up the scenery."

Chic Sale

Among the most ignominious fates suffered by an American actor befell vaudeville comedian Chic Sale, an early-twentieth-century performer whose act was very popular throughout the country. Sale was noted for his comedy routine about building an outhouse, and he even wrote a book about his "specialty." He is rarely even mentioned in theater histories today, but since the 1920s his name has lived on as a synonym for an outhouse.

Cineast

A French word for a devoted movie fan. (*See* AUTEUR).

Cinema Verité

Documentary filmmaking in which the camera records events without directional control. The technique was introduced in France from one developed by Russian filmmaker Dziga Vertov (1896–1954). It can also mean any film using this technique or a simulation of it.

Cowabunga!

Cowabunga! has recently come to be used as a general cry of delight, due to its popularization by the cartoon character Bart Simpson of television fame. Originating in Australian surfing sometime in the 1930s, *cowabunga!* is still shouted by surfers at the beginning of a good wave.

Critic

Critic, referring to someone who passes judgment on something, was first recorded by Shakespeare in *Love's Labour's Lost* (1588), but we don't know if the Bard coined the word, which is based ultimately on a Greek term meaning the same. Shakespeare is said to have been the first to record more than seventeen hundred words.

Cry All the Way to the Bank

An expression usually said by or of someone who may not be a critical success but nevertheless makes lots of money. The origin of the saying is unknown, but it is often attributed to the popular American pianist Liberace, who frequently used it.

Curtain Call

The appearance of the performers or a single performer at the close of a play in response to the applause of the audience, as in, "She took three curtain calls."

Curtain Speech

The final speech of an act or scene in a play, or in the play itself. Also a brief speech by an actor, author, or producer, etc., after the end of a play in front of the closed curtain.

Cut

A film director's instruction to stop camera action; also the process of shortening a scene or scenes in a movie. Often used in expressions like *cut to the chase*.

Cutaway

A camera shot that switches from one scene to another in order to show simultaneous or related action or to create suspense. Also called a *cutaway shot*.

Cyrano

Bearer of the most famous proboscis in history. Anyone with a prodigious nose is likely to be called a *Cyrano* after the eponymous hero of Edmond Rostand's play of the same name (1897). Rostand's hero was based on the very real Savinien de Cyrano de Bergerac (1619–55), who had a nose as long as his fictional counterpart's and whose exploits were even more remarkable. This historical Cyrano was a brave soldier, great lover, and eloquent, influential writer of comedies and tragedies. This swaggering swordsman fought countless duels with those foolish enough to insult or even mention his nose, and his duel singlehandedly against one hundred enemies while serving as an officer in the Guards is a well-documented fact. Cyrano's exploits became legend long before Rostand fictionalized him. Surprisingly, he did not perish on the wrong end of a sword. Cyrano died as a result of a wound caused by a falling beam or stone while staying at the home of a friend.

Dark

Said of a theater that is closed, or in which no performances are given, as in, "The theaters in the city are dark on Sunday."

Diddle

In its sense of "to cheat or deceive" *diddle* derives from the name of the main character in James Kenny's farce *Raising the Wind* (1803). In the play Jeremy Diddler continually borrows small sums from other people and fails to pay them back. Since the late nineteenth century *diddle* has been slang for "to fornicate," making Mr. Diddler perhaps the only theatrical character so honored.

Dissolve

To fade out one camera shot or scene while simultaneously fading in the next, overlapping the two during the process. Used in films to effect a transition.

"Don't Bogart That Joint"

In his films Humphrey Bogart often left cigarettes dangling from his mouth without smoking them. This led to the counterculture expression *Don't bogart that joint*; that is, "don't take so long with, don't hog that stick of marijuana; smoke and pass it on to the next person." The term became widely used after appearing in a song in the film *Easy Rider*. Among those who practice the long-standing, widespread habit of communally smoking marijuana cigarettes, bogarting is considered both selfish and a waste of the expensive weed. Bogart's name, in the form of *Bogard*, also became innercity slang for "to act tough or in a forceful manner" in the 1950s, deriving from the tough-guy heroes Bogart portrayed.

"Don't Fence Me In"

An expression meaning "give me freedom, elbow room"—from a song often associated with the American West. Originally *don't fence me in* was a line in a poem written by Bob Fletcher, a Westerner. Cole Porter bought the rights to the poem, revised the lyrics, and wrote the music for the song, which wasn't used until a decade later, in the film *Hollywood Canteen* (1944). The next year it was featured in Roy Rogers's movie *Don't Fence Me In*. "Meanwhile, in a sad irony," Frank Richard Prassel notes in *The Great American Outlaw* (1993), "Porter had been left crippled by a riding accident."

Downstage

Used by theater folk to describe the part of the stage nearest the audience.

Dr. Pangloss

Any incurable optimist is called a *Dr. Pangloss* after the pedantic old tutor of the same name in Voltaire's *Candide, or The Optimist* (1759), which was an attack against Rousseau's philosophy and later became a popular stage play. Dr. Pangloss remained optimistic to the end, despite all his numerous misfortunes, believing "all is for the best in this best of all possible worlds."

Drop

A painted piece of large fabric that is used as scenery in a play.

Entr'acte

The interval between two acts of a theatrical performance; or any performance given between two acts.

E.T.

H. G. Wells first recorded and perhaps invented *extraterrestrial* as an adjective at the turn of the century. Meaning "outside the limits of the earth," the word was first used as a noun by American author L. Sprague de Camp in the May 1939 issue of *Astounding Science Fiction*; the author invented the abbreviation e.t. in the same article. E.T. has since become the name of the extraterrestrial being in the popular film *E.T. the Extra-Terrestrial*. Wells, or someone before him, may have patterned *extraterrestrial* on the word *extraterritorial*, which dates back to at least 1665.

Fade-Out

A gradual decrease in the visibility of a scene from full exposure to black. A *fade-in* is a gradual increase in the visibility of a scene from black to full exposure.

Fairbanks

Movie actor Douglas Fairbanks Jr. was said to take great pleasure in the company of royalty. Picking up on this, contract bridge players dubbed a hand chock full of kings and queens a *fairbanks*.

Family Hour

The television time slot between six P.M. and eight P.M. during which programs are supposed to be free of violence and sex, though this seems at best improbable considering that most news programs are aired at this time.

Fly

The space above a theater's stage used mainly for storing scenery and equipment.

Frame

One of the successive images on a strip of film, the standard American film speed being twenty-four frames a second.

Friday the Thirteenth

In the theater the widespread Friday the thirteenth bad luck tradition applies only to opening nights. According to theatrical tradition, a show should never open on Friday the thirteenth. The reasons behind the tradition, if there are any, are unknown to history.

The Ghost Walks

An expression meaning, "It's payday and all the salaries will be paid." It is said to have originally been a nineteenth-century British theatrical expression. As the story goes, a British company doing *Hamlet* hadn't been paid for a month or so. When during a performance Hamlet exclaimed, "Perchance 'twill walk again," the actor playing the ghost answered from the wings, "No, I'll be damned if the ghost walks anymore until our salaries are paid." That night the salaries were finally paid.

Grable-Bodied Seamen

Movie actress Betty Grable, her "million-dollar legs" insured by Lloyd's of London, was the pinup girl par excellence during World War II. British sailors used the term *Grable-bodied seamen* to describe long-stemmed lovelies in the Wrens (Women's Royal Naval Service) who fit the description.

Grip

A general movie crewman who helps shift scenery, operates cranes and dollies, etc., or a stagehand in the theater who works on the stage floor. The head grip is called the *key grip*. Grips are probably so named for their strong grips (that is, their strength) in handling the heavy equipment on movie sets. (*See* BEST BOY.)

Improvisator

An *improvisator* is someone who composes, acts, sings, etc., on the spur of the moment, without preparation. The word derives from the Italian *improvvisatore*, which originally referred only to a person who extemporized verse. Petrarch is supposed to have introduced the game of inventing poems on the spot for a particular occasion and to have received a laurel crown for extemporizing in verse. Among many others famous for this talent were Italian poet Angelo Mazza (1741–1817), whom Napoléon made imperial poet to celebrate his victories in verse; English poet Thomas Hood, author of "The Bridge of Sighs"; William Cowper; and Alexandre Dumas *père*.

Jim Crow

Blackface minstrel Thomas D. Rice, the Father of American Minstrelsy, introduced the song "Jim Crow" in 1828, claiming to have patterned it on the song and dance of an old field hand named Jim Crow he had observed in Kentucky. Rice's routine, part of a skit called "The Rifle," became so familiar here and on tour in England that a few years later a British antislavery book was titled *The History of Jim Crow*. It is from this book and similar uses of *Jim Crow* to signify a black person that the discriminatory laws and practices take their name, though the first Jim Crow laws weren't enacted until 1875 in Tennessee.

Kinescope

The filmed record of a television program. The kinescope device was invented in the 1930s, and the word once enjoyed trademark status.

Langtry Fever

America was seized by what was called *Langtry Fever* in 1882 when the violet-eyed English actress Lillie Langtry first appeared on the American stage. Huge crowds turned out everywhere to see the beautiful Jersey Lily, who was better known for her liaison with the Prince of Wales than for her acting ability. The daughter of a clergyman, she married a wealthy aristocrat and became one of the first English society women to act on the stage.

Lavaliere

Louis XIV, the Sun King, had a voracious appetite for women as well as food. Louise-Françoise de La Baume le Blanc, whom he later made Madame la Duchesse de La Vallière, was only his first *maitresse en titre*, or official mistress to the king. Louise, an innocent girl, never asked for anything, and it was only toward the end of their affair in 1667 that Louis made her a duchess, granting her the estate of Vaujours. Long before that she had become famous throughout Europe for her great beauty and the glamorous fashions she introduced. One of these, called the *lavallière* in her honor, was the ornamental jeweled pendant, usually worn on a chain around the neck, that we know as the *lavaliere*. Today the small TV microphone that hangs on a cord from the neck is also called a lavaliere, taking its name from the pendant necklace that honors the famous beauty.

"Lili Marleen"

One of the few songs or poems whose real-life origins are known. The lyrics for this song, called "the most beautiful love song of all time" by John Steinbeck, were written in the early years of World War I by German officer cadet and poet Hans Leip. He took the woman's name in the title from a girl he loved back home named Lili, a grocer's daughter, and a green-eyed beauty named Marleen whom he'd met in a Berlin art gallery. The poem was not published for another twenty years and only became popular in 1939 when Berlin composer Norbert Schultze set it to music and singer Lale Anderson recorded it. The whole story of the song, which became popular the world over, is told in Carlton Jackson's book *The Great Lili* (1995).

Lone Ranger

This fictional masked rider of the plains, with his "faithful Indian companion, Tonto" and his "great horse, Silver," was a champion of justice to a generation of devoted followers on radio, in the movies, and on TV. The enduring symbol of the imaginary West was born in 1933 on Detroit radio station WXYZ. He shot pure silver bullets, never shot to kill, and at the end of each program always shouted a hearty "Hi-ho, Silver!"

MC; Emcee

In this case the initials became the word. MC, an abbreviation of master of ceremonies, came first. This began to be used as a verb in the early 1940s and was spelled *emcee*. The term *femcee* for a female emcee never caught on.

Meanwhile Back at the Ranch

An expression that originated as a movie caption in the silent-film era at the beginning of the century, these words are used humorously today when someone wants to get back to a story after going off on a tangent.

Momus

Momus, the Greek god of ridicule, was banished from heaven for his censures upon the gods—he once blamed Zeus for not having put a window in the breast of a man that Zeus had made. His name has been used in English for a faultfinder or captious critic at least since the sixteenth century.

"The Most Unkindest Cut of All"

"This was the most unkindest cut of all," Shakespeare had Antony say in *Julius Caesar*. This most famous of literary double superlatives wasn't the only such "grammatical crudity" he used. The double superlative and double comparative ("more larger") were considered excellent devices for emphasis by Elizabethan dramatists. So were multiple negatives like the Bard's "Thou hast spoken no word all this while—nor understood none either."

Munchkin

Munchkins were once only the little people who lived in Oz, a land invented by L. Frank Baum in *The Wizard of Oz* (1900). But with the great popularity of the book and the motion picture that starred Judy Garland made from it, the word became a synonym for any little person, especially a small, adorable child.

Never-Never Land

Today *never-never land* usually signifies an unreal, imaginary, or ideal condition or place, as in "the never-never land of the movies." Originally however, it was Australian slang for an isolated, sparsely settled region and was first applied to all of Australia and then to the remote Australian outback of Western Queensland and central Australia. This region was probably called *never-never land*, or *country*, because those who visited there vowed "never, never" to return. Sir James Barrie first gave the meaning of an imaginary place to *Never-Never Land* in his play *Peter Pan*, having Peter teach the Darling children to fly away to the wonderful realm of a child's imagination. Today the British sometimes call installment plans *never-never plans*, because one's ownership of the goods bought on such plans lies far in the distance in never-never land. (See PETER PAN.)

Not a Dry Seat in the House

The drama critic's cliché *there wasn't a dry eye in the house*, to describe a moving play, suggested this humorous expression, which has been fairly common in England since about 1930 for a play or movie so funny that the audience was helpless with laughter—in fact, wet their pants laughing.

Old Chestnut

English playwright William Diamond's melodrama *The Broken Sword* (1816) is all but forgotten, along with its characters, plot, and dialogue, and the author himself isn't remembered in most theater guides. Yet Diamond has found immortality of sorts in the expression *an old chestnut*, "a stale joke or story," which probably derives from an incident in his play. *The Broken Sword*'s principal character is crusty old Captain Xavier, who is forever spinning the same yarns about his highly unlikely experiences. He begins to tell the following one to Pablo, another comic character:

> *Captain Xavier:* I entered the woods of Golloway, when suddenly from the boughs of a cork tree—
> *Pablo:* A chestnut, Captain, a chestnut!
> *Captain Xavier:* Bah, I tell you it was a cork tree.
> *Pablo:* A chestnut; I guess I ought to know, for haven't I heard you tell this story twenty-seven times?

Fame didn't come immediately. The lines lay at rest in Diamond's play for almost seventy years before American actor William Warren Jr. repeated them at a stage testimonial dinner in Boston, after hearing another speaker tell a stale joke. Other actors present adopted Warren's *chestnut*, elaborated on it, and it became the timeworn *old chestnut*.

One-Man Tango

A name for someone supremely self-confident, who looks like he could dance the grand tango all alone. In his autobiography *One Man Tango* (1955), actor Anthony Quinn claims Orson Welles gave him this nickname. Whether Welles invented the words or not isn't established, but the expression does deserve to be recorded.

Oprah

Oprah has become synonymous for a television talk show host, honoring Emmy Award–winning Oprah Winfrey (b. 1954), American talk show host, actress, and producer, whose "Oprah" has the highest viewer ratings in history, making her one of the world's highest paid, most influential entertainers. The actress also received a best supporting actress nomination for her performance in the film *The Color Purple* (1985).

Oscar

The real-life person for whom the Academy Award Oscar is named is covered in Chapter 8, along with several real-life Oscars who were nominated for Oscars (like Oscar Hammerstein). Another famous Oscar is Australian Oscar Asche (1872–1936), a musical-comedy star who made a tidy fortune on the stage and whose full name therefore became Australian rhyming slang for cash. Oscar Asche for cash was eventually shortened to *Oscar*, making Oscar Asche the only man whose first name means money in a generic sense.

Outtake

A segment of film edited out of the final version of a film or videotape, often because of a technical error.

Pan

To photograph part of a film while rotating the camera on its horizontal or vertical axis. Used to keep a moving person or object in view or to record a panorama, as when a football field is panned from one end of the field to the other at the beginning of the game.

Peter Pan

Peter Pan, the boy who refused to grow up, has been familiar to readers and theatergoers for several generations. We now use his name to describe a person who retains in mature years the naturalness of spirit and charm associated with childhood, or one who absolutely refuses to escape from the comfortable irresponsibility of childhood. British dramatist and novelist Sir James M. Barrie introduced his immortal character on the stage in the play *Peter Pan* (1904), although the fantastic world of Peter Pan had previously been presented in his *Little White Bird* (1902). *Peter Pan*, a poetical pantomime, as it has been called, charmed audiences from the night it first appeared. Peter has since been played by many great stars, ranging from Maude Adams to Mary Martin, and a statue of him stands in Kensington Gardens, London. Barrie, who described his business as "playing hide and seek with angels," named Peter for one of his nephews, for whom he wrote the story, giving the character his last name from the name of Pan, god of forests, meadows, flocks, and shepherds. Wendy, Peter's girlfriend, also borrowed her name from a real person. This was Barrie's own nickname, bestowed upon him by the daughter of his friend, poet W. E. Henley. Little Margaret Henley called him Friendly, then Friendly-Wendy, and this ultimately became Wendy, the name he dubbed his character. (*See* NEVER-NEVER LAND.)

Pit

In England this is the main floor of a theater beyond the stalls. In America it is the section below the stage where the musicians sit and is also called the orchestra pit.

Playing to the Haircuts

An expression used by performers for the closing act of a vaudeville bill. Such an act would still be playing as the audience was leaving—with the backs of their heads facing the performers.

Poo-Bah

A politician who holds several offices or a pompous, self-important person is sometimes called a poo-bah. In Gilbert and Sullivan's operetta *The Mikado* (1885) Poo-Bah is the personal name of the arrogant Lord High Everything Else, this being the source of the word.

Pratfall

Pratfall is old show business slang for a fall on the buttocks taken by a comedian to obtain laughs. *Pratts*, or *prats*, is simply rogues' cant for "the buttocks." No one knows the origin of the term, which dates back to the sixteenth century, and there seems to be no connection between it and the older *prat*, for "a trick or prank."

Proscenium

The arch that separates a stage from the auditorium; also called the *proscenium arch*. It was once a term for the stage itself.

Protean

Protean, for "something that is constantly changing, or an actor who assumes many roles," derives from the name of Proteus, herdsman of Neptune, Greek god of the sea. Wise old Proteus lived in a huge cave tending his herd of sea calves, and no one was able to catch the great prophet because he could rapidly change himself into different shapes.

Proud as Punch

The Punch-and-Judy show originated in early seventeenth-century Italy, where the main character's name was Pulcinello, a vain, pompous character with a shrewish wife, Judy. When the shows became popular in England Pulcinello's name was corrupted to Punchinello and then shortened to Punch, but his personality remained the same, as is reflected in the old saying *proud as Punch*, "being proud over a victory," as Punch was when he bested Judy.

Pull a Boner

"Mistah Bones" in American minstrel shows was the end man in the line who rhythmically played a pair of bones, originally polished rib bones from an animal. It is said that "Mistah Interlocutor," the middle man in the line, fired questions at him designed to evoke ridiculous or stupid answers, which became known as *pulling boners.*

Pull Strings

This expression was inspired by puppet masters of days past, who manipulated strings or wires on their marionettes from behind a curtain. Unseen, they completely controlled the actions of their puppets, so in the mid-nineteenth century *pulling the strings* or *wires* came to mean controlling the affairs of humans invisibly or from a distance as if they were puppets.

Pumping Iron

Lifting weights. The expression, dating back only to the 1970s, became a household term mainly due to the efforts and example of weight lifter and movie star Arnold Schwarzenegger.

Put a Sock in It

Seldom heard anymore, this phrase goes back to the days of early phonographs, invented by Thomas Edison in 1877. The first phonographs had no form of volume control and in order to hold the volume down, people were told to put a sock in the horn to mute the sound. To *put a sock in it* came generally to mean "to stop anyone from talking too much or too loudly."

QT

A British broadside ballad (1870) contained the line "Whatever I tell you is on the QT." This is the first record of QT for "on the quiet, in confidence" recorded in English, but no one has established whether the broadside's anonymous author was the first person to use the initials QT to stand for quiet. *On the* QT gained more popularity when it appeared in an 1891 minstrel show number called "Ta-ra-ra-boom-de-ay." London "went stark mad over the refrain," which was written by Henry J. Sayers and sung by Lottie Collins. The first stanza follows:

> *A sweet Tuxedo girl you see,*
> *Queen of swell society,*
> *Fond of fun as fun can be*

When it's on the strict QT
I'm not too young, I'm not too old,
Not too timid, not too bold,
Just the kind of spirit I'm told—
Ta-ra-ra-boom-de-ay . . .

If your or your children grew up with TV's "Howdy Doody Show," you'll notice the similarity between "Ta-ra-ra-boom-de-ay" and Howdy's theme song.

A Quiz on Quiz

Who invented the word *quiz*? Though the tale may be apocryphal, it's said that toward the end of the eighteenth century, Dublin theater manager and playwright James Daly bet that he could introduce a new meaningless word into the language almost overnight. He proceeded to pay Dublin urchins to chalk the word *quiz* on every wall in town. By morning almost all Dubliners had seen the word and because no one knew what it meant, the meaningless *quiz* came to mean "a test of knowledge." Others say the word is a play on *inquisition*.

Rat Pack

The term *rat pack* was first applied to singer Frank Sinatra (1915–98) and his close friends (Dean Martin, Peter Lawford, Sammy Davis Jr., etc.) by Republicans angry at Sinatra for the help he gave John F. Kennedy in the 1960 presidential campaign. Later, angry at Kennedy, Sinatra supported Nixon, Reagan, and the Republicans. Sinatra ("Chairman of the Board," "The Voice," "Frankie Boy," "Old Blue Eyes") was of course a legend in his own time. The singer won an Oscar for his portayal of Maggio in *From Here to Eternity*. Sinatra himself called the rat pack his "pallies."

Rhubarb

Speculation has been rife for years about how the slang term *rhubarb*, "a heated argument," arose from the name of a popular vegetable. Since the word is often associated with baseball, many writers say it has its origins there. But probably the best explanation, advanced about fifty years ago by a veteran actor familiar with theatrical traditions, is that actors simulating angry talk in crowd scenes for "the noise without" gathered backstage and "intoned the sonorous word 'rhubarb.'" The actor-etymologist Alexander McQueen advised that the word produces such an effect "only if two or three work at it," and claimed that this theatrical tradition went back to Shakespearean times, though the slang *rhubarb* for an argument arose only in the late nineteenth century.

Rock 'n' Roll

The best guess is that *rock 'n' roll* "reflects a sexual metaphor," as one writer puts it, quoting the lyrics "My baby rocks me with one steady roll." Rock and roll music, an outgrowth of African American culture in America, of course dates back much earlier than the first recorded use of the term in the early 1950s, deriving from black rhythm and blues. The first major film to use rock and roll music was *Blackboard Jungle* (1955). Director Richard Brooks bought the rights to use the song "Rock Around the Clock" in the film for $4,000. He could have bought the song outright for another $1,000, but the studio refused to pay. "Rock Around the Clock" went on to sell 1.5 million records that year, becoming one of the biggest hits of all time.

Romeo and Juliet

Not much is known about Romeo and Juliet, but they were real lovers who lived in Verona, Italy, and died for each other in about the year 1303. The Capulets and Montagues were among the inhabitants of the town at that time, and as in Shakespeare's play, Romeo and Juliet were victims of their parents' senseless rivalry. Their story was told in many versions before the Bard of Avon wrote of his "star-crossed lovers." The tale can be traced to Masuccio's *Il Novellino* (1476). Shakespeare found the tale in Arthur Brooke's poem *The Tragical History of Romeus and Juliet*, containing "a rare example of love constancie . . ." (1562). Romeo alone means a male lover today and has a derisive ring, but *Romeo and Juliet* still means a pair of youthful, often helpless lovers.

Rush

Often called a *daily*, a *rush* is a series of hastily printed camera shots from a day's shooting viewed by the director for possible use in the film he is making.

The Scottish Play

For some reason lost to history, actors consider it unlucky to mention the name Macbeth. Instead they call Shakespeare's tragedy "the Scottish play."

Seven-Year Itch

Used to describe a husband's or wife's urge to stray from his or her mate after seven years of marriage, this expression appears to have been invented by American playwright George Axelrod in his play *The Seven Year Itch* (1952) and further popularized by the film version starring Marilyn Monroe (1955). No one has turned up any earlier use of the words in a sexual context.

Shot

A single unedited unit of film by a single movie camera.

The $64 Question

On the radio quiz program "Take It or Leave It," which premiered in 1941 and was emceed by Bob Hawk, topics were chosen by contestants from the studio audience and questions on these topics were answered by each contestant on seven levels. The easiest question was worth two dollars and the questions progressed in difficulty until the ultimate $64 question, which eventually came to mean "any question difficult to answer" or "the key question." "Take It or Leave It" inspired a slew of similar quiz shows. A decade later came television's "$64,000 Question" with its plateaus instead of levels, its isolation booth, and its scandals involving prominent contestants who cheated in cahoots with the producers. Then, after a long hiatus, there was the "$128,000 Question," but despite these programs with their inflated prizes, *$64 question* retains its place in the national vocabulary.

Skit

No one really knows the origin of the word *skit*, for "a short comical act in a variety show." A good guess is the Swedish *skjuta*, one of whose meanings is "full of frisks or capers." *Skit*, first recorded in 1820, may also be a back-formation from *skittish*, in its sense of "lively, humorous."

Soul Kiss

Actress Olga Nethersole's long passionate onstage kiss in Dandot's *Sapho* in the late 1880s led to her prosecution for obscenity. It is said that her "intra-oral and interlingual" kiss, or French kiss, as it is also called, inspired the term *soul kiss*, from a shortening of the name Nether*sole*. A good theory, but the expression wasn't recorded until the 1930s, almost half a century after Nethersole's famous kiss.

Spaghetti Western

Cheap Western movies made in Italy in the 1960s usually featured bloody violence more prominently than plot or character. They came to be called *spaghetti Westerns*, a term used to describe any cheap Western today.

Steadi Cam

A traditional harness device that holds a camera steady to the cameraman's body enabling him to take smooth shots without any jerking or shaking. The first Steadi Cams were used in the Oscar-winning film *Rocky* (1976).

Storyboard

A panel on which a sequence of rough sketches shows the progression of the plot and characters of a film.

Suits

A term first used in Hollywood for studio executives that is now used to describe all business executives.

Superman

George Bernard Shaw, not Friedrich Nietzsche, coined *superman*, never expecting a movie to be made about such a character. The German philosopher's word for a dominant man above good or evil, introduced in *Thus Spake Zarathustra* (1883–91), was *übermensch*, "overman" or "beyondman." Shaw didn't like the sound of Nietzsche's word and so translated its German prefix *über-* into the Latin *super-* then added to it the English *man*, translated from the German *mensch*. Shaw used the new word for the first time in his play *Man and Superman* (1903). The word was widely popularized by an American comic book character of the same name who made his debut in the 1930s.

Surfing

A name for the use of a television remote control device to switch from channel to channel to see what is playing or to escape relentless unimaginative commercials.

"Sweet Adeline"

The "Sweet Adeline" in the song of the same name was originally "Sweet Rosalie." Songwriters Richard Gerard and Henry Armstrong wrote "You're the Flower of My Heart, Sweet Rosalie" in 1903, tried to sell it, and couldn't. When they decided to name the song's heroine in honor of popular prima donna Adelina Patti and shortened the title to "Sweet Adeline," it sold and eventually became the barbershop quartet hit of all time.

Teleprompter

This trademarked device, hidden from the audience, provides television performers with a magnified script he or she can read line by line. Its counterpart in the theater is the human prompter (*see* Chapter 2).

"There's a Sucker Born Every Minute"

Showman P. T. Barnum lived by this principle, but he probably didn't invent the phrase so often attributed to him. Since there is no recorded instance of Barnum uttering the words, they must be credited to Anonymous, like another famous American cynicism, *Never give a sucker an even break*, which was the title of a W. C. Fields movie. Terms that Barnum did coin or help popularize include *jumbo, bandwagon, Siamese twins, bearded lady, wild man of Borneo, Swedish Nightingale, Tom Thumb, three-ring circus*, and *The Greatest Show on Earth*.

Thumbs Down

First, we have the traditional story: *Habet!* or "He's had it," Roman spectators shouted when they wanted a defeated gladiator to be killed. Their shouts were accompanied by a thumbs-down gesture that is believed to be the ancestor of the same gesture we use today and of our expression *thumbs down* for "no!" Some Latinists, however, say that thumbs down is a mistranslation of the Latin phrase *pollice verso*, which means "thumbs turned." According to this theory spectators made the gesture *pollice primo*, "thumbs in front," when a gladiator fought a good fight, and made the gesture *pollice verso* if he fought poorly and they wanted him killed. The idea that *pollice verso* meant "thumbs down," this story holds, seems to have been first suggested by a painting of nineteenth-century French artist Jean-Léon Gérôme that depicted scowling Roman spectators holding their thumbs down at the end of a gladiatorial contest.

Tournedos

Tournedos are small round pieces of thick beef, served with a number of sauces and garnished. The Italian composer Gioacchino Antonio Rossini (1792–1868), best known for *The Barber of Seville* (1816), is said to have invented the cut of beef when he conceived tournedos à la Rossini at the height of his popularity. According to the old tale, Rossini was dining at the Café Anglais in Paris. Tired of the beef dishes on the menu, he gave instructions for his meat to be prepared in a different way. "Never would I dare to offer such a thing—it is unpresentable!" the maître d'hotel protested. "Well then, arrange not to let it be seen!" the composer countered. Ever after, we are told, tournedos were to be served not before the eyes, but behind the diner's back. Hence the name in French: *tournedo le dos* ("turn the back"). There is no doubt anyway, that tournedos à la Rossini is named in the composer's honor: succulent slices of fried fillet of beef set on fried bread, capped with foie gras, crowned with truffles, and coated with Perigueux sauce. It is one of the richest, most expensive dishes in the world and a favorite of at least one portly opera singer.

Trap

A trap door that is used to project scenery and actors onto the stage from below. There are many complicated varieties of them, one of the most famous the Grave Trap traditionally used in the grave scene in *Hamlet*.

Travelogue

A lecture, slide show, or motion picture describing travels. The word was coined in 1903 by writer Burton Holmes, who fashioned it from *travel* and mono*logue*. Some scholars objected that it was "irregularly formed" because its first half is French and its second Greek, but *travelogue* has stood the test of time.

TV Dinner

Few people realize that the ubiquitous frozen TV dinner was a trademark name of the C. A. Swanson Company. It was coined in 1953, during the early days of television, when people first began to sit around their TV sets and eat prepared dinners that were easily heated in the oven.

Upstage

The back of the stage. The expression *to upstage* comes from the practice of an actor overshadowing another actor by moving upstage and forcing him to play with his back to the audience.

Video

Video, the Latin for "I see," has been used as a term for television since the 1950s. *Video* is also shorthand for *videocassette*. Another recent coinage, dating to the early 1960s, is *videotape*, which first meant a picturephone, a telephone with a small TV screen on which callers can see each other. The system has so far proved too expensive to put into general use but promises to be commonplace in the near future.

Voice-Over

The voice of an unseen narrator or an unseen actor speaking in a movie. Also very common in television commercials.

Warren

Just as George Bernard Shaw's play *Mrs. Warren's Profession* resulted in the coining of *Comstockery* for prudish censorship (after censor Anthony Comstock), it also gave rise to the word *warren*, for "a prostitute," after the title character in the play. The earlier *warren* for "a brothel," origin unknown but dating back to the late seventeenth century, may have reinforced the usage.

Well-Made Play

Apparently this expression, for "an entertaining, carefully constructed play with more attention given to plot than characters," is a literal translation of the French *pièce bien faite*, which was applied to the well-made plays of Scribe and Sardou in the nineteenth century.

"What Time Does the Next Swan Leave?"

According to the old story, a boat drawn by a swan used in a performance of Wagner's *Lohengrin* was pushed onto the stage before the actor playing Lohengrin could get into it. The perfectly composed tenor quipped, "What time does the next swan leave?" This famous remark has been attributed to a number of famous singers over the years, but it actually goes back to the first tenor to sing the role, over a century ago.

White Slavery

The White Slave (1882), a play by Barley Campbell, popularized the term *white slavery* for "prostitution." The term is also used as a synonym for the widespread indentured servitude (a form of slavery) in Colonial America.

"Win One for the Gipper"

This phrase is well known, of course, because President Ronald Reagan played George Gipp, the "Gipper," in a movie about Knute Rockne and his football team at Notre Dame (*Knute Rockne—All-American*, 1940). Rockne urged his team to go out and "win this game for the Gipper," who on his deathbed had requested that the team win a game in his honor—and Notre Dame proceeded to do it. Actually Gipp had made this request of Rockne in 1920 when dying of pneumonia, and the coach had used the same appeal several other times before the 1928 game with heavily favored Army that is depicted in the film.

Wings

The unseen backstage part on both sides of the stage of a PROSCENIUM theater. The expression *in the wings* has come to mean someone waiting in the wings, like an actor ready to go onstage, someone available on short notice, as in "At least one presidential candidate is waiting in the wings."

Wireless

This is an old British name for the radio that never really caught on in the United States, though it has had limited use here. The word derives directly from the name of the Marconi Wireless Telegraph Company. Guglielmo Marconi (1874–1937) was an Italian inventor in the field of wireless telegraphy, and his company tried to establish a monopoly in the North Atlantic. Eventually the British applied the name for his wireless telegraph to the wireless radio, though now they too generally say *radio*.

Yes-Man

In a 1913 cartoon the great sports cartoonist T. A. Dorgan depicted a newspaper editor and his assistants looking over sheets fresh from the press. The assistants, all praising the edition, are labeled *yes-men*, leading many authorities to credit T.A.D. with the coinage. The expression quickly became a name for assistant directors in Hollywood (Wilson Mizner's "land where nobody noes")—*Variety* labeling one unfortunate director "super-yes-man"—and was well known enough in general speech for *Yes-Man's Land* to be used as the title for a book in 1929. Another theory is that *yes-man* may be of German origin, a translation of *Jaherr*, "a compliant person, one unable to say no," which was used by a German author who wrote about America in 1877. In any case, Dorgan certainly popularized the expression.

"You Ain't Heard Nothin' Yet"

This commonly used phrase is an Americanism and the title of a 1919 popular song but probably dates back fifty years or more before that. It was popularized in Al Jolson's movie *The Jazz Singer* (1927) and again in the 1940s in two film biographies of Jolson's life.

XI

FINAL CUTS AND CURTAIN FALLS: THE STRANGE DEATHS AND LAST WORDS OF FAMOUS THESPIANS

A-1 Actors at Lloyd's

The world-famous Lloyd's of London insurance association has frequently insured the lives and trademark features of many Hollywood stars and models over the past century. Some interesting policies in its risky history include: Betty Grable's legs insured for $250,000 (not $1 million, as is often claimed); Jimmy Durante's nose for $140,000; silent-film comedian Ben Turpin's crossed eyes for $500,000; flamenco dancer José Greco's special trousers insured against splitting at $980 a pair; Fred Astaire's legs for $650,000; Zorina's toes at $25,000 per digit; Abbott and Costello insured for $250,000 against career disagreement over a five-year period; actress Julie Bishop, a $25,000 policy against her gaining four inches around the hips or waist over a seven-year period; and a $250,000 policy on the forty-two-inch bust of an unnamed English actress.

Lloyd's has also written a $100,000 "love insurance" policy that provided payment if a certain photographer's model married (she did, but after the policy expired) and a "happiness policy" that insured against "worry lines developing on a model's face."

The American author and scourge of Victorian society Frank Harris (1856–1931), who wrote several plays, regarded himself as "the greatest Shakespearean" and greatest lover of his day. Harris had Lloyd's of London insure the card file of two thousand women he claimed he'd seduced in his lifetime for $150,000. Whether he insured Dirty Banshee—the card game he invented, complete with playing cards depicting variations of the sexual act—remains unknown.

Risks Lloyd's turned down include a policy insuring the back teeth of an acrobat, who hung from them in her act, and a request by a European gentleman to insure his actress-daughter's virginity.

Many other insurance companies offer similar coverage today. There are even policies in force insuring the physical attributes of male and female porno stars. The most X-rated insurance coverage is the $1 million policy the porno movie production company Vivid Video took out in 1996 on porn star Steven St. Croix's genitalia. Vivid Video reportedly got a little nervous when St. Croix announced he had purchased a motorcycle.

Guess Who—and Your Guess Is as Good as Mine

Nine major insurance companies joined forces to insure the life of a leading Hollywood entertainment industry figure for $100 million in 1990. This was the largest life insurance policy ever written on the life of anyone in any profession. It was bought by a major entertainment corporation, which required that its name and the name of the insured be kept secret. Presumably, the policy still remains in force.

The Sunshine Boys and Girls: Long-Lived Thespians

The oldest person ever to appear on the stage or screen was Louise Calment (1875–1997), a French-Canadian woman and at the time the world's oldest living person, who appeared as herself in the Canadian film *Vincent and Me* (1990) when she was 115. Unlike Mr. Broadway she was not a professional thespian. "Mr. Broadway" was the nickname of George Abbott, prizewinning American actor, playwright, director, and producer, who died in 1995, age 108! Over his long theatrical career (from c. 1912 to 1990), probably longer than any professional theater person anywhere, Abbott won Tony Awards for writing the musicals *The Pajama Game* (1955), *Damn Yankees* (1956), and *Fiorello!* (1960); a Tony for directing *A Funny Thing Happened on the Way to the Forum* (1963); a special lifetime Tony Award (1987); and a Pulitzer Prize and New York Drama Critics Circle Award for *Fiorello!* Abbott had an acting, writing, directing, or producing hand in over 120 plays, more than one for each year of his long life.

Other long-lived theater people (nine more of them over 100) include:

Age of Death

109—Jean Frédéric, comte de Waldec (1766–1875), a novelist and playwright who published his second book when 100; dropped dead on a Paris street just after turning to eye a pretty woman.

104—Isabel Kambert (1892–1996), opera singer, banned from singing in Germany after she refused to join the Nazi party.

101—Estelle Windwood (1883–1984), American actress whose career spanned more than seventy years.

101—Irving Berlin (1888–1989), legendary American songwriter and playwright.

100—Eubie Blake (1883–1983), American composer and performer.

100—Charles Macklin (c. 1697–1797), English actor and playwright, who may have actually lived until he was 107, according to some accounts.

100—George Burns (1896–1996), American comedian and straight man for his wife, Gracie Allen.

100—Bernard Le Bovier (c. 1657–c. 1757), French poet and dramatist.

98—Eden Phillpotts (1862–1960), English novelist and playwright.

96—George Broadhurst (1866–1952), British-born American playwright and producer after whom Broadway's Broadhurst Theatre was named.

96—Lynn Fontanne (1887–1983), of the great acting team of Lunt and Fontanne; her husband Alfred Lunt died in 1980, age 88.

95—John Payne Collier (c. 1788–1883), British drama critic said to have forged entries in Elizabethan theatrical documents solely for the vanity of being their discoverer.

95—Guy Bolton (1884–1979), American playwright.

94—Pelham Grenville Wodehouse (1881–1975), English novelist and playwright; often collaborated with Bolton, above.

94—George Bernard Shaw (1856–1950), Irish playwright.

94—Lyle Talbot (1902–96), American character actor in more than 150 films.

94—Joe Howard (1867–1961), American composer and performer, who was still performing up to the day he died.

93—Helen Hayes (1900–93), American stage and screen actress whose first film was made when she was 10 and whose last film was made when she was 88, the world's longest screen career for a woman so far.

92—Michael Leavitt (1843–1935), American performer and theater owner.

91—Curt Bois (1900–91), German actor who appeared in movies from the time he was 8 until he was 88, the world's longest screen career.

91—Joris Ivens (1898–1989), Dutch director who made his last film when 88, becoming the oldest director to make a movie.

91—Somerset Maugham (1874–1965), English novelist and dramatist.

91—Albert Edward "Matty" Matthews (1869–1960), English player who acted up until the day of his death. When he died he was thought to be much younger, for he always cut ten years off his age when applying for a part.

91—Tom Helmore (1904–95), American actor and author.

91—Marc Connelly (1890–1981), American playwright, director, and actor.

91—Claudette Colbert (1905–96), Academy Award–winning American actress.

90—Sophocles (496–406 B.C.), immortal Greek tragedian who finished his Oedipus plays in his eighties.

90—Marcus Pacuvius (c. 220–130 B.C.), Roman dramatist.

90—Olga Knipper (1869–1959), Russian actress and Chekhov's wife; created the part of Madame Ranevsky in *The Cherry Orchard* (1904) and played it for forty years.

90—John Patrick (1905–95), American Pulitzer Prize–winning playwright.

90—Brigitte Helm (1906–96), German actress who played the robot director in Fritz Lang's classic film *Metropolis*.

90—Brooks Atkinson (1894–1984), drama critic of the *New York Times* for thirty-four years.

89—Otto Kruger (1885–1975), popular American leading man.

89—John Masefield (1878–1967), English poet laureate, novelist, and dramatist.

88—Fred Astaire (1899–1987), American dancer and actor.

88—Crébillon (1674–1762), French dramatist.

88—Thomas Hardy (1840–1928), renowned English poet, novelist, and dramatist.

88—Mae West (1892–1980), American actress and sex symbol supreme who boasted of her active sex life well into her eighties.

Many of these long-lived thespians are covered more fully elsewhere in these pages.

Old Playwrights Who Played Around

- When he was approaching his one hundredth birthday in 1757, French poet and dramatist Bernard Le Bovier, sieur de Fontanelle, abruptly entered the dressing room of Comtesse Anne Catherine de Ligniville d'Autricourt, a famous beauty of thirty-two, and found her almost completely naked. Very politely he backed out of the room, bowing and saying, "Ah, madam, if only I were eighty years old again."

- It is said that English playwright William Wycherley (1640–1716) continued "chasing women beyond his capacity into a bad old age." His last amorous adventure may have been undertaken out of spite, in order to thwart his nephew, the next in line to his family property. In any case, at the age of seventy-five he married a twenty-year-old girl. All the excitement proved too much for him, and he died a few days later.

- In his later years Alexander Dumas *père* was reproached for holding a young actress on his lap while two others rumpled his hair. "Sixty is twenty times three," he replied, "which makes me twenty years old for each of these three young ladies." Dumas, well-named *père*, claimed to have fathered five hundred illegitimate children, one of whom is generally known as Alexandre Dumas *fils*, author of *La Dame aux Camélias*.

Pompadour's Priapic Playwright

Madame de Pompadour, a cultured woman whose library numbered some 3,500 volumes, saved the old playwright Prosper Jolyot de Crébillon from starving to death in the attic where he lived with his ten dogs, fifteen cats, and several ravens. When he went to Versailles to thank her for the pension she had awarded him, la Pompadour received him while in bed. Crébillon bent down to kiss her hand, but at this exact moment Louis XV entered the room. "Madam," the old but still quite masculine man cried, "I am undone; the king has surprised us together!" Louis so admired his witticism that he helped him produce his next play, finished when he was eighty.

"The End of My Heart": Long-Lived Lovers

Many thespians have suffered in marriage, including Shakespeare, Aristophanes, Euripides, Ben Jonson, John Dryden, Racine, and Molière, to name just a few great dramatists. On the other hand, there have been many supremely happy long-lived marriages in theatrical history.

Alfred Lunt and Lynn Fontanne, perhaps America's greatest acting team, were married for fifty-eight years before Lunt died in 1980, age eighty-eight. Lynn Fontanne lived on another three years, until she was ninety-six. The team's farewell performance had come in 1958, when both triumphed in Friedrich Dürrenmatt's *The Visit*. At the time, Lunt was sixty-six and Fontanne was seventy-one. Broadway's Lunt-Fontanne Theatre honors them today.

Tiny, big-voiced Nora Bayes (born Dora Goldberg) was one of the most dramatic singers in vaudeville and went on to star in the Ziegfeld Follies, among many other shows. In 1908 she married and teamed up with Jack Norworth (born John Knauff), a little song and dance man whose "Take Me Out to the Ballgame" and, especially, "Shine on Harvest Moon" they often sang together. Nora died in 1928 when she was only forty-eight, but Jack, the same age, lived on without her until he was eighty. The team is still remembered for their billing, among the most memorable in show business:

> NORA BAYES
> *Assisted and Admired by Jack Norworth*

Other famous long-lived pairs include, among many others, Katharine Cornell and Guthrie McClintic, and Hume Cronyn and Jessica Tandy. The legendary actress Helen Hayes, after whom Broadway's Helen Hayes Theatre is named, lived on thirty-seven years after her husband, playwright Charles MacArthur (1895–1956); she died in 1993, age ninety-three. She never remarried, as might be expected reading her touching remembrance in her autobiography of how she met her husband:

> *I was at a party feeling very shy because there were a lot of celebrities around, and I was sitting in a corner alone and a very beautiful young man came up to me and offered me some salted peanuts and said "I wish they*

were emeralds" as he handed me the peanuts and that was the end of my heart. I never got it back.

Unrequited Love

The French poet, playwright, and novelist Alfred de Musset's liaison with George Sand is said to have taught him the tragedy of unrequited love. Sand angered the French author in many little ways, but he hated most her habit of getting up immediately after they had enjoyed a long night of love and sitting right there in the bedroom working on her latest novel. His lover would never put him before her work, Musset knew, and he could do nothing about it. His anger turned to hate when George Sand left him for another man, and he finally wrote the pornographic novel *Gamiani* about her.

243 Years on the Stage

Highly regarded British actor George Frederick Cooke (1756–1812) "seemed to play better when drunk and was probably somewhat insane with constant inebriation," according to one critic. The eccentric Cooke was considered "the greatest of actors" by famed player Edmund Kean, who erected a monument to him and stole one of his toe bones as a relic when his grave was moved. Byron wrote of him that it was marvelous "that a man should live so long drunk." Cooke, in a way, may still be performing today—his skull was willed to a troupe of American actors for use in *Hamlet*'s graveyard scene ("Alas, poor Yorick . . .") and may somewhere be playing its 243rd year on the stage.

The Real Yorick

> *Alas, poor Yorick! I knew him, Horatio, a fellow of infinite jest, of most excellent fancy. He hath bore me on his back a thousand times; and now, how abhorr'd in my imagination it is! my gorge rises at it. Here hung those lips that I have kiss'd I know not how oft. Where be your jibes now, your gambols, your songs, your flashes of merriment, that were wont to set the table on a roar? Not one now to mask your own grinning—quite chop-fall'n. Now get you to my lady's chamber, and tell her, let her paint an inch thick, to this favour she must come; make her laugh at that.*

This famous passage from *Hamlet* where the Prince holds the old jester's skull in his hand and reflects on the vanity of life is thought by many to be a funeral oration commemorating the most noted of English clowns, Richard Tarlton (d. 1588). A very short, broad man who was one of the queen's players, Tarlton was immensely popular in his day for his quick wit, jests, jig-dancing, singing, and comic acting. Shakespeare may well have known him when he was a boy, and Tarlton may even have carried little Willie on his back on one of his visits to Stratford as a traveling actor.

Here, but Not for Long: Short-Lived Thespians

Age at death

- 21—Terence (c. 180–159 B.C.), a Roman slave of an unknown African tribe who was freed and became a great comic playwright; he is said to have been lost at sea. (May have been ten years older.)
- 23—Selena (Quintanilla Perez, b. 1971), popular American singer shot by the deranged president of her fan club; a movie was made of her brief life.
- 24—James Dean (b. 1931), American movie star, died in an automobile accident.
- 26—John Wilkes Booth (b. 1839), the most infamous actor anywhere.
- 27—American playwright Thomas Godfrey (b. 1736), author of *The Prince of Parthia* (1759), the first American play to be produced professionally.
- 29—Christopher Marlowe (b. 1564), English playwright and poet, killed in a tavern brawl.
- 29—George Farquhar (b. 1678), Irish dramatist, died of unrecorded illness caused by extreme poverty.
- 30—Thomas Randolph (b. 1605), English poet and playwright.
- 30—Thomas Heggen (b. 1919), American novelist and playwright, author of *Mister Roberts*, who died a year after the play opened.
- 31—Rudolph Valentino (b. 1895), American movie star.
- 32—Francis Beaumont (b. 1584), English dramatist of "Beaumont and Fletcher" fame, died of "overwork of the brain."
- 32—Robert Greene (b. 1560), English dramatist and Shakespeare's antagonist, died of "a surfeit of pickled herrings and Rhinish wine."

33—Nathan Field (b. 1587), English actor; kidnapped as a child for use as a child actor, he went on to become one of the best players of his day, possibly succeeding Shakespeare when the Bard retired from the King's Company troupe, but his wild dissolute ways led to his early death.

33—Thomas Otway (b. 1652), English playwright and poet, choked to death on a piece of bread he had begged money to buy.

33—John Suckling (b. 1609), English playwright and poet who invented the game of cribbage; said to have committed suicide.

33—John Daly Burke (b. 1775), English playwright, killed in a duel.

34—Heinrich von Kleist (b. 1777), German dramatist, committed suicide.

34—Thomas Nash (b. 1567), English dramatist, died in poverty after being forced into retirement for his satires.

34—John Augustus Stone (b. 1800), the first prizewinning American playwright (*see* Chapter 3); committed suicide.

34—Antonio José da Silva (b. 1705), Portuguese playwright.

34—Gros Guillaume (Robert Guérin, b. 1600), French comedian.

35—Jonathan Larson (b. 1961), struggling American playwright and composer who died a week before his rock opera *Rent* opened Off-Broadway; *Rent* went on to win the Tony Award for best musical and the Pulitzer Prize for drama.

36—Shelley Hull (b. 1883), American actor.

36—Marilyn Monroe (Norma Jean Baker, b. 1926), American movie star.

38—Nathanael West (Nathan Wallenstein Weinstein, b. 1903), American novelist and screenwriter known for his satire of Hollywood life *The Day of the Locust* (1939); died in a car crash.

38—Rachel (Elisa Félix, b. 1820), the great French actress who died of tuberculosis after her successful American tour.

38—Federico García Lorca (b. 1898), Spanish poet and playwright; assassinated during the Spanish Civil War.

39—William Conway (b. 1789), excellent but thin-skinned British actor who committed suicide by jumping off a ship at sea.

39—Charles Hoyt (b. 1860), American actor who died shortly after being committed to a lunatic asylum when his mind snapped over severe panning of his last play.

39—Nathaniel Lee (b. 1653), English actor and playwright.

39—Dylan Thomas (b. 1914), Welsh poet, playwright, and filmmaker who died of wild living and hard drinking.

Many theatrical greats in days past died while still in their forties, including Anton Chekhov (b. 1860), the immortal Russian dramatist, who died of tuberculosis at the age of 44.

"If You Need Anything, Just Whistle"

When Humphrey Bogart died and was cremated in 1957 his wife, Lauren Bacall, placed a small gold whistle in the urn with his ashes. Inscribed on the whistle is a variation on the famous line she delivered to Bogey in their first film together, *To Have and Have Not*: "If you need anything, just whistle."

Another actor buried with a beloved object is Bela Lugosi, whose last wish was to go to the grave in the black cape he wore in his Dracula films. On his deathbed silent-film star Rudolph Valentino insisted that he be buried wearing the slave bracelet his wife, Natasha, had given him, even though slave bracelets were considered effeminate at the time.

Dramatic Last Exits of Noted Thespians

- Legend has it that the famed Greek dramatist Aeschylus was killed when an eagle dropped a tortoise on his bald head, mistaking it for a rock to break open its prey upon.
- While swimming at the Pireaus, the Greek dramatist Menander developed a cramp and drowned.
- The Greek dramatist Sophocles may have died when his breath failed him because he had no time to pause while reading a long passage from his tragedy *Antigone.*
- Euripides is said to have been torn to death by the King of Macedonia's hunting dogs, when he served as the king's court poet, or to have been ripped apart by a mob of women who objected to one of his plays.
- The Greek dramatist Philemon is supposed to have died of laughter over a joke he'd just made.
- The great French comedian Gros Guillaume (Robert Guérin) is said to have mocked a certain judge while playing the part of a magistrate on

stage. The judge happened to be in the audience and later had him thrown in jail, where he died months later.

- British playwright Thomas Otway, mired in poverty, left his room one morning to beg for bread. A passerby gave him a guinea. He hurried to a nearby baker's shop, where he bought a loaf of bread and began stuffing it in his mouth to satisfy his ravenous hunger, but he choked to death on the first mouthful.
- French actor Nicolas Dauvilliers (d. 1690), a master at tragedy, is said to have gone mad while playing a part onstage and tried to kill himself with a prop sword, running himself through. He later died in an asylum.
- English actor and dramatist Nathaniel Lee died insane in a drunken fit while trying to escape from Bedlam.
- Considered the best Portuguese playwright of his day, Antonio José da Silva was arrested with his mother in 1726 for being a Jew. His mother was burned at the stake, but he was released upon renouncing his religion. Thirteen years later he was charged with secretly practicing Judaism and burned at the stake himself. On the day of his execution one of his plays was being performed in Lisbon.
- English dramatist Theophilus Cibber (1703–58) led a controversial life like his playwright father, Colley Cibber, before him. As rude and vain as his father, with much less to be vain about, he was involved in financial dishonesty concerning the Drury Lane Theatre and provoked great scandal by encouraging his attractive actress wife to have an affair with a rich man for mercenary reasons. It is common knowledge that American author Mark Twain came in and went out with Halley's Comet. Cibber, who led such a stormy life, was born during the Great Storm of 1703 and died in the Great Storm of 1758; he drowned when his ship went down while sailing to Dublin to keep a theatrical engagement.
- George Garrick (d. 1770), David Garrick's brother and faithfully available right-hand man at the Drury Lane Theatre, died three days after David. The cause of George's death, according to a wit of the day, was that "Davy wanted him."
- British playwright John Daly Burke was killed in a duel with a Frenchman after insulting Napoléon's name.
- Russian poet and dramatist Aleksandr Pushkin (1799–1837) died in a duel, as did Russian poet Mikhail Lermontov (1814–41), who had been inspired by Pushkin's death to write the poem "On the Death of a Poet."

- Scottish poet John Davison (1857–1909) was loaned £250 by George Bernard Shaw to finish his trilogy *God and Mammon*. Davison instead wrote a historical melodrama to repay the loan, and when the play failed, he was so embarrassed that he drowned himself in the English Channel.
- W. S. Gilbert of Gilbert and Sullivan fame died of a heart attack after saving a little girl from drowning in a lake. He was seventy-five at the time.
- Russian composer Aleksandr Scriabin (1872–1915) died, at only forty-three, of blood poisoning after picking a pimple on his lip.
- German-born performer Eugene Sandow (1867–1925), billed as the "World's Strongest Man," died after trying to lift an automobile from a ditch.
- Dancer Isadora Duncan (1877–1927) died when her long scarf got entangled in the rear wheel of a car she was riding in, breaking her neck.
- English novelist and playwright William Saroyan (1908–81) wrote in a suggested posthumous statement to the Associated Press five days before his death: "Everybody has got to die, but I have always believed an exception would be made in my case. Now what?"
- *On the Eve* (1941), the Russian dramatist Alexander Nikolayevich Afinogenov's final play, depicted a German attack on the Soviet Union. A month after its first performance the playwright himself was killed in a German air raid on Moscow.
- Suave, urbane British actor George Sanders committed suicide and left behind a note saying his reason was that he was "bored by it all."
- One American actor—anonymous here—is said to have died "the sweet death" while making love.

Hardy's Heart

Thomas Hardy's heart was to be buried in Stinsford, England, his birthplace, after the rest of his body was cremated in Dorchester. All went according to plan until Hardy's sister's cat snatched the heart off her kitchen table and disappeared into the woods with it.

Deaths Onstage

- When he was seventy-five, English actor Charles Farrel (b. c. 1620) performed the highland broad dance on stage. After one wrong step he wounded himself in the thigh with a sword he carried. Though he carried on his performance, blood streaming over the stage, he died shortly afterward.

- Molière, the immortal French dramatist, died a few hours after playing the part of a hypochondriac onstage, where he had a fit of coughing blood but finished the performance. The comedy was entitled *Le Malade Imaginaire.*
- British actor John Palmer the Younger (1742–98), ironically nicknamed "Plausible Jack" for his constant lying, died onstage while performing in a Liverpool production of *The Stranger.*
- In the worst of theater disasters that have claimed the lives of actors (*see* Chapter 7) fifteen people were killed and twenty badly injured when the Royal Brunswick Theatre (badly reconstructed after a fire) collapsed on February 25, 1828, while the company was rehearsing a play.
- British actor Fred Emney (1865–1917) slipped in soap suds on the stage during a scene in *Cinderella* and died of the injuries he sustained.
- Vaudeville tramp comic Joe Jackson (1880–1942) fell down dead the instant after he took his last curtain call in a New York theater. Smiling at the applause, he died as the curtain closed.
- American opera singer Leonard Warren (1911–60) was starring in Verdi's *La Forza del Destino* at New York's Metropolitan Opera House. The next line of the aria he was to sing was "O fatal urn of my destiny." Warren fell down, dead of a heart attack, just as he sang the word "fatal."

Dead Asleep Onstage

In one of the most famous scenes in ancient Roman tragedy, the male actor playing Iliona in Marcus Pacuvius's play of that name was supposed to be sleeping and awakened by the ghost of his character's murdered son calling out "Mother, I cry to thee!" During one performance the boy cried these words again and again, but the actor didn't move—he had gotten drunk and really fallen asleep on the stage. Iliona didn't awaken until the entire audience finally took up the boy's words, the whole theater thundering "Mother, I cry to thee! Mother, I cry to thee!"

A Curtain Rung Cruelly Down: Barrymore's Last Days

Maurice Barrymore (1847–1905), the founder of the important family of American actors, changed his name from Herbert Blythe early in his career, taking his new name from a playbill he noticed hanging on a theater wall. Born in

India and schooled at Cambridge, the handsome Barrymore was well known as a boxer before turning to the stage. After a distinguished twenty-five years as an actor in America he became a vaudeville star toward the close of his life, until mental illness struck and finished his career. Though there were signs before, the end came while he was onstage at the Lion Palace Music Hall in New York. A news item in *Billboard* (April 6, 1901) tells the story:

> There was a large audience present at the Lion Palace on Thursday night when Maurice Barrymore went insane. They were drawn there chiefly by the not yet departed vogue of the once great actor and in part by the stories of his ardent advocacy of the cause of the White Rats, the organization of vaudeville artists that is warring upon the theatrical trust.
>
> Barrymore looked strange in spite of his make-up. His eyes were large and staring. He looked unkempt and his hands twitched nervously. He stepped to the front of the stage, and, instead of speaking the lines, his monologue, began a wild harangue against the Theatrical Trust. He talked so fast and so indistinctly that only those in the front rows heard the words.
>
> "Down with the trust! Death to the syndicate! Charles Frohman is doomed!"
>
> The stage manager ordered him off the stage, but he either did not hear or would not obey. He went on haranguing, tossing his arms above his head and striding from one side of the stage to the other.
>
> At first the audience stared; then it tittered. At last a woman screamed, and the curtain was rung down.
>
> The actor raved about the White Rats and George Fuller Golden and Charlie Frohman, but seemed to know nothing of the fiasco of his act. He hurried from the theater, and almost ran to the Ft. Lee ferry, at the foot of One Hundred and Thirtieth street, followed by his son John.
>
> Barrymore was hospitalized at a sanatorium in New York but never really recovered.

Mock Epitaphs of Stage and Movie Stars

Mock epitaphs are humorous words usually invented by someone for his or her gravestone, though not for actual use. They are hardly a modern phenomenon, dating back to ancient times, but have never been more popular than they are today. Here's a good selection from theater folk:

- "Well, I've played everything but a harp."   —actor Lionel Barrymore
- "All my old junk gone to the storehouse, / Here I am, God, starting for your house. / In order to prevent possibility of ruction / Am

- bringing you back your original production." —British actor George Arliss
- "On the whole I'd rather be in Philadelphia" is a mock epitaph first printed as a joke in *Vanity Fair* in the 1920s. It was not coined by W. C. Fields and is not inscribed on his tomb as is frequently stated.
- "Here's something I want to get off my chest." —actor William Haines
- "This is too deep for me." —movie star Hedy Lamarr
- "This is just my lot." —actor Fredric March
- "Back to the silents." —movie star Clark Gable
- "This is all over my head." —critic, screenwriter, and actor Robert Benchley
- "He was an average guy who could carry a tune." —singer-actor Bing Crosby
- "Of this quiet and peace / I'm very fond; / No more remarks— / She's a platinum blonde." —movie siren Jean Harlow
- "There is something / to be said / For being dead." —playwright Eugene O'Neill
- "Did you hear about my operation?" —movie actor Warner Baxter
- "I knew if I stayed around long enough, something like this would happen." —playwright George Bernard Shaw
- "Pardon my dust." —screenwriter Dorothy Parker
- "This is on me." —Dorothy Parker again
- "Here in nature's arms I nestle, / Free at last of George Jessel." —singer and actor Al Jolson, who had a long feud with Jessel
- "Do not disturb." —actress Constance Bennett

Aretino's Epitaph

Italian dramatist Pietro Aretino (1492–1556) started out as a lackey and nearly became a Catholic cardinal, despite all the scandal attached to him. Aretino's *Sonnetti Lussuriosi* (1524) was an early *Joy of Sex*, a collection of verses and erotic drawings showing positions for sexual intercourse. It was an underground favorite in Europe for centuries. The engravings were actually made by Marcantonio Raimondi from drawings by Giulio Romano. Critics were astute in England—John Donne, for one—observing that some "postures" were left out. At least six courtesans (perhaps the original groupies) were so proud to have slept with Aretino that they called themselves *Aretines*. But many hated the satirist, one critic of the day writing this mock epitaph on him:

> Here lies Tuscan Aretino
> Who evil spoke of everyone but God,
> Giving as his excuse, "I never knew him."

Shadwell's Epitaph

The British poet laureate and dramatist Thomas Shadwell (1642?–92) is said to have died of an overdose of opium when about fifty. Satirist Thomas Brown, who had also lampooned Shadwell's enemy John Dryden, "eulogized" him with the following wit:

> Tom writ, his readers still slept o'er his book;
> For Tom took opium, and they opiates took.

Arrested After Death

A friend recorded in his diary how a certain Mr. Vaughan found the starving Richard Brinsley Sheridan and his wife in the British playwright's terrible last few days:

> He said that he found him and Mrs. Sheridan both in their beds, both apparently dying, and both starving! It is stated in Mr. Moore's book that Mrs. Sheridan attended her husband in his last illness; it is not true. She was too ill to leave her own bed, and was in fact already suffering from the disease [cancer] of which she died a couple of years after. They had hardly a servant left. Mr. Sheridan's maid she was about to be sent away, but they could not collect a guinea or two to pay the woman's wages. When Mr. Vaughan entered the house, he found all the reception rooms bare, and the whole house in a state of filth and stench that was quite intolerable. Sheridan himself he found in a truckle bed in a garret with a coarse blue and red coverlet, such as one sees as horse-cloths, over him; out of this bed he had not moved for a week, not even for the occasions of nature, and in this state the unhappy man had been allowed to wallow, nor could Vaughan discover that anyone had taken any notice of him, except one lady, whose name I hardly know whether I am authorized to repeat, Lady Bessborough, who sent 20 pounds.

After his death the brilliant but destitute Sheridan was laid out at a relative's house in London. In a few days a well-dressed man called and, claiming he had come a long way and was an old friend of Sheridan's, asked to view his remains. On his insistence Sheridan's coffin was opened and the corpse unshrouded. The man promptly drew his bailiff's wand, touched Sheridan on the forehead, and declared that he was arresting him in the name of the king for a debt of five hundred pounds. Since the corpse was arrested, the funeral and burial could not go on until George Canning and another of the long-suffering Sheridan's friends pulled out their purses and paid the man.

"He's Gone, and with Him What a World Is Dead"

These words are from an elegy on actor Richard Burbage when he died on May 13, 1619. Burbage's death brought on such grief in London that people forgot the death of Queen Anne, wife of James I, a few weeks before. "The deaths of men who act over Queens and Kings / Are now more mourned than are the real things," another elegy declared. Still another dirge claimed that if Burbage with his "enchanting tongue" had been able to speak to Death he would with his "all-charming art" have convinced the Grim Reaper to let him remain alive, but Death knew this and seized his tongue first. According to the elegy, this explained Burbage dying of a paralysis that began with his tongue and gradually extended to his entire body:

> *Death first made seizure on thy wondrous tongue,*
> *Then on the rest, 'twas easy; by degrees*
> *The slender ivy twines the hugest trees.*

"Our Revels Now Are Ended": Real Epitaphs of Famous Thespians

Epitaph for a Long-Forgotten Fool

> *Here lies the Earl of Suffolk's fool, men called*
>   *Him Dicky Pearce,*
> *His folly served to make men laugh when wit and mirth*
>   *Were scarce.*
> *Poor Dick alas is dead and gone, what signifies to cry.*
> *Dickys enough are still behind to laugh at by and by.*

Shakespeare's Epitaph

It is not certain that Shakespeare himself wrote the famous epitaph on his gravestone at Holy Trinity Church in Stratford, but the words are generally attributed to him:

> *Good friend for Jesus sake forbeare*
> *To dig the dust enclosed here!*
> *Bleste be ye man that spares thes stones,*
> *And curst be he that moves my bones.*

O Rare Ben Jonson

Legend has it that the epitaph "O rare Ben Jonson" over the grave of the great Elizabethan dramatist is actually the mistake of a stonecutter who didn't know Latin and carved the words instead of *Orare Ben Jonson* ("Pray for Ben Jonson"). But the carving was actually commissioned by Sir John Young, who wrote it. Jonson once remarked in jest that he wanted to be buried standing up. When he died, James I took him at his word and today he still stands below one square foot of Westminster Abbey.

Gay's Sad Epitaph

The English poet and playwright John Gay, author of the long-popular ballad-opera *The Beggar's Opera* (1728), is buried in Westminster Abbey under a real epitaph written by himself:

> *Life is a jest, and all things show it;*
> *I thought so once and now I know it*

Poor Scarron's Epitaph

The terribly afflicted French playwright Paul Scarron (*see* Chapter 3) composed his own epitaph shortly before his death:

> *He who lies here*
> *Awoke more pity than envy,*
> *And suffered death a thousand times*
> *Before losing life.*
> *Passing, make here no noise,*
> *Take care not to wake him;*
> *For this is the first night*
> *That poor Scarron sleeps.*

Wilde's Resting Place

The Irish playwright Oscar Wilde is buried in the Père Lachaise Cemetery in Paris, his gravestone, according to one writer, "a huge rectangular tomb dominated by the figure of a nude Egyptian-like male angel in flight, the penis partially chopped off by vandals."

Norma Jean's Grave

Marilyn Monroe (Norma Jean Baker) lies buried in Los Angeles's Westwood Memorial Park in a pink marble crypt with a bronze nameplate. Her former husband Joe DiMaggio ordered red roses to be placed on her tomb three times a week in perpetuity.

Rin Tin Tin's Epitaph

The legendary German shepherd silent-movie star (*see* Chapter 5) is buried in the Cimetière du Chiens in Paris, France. He lies under a black onyx stone inscribed:

The Greatest Movie Star

Vagrant Actor

"Barefooted and tattered, Charles Howard, the famous old-time minstrel, was picked up in Baltimore on the night of July 30th . . . and the following morning Justice Lewis sent him to Bayview Asylum on the charge of vagrancy. 'Thank you,' said the old man when sentence was passed, for he knew that fate had nothing better in store for him. . . . He was barefooted when found . . . and home was a place which had long been forgotten by the minstrel. His clothes were ragged and one foot and leg were bandaged. . . . Howard was one of the original minstrels and was familiar to all theater-goers of a generation ago. He traveled with his troupe from city to city and was well-known everywhere. . . . Like many others who pursue the same means of livelihood, he was prodigal of his money, and when his days before the footlights were over he had very little saved. This little soon disappeared. When arrested he gave his age at 65 years, but those who remember him believe him to be much older."

—*from a news story in* Billboard, *August 23, 1902*

Curtain Speeches: Theatrical Last Words

For his last words, before he embraced his wife, Livia, and died, the Roman emperor Augustus, a great theater fan, chose a phrase often used at the conclusion of Roman comedies: "Since well I've played my part, clap now your hands, and with applause dismiss me from the stage." Since that time history has recorded the last words of many players, playwrights, and others connected with theater and films. Here, arranged chronologically, is a large selection ranging from the absurd to the tragic.

- "A libation to [the god] Jupiter the liberator!" —Roman poet and dramatist Lucius Seneca (3 B.C.–A.D. 65), after splashing water from a pool on people standing by its edge

- "Oh, what an artist dies in me." —Roman emperor Nero (A.D. 37–68), who thought himself a great singer and actor

- "Keep the rats away from me now that I am greased up." —Italian dramatist Pietro Aretino (1472–1557), after receiving the last rites

- "I am happy that I die in the bosom of my country—nay, in that I am dying with her," —Portuguese poet-dramatist Luiz Vaz de Camões (1525–80)

- "There is no need to be frightened. You have seen me spit more blood than that and [some] to spare. Nevertheless, go and ask my wife to come up to me." —French playwright Molière (1622–73)

- "Do you wish to hasten my last hours?" —French critic Nicolas Boileau-Despréaux (1636–1711), to a young playwright trying to read him his new play

- "No, it is not." —English playwright Oliver Goldsmith (1728–74), when asked on his deathbed if his mind was at ease for the final journey

- "In the name of God, let me die in peace." —French philosopher-playwright Voltaire (1694–1778), to a cleric attending him and trying to convert him

- "Well, Tom, I shall do very well yet and make you amends for all this trouble." —English actor David Garrick (1717–79), to his servant

- "Calmer and calmer." —German poet and playwright Friedrich von Schiller (1757–1805), on being asked how he felt

- "I am absolutely undone and brokenhearted." —English playwright Richard Brinsley Sheridan (1751–1816)

- "The damned doctors have drenched me so that I can scarcely stand. I want to sleep now. Shall I sue for mercy? Come, come, no weakness. Let me be a man to the last." —English poet-dramatist Lord Byron (1788–1824)
- "Friends, applaud, the comedy is over." —German composer Ludwig von Beethoven (1770–1827)
- "More light! More light!" —German poet-dramatist Johann Wolfgang von Goethe (1749–1832)
- "There is probably no hell for authors in the next world—they suffer so much from critics in this." —French playwright Christian Nestell Bovée
- "Give another horse. . . . Howard!" —English actor Edmund Kean (1789–1833)
- "I am ready." —English comedian Charles Mathews (1776–1835)
- "Farewell, my friends." —Russian poet and dramatist Aleksandr Pushkin (1797–1837) while staring at his books
- "Tell my mother I died for my country. . . . I thought I did for the best. . . . Useless!" —American actor John Wilkes Booth (1838–65), the assassin of Abraham Lincoln
- "Dear friends and gentle hearts." —American composer Stephen Foster (1826–64)
- "Good-bye, Jeanne, good-bye." —French novelist-dramatist Victor Hugo (1802–85) to his wife
- "How were the circus receipts tonight at Madison Square Garden?" —American showman Phineas T. Barnum (1810–91)
- "I am dying, as I have lived, beyond my means." —Irish playwright Oscar Wilde (1856–1900), while calling for champagne on his deathbed
- "I am dying. . . . I haven't drunk champagne for a long time." —Russian dramatist Anton Chekhov (1860–1904), who had been given a glass of champagne by his doctor
- "On the contrary." —Norwegian playwright Henrik Ibsen (1828–1906) in reply to his nurse, who had said he was looking better
- "It's no use fighting death any longer." —Irish dramatist John Millington Synge (1871–1909)
- "I love to see the reflection of sun in the bookcase." —American novelist-playwright F. Marion Crawford (1854–1909)

- "Everything is atoned for."   —Swedish dramatist August Strindberg (1849–1912), holding a Bible to his heart
- "Why fear death? It is the most beautiful adventure in life."   —American producer Charles Frohman (1860–1915), who died in the sinking of the *Lusitania* by a German submarine
- "I shall not need to study the part at all. I know it already."   —English actor Herbert Beerbohm Tree (1851–1917), speaking of a coming role
- "Well, let's forget about it and play High Five. I wish Johnny would come."   —American impresario Buffalo Bill Cody (1846–1917)
- "Dorio, I can't breathe!"   —Italian tenor Enrico Caruso (1873–1921)
- "We must stir ourselves. Move on! Work! Work! Cover me! Must move on! Must work! Cover me!"   —Italian actress Eleonora Duse (1859–1924)
- "Don't pull down the blinds! I feel fine. I want the sunlight to greet me."   —Italian screen legend Rudolph Valentino (1895–1926)
- "Adieu, my friends, I go on to glory!"   —American dancer Isadora Duncan (1878–1927)
- "I'm going to Dr. Caldwell's for one of my regular treatments."   —American actress Jeanne Eagels (1894–1929) before her sudden death, possibly from drug addiction
- "It's very beautiful over there."   —American inventor and motion picture pioneer Thomas Edison (1847–1931)
- "Everything has gone wrong."   —British novelist-dramatist Arnold Bennett (1867–1931)
- "Get my Swan costume ready!"   —Russian prima ballerina Anna Pavlova (1885–1931)
- "Curtain! Fast music! Light! Ready for the finale! Great! The show looks good, the show looks good."   —American showman Florenz Ziegfeld (1869–1932)
- "Why should I talk to you? I've just been talking to your boss."   —Hollywood wit Wilson Mizner (d. 1933) to a priest in attendance
- "I have enjoyed too pleasant circumstances."   —English novelist-dramatist John Galsworthy (1867–1933)
- "The hearse, the horse, the driver, and—enough!"   —Italian playwright Luigi Pirandello (1867–1936)

- "I can't sleep."   —English playwright James Barrie (1860–1937)
- "I've lots to say to her, not just something. But not now. I'm sure to get it all mixed up."   —Russian director Konstantin Stanislavsky (1863–1938), on being asked if he wanted to send a message to his sister
- "I never felt better!"   —American actor Douglas Fairbanks Sr. (1883–1939)
- "I'm going to Schwab's to get some ice cream. . . ."   —American novelist-screenwriter F. Scott Fitzgerald (1896–1940), before suddenly collapsing outside his Hollywood hotel
- "Tell me, Gene, is it true that you're the illegitimate son of Buffalo Bill?"   —American actor John Barrymore (1882–1942), to his friend, writer Gene Fowler
- "You can keep the things of bronze and stone and give me one man to remember me just once a year."   —American author-playwright Damon Runyon (1884–1946)
- "For me this is quite natural. It is for you that I am concerned."   —Belgian poet-dramatist Maurice Maeterlinck (1862–1949), to his wife
- "This is it. I'm going, I'm going."   —American singer-actor Al Jolson (1886–1950)
- "Sister, you're trying to keep me alive as an old curiosity. But I'm done. I'm finished. I'm going to die."   —Irish dramatist George Bernard Shaw (1856–1950)
- "Mamasha!"   —Russian ballet dancer Vaslav Nijinsky (1890–1950)
- "C'est bien."   —French novelist and dramatist André Gide (1869–1951)
- "See that Yul gets star billing. He has earned it."   —British actress Gertrude Lawrence (1898–1952), who had played with Yul Brynner in *The King and I*
- "I've had eighteen straight whiskies. I think that's the record."   —Welsh poet-dramatist Dylan Thomas (1914–53)
- "Thanks for everything."   —English author and critic Max Beerbohm (1872–1956)
- "I want that fifty bucks you owe me and I want it now!"   —American actor Carl "Alfalfa" Switzer (1926–59) (*See* Chapter 7.)
- "I'm not afraid anymore."   —American playwright George S. Kaufman (1889–1961)

- "Dying is a very dull, dreary affair. And my advice to you is to have nothing whatever to do with it."   —British novelist-playwright Somerset Maugham (1874–1965)
- "Let it roll, let it roll!"   —American jazz musician Jimmy Lee Laine (d. 1970), who died while playing the piano
- "And now, in keeping with Channel 40's policy of always bringing you the latest in blood and guts, in living color, you're about to see another first—an attempted suicide."   —American broadcaster Chris Hubbock (d. 1970) before shooting herself to death while anchoring an evening news program
- "Goodnight, my darlings, I'll see you in the morning."   —English actor-playwright Noël Coward (1899–1973)
- "I never thought I'd live to see the day."   —attributed to American producer Samuel Goldwyn (1882–1974), but probably apocryphal
- "That was a great game of golf, fellers."   —American singer and actor Bing Crosby (1904–77)
- "The only place I feel alive is the high wires."   —German trapeze artist Karl Wallenda (d. 1978) of the Flying Wallendas, shortly before he fell to his death while performing on the high wire in Puerto Rico
- One fifty-year-old Hollywood actor, an alcoholic and who will remain anonymous here, couldn't make it to the top again. He left the following suicide note:

    I tried so hard
    To make a comeback.
        Exit, Act III

- And finally, the last *word* of radiant British actress Ellen Terry (1847–1928), a word written in the dust on her bed table before she died in her sleep: HAPPY.

So there as our revels end and the acting stops and the curtain drops, fellow players, we have for once a true happy ending.

Exeunt Omnes

BIBLIOGRAPHY

Here's a selection of excellent books about various aspects of show business that you may want to read or add to your reference shelf. In addition to these works, numerous biographies of entertainment figures have been consulted as well as many issues of newspapers and magazines, including: *American Movie Classics Magazine, American Theatre, Back Stage, Billboard, Dance Magazine, Entertainment Weekly, Film Quarterly, Hollywood Reporter, New York Post, New York Times, New Yorker, Photoplay, Playboy, Theater Week, TV Guide,* and *Variety.*

Adamson, Joe. *Groucho, Harpo, Chico and Sometimes Zeppo: A History of the Marx Brothers and a Satire on the Rest of the World.* New York: Simon & Schuster, 1973.

Agee, James. *Agee on Film.* New York: McDowell, Obolensky, 1968.

Anger, Kenneth. *Hollywood Babylon.* New York: Dell Publishing, 1981.

Arkof, Sam and Richard Trubo. *Flying Through Hollywood by the Seat of My Pants.* Secaucus, NJ: Carol Publishing, 1992.

Asbury, Herbert. *Gangs of New York.* New York: Marlowe & Co., 1994.

Asplund, Uno. *Chaplin's Films.* Trans. Paul Britten Austin. S. Brunswick, NJ: A. S. Barnes, 1973.

Aylesworth, Thomas G. and John S. Bowman. *The World Almanac of Who's Who of Film.* New York: World Almanac, 1987.

Bainbridge, John. *Garbo.* New York: Holt, Rinehart & Winston, 1971.

Baldwin, Neil. *Edison: Inventing the Century.* New York: Hyperion, 1996.

Barnum, P. T. *The Humbugs of the World: An Account of Humbugs, Delusions, Impositions, Quackeries, Deceits, and Deceivers Generally, in All Ages.* New York: Carleton, 1865.

Barrymore, John. *Confessions of an Actor.* N. Stratford, NH: Ayer Company Publishers, 1926.

Benchley, Robert. *My Ten Years in a Quandary and How They Grew.* New York: Harper & Brothers, 1936.

Bernhardt, Sarah. *The Art of the Theatre.* N. Stratford, NH: Ayer Company Publishers, 1972.

Biskind, Peter. *The Godfather Companion: Everything You Ever Wanted to Know About All Three Godfather Films.* New York: HarperPerennial, 1990.

Bogdanovich, Peter. *Who the Devil Made It?* New York: Ballantine Books, 1998.

Boller, Paul F., Jr., and John George. *They Never Said It: A Book of Fake Quotes, Misquotes, and Misleading Attributions.* New York: Oxford Univ. Press, 1989.

Bowman, W. P. and Robert H. Ball. *Theatre Language: A Dictionary of Terms in English of the Drama and Stage from Medieval to Modern Times.* New York: Theatre Arts Books, 1961.

Brosnan, John. *Movie Magic: The Story of Special Effects in the Cinema.* New York: St. Martin's Press, 1974.

Brown, Karl. *Adventures with D. W. Griffith.* New York: Da Capo Press, 1976.

Brownlow, Kevin. *Hollywood: The Pioneers.* New York: Knopf, 1979.

———. *The Parade's Gone By.* New York: Knopf, 1968.

Bukowski, Charles. *Hollywood.* Santa Rosa, CA: Black Sparrow Press, 1998.

Callow, Simon. *Orson Welles: The Road to Xanadu.* New York: Viking Penguin, 1996.

Chaplin, Charles. *My Autobiography.* New York: NAL Dutton, 1992.

Cheney, Sheldon. *The Theatre: Three Thousand Years of Drama, Acting, and Stagecraft.* New York: McKay, 1972.

Clurman, Harold. *The Fervent Years: The Group Theatre and the Thirties.* New York: Da Capo Press, 1949.

Csida, Joseph and June Bundy Csida. *American Entertainment: A Unique History of Popular Show Business.* New York: Watson-Guptill Publications, 1978.

Didion, Joan. *Slouching Towards Bethlehem.* New York: Farrar, Straus & Giroux, 1990.

Dunne, John Gregory. *The Studio.* New York: Vintage Books, 1998.

Ebert, Roger. *A Kiss Is Still a Kiss.* Kansas City, MO: Andrews, McMeel & Parker, 1984.

———. *Roger Ebert's Book of Film: From Tolstoy to Tarantino—The Finest Writing from a Century of Film.* New York: W. W. Norton & Co., 1996.

Federal Writers' Project Staff. *New York Panorama: A Comprehensive View of the Metropolis, Presented in a Series of Articles.* New York: Somerset Publishers, 1981.

Finch, Christopher and Linda Rosenkrantz. *Gone Hollywood.* Garden City, NY: Doubleday, 1979.

Fitzgerald, F. Scott. *The Last Tycoon.* New York: MacMillan Library Reference, 1977.

Fowler, Gene. *Good Night, Sweet Prince: The Life and Times of John Barrymore.* Cutchogue, NY: Buccaneer Books, 1978.

Freedley, George and John A. Reeves. *A History of the Theatre.* New York: Crown Publishers, 1968.

Gabler, Neal. *Life, The Movie: How Entertainment Conquered Reality.* New York: Knopf, 1998.

Gelb, Arthur and Barbara Gelb. *O'Neill.* New York: Harper, 1962.

Gielgud, John. *Stage Directions.* Westport, CT: Greenwood Press, 1979.

Gilbert, David. *American Vaudeville, It's Life and Times.* New York: Dover Publications, 1963.

Givens, Bill. *Roman Soldiers Don't Wear Watches: 555 Film Flubs.* Secaucus, NJ: Carol Publishing, 1996.

Granville, Wilfred. *A Dictionary of Theatrical Terms.* London: A. Deutsch, 1952.

Greenfield, Jeff. *Television: The First Fifty Years.* New York: H. N. Abrams, 1977.

Grobel, Lawrence. *The Hustons.* New York: Avon Books, 1990.

Gurr, Andrew with John Orrell. *Rebuilding Shakespeare's Globe.* New York: Routledge, 1989.

Guthrie, Tyrone. *In Various Directions: A View of Theatre.* Westport, CT: Greenwood Press, 1979.

Hartnoll, Phyllis. *The Theatre: A Concise History.* New York: Thames & Hudson, 1985.

Hartnoll, Phyllis and Peter Found, eds. *The Concise Oxford Companion to the Theatre, Second Edition.* New York: Oxford Univ. Press, 1992.

Hecht, Ben. *A Child of the Century.* New York: Simon & Schuster, 1954.

Hemstreet, Charles. *When Old New York Was Young.* New York: Scribner & Sons, 1902.

Hope, Bob and Bob Thomas. *The Road to Hollywood: My Forty-Year Love Affair with the Movies.* Garden City, NY: Doubleday, 1977.

Houseman, John. *Run-Through: A Memoir.* New York: Simon & Schuster, 1972.

Howatson, Margaret. *The Oxford Companion to Classical Literature, Second Edition.* New York: Oxford Univ. Press, 1989.

Hughes, Glenn. *A History of the American Theatre: 1700–1950.* New York: S. French, 1951.

Huston, John. *An Open Book.* New York: Da Capo Press, 1994.

Jacobs, Lewis. *The Rise of the American Film: A Critical History.* New York: Harcourt Brace & Co., 1939.

Johnson, James Weldon. *Black Manhattan.* N. Stratford, NH: Ayer Company Publishers, 1969.

Kael, Pauline. *Deeper into Movies.* Boston: Little, Brown, 1973.

———. *I Lost It at the Movies: Film Writings, 1954–1965.* New York: Marion Boyars Publishers, 1993.

Koch, Howard. *As Time Goes By: Memoirs of a Writer.* New York: Harcourt Brace Jovanovich, 1979.

Lahr, John. *Astonish Me: Adventures in Contemporary Theater.* New York: Viking Press, 1973.

Lahr, John and Jonathan Price. *Life-Show: How to See Theater in Life and Life in Theater.* New York: Limelight Editions, 1989.

Lawrence, Hoe R. and Otto Hufeland. *Valentine's Manuals: A General Index to the Manual of the Corporation of the City of New York, 1841–1870.* Harrison, NY: Harbor Hills Books, 1981.

Levant, Oscar. *The Memoirs of an Amnesiac.* Hollywood, CA: Samuel French, 1989.

Mailer, Norman. *Marilyn: A Biography.* New York: Perigee Books, 1987.

Maltin, Leonard. *The Disney Films, Third Edition.* New York: Hyperion, 1995.

———. *The Great Movie Comedians: Updated Edition from Charlie Chaplin to Woody Allen.* New York: Harmony Books, 1982.

Mantzuis, Karl. *A History of the Theatrical Art in Ancient and Modern Times.* Magnolia, MA: Peter Smith Publishers, 1990.

Marx, Groucho. *The Groucho Letters: Letters from and to Groucho Marx.* New York: Da Capo Press, 1994.

Mulay, James J., ed. *The Horror Film: A Guide to More than 700 Films on Videocassette.* Evanston, IL: CiteBooks, 1989.

Norman, Barry. *The Story of Hollywood.* New York: NAL Books, 1988.

Peary, Danny. *Alternate Oscars: One Critic's Defiant Choices for Best Picture, Actor, and Actress from 1927 to the Present.* New York: Delta, 1993.

Perelman, S. J. *The Road to Miltown.* New York: Simon & Schuster, 1957.

Quinlan, David, ed. *The Film Lover's Companion: An A to Z Guide to 2,000 Stars and the Movies They Made.* Secaucus, NJ: Carol Publishing, 1999.

Rankin, Hugh F. *The Theater in Colonial America.* Chapel Hill, NC: Univ. of North Carolina Press, 1965.

Rebello, Stephen. *Alfred Hitchcock and the Making of Psycho.* New York: St. Martin's Press, 1999.

Reed, Rex. *Do You Sleep in the Nude?* New York: NAL Books, 1968.

Renoir, Jean. *My Life and My Films.* Trans. Norman Denny. New York: Da Capo Press, 1991.

Rosten, Leo C. *Hollywood: The Movie Colony, the Movie Makers.* N. Stratford, NH: Ayer Company Publishers, 1975.

Schemering, Christopher. *The Soap Opera Encyclopedia.* New York: Ballantine Books, 1988.

Schoenbaum, Samuel. *William Shakespeare: A Compact Documentary Life.* New York: Oxford Univ. Press, 1987.

Sennett, Mack. *King of Comedy.* Garden City, NY: Doubleday, 1954.

Shipman, David. *The Story of Cinema: A Complete Narrative History from the Beginnings to the Present.* New York: St. Martin's Press, 1986.

Simon, John. *Movies into Film: Film Criticism, 1967–1970.* New York: Dial Press, 1971.

Steinberg, Cobbett. *Reel Facts: The Movie Book of Records.* New York: Vintage Books, 1982.

Taubman, Howard. *The Making of the American Theatre.* New York: Coward-McCann, 1967.

Taylor, Robert L. *W. C. Fields.* New York: St. Martin's Press, 1989.

Terry, Ellen. *The Story of My Life.* New York: Schocken Books, 1982.

Truffaunt, Francois. *Hitchcock.* New York: Simon & Schuster, 1985.

Tynan, Kenneth. *Curtains: Selections from the Drama Criticism and Related Writings.* New York: Atheneum, 1961.

———. *Show People: Profiles in Entertainment.* New York: Simon & Schuster, 1979.

Urban, Joseph. *Theatres.* New York: Theatre Arts Books, 1929.

Wallace, Irving and David Wallechinsky. *The People's Almanac.* Garden City, NY: Doubleday, 1975.

Index

Aasen, Ivar Andreas, 112
Abbott, George, 326, 390
Abbott and Costello, 389
Abbott and Costello Meet Dr. Jekyll and Mr. Hyde, 204
Abide with Me, 345
Abie's Irish Rose, 148
Academy Award, 375
Academy of Motion Picture Arts and Sciences, 253
Acrobats, 362–63
The Actors Studio, Inc., 55
Addison, Joseph, 334
Adler, Jacob P., 19
The Adventures of Don Juan, 69
The Adventures of Priscilla, Queen of the Desert, 71
Aeschines, 335
Aeschylus, 85, 162, 398
Aesopus, 3
Afinogenov, Alexander Nikolayevich, 400
The African Queen, 75
African American actors and actresses, 53
L'Age d'Or (Buñuel and Dalí), 245
The Age of Innocence, 71
Agésilas (Pierre Corneille), 103
Ah, Wilderness! (Eugene O'Neill), 123, 153
Alabama, 150
"Alan Smithee," 173
An Alan Smithee Film: Burn Hollywood Burn, 173
Albee, Edward, 305
Aldridge, Ira, 53
Algiers, 361
Ali, George, 181
Ali, Hadji, 26
Alien, 202
All About Eve, 69, 279
All Quiet on the Western Front, 246
All That Jazz, 71
All the King's Men, 74
Allen, Fred, 48, 160

Allen, Gracie, 360
Amadeus, 71, 326
Ameche, 363
American Academy for Dramatic Arts, 55
An American in Paris, 69, 81
An American Tragedy, 154
An American Werewolf in London, 65, 197
Amorous Widow (Thomas Betterton), 7
The Amours of Philander and Sylvia (Aphra Behn), 105
Anchor, 363
Anderson, Eddie, 53
Anderson, Maxwell, 342
André (William Dunlap), 111–12
Androboros (Robert Hunter and Lewis Morris), 305
The Andromeda Strain, 201
Andromède (Pierre Corneille), 103
Anecdotes sur Fréron (Voltaire), 108
Animal actors, 175–82
Anna, 280
Anna & Bella, 191
Anna and the King of Siam, 80
Anna Christie, 41, 359
Anna Karenina (film), 41
Anne of a Thousand Days, 70
Annie Get Your Gun, 137
Annie Oakley, 363
Ann-Margret, 72
Antheil, George, 244–45
Anthony Adverse, 80
Antigone, 87, 398
Antiphanes, 87
Anvil Chorus, 364
The Apartment, 254
Apocalypse Now, 82
Arbuckle, Roscoe "Fatty," 232–33, 353
Aretino, Pietro, 403–4, 408
Aristophanes, 87, 394
Arliss, George, 403
Arms and the Man (George Bernard Shaw), 120

Arness, James, 199–200, 204
Arnold, Jack, 205
Aronson, Max, 138
Around the World in 80 Days, 81
L'Arroseur Arrosé, 137
As Good as It Gets, 360
Asner, Ed, 330
Astaire, Fred, 389, 393
Astor Place Riots, 240–41
Atkinson, Brooks, 392
The Attack of the Killer Tomatoes, 203
Attenborough, Richard, 62
Attila (Pierre Corneille), 103
The Auctioneer, 78–79
Augustus, 408
Auteur, 364
Avery, Tex, 191
Axelrod, George, 381

Bacall, Lauren, 55, 357, 398
Bacon, Francis, 93, 96, 346
Bad acting, 23–29
The Bad and the Beautiful, 69, 81
Bailey, Pearl, 53
Balance, 191
Baldwin, William, 92
Ball, Lucille, 72
Bambi, 187
Bancroft, Anne, 55
Bankhead, Tallulah, 345–46
Bara, Theda, 38
The Barber of Seville, 383
Bard, Wilkie, 31–32
Barnes, Clive, 345
Barnstorming, 224
Barnum, P. T., 134, 178, 247, 383, 409
Barrie, Sir James, 127–28, 374, 376, 411
Barry, Joan, 45
Barry Lyndon, 71, 82
Barrymore, Drew, 54
Barrymore, Ethel, 54
Barrymore, John, 38, 140, 164, 179, 204, 225, 345, 348, 362, 411
Barrymore, Lionel, 359, 402
Barrymore, Maurice, 54, 401–2
Bart Simpson, 367
Bassett, Angela, 53
Battle of Angels, 347
Battleground, 81
Baum, L. Frank, 374
Baxter, Warner, 403
Bayes, Nora, 394

"Beam Me Up, Scotty," 364
The Beast from 20,000 Fathoms, 200
Beat the Devil, 359
Beatty, Warren, 360
Beau Geste, 283
Beaumont, Francis, 396
Beaumont and Fletcher, 98–99, 215
Beauty and the Beast, 189, 254
Beauvoir, Simone de, 131
Beckett, Samuel, 129–30
Beddoes, Thomas Lovell, 99
Bedtime for Bonzo, 180
Beerbohm, Max, 341, 411
Beethoven, Ludwig van, 409
Beetlejuice, 66
Before Breakfast (Eugene O'Neill), 5
The Beggar's Opera, 250, 406
Behan, Brendan, 346
"Behind the scenes," 212
Behn, Aphra, 105
Bel Canto, 364
Benchley, Robert, 155, 342–43, 403
Benét, Stephen Vincent, 160
Ben-Hur, 55, 70, 81
Benjy, 178
Bennett, Arnold, 410
Bennett, Constance, 403
Bergen, Edgar, 281
Bergman, Ingrid, 56, 358
Berle, Milton, 330
Berlin, Irving, 344, 391
Bernard, Tristan, 130
Bernhardt, Sarah, 19–21, 140, 338, 341, 361
Best Boy, 364
The Best Years of Our Lives, 141, 197
Betterton, Thomas, 7, 27
Betty, William Henry West, 9
Betty Boop, 188
Beyond a Reasonable Doubt, 169
Beyond the Forest, 360
Beyond the Horizon (Eugene O'Neill), 123
The Bicycle Thief, 55
Big Daddy, 365
The Big Parade, 165
The Bird of Paradise (Richard Walton Tully), 130
The Birds, 167, 202
Birds Anonymous, 190
The Birth of a Nation, 155, 163, 353
Bishop, Julie, 389
The Biter (Nicholas Rowe), 107
The Black Crook, 219–20

INDEX   421

Black Narcissus, 80
The Black Swan, 79, 80
Blackboard Jungle, 380
Blacklist, 161–62
Blackmail, 166
Blackout, 365
Blacula, 201
Blair, Linda, 74
Blake, Eubie, 391
Blanc, Mel, 191
Blithe Spirit (Noël Coward), 110
The Blob, 200
Blondin, 16
Blood and Sand, 80
The Blood Beast Terror, 203
The Blood-Red Knight, 177
Blue Movies, 365
Boards, 365
Bob's Birthday, 191
Bogart, Humphrey, 56, 75, 203, 357–59, 361, 369, 398
Bogdanovich, Peter, 77, 166
La Bohème (Puccini), 34
Boileau-Despréaux, Nicolas, 408
Bois, Curt, 392
Bolton, Guy, 391
Bonanza, 204
Bonnie and Clyde, 82, 360
Bonzo, 179–80
Booth, Edwin, 13, 54
Booth, John Wilkes, 13, 54, 232, 234–37, 396, 409
Booth, Junius Brutus, 54
Born Yesterday, 72
Bound East for Cardiff (Eugene O'Neill), 221
Bound for Glory, 82
Bovée, Christian Nestell, 409
Bow, Clara, 38
Bowdler, Thomas, 349
Bowdlerization, 349–50
Bowery Theatre, 217, 239, 242
The Box, 190
Box office, 214
Boxes, 214
Boyer, Charles, 361
Bracegirdle, Anne, 7
Bram Stoker's Dracula, 66, 71, 192
Brandes, Georg Morris, 335–36
Brando, Marlon, 51, 56, 69, 279, 283, 359
Braveheart, 66, 83
Break a Leg!, 365

Breakfast at Tiffany's, 69
Brecht, Bertolt, 56, 169, 209
Brennan, Walter, 279, 360
Brewster's Millions (Winchell Smith), 63
Brice, Fanny, 135
The Bridge on the River Kwai, 81
Brief Encounter, 286
"Bringing down the house," 214–15
Broadcast News, 280
Broadhurst, George, 391
Broadway, origins of, 219–20
The Broadway Melody, 254
Broadway Melody of 1938, 43
Broadway theaters, 220–21
The Broken Sword, 374–75
Bronson, Charles, 204
Brooks, Louise, 72
Brooks, Richard, 133, 380
The Brotherhood of Passion, 209–10
Broun, Heywood, 28
Brown, Joe E., 225
Bruno, Giordano, 335
Brynner, Yul, 75, 201, 285, 411
Buffalo Bill. *See* Cody, Buffalo Bill
Bugs Bunny, 191
Bugsy, 71
Bulwer-Lytton, Edward George, 339
Bunker, Chang and Eng, 14–15
Bunny, 191
Buñuel, Luis, 245
Burbage, James, 22, 210–11
Burbage, Richard, 5–6, 22, 210, 215, 405
Burke, John Daly, 397, 399
Burlesque, 33
Burns, George, 1, 280, 360, 391
Burton, Richard, 282
Bushman, Francis X., 39
Butch Cassidy and the Sundance Kid, 82
Buying Back the Nut, 366
Byron, Lord, 109, 333, 409

Cabaret, 82
Cabin in the Cotton, 359
The Cabinet of Dr. Caligari, 198–99
Cagney, Jimmy, 357, 361
Caine, Michael, 57
Caligula, 234–35
Call Me Madam, 359
Calment, Louise, 390
Camelot, 70
Cameramen, 79–83
Camille, 41, 126

Camoes, Luiz Vaz de, 408
Campbell, Barley, 385
Camus, Albert, 131
Cancan, 366
Candide, 369
Cannes Film Festival, 286–97
Cantor, Eddie, 135
Cantzen, Conrad, 50
Canutt, Yamika, 63
Capek, Karel, 197
Capra, Frank, 43, 145
The Captain Hates the Sea, 148
The Capture of Meletus (Phrynichus), 86
The Caravan, or The Driver and His Dog (Frederick Reynolds), 176–77
The Careless Husband (Colley Cibber), 104
Carey, Henry, 30
Carey, Jim, 49
Carlton, Henry Guy, 122–23
Carmen (Bizet), 28
Carousel, 137
Carrie, 327
Carroll, Leo G., 200
Carroll, Madeleine, 358
Cartoon characters, 182–92
Caruso, Enrico, 28, 34–35, 410
Casablanca, 56, 358
"Casey at the Bat" (Ernest Laurence Thayer), 18
The Cat Concerto, 189
Cat People, 199
Catcher in the Rye (J. D. Salinger), 225–26
Cather, Willa, 156
Catherine the Great, 104, 361
Catherine Was Great, 357
Cats, 74, 304
Caviar to the General, 366
Censors, 352–55
Censorship, 349–51
Cervantes, Miguel, 100–101
Chairman of the Board, 366
Champ, 225
The Champ, 165
Chaney, Lon, Jr., 196–97
Chaney, Lon, Sr., 65–67, 192
Chaplin, Charlie, 42–45, 50, 59, 166, 246, 280, 331, 344
Charade, 191
Chariots of Fire, 71
Chatrain, Alexander, 98
Chauvin, Nicolas, 113
Che!, 285

Chekhov, Anton, 115–16, 339, 347, 398, 409
Cher, 280
The Cherry Orchard, 392
Cherry Sisters, 24–25
Chew Up the Scenery, 366
Chic Sale, 366–67
Chikamatsu Monzaemon (Sugimori Nobunori), 97–98, 229
Children Shouldn't Play with Dead Things, 204
Chimes at Midnight, 169
Choreography, 172–73
Christie, Agatha, 128, 304
A Christmas Carol, 190
Chrononhotonthologos, the Most Tragical Tragedy That Ever Was Tragedized by Any Company of Tragedians (Henry Carey), 30
Churchill, Winston, 361
Cibber, Colley, 27, 104, 399
Cibber, Theophilus, 399
Cinderella, 401
Cineast, 367
Cinema Verité, 367
Citizen Kane, 42, 169–70
City Lights, 44
Claque(s), 60
Clarke, Creston, 345
Cleopatra, 70, 79–81
Cleopatre Captive (Etienne Jodelle), 4
Close, Glenn, 280
Close Encounters of the Third Kind, 82, 202
A Close Shave, 191
Closed Mondays, 190
Coates, Ronald, 23–24
La Cocarde Tricolor (Cogniard, Charles and Jean), 113
Cocking, George, 305
The Cocoanuts, 344
Cody, Buffalo Bill (William Frederick), 50, 136, 139, 410
Cohan, George M., 129, 141, 153
Cohn, Harry, 145, 148
Colbert, Claudette, 359, 392
Colette, 243
Collaborators, 98
Collier, John Payne, 391
The Color Purple, 375
Colosseum, 207–8
Come and Go (Samuel Beckett), 129
The Comédie-Française, 210

Comedy in Music, 304
Computers, 75
Comstock, Anthony, 352
Comstockery, 385
Congo, 181
Connelly, Marc, 392
Connery, Sean, 358
The Conqueror, 285
Conquest, Fred, 182
The Conquest of Canada, or The Siege of Quebec (George Cocking), 305
The Contrast (Royall Tyler), 305
Convent Garden Theatre, 238
Conway, William, 397
Coogan, Jackie, 48–49, 59
Cooke, George Frederick, 395
Cooper, Gary, 64, 254, 279, 358, 359
Cooper, Gladys, 56
Cooper, Jackie, 179
Coquette, 362
Corneille, Pierre, 103–4
Cornell, Katharine, 394
The Corpse Grinders, 204
Cosby, Bill, 53
Costner, Kevin, 284
Costume design, 68–72
The Count of Monte Cristo, 28, 170
Countdown, 169
The Country Cousin, 189
The Country Wife (William Wycherly), 105
Covent Garden Theatre, 246
Cowabunga!, 367
Coward, Noël, 50, 110, 125–26, 341, 412
Crac, 191
Crane, Cheryl, 233
Crawford, Cheryl, 55
Crawford, F. Marion, 409
Crawford, Joan, 42, 72–73, 281
Creature Comforts, 191
The Creature from the Black Lagoon, 205
Crébillon, Prosper Jolyot de, 335, 393–94
Cries and Whispers, 82
Critic, 367
The Critic, 27, 109, 190, 336, 337
Critics, 333–51
Cromwell, 70
Cronyn, Hume, 55, 394
Crosby, Bing, 403, 412
Crosland, Alan, 140
The Crowd, 62, 165
Cruise, Tom, 49, 284

The Crunch Bird, 190
Cry All the Way to the Bank, 367
Cukor, George, 166, 280
Cullum, John, 326
Cumberland, Richard, 337
The Curse of Dracula, 193
Curtain Call, 367
Curtain Speech, 368
Curtis, Tony, 358
Cut, 368
Cutaway, 368
Cutthroat Island, 148, 284
Cyrano de Bergerac (Edmond Rostand), 71, 126–27, 129, 368

Da Silva, Antonio José, 397, 399
Dadaists, 244
Dafne (Ottavio Rinuccini), 92
Dalí, Salvador, 245
La Dame aux Camélias, 20, 21, 393
Damn Yankees, 390
The Dance of the Vampires, 201
Dances with Wolves, 82
Dane, Clemence, 110–11
Danger, 149
Dangerous Liasons, 71
D'Annunzio, Gabriele, 21, 230
Dark, 368
Dark Victory, 283
Darling, 70
Darwell, Jane, 360
Dauvilliers, Nicolas, 399
D'Avenant, Sir William, 95
Davies, Marion, 42
Davis, Bette, 55, 359, 360
Davis, Ossie, 53
Davis, Sammy, Jr., 53, 379
Davison, John, 400
The Day the Earth Stood Still, 200
Days of Heaven, 82
De Havilland, Olivia, 254
De Niro, Robert, 51
De Sade, 163
De Sica, Vittorio, 55
De Vega (Carpio), Lope (Felix), 99–100
Deacon Brodie, or The Double Life, 198
The Dead, 174
Dean, James, 69, 396
Death on the Nile, 71
Deaths, 389–411
Deed, André, 45
The Deer, 245

The Defiant Ones, 81
DeMille, Cecil B., 73, 148, 173
Dennis, John, 334
Desire Caught by the Tail (Pablo Picasso), 131
Desire Under the Elms (Eugene O'Neill), 221
Le Desrin de Pierre, 361
deus ex machina, 209
The Devil Tavern, 215
Diamond, William, 374–75
The Diary of Anne Frank, 81
DiCaprio, Leonardo, 49
Dick Tracy, 66
Dick Turpin's Ride to York, 177
Diddle, 368
Dietrich, Marlene, 38, 69, 360
Digital film restoration, 83
DiMaggio, Joe, 407
Dinsdale, Shirley, 330
Directors, 162–74
Dish houses, 225
Disney, Walt, 182–87, 189–90, 279, 281, 355
Dissolve, 369
Doctor Zhivago, 70, 82
The Doctor's Experiment, or Reversing Darwin's Theory, 198
Dodsworth, 141
The Dog of Montargis (Guilbert de Pixérecourt), 177
La Dolce Vita, 70
A Doll's House, 339
Domingo, Placido, 61
Don Giovanni, 361
Don Juan, 140
Don Quixote, 100–101, 177
Donne, John, 403
"Don't Bogart That Joint," 369
"Don't Fence Me In," 369
Dostoyevsky, Fyodor, 5, 334
The Dot and the Line, 190
Double Indemnity, 174, 359
Douglas, Kirk, 204
Downstage, 369
Dr. Faustus (film), 169
Dr. Jekyll and Mr. Hyde, 197–98, 204
Dr. Pangloss, 369
Dr. Terror's House of Horror, 203
Dracula, 192–93
Dracula movies, 193–94
The Drama of King Shotaway, 53
Dressler, Marie, 49

Drew, Georgiana, 54
Drew, John, 54
Dreyfuss, Richard, 280
Driscoll, Bobby, 281
Driving Miss Daisy, 66, 280
Drop, 369
Drums Along the Mohawk, 283
Drury Lane Theatre, 12, 109, 176, 213, 228, 234, 246, 248, 252, 399
Dryden, John, 1, 5, 98, 212, 232, 334, 394, 404
Duel in the Sun, 165
The Duenna (Richard Brinsley Sheridan), 108–9
Dumas, Alexandre *fils*, 126
Dumas, Alexandre *père*, 11, 340, 371, 393
Duncan, Isadora, 50, 400, 410
Dunlap, William, 111
Durante, Jimmy, 225, 362, 389
Durbin, Deanna, 281
Dürrenmatt, Friedrich, 394
Duse, Eleonora, 1, 20–21, 67–68, 230, 410
Duvall, Robert, 51
Dwan, Allen, 77
The Dying Swan, 62

Eagels, Jeanne, 410
Eastwood, Clint, 170, 359
Easy Rider, 369
Ebsen, Buddy, 55
L'Ècole des Femmes (Molière), 241
The Ed Sullivan Show, 178
Ed Wood, 66
Edison, Thomas, 139, 237, 378, 410
El Burlador de Sevilla, 361
Electra (Euripides), 87
The Elephant Man, 68
L'Elisir d'amore, 61
Elizabeth, 66
Elmer Fudd, 191
Emcee, 373
The Emmys, 330
Emney, Fred, 401
The Emperor Jones (Eugene O'Neill), 221
Empire, 285
The Empire Strikes Back, 49
The English Patient, 71, 83
The Entertainer, 51
Entr'acte, 370
Epitaphs, 403–7
Erckmann, Emile, 98
Erkmann Chatrain, 98

Ersatz (The Substitute), 190
L'Escossaise (Voltaire), 108
E.T. the Extra-Terrestrial, 198, 202, 370
Etherege, George, 234
Euripides, 87–88, 162, 335, 394, 398
Evans, Maurice, 201
Every Which Way but Loose, 180
Exiles (Tristan Bernard), 130
The Exorcist, 74

The Facts of Life, 70
Fade-Out, 370
The Fair Jilt (Aphra Behn), 105
Fairbanks, 370
Fairbanks, Douglas, Jr., 370
Fairbanks, Douglas, Sr., 411
Falling in Love Again, 166
Family Hour, 370
Fanny and Alexander, 71, 82
Fantasia, 83
The Fantasticks, 304
A Farewell to Arms, 80
The Farmer's Daughter, 281
Farquhar, George, 5, 216, 396
Farrel, Charles, 400–401
Farren Riots, 242
Fatal Attraction, 280
The Father (William Dunlap), 111
Faulkner, William, 156
Federico Fellini's 8½, 70
Fellini's Casanova, 71
Ferber, Edna, 54
Ferdinand the Bull, 189
Feydeau, Georges, 348
Fictitious names, 63
Fiddler on the Roof, 82
Field, Eugene, 345
Field, Nathan, 397
Fielding, Henry, 104
Fields, W. C., 46–47, 53, 56, 135, 159, 403
Fifteen Years of a Drunken Life, 340
Film, longest, 285
Films, worst, 285
Finch, Peter, 360
Fires, 246–50
Fitzgerald, F. Scott, 160–61, 411
Fitzgerald, Zelda, 160
The Flame and the Arrow, 64
Flowers and Trees, 189
Fly, 370
The Fly, 66, 191, 200
Flynn, Errol, 55, 164

Fonda, Bridget, 53
Fonda, Henry, 53, 280
Fonda, Jane, 53
Fonda, Peter, 53, 69
Fontaine, Joan, 254
Fontanne, Lynn, 391, 394
Foote, Samuel, 5, 29, 212, 351
For Scent-Imental Reasons, 189
Ford, Harrison, 49, 69
Ford, John, 279
Ford's Theatre, 235, 237
Forrest, Edwin, 112, 240–41
Forrest Gump, 360
Forty-Five Minutes from Broadway (George M. Cohan), 129
La Forza del Destino, 401
Foster, Stephen, 409
The Fountainhead, 165
The Four P's (William Baldwin), 92
Fourth Network of Noise (Luigi Russolo), 244
Fowler, Gene, 411
Fox, George Washington Lafayette, 67, 229–30
Fox, Vivica A., 53
Frame, 370
Frank Film, 190
Frankenstein, 194–97
Frankenstein films, 196
Frédéric, Jean, 391
Frederick, William. *See* Cody, Buffalo Bill
A Free Soul, 54
Free Willy, 180
Freeman, Morgan, 53
French Revolution, 237–38
Fréron, Eli Catherine, 108
Friars Club, 23
Friday the Thirteenth, 371
Frohman, Charles, 410
From Here to Eternity, 72, 81
Der Führer's Face, 189
A Funny Thing Happened on the Way to the Forum, 390

Gable, Clark, 42–43, 69, 357, 403
Gabor, Zsa Zsa, 39
Gallagher and Shean, 32
Galloping Gaucho, 184
Galsworthy, John, 410
Gambling, John, 331
Gandhi, 62, 71, 82

Garbo, Greta, 38, 40–42, 55, 69, 72–73, 359
Gardiner, Charles A., 63
Gardner, Ava, 72–73
Garland, Judy, 43, 59, 281
Garner, Peggy Ann, 281
Garrick, David, 8–9, 22, 30, 122, 213, 337, 399, 408
Garrick, George, 399
Garson, Greer, 254
Gate of Hell, 69
Gauguin, Paul, 254
Gay, John, 250, 406
The General Died at Dawn, 358
Gentle Ben, 179
Gentleman Jim, 164
Gentleman's Agreement, 281
Gentlemen Prefer Blondes, 154, 358
George II, 333
"George Spelvin," 63
Gerald McBoing-Boing, 190
Geri's Game, 191
The Ghost Walk, 371
Ghosts, 339
Gibbs, Wolcott, 345
Gibson, Mel, 49
Gide, André, 411
Gigi, 70, 79, 81
Gil Blas (Alain-René Lesage), 106
Gilbert, John, 39, 41, 55, 148
Gilbert and Sullivan, 98, 118–19, 377, 400
Gilda, 71, 358
Gilpen, Charles, 53
Un Giorno di Regno (Verdi), 113
The Girl from Rector's (Paul Potter), 251
Globe Theatre, 211–12, 246
Glory, 82
God and Mammon, 400
The Godfather, 174, 359
The Godfather: Part II, 359
The Godfather: Part III, 359
Godfrey, Thomas, 10, 396
Godfrey, Thomas, the Younger, 305
Goethe, Johann Wolfgang von, 409
Gogol, Nikolai, 5
The Gold Rush, 44
"The Goldbergs," 331
Goldblum, Jeff, 200
Goldoni, Carlo, 107
Goldsmith, Oliver, 122, 408
Goldwyn, Samuel, 54, 141–45, 147, 412
Goldwyn, Tony, 54
"Goldwynisms," 141–44
The Golem, 194
Goncourt, Edmond and Jules, 98
Gondibert, 95
Gone with the Wind, 42–43, 55, 80, 147, 165, 254, 283, 284, 357, 360
The Good Earth, 80
Goodbye, Mr. Chips, 283
The Goodbye Girl, 280
Gooding, Cuba, Jr., 53
Goodman, Cardonell "Scum," 228
Gordon, Ruth, 55
Gorillas, 181
Gorillas in the Mist, 181
Gorky, Maksim, 50
Gossett, Lou, Jr., 53
Gösta Berlings Saga, 40
Gould, Elliott, 166
Grable, Betty, 225, 371, 389
Grable-Bodied Seamen, 371
Grand Illusion, 246
"Grand Old Opry," 331
Grant, Cary, 51, 54, 55, 357
Grant, Jennifer, 54
The Grapes of Wrath, 360
Grauman's Chinese Theater, 225
Gravelet, Jean François, 16
Grayson, Kathryn, 72
Great, 190
The Great Dictator, 44, 246
Great Expectations, 80
The Great Gatsby, 71
The Great Train Robbery, 138, 347
The Great Waltz, 79, 80
Great White Way theaters, 220–21
Greco, José, 389
Greece, ancient, 1–2, 162, 207–8
Greek drama, 85–91
A Greek Tragedy, 191
Greene, Robert, 334, 396
Greenroom, 213
Greenstreet, Sydney, 358, 360
Greville, 9
Greystoke: The Legend of Tarzan, Lord of the Apes, 66
Grier, Rosey, 201
Griffith, D. W., 154–55, 163–64, 346, 353
Grimaldi, Joseph, 12
Grip, 371
Guillaume, Gros, 397, 398, 399
Guitry, Lucien, 337–38
Gulliver on His Travels, 176

INDEX

Gunga Din, 283
Gunsmoke, 204
Guy Domville, 347
Guys and Dolls, 141

Haines, William, 403
Hairstyling, 72–73
The Hairy Ape, 181, 221
Haley, Bill, 245
Haley, Jack, 55
Hall, Irma, 53
Hamlet, 4, 5, 20, 69, 333, 346, 371, 395–96
Hammerstein, Oscar, 31, 136
Hammerstein, Oscar, II, 137, 281
Hammond, Percy, 346
Hangmen Also Die, 169
Hanks, Tom, 51, 279, 360
Hans Christian Andersen, 69
Hardy, Alexandre, 101
Hardy, Thomas, 393, 400
Harlow, Jean, 156, 358, 403
Harrigan and Hart, 32
Harris, Frank, 389–90
Harris, Jed, 362
Harris, Julie, 55, 326
Harry and the Hendersons, 66
"Harry Selby," 63
Hart, Charles, 6
Hart, Moss, 57
Hasty Pudding Club, 23
Hattan, Rondo, 68
Hawk, Bob, 381
Hawks, Howard, 156
Hayes, Helen, 362, 392, 394
Hays, Will Harrison, 353
Hays Code, 353
Hayward, Susan, 281
Hayworth, Rita, 71, 145, 358
Head, Edith, 68–72, 279
Hearst, William Randolph, 42
The Hearts of Age, 169
Hearts of the World, 163
Hedda Gabler, 116, 339
Heggen Thomas, 396
Heiberg, Gunnar, 27–28
The Heiress, 69
Held, Anna, 18–19, 135
Hellman, Lillian, 130–31
Hell's Angels, 358
Helm, Brigitte, 392
Helmore, Tom, 392
Hemingway, Ernest, 156

Hemion, Dwight, 330
Hemmond, Percy, 343
Hendrickson, Robert, 346
Henry, John, 10
Henry IV, 93, 97–98
Henry V, 71
Henry VI, 215
Henry VIII, 93, 98, 211
Hepburn, Audrey, 69
Hepburn, Katharine, 69, 279, 345
Herb Alpert and the Tijuana Brass Double Feature, 190
Hernani (Victor Hugo), 242
Herod and Mariamme (Samuel Pordage), 232
Heston, Charlton, 55
Hewlett, James, 53
Heywood, Thomas, 100–101
High Sierra, 56
"Hill Street Blues," 330
Une Histoire de Vent, 166
Histrionics, 3
Hitchcock, Alfred, 75, 166–69
H.M.S. Pinafore (Gilbert and Sullivan), 118
Hoffenstein, Samuel Gordon, 154
Hoffman, Dustin, 51, 279, 353
Hold Back the Dawn, 254
The Hole, 190
Holland, George, 223–24
Holly, Ellen, 53
Hollywood, 225
Hollywood Canteen, 369
Holmes, Burt, 384
Holtei, Karl Eduard von, 5
Hood and Ladder, 345
The hook, 218–19
Hootchie-kootchie, 34
Hope, Anthony, 346
Hope, Bob, 331
Hopkins, Anthony, 51, 358
Hopper, De Wolf, 18
Horne, Lena, 72
The Horror of Party Beach, 203, 285
Horses, 177, 181
Houdini, Harry, 36
House of Wax, 204
House on Fire, 75
How Green Was My Valley, 80
How to Sleep, 155
Howard, Charles, 407
Howard, Joe, 391
Hoyt, Charles, 397
Hubbock, Chris, 412

Hud, 81
Hughes, Margaret, 6
Hughes, Richard, 148–49
Hugo, Victor, 242, 409
Hull, Shelley, 397
Hume, David, 334
Humpty Dumpty, 230
The Hunchback of Notre Dame, 66, 199
Hunter, Holly, 280
Hunter, Kim, 201
Hurricane in Galveston, 166
Hurt, John, 68
The Hustler, 81
Huston, John, 69, 174
Hyder Ali, or The Lions of Mysore, 176

I Married a Monster from Outer Space, 200
I Remember Mama (Rodgers and Hammerstein), 137
I Walked with a Zombie, 199
I Was a Teenage Werewolf, 204
Ibsen, Henrik, 116–17, 338–39, 409
The Iceman Cometh (Eugene O'Neill), 50
Ilgenfritx, McNair, 129
I'll Cry Tomorrow, 70
Improvisator, 371
In Praise of Love (Terence Rattigan), 130
The Incredible Shrinking Man, 200
Indian Emperor (John Dryden), 5
The Inspector General (Nikolai Gogol), 5
Insurance, 389
Intermezzo, 283
Intolerance, 154, 163
The Invisible Man, 199
The Ireland Hoax, 239–40
Irene, 8
Ironweed, 280
Iroquois Theatre fire, 248–49
Is It Always Right to Be Right?, 190
The Island of Lost Souls, 358
It Came from Beneath the Sea, 203
It Happened One Night, 43, 69, 254, 359
It's So Nice to Have a Wolf Around the House, 191
It's Tough to Be a Bird, 190
Ivens, Joris, 166, 392

Jackson, Joe, 401
James, Henry, 347
James Bond, 358
Jandl, Ivan, 281
Jarman, Claude, Jr., 281

Jarry, Alfred, 119–20
Jason and the Argonauts, 197
Jaws, 198, 201–2
The Jazz Singer, 55, 140, 387
Jeritza, Maria, 28
Jerrold, Douglas, 340
Jessel, George, 55, 140, 403
JFK, 82
Jim Crow, 372
Joan of Arc, 80
Jodelle, Etienne, 4
"The Joe Franklin Show," 331
Johann Mouse, 190
Johnson, Nunnally, 154
Johnson, Samuel, 8, 27, 333
Jolie, Angelina, 54
Jolson, Al, 55, 140, 225, 387, 403, 411
Jones, George, 12
Jones, James, 155
Jones, James Earl, 53
Jones, Tommy Lee, 49, 69
Jonson, Ben, 4, 5, 95–96, 98, 215, 231, 334, 394, 406
Juan, Don, 361
Julius Caesar, 374
Jumbo, 178
Jurassic Park, 198, 202, 284

Kael, Pauline, 347
Kaiser, George, 128–29
Kalidasa, 91
Kambert, Isabel, 391
Kane, Helen, 188
Kanin, Garson, 345
Karl the Peddler (Charles A. Gardiner), 63
Karloff, Boris, 194–97, 199
Kaufman, George S., 29, 54, 57, 156, 343–44, 362, 411
Kazan, Elia, 55–56, 153
Kean, Edmund, 11, 22, 395, 409
Kean (Alexandre Dumas), 11
Keaton, Buster, 46
Kelly, Grace, 72–73
Kendrick, Rhonda Ross, 54
Kennedy, John F., 71, 331, 379
Kennedy, Madge, 28
Kenny, James, 368
Kern, Jerome, 137, 281
Kerr, Walter, 345
Key Largo, 133, 359
The Kid, 44, 48, 59
Kiley, Richard, 326

The Killing Fields, 82
Kinescope, 372
King, Henry, 64
The King and I, 70, 137
King George III, 234
King Kong, 73–74, 79, 199
King Lear, 349
King Lion, 345
King Solomon's Mines, 81
The King's Henchman, 92
Kingsley, Ben, 62
Kirby, J. Hudson, 26–27
Kirkland, Sally, 280
Kleist, Heinrich von, 397
Klieg lights, 77–78
Knighty Knight, Bugs, 190
Knipper, Olga, 392
Knute Rockne—All-American, 386
Kotzebue, August von, 232
Kreisler, Fritz, 244
Kronenberger, Louis, 346
Kruger, Otto, 392

Laban, Rudolph, 172–73
Labanotation, 172–73
Lady Be Good, 281
Lady in the Moon, 169
Laine, Jimmy Lee, 412
Lake, Veronica, 73
Lamarr, Hedy, 73, 403
Lamb, Charles, 348
Lambs Club, 23
Lancaster, Burt, 55, 64
Landis, John, 250
Landon, Michael, 204
Lang, Fritz, 169, 392
Langtry, Lillie, 372
Langtry Fever, 372
Lapine, James, 326
Larson, Jonathan, 397
Lassie, 179
The Last Chance, 286
The Last Emperor, 71, 82
The Last Will of Dr. Mabuse, 169
Last words, 389–411
Laughton, Charles, 358
Laura, 80
Laurel and Hardy, 46
Lavaliere, 372
Lawford, Peter, 379
Lawrence, Florence, 151–52
Lawrence of Arabia, 81

"Lay them in the aisles," 223
Le Bovier, Bernard, 391, 393
Leave Her to Heaven, 79, 80
Leavitt, Michael, 392
Lee, Canada, 53
Lee, Christopher, 193
Lee, Gypsy Rose, 33
Lee, Nathaniel, 106, 398, 399
Legends of the Fall, 83
Leigh, Vivien, 360
Leighton, Jan, 51
Leisure, 190
Lend a Paw, 189
Leonardo da Vinci, 75
Les Girls, 70
Lesage, Alain-René, 106
Lessing, Gotthold Ephriam, 108
Lettieri, Al, 359
Lewis, Robert, 55
Lewis, Rudolf, 343
Lex the Wonderdog, 166
The Liar (Samuel Foote), 212
The Life of an American Fireman, 138
Life with Father, 343
Lifeboat, 167
"Lili Marleen," 373
Lillies of the Field, 254
Limelight, 78
Limelight, 44
Lincoln, Abraham, 54, 232, 234–37
Lind, Jenny, 14
Linder, Max, 45
Ling, Sydney, 166
The Lion King, 187
Little Big Man, 65
Little Caesar, 359
The Little Foxes, 141
Little House on the Prairie, 204
The Little Orphan, 189
Little White Bird, 127, 376
Lloyd, Harold, 46
Lloyd's of London, 389
The Lodger, 166
Lohengrin, 385
Lombard, Carole, 43
London After Midnight, 192
Lone Ranger, 331, 373
Long Day's Journey into Night, 123–24
The Longest Day, 81, 155
Longest film, 285
Longest words, 30
Loos, Anita, 154

Lorca, Federico García, 397
Lorre, Peter, 153, 360
Lost Horizon (remake), 285
A Lost Lady, 156
The Lost Weekend, 286–87
Louis XIV, 372
Louisiana Story, 308
Love Is a Many-Splendored Thing, 70
Love's Labor's Lost, 96
Love's Last Shift (Colley Cibber), 104
Luce, Clare Booth, 345
Lugosi, Bela, 192–93, 195–96
Lunt, Alfred, 394
Lust for Life, 254
Lynch, David, 68

MacArthur, Charles, 394
Macbeth, 380
Macbeth, 76, 169, 177, 349
Macguffin, 168–69
Macklin, Charles, 76, 228–29, 391
MacMurray, Fred, 359
Macready, William Charles, 240–41
Mad Max, 284
Maeterlinck, Maurice, 145, 411
The Magnificent Ambersons, 169
Mailer, Norman, 43
Makeup, and makeup artists, 64–68
Le Malade Imaginaire (*The Imaginary Invalid*) (Molière), 103
Malaprop(s), 110–11
The Maltese Falcon, 56, 360
Man and Superman, 120, 382
A Man For All Seasons, 70, 82, 326
The Man Inside (Roland Molineaux), 231
Man of a Thousand Faces, 67
The Man of Mode (George Etherege), 234
The Man They Could Not Hang, 199
The Man Who Came to Dinner (Moss Hart and George S. Kaufman), 57
The Man Who Knew Too Much, 166
The Man Who Planted Trees, 191
The Man with the Golden Arm, 56
Manipulation, 191
Mann, Thomas, 157
Manson, Charles, 201, 233
March, Fredric, 197, 204, 279, 403
Marcus, Lawrence B., 64
María Candelaria, 286
Marie Antoinette, 72
Marlowe, Christopher, 93, 214, 231, 396
Martin, Dean, 379

Martin, John, 10
Le Martyre de Saint Sebastien (Gabriele D'Annunzio), 230
Marx, Groucho, 146
Marx Brothers, 47–48, 146, 344
"The Mary Tyler Moore Show," 330
Masefield, John, 392
Mask, 66
The Master Builder, 116, 339
Mastroianni, Chiara, 54
Mastroianni, Marcello, 54
Mata Hari, 36
Mathews, Charles, 409
Matthews, Albert Edward "Matty," 392
Mature, Victor, 73
Maugham, Somerset, 56, 392, 412
Mayer, Louis B., 72, 140–41
Mazeppa, 177
Mazza, Angelo, 371
MC, 373
McCambridge, Mercedes, 74
McCarey, Leo, 168
McCarthy, Charlie, 281
McClintic, Guthrie, 394
McDaniel, Hattie, 53, 254
McDowell, Roddy, 201
McGuire, Dorothy, 281
McQueen, Steve, 200
Meanwhile Back at the Ranch, 373
"Meet the Press," 331
Melba, Dame Nellie, 35–36
Men In Black, 66
Men Without Wings, 286
Menander, 88–89, 398
The Merchant of Venice, 228, 349
Méreimée, Prosper, 112–13
The Mermaid (tavern), 215
Merman, Ethel, 359
Merrick, David, 346
Merrie Melodies, 191–92
The Merry Wives of Windsor, 94
Metamora, or The Last of the Wampanoags (John Augustus Stone), 112
The Metaphor, 165
Method school, 55
Metro-Goldwyn-Mayer, 140–41, 147, 153
Metropolis, 392
Mickey Mouse, 182–86, 225, 355
Midnight Cowboy, 254, 353
A Midsummer Night's Dream, 80, 333
The Mikado, 118, 377
The Milky Way, 189

INDEX 431

Milland, Ray, 201
Millay, Edna St. Vincent, 92
Miller, Arthur, 112
Miller, Joe (Josias), 7–8
Miller, Marilyn, 135
Mills, Hayley, 281
Ming Huang, 209
Minzner, Wilson, 410
The Miracle, 341
Miracle on 34th Street, 158
Le Misanthrope (Molière), 4
The Misfits, 43
The Mission, 82
Mississippi Burning, 82
Mister Magoo's Puddle Jumper, 190
Mizner, Wilson, 159
Mnester, 234–35
Mock epitaphs, 402–3
Modern Times, 44
Moguls, 133–74
Moguls, first, 137–38
Mohammed, Messenger of God, 245
Molière, Jean-Baptiste Poquelin, 4, 102–3, 213–14, 335–36, 361, 394, 401, 408
Molineaux, Roland, 231
Molnár, Ferenc, 338
Momus, 373
Mona Lisa Descending a Staircase, 191
Monroe, Marilyn, 38, 40, 43, 55, 71–73, 357, 358, 381, 397, 407
Monsieur Verdoux, 44
Monsters, 192–205
Montez, Lola, 13–14
Moonbird, 190
Moonstruck, 280
Moron(s), 103
Morris, 179
Morrow, Vic, 250
Morton, Thomas, 111
"The Most Unkindest Cut of All," 374
Mother Courage, 56
Mourning Becomes Electra, 281
Mouse Trouble, 189
The Mousetrap, 128, 304
Mozart, 361
Mr. Smith Goes to Washington, 283, 360
Mrs. Doubtfire, 66
Mrs. Miniver, 79, 80, 254
Mrs. Warren's Profession, 351–52, 385
Much Ado About Nothing, 110
The Mummy, 199
Munchkin, 374

Munden, Joseph, 68
Munro, 190
Murder, 227–37
Murnau, F. W., 192
Murray, James, 62
Muses, 89–90
Musset, Alfred de, 395
Mutiny on the Bounty, 43
My Fair Lady, 70, 81, 280
My Son John, 168
Myer, Russ, 3554
Myra Breckinridge, 285

The Naked City, 80
Nash, Thomas, 397
Nathan, George Jean, 135, 153, 160, 345–46
National Film Registry: 150 Great Movies, 297–302
Neecha Nagar, 286
Nero, 3, 227, 408
Nethersole, Olga, 381
Network, 360
Never give a sucker an even break, 383
Never-Never Land, 374
New Theater (NYC), 216
New York Drama Critics Circle Awards, 327–29
New York Herald, 351
New York Times, 342, 346, 347, 351, 355, 392
New York Tribune, 28, 343
Newman, Alfred, 279
Newman, Paul, 55
Nicholas and Alexandra, 70
Nichols, Mike, 326
Nicholson, Jack, 49, 51, 197, 204, 279
Nickels, Ted, 204
Nielsen Ratings, 329–30
Nietzsche, Friedrich, 382
A Night in Casablanca, 146
Night of the Iguana, 70
Night of the Living Dead, 201
Nijinsky, Vaslav, 411
Ninotchka, 283
Niven, David, 281
No Man of Her Own, 43
Nobel Prize, 131–32
Nolte, Brawley, 54
Nolte, Nick, 54
None but the Lonely Heart, 54
Norworth, Jack, 394
Nosferatu, 192

Not a Dry Seat in the House, 374
Notorious, 167
Il Novellino, 380
The Nutty Professor, 66

Oakley, Annie, 139, 363
Oberammergau Passion Play, 304
The Obies, 329
O'Brien, Margaret, 281
O'Casey, Sean, 50, 245
Odets, Clifford, 344
Oedipus at Colonus (Sophocles), 86
Of Mice and Men, 283
Off-Broadway, 221
Ogle, Charles, 195
Oh! Calcutta!, 4, 345
Old Chestnut, 374–75
The Old Mill, 189
Olivier, Sir Laurence, 22, 51, 55
On Golden Pond, 280
On the Eve, 400
On the Spot, 101
On the Waterfront, 56, 81
One Flew Over the Cuckoo's Nest, 254
One Million Years B.C., 200
O'Neal, Tatum, 280
O'Neill, Eugene, 5, 28, 50, 123–24, 153, 156, 181, 221, 305–7, 341–42, 352, 403
O'Neill, James, 28, 123
One-Man Tango, 375
Oofty Goofty, 16–17
Opera, 61, 92
Opera stars, 34–35
Oprah, 375
The Optimist, 369
The Orphan (Thomas Otway), 7
Orphans of the Storm, 163
Orpheus Descending, 347
Oscar, 375–76
Oscars, cartoon, 189
Otello, 61
Othello, 169
O'Toole, Peter, 64, 282
Otway, Thomas, 7, 397, 399
Our Daily Bread, 165
Our Gang, 233
Out of Africa, 82
Outtake, 376

Pacino, Al, 359
Pacuvius, Marcus, 392, 401
Page, Geraldine, 55

The Pajama Game, 390
Palance, Jack, 285
Palmer, John, the Younger, 401
Pan, 376
Pancho Villa, 139
Pantomime, 3
Paper Moon, 280
Paquin, Anna, 280
A Parisian Model (Ziegfeld), 135
Parker, Dorothy, 40, 157–59, 345, 366, 403
A Parlor Match (Ziegfeld), 135
Patrick, John, 392
Paul, Steven, 166
Le Pauvre Diable (Voltaire), 108
Pavlova, Anna, 62, 410
Pavarotti, Luciano, 61
Payton, Corse, 24
Pepys, Samuel, 333
Peter Pan, 376
Peter Pan, 127–28, 346, 374, 376
Phantom of the Opera, 66–67, 80, 199
Philadelphia Inquirer, 347
Philemon, 89, 398
Phillpotts, Eden, 391
Phrynichus, 86
The Piano, 280
Picasso, Pablo, 131
The Picture of Dorian Gray, 65, 80
Pierce, Jack, 195, 197
The Pink Phink, 190
Pinocchio, 187–88
Pinter, Harold, 5
Pippa Passes, 346
Pirandello, Luigi, 410
Pirates, 79
The Pirates of Penzance, 118
Piron, Alexis, 337
Pit, 376
Pixérecourt, Guilbert de, 177
A Place in the Sun, 69, 81
The Plain Dealer (William Wycherly), 105
Plane Crazy, 184
Planet of the Apes, 65, 201
The Playboy of the Western World (John M. Synge), 243
Playing to the Haircuts, 377
Plays, long-running, 304
Playwrights, 85–132
The Pleasure Garden, 166
The Plough and the Stars (Sean O'Casey), 245

Poitier, Sidney, 53, 254
Polanski, Roman, 201
Poltergeist, 75
Poo-Bah, 377
Pope, Alexander, 333
Pordage, Samuel, 232
Porgy and Bess, 141
Porky Pig, 192
Porter, Cole, 369
Porter, Edwin S., 138
Possessed, 281
Il Postino (*The Postman*), 284
The Postman, 284
Potter, Paul, 251
Powers, Tyrone, 54
Pratfall, 377
Les Précieuses Ridicules, 102, 336
Preston, Robert, 326
Price, Vincent, 204
Pride of the Yankees, 141
Prince, Harold, 326, 327
The Prince of Parthia, 10, 305
La Princesse d'Èlide (Molière), 103
Private Lives, 341
The Prize, 286
Props, 78–79
Proscenium, 377
Protean, 377
Proud as Punch, 377
Prynne, William, 350
Pryor, Richard, 53
Psycho, 167–68, 202
Psychomania, 201
Puffery, 336
Pujol, Joseph, 26
Pulitzer Prize(s), 305–9
Pull a Boner, 378
Pull Strings, 378
Pumping Iron, 378
Punch-and-Judy, 377
Pushkin, Aleksandr, 399, 409
Put a Sock in It, 378
Pygmalion, 120–22, 280, 351

QT, 378–79
Queen Christina, 41, 55
Queen Elizabeth, 20
Quest, 191
Quest for Fire, 65
The Quiet Man, 81
Quiet Please!, 189
Quinn, Anthony, 254, 375

Quiz, 379
Quo Vadis, 62, 138

R.U.R. (Karel Capek), 197
Rachel, 12–13, 60, 397
Racine, Jean, 228, 334, 394
Radio City Music Hall, 226
Radio shows, 331
Raft, George, 56
Raiders of the Lost Ark, 49, 69
Rains, Claude, 358, 360
Raising the Wind, 368
"Rambling with Gambling," 331
Ran, 71
Randolph, Thomas, 396
Rappe, Virginia, 232
The Raspberry Awards, 284
Rat Pack, 379
Rattigan, Terence, 130
Die Rauber in den Abruzzen, 177
The Raven, 204
Reagan, Ronald, 56, 147, 285, 386
Rear Window, 167
Rebecca, 80, 167
The Recruiting Officer (George Farquhar), 216
The Red Earth, 286
Red Scare, 355
Redford, Robert, 55
Redgrave, Corin, 54
Redgrave, Jemma, 54
Redgrave, Lynn, 54
Redgrave, Michael, 54
Redgrave, Roy, 54
Redgrave, Vanessa, 54
The Red-Nosed Monster or The Tyrant of the Mountains, 216
Reds, 82
Redwitz, Oscar von, 114
Reger, Max, 343
Reitz, Edgar, 285
Rent, 397
Restoration, 71
The Return of Dr. X, 203
Return of the Jedi, 49, 198
The Revolt of Mamie Stover, 164
Reynolds, Frederick, 176
Rhubarb, 379–80
Rice, Thomas D., 372
Rich, Richard, 64
Rich and Famous, 166
Richard II, 348

Richard III, 138, 177, 208
Richardson, Joely, 54
Richardson, Natasha, 54
Rigoletto, 113–14, 337
Rin Tin Tin, 179, 407
Rinuccini, Ottavio, 92
Riots, 240–46
Rites of Spring (Stravinsky), 243
The Rivals (Richard Brinsley Sheridan), 27, 109–10
A River Runs Through It, 82
Robards, Jason, Jr., 55
Robbing Cleopatra's Tomb, 198
The Robe, 69
Roberts, Julia, 49
Robeson, Paul, 53
Robinson, Edward G., 55, 359
Robot Monster, 203, 285
Robots, 197
Rock Around the Clock, 245
Rock 'n' Roll, 380
Rocky, 382
Rodgers, Richard, 137
Rodgers and Hammerstein, 98, 137
Rogers, Ginger, 72
Rogers, Roy, 51, 181
Rogers, Will, 135
Roman Holiday, 69
Romberg, Sigmund, 137
Rome, ancient, 2–4, 175, 207–8, 227–28, 234–35, 408
Romeo and Juliet, 70, 82, 126, 169, 349, 380
Rome—Open City, 286
A Room with a View, 71
Rooney, Mickey, 281
"Roots," 330
Roscius, 9, 22
Roscius, Quintus Gallus, 2
Rose, George, 326
The Rose Tattoo, 81
Ross, Diana, 54
Ross, Tracee, 54
Rossini, Gioacchino Antonio, 383–84
Rostand, Edmond, 126–27, 129, 368
Rosten, Leo, 145
Roundtree, Richard, 53
The Rover (Aphra Behn), 105
Rowe, Nicholas, 107
Royal Brunswick Theatre, 401
The Royal Family, 54
Ruby Gentry, 165
Runyon, Damon, 411

Rush, 380
Russell, Lillian, 17
Russell, Rosalind, 55, 281
Russolo, Luigi, 244
Ryan's Daughter, 82

Sabrina, 69
Sade, Marquis de, 162–63
Sadie Thompson, 164
Saint, Eve Marie, 56
Sale, Chic, 366–67
Salinger, J. D., 225–26
Samson and Delilah, 69, 73
Sand, George, 395
The Sand Castle, 190
Sanders, George, 400
Sandow, Eugene, 400
Santa Claus Conquers the Martians, 203, 285
Sapho, 381
Sarcey, Francisque, 348
Sardou, Victorien, 114–15, 338
Saroyan, William, 305–6, 400
Sartre, Jean-Paul, 131
Saunders, John Mark, 160–61
Saving Private Ryan, 83
Scarron, Paul, 101–2, 406
The Scent of Mystery, 150
Schiller, Friedrich von, 408
Schindler's List, 82
The School for Scandal, 108–9, 337
Schwarzenegger, Arnold, 360, 378
Scott, George C., 283
The Scottish Play, 380
Screenwriters, 154–59
Scriabin, Aleksandr, 400
The Sea Gull, 347
The Seagull (Chekov), 115
The Secret Agent, 166
The Secret Life of Walter Mitty, 141
Selena, 396
Selznick, David O., 55
Seneca, Lucius, 408
Sentimental Journey, 154
"Sesame Street," 330
Settle, Elkanah, 106–7
The Seven Faces of Dr. Lao, 65
The Seven Year Itch, 381
Seven-Year Itch, 381
Sex, 352
Shadow, 331
Shadow of a Doubt, 167
Shadwell, Thomas, 404

Shakespeare, William, 4–6, 75, 92–97, 110, 208, 210–11, 215, 231, 333–34, 346, 348–49, 366, 367, 374, 380, 394, 396, 406
Shakespeare in Love, 71
Shakuntala, 91
Shane, 81, 174
Shanghai Express, 80
Shaw, George Bernard, 1, 120–22, 147, 174, 280, 282–83, 334, 338, 339, 341, 347, 351–52, 382, 385, 391, 400, 403, 411
She Done Him Wrong, 357, 360
She Stoops to Conquer (Oliver Goldsmith), 122
She Wore a Yellow Ribbon, 81, 359
She Would and She Wouldn't, 234
Shearer, Norma, 72
Shelley, Mary, 194
Shepard, Sam, 5
Sheridan, Ann, 56
Sheridan, Richard Brinsley, 27, 108–10, 176, 336, 337, 361, 404–5, 408
Sheridan, Thomas, 27
Sherwood, Robert E., 305–6
The Shining, 204
Ship of Fools, 82
Shore, Dinah, 330
Shot, 381
Show Boat, 137
Siamese twins, 14–15
Siege of Rhodes, 95
Silence of the Lambs, 202, 254, 358
Silvers, Phil, 326
Simon, Simone, 199
Sinatra, Frank, 56, 379
The $64 Question, 381
Skelton, Red, 145
Skinners Baby, 48
Skippy, 280
Skit, 381
Slang, 362–87
Sleep, 285
Slowacki, Juliusz, 104
Smash-Up: The Story of a Woman, 158, 281
Smith, Will, 49, 69
Smith, William, 234
Smith, Winchell, 63
Snipes, Wesley, 53
Snow White and the Seven Dwarfs, 281, 284
Soap opera, 149–50
The Solid Gold Cadillac, 70, 72
Solomon and Sheba, 165, 285

Some Like It Hot, 70, 358
Somebody Up There Likes Me, 79, 81
Someone in the House, 344
Son of the Blob, 200
Sondheim, Stephen, 327
The Song of Bernadette, 80
Sonnetti Lussuriosi, 403
Sons and Lovers, 81
Sophocles, 86–87, 162, 392, 398
Soul kiss, 381
Soumet, Alexander, 340
Sound effects, 77
The Sound of Music, 137
Sousa, John Philip, 50
South Pacific, 137
Spaghetti Western, 382
Spartacus, 70, 81, 174
Special Delivery, 190
Special effects, 73–76
Speed the Plow (Thomas Morton), 111
Speedy Gonzales, 190
Spellbound, 167
Spenser, Gabriel, 231
Spielberg, Steven, 75, 166, 202, 284
Splinter, Judy, 330
The Squall, 342
The Squaw Man, 141
Sssnake, 201
Stage Door Canteen, 222–23
Stage mothers, 59
Stage names, 51–52
Stagecoach, 283
Stanislavsky, Konstantin, 55, 76, 163, 347, 411
Stanley, Kim, 55
Stapleton, Maureen, 55
A Star Is Born, 41, 72, 158
"Star Trek," 364
Star Wars, 49, 71, 83, 198, 202, 284
State Fair, 281
Steadi Cam, 382
Steamboat Willie, 184
Stella Dallas, 165, 331
Stevenson, Robert Louis, 197–98
Stewart, Jimmy, 147, 160
Stiller, Mauritz, 40
The Sting, 70
Stoker, Bram, 192
Stone, John Augustus, 112, 397
Stone, Sharon, 360
The Story of Alexander Graham Bell, 363
Storyboard, 382

Strangers on a Train, 167–68
Strasberg, Lee, 55
Stravinksy, Igor, 243
Streep, Meryl, 280
Strindberg, August, 117–18, 410
Stripteasing, 33
The Stunt Man, 64
Stuntmen and stuntwomen, 63
Suckling, John, 397
Sudden Impact, 359
Sudermann, Hermann, 340
Suits, 382
Sundae in New York, 191
Sundance Film Festival Awards, 303
Sunrise, 79
Sunset Boulevard, 359
The Sunshine Boys, 280
Superman, 382
Surfing, 382
Suspicion, 254
Swanson, Gloris, 359
"Sweet Adeline," 382
Sweet Eros, 280
Switzer, Carl "Alfalfa," 233, 411
La Symphonie Pastorale, 286–87
Synge, John M., 243, 409

Tabu, 80
"Take It or Leave It," 381
Talbot, Lyle, 391
A Tale of Possessors Self-Dispossessed (Eugene O'Neill), 124
Tales from the Crypt, 201
Talmadge, Norma, 225
Tandy, Jessica, 280, 394
Tango, 191
Tarantula, 200
Tartuffe (Molière), 102–3
Tarzan, 357
Tarzan of the Apes, 152–53
Tate, Sharon, 201, 233
Taurog, Norman, 280
Taylor, Elizabeth, 72–73
Teleprompter, 383
Téllez, Gabriel, 361
The Tempest, 95
Temple, Shirley, 48–49, 280, 281
The Ten Commandments, 148
Terence, 396
Terminator 2, 66
Terpander, 335
Terrence, 89

Terris, William, 232
The Terror of Tiny Town, 285
Terry, Ellen, 412
Tess, 71, 82
Tetrazzini, Luisa, 35
Thackeray, William Makepeace, 150–51
That Hagen Girl, 285
Thayer, Ernest Laurence, 18
Theaters, 207–26
Le Théâtre de Clara Gazul (Prosper Mérimée), 112–13
Theatrical clubs, 23
Them, 200
"There's a Sucker Born Every Minute," 383
There's No Business Like Show Business, 357
Thesiger, Ernest, 56
Thesmophoriazusae (Aristophanes), 87
Thespis, 1–2, 22
They Died with Their Boots On, 164
The Thief of Bagdad, 80
The Thin Man, 180
The Thing, 199, 204
The Thing with Two Heads, 201
The Third Man, 81, 169
The 30 Foot Bride of Candy Rock, 203
The Thirty-Nine Steps, 166
Thomas, Dylan, 221, 354, 398, 411
Thomson, Virgil, 308–9
Three Coins in the Fountain, 81
The Three Faces of Eve, 56, 154
The Three Little Pigs, 189
Three Orphan Kittens, 189
The Threepenny Opera, 209
Thumbs Down, 383
Thurber, James, 48
Thus Spake Zarathustra, 382
Time After Time, 202
The Time of Your Life, 305–6, 327
Timour the Tartar, 177
Tin Pan Alley, 222
Tin Pan Alley, 222
Tin Toy, 191
Titanic, 71, 83, 148, 279, 284
To Be or Not to Be, 360
To Catch a Thief, 81
To Have and Have Not, 156, 357, 360
Todd, Mike, 150
The Tonight Show, 178
Tony Awards, 309–27
Toot, Whistle, Plunk and Boom, 190
Topsy, 237

INDEX 437

The Tortoise and the Hare, 189
Total Recall, 360
Touch of Evil, 169, 360
Tournedos, 383–84
The Towering Inferno, 63–64, 82, 249
Tracy, Spencer, 55, 204, 279
The Tragicall History of Dr. Faustus (Marlowe), 214
Trap, 384
Trapeze artists, 15–16
Travelogue, 384
Travels with My Aunt, 70
Travolta, John, 49
The Treasure of the Sierra Madre, 359
Tree, Sir Herbert Beerbohm, 338, 410
The Trial, 169
Trigger, 225
Truckline Café, 342
True Grit, 357
Truman, Harry, 233–34, 281
Truman, Margaret, 233–34
Tully, Richard Walton, 130
Turcaret (Alain-René Lesage), 106
Turner, Lana, 72, 233
Turpin, Ben, 389
TV Dinner, 384
Twain, Mark, 399
Tweetie Pie, 189
Twilight Zone: The Motion Picture, 250
Two Mouseketeers, 190
2001: A Space Odyssey, 201
Tyler, Royall, 305
Tynan, Kenneth, 4

Ubu Roi (Alfred Jarry), 119
The Ugly Duckling, 189, 283
Under Milk Wood, 221, 355
The Undertaker and His Pals, 204
Union Pacific, 283
Upstage, 384
Urban, Joseph, 135

Vaché, Jacques, 335
Valentino, Rudolph, 37–38, 251, 396, 398, 410
Variety, 347
Vaudeville, 30–32
Veidt, Conrad, 199
Verdi, Giuseppe, 113–14, 337, 401
Vertigo, 167
Vertov, Dziga, 367
Video, 384

Vidor, King, 41, 62, 165–66
Vincent and Me, 390
The Virginian, 359
The Visit, 394
Vitascope, 346–47
Voice-Over, 385
Voight, Jon, 54, 353
Voltaire, 108, 213, 369, 408
Voss, Richard, 340
Voyage to the Moon, 198

Wagner, Natasha, 54
Wagner, Richard, 385
Wagner, Robert, 54
Wagner, Walter, 283
Walker, Robert, 168
Wallace, Edgar, 101
Wallenda, Karl, 412
Walpole, Hugh, 334
Walsh, Raoul, 164–65
"Walter Plinge," 63
War and Peace, 165
War of the Worlds, 169
Warburton, John, 107
Warde, Frederick Barkham, 138
Warhol, Andy, 285
Warner, Jack, 133, 146–47, 203–4
Warren, 385
Warren, Leonard, 401
Warren, William, Jr., 375
Washington, Denzel, 53
Watts, Richard, 345
Wayne, John, 51, 285, 357, 359
Wegener, Paul, 194
Weissmuller, Johnny, 357
Welch, Raquel, 200
Welles, Orson, 166, 169–70, 331, 361, 375
Well-Made Play, 385
Wellman, William, 145
Wells, H. G., 202, 347, 370
Werewolves, 196–97
West, Mae, 37–40, 346, 352, 357, 360, 361, 393
West, Nathaniel, 397
West Side Story, 70, 81
Westworld, 75, 201
What Price Glory, 164, 165
"What Time Does the Next Swan Leave?", 385
Whatever Happened to Baby Jane?, 70
Wheeler, Hugh, 326
When Husbands Flirt, 145

When Magoo Flew, 190
Where the Cross Is Made (Eugene O'Neill), 123
Whitaker, Forest, 53
White Heat, 357
White Rats, 23
White Shadows in the South Seas, 79
The White Slave, 385
White Slavery, 385
White Wings, 181–82
Whitefield, George, 30
Whitely, Jon, 281
Whitfield, Lynn, 53
Whitney, John Hay, 342–43
Who's Afraid of Virginia Woolf?, 70, 82, 326
Wiest, Dianne, 279
Wild Man of Borneo, 16–17
Wilde, Oscar, 340–41, 407, 409
Wilder, Billy, 279
William Tell, 67
Williams, Bert, 53, 135
Williams, Robin, 49
Williams, Tennessee, 124–25, 347–48, 365
Williams, Vanessa, 53
Wilson, 79, 80
Wilson, Dooley, 358
"Win One for the Gipper," 386
Windwood, Estelle, 391
Winfrey, Oprah, 53, 331, 375
Wings, 386
Wings, 254
Winnie the Pooh and the Blustery Day, 190
The Winning of Barbara Worth, 64
Winter, Vincent, 281
Winters, Shelley, 279
Wireless, 386
Wise, Robert, 201
With Byrd at the South Pole, 80
The Wizard of Oz, 55–56, 72, 165, 180, 283, 374

Wodehouse, P(elham) G(renville), 391
Wolf, 197, 204
The Wolf Man, 196–97
Womaneater, 203
The Wonderful World of the Brothers Grimm, 70
Wood, Natalie, 54
Woodard, Alfre, 53
Woodward, Joanne, 55, 56
Woollcott, Alexander, 28, 57, 165, 343, 345, 350
Woolley, Monty, 225
Words, longest, 30
Words and Phrases, Show Biz, 362
The Worm Eaters, 204
Worst movies, 285
Wray, Fay, 73
The Wrong Box, 174
The Wrong Trousers, 191
Wuthering Heights, 80, 141, 283
Wycherley, William, 105, 393
Wynn, Ed, 330

Yankee Doodle Dandy, 189
The Yearling, 80
Yes-man, 386–87
The Yiddish King Lear, 19
York, Susannah, 166
"You ain't heard nothin' yet," 387
Young, Loretta, 72, 281
Young Roscius, 9

Zanuck, Darryl, 155
Ziegfeld, Florenz, 18, 135, 343, 410
Ziegfeld Follies, 53, 394
Zleger, Charles, 67
Zorba the Greek, 81
Zorina, 389
Die Zweite Heimat, 285